5th Workshop on NLP for Conversational AI (NLP4ConvAI 2023)

Toronto, Canada
14 July 2023

ISBN: 978-1-7138-8230-5

Printed from e-media with permission by:

Curran Associates, Inc.
57 Morehouse Lane
Red Hook, NY 12571

Some format issues inherent in the e-media version may also appear in this print version.

Association for Computational Linguistics
209 N. Eighth Street
Stroudsburg, Pennsylvania 18360

Phone: 1-570-476-8006
Fax: 1-570-476-0860

acl@aclweb.org

Additional copies of this publication are available from:

Curran Associates, Inc.
57 Morehouse Lane
Red Hook, NY 12571 USA
Phone: 845-758-0400
Fax: 845-758-2633
Email: curran@proceedings.com
Web: www.proceedings.com

NLP4ConvAI 2023

The 5th Workshop on NLP for Conversational AI

Proceedings of the Workshop

July 14, 2023

Order copies of this and other ACL proceedings from:

Association for Computational Linguistics (ACL)
209 N. Eighth Street
Stroudsburg, PA 18360
USA
Tel: +1-570-476-8006
Fax: +1-570-476-0860
acl@aclweb.org

Introduction

We are excited to welcome you to NLP4ConvAI 2023, the 5th Annual Workshop on NLP for Conversational AI, co-located with ACL 2023 at Toronto, Canada.

The goal of this workshop is to bring together NLP researchers and practitioners in different fields, alongside experts in speech and machine learning, to discuss the current state-of-the-art and new approaches in conversational AI, and to shed light on future directions. Following the success of the four previous editions of NLP for Conversational AI workshops at ACL & EMNLP, NLP4ConvAI 2023 is a one-day workshop including keynotes, oral presentations and posters.

We received 53 submissions this year, consisting of 38 long papers and 15 short papers. We had a total of 54 program committee (PC) members. At least three PC members reviewed each of the papers. We accepted 20 papers: 15 long papers and 5 short papers. These numbers give an overall acceptance rate of 38%, with the long and short papers acceptance rate being 39% and 33% respectively. Out of the 20 accepted papers, six are being presented as oral presentations and the remaining in a poster session. We have also identified one best paper (Generating Video Game Scripts with Style) and two outstanding papers (On the Underspecification of Situations in Open-domain Conversational Datasets, and Conversational Recommendation as Retrieval: A Simple, Strong Baseline).

In addition, the workshop program consists of five invited talks given by leading practitioners in industry and academia. We thank our five keynote speakers, Diyi Yang (Stanford University), Larry Heck (Georgia Institute of Technology), Vipul Raheja (Grammarly), Nurul Lubis (Heinrich Heine University Düsseldorf) and Jason Weston (Meta AI) for their inspiring, informative and thought provoking talks. We would also like to thank all the authors for submitting their work at the workshop, the program committee members for diligently reviewing the submissions and giving valuable feedback to the authors, and the ACL organizing committee for supporting us throughout the process.

We hope you will enjoy NLP4ConvAI 2023 at ACL and contribute to the future success of our community!

NLP4ConvAI 2023 Organizers
Abhinav Rastogi, General Chair
Georgios Spithourakis, Program Chair
Yun-Nung (Vivian) Chen and Bing Liu, Publication chairs
Yu Li, Diversity & Publicity Chair
Elnaz Nouri, Sponsorship Chair
Alon Albalak, Shared Task Chair
Alexandros Papangelis, Advisory Board

Organizing Committee

General Chair

Abhinav Rastogi, Google Research

Program Chair

Georgios Spithourakis, ex-PolyAI, Entrepreneur First

Publication Chairs

Yun-Nung Chen, National Taiwan University
Bing Liu, Meta

Diversity and Publicity Chair

Yu Li, Columbia University

Sponsorship Chair

Elnaz Nouri, Microsoft Research

Shared Task Chair

Alon Albalak, University of California, Santa Barbara

Advisory Board

Alexandros Papangelis, Amazon Alexa AI

Program Committee

Yun-Nung Chen, National Taiwan University
Bing Liu, Meta
Elnaz Nouri
Alexandros Papangelis, Amazon
Abhinav Rastogi, Google
Georgios P. Spithourakis, ex-PolyAI, Entrepreneur First
Yu Li, Columbia University
Alon Albalak, University of California, Santa Barbara
Abhinav Arora, Meta
Kartikeya Badola, Google Research
Mukul Bhutani, Carnegie Mellon University, Apple, Google
Alexandra Birch, University of Edinburgh
Jie Cao, University of Colorado
Yuan Cao, Google Brain
Guan-Lin Chao, Microsoft
Maximillian Chen, Columbia University
Nina Dethlefs, University of Hull
Ashwinkumar Ganesan, Amazon Alexa AI
Shubham Garg, Amazon.com
Christian Geishauser, Heinrich Heine University Duesseldorf
Alborz Geramifard, Facebook AI
Liane Guillou, The University of Edinburgh
Raghav Gupta, Google Inc.
Shachi H Kumar, Intel Labs
Dilek Hakkani-Tur, Amazon Alexa AI
Michael Heck, Heinrich Heine University
David M. Howcroft, Edinburgh Napier University
Songbo Hu, University of Cambridge
Chao-Wei Huang, National Taiwan University
Rishabh Joshi, Google
Mihir Kale, Google
Saarthak Khanna, Amazon
Seokhwan Kim, Amazon Alexa AI
Stefan Larson, Vanderbilt University
Hsien-chin Lin, Heinrich Heine University
Liangchen Luo, Google
Wolfgang Maier, Mercedes-Benz AG
Sneha Mehta, Bloomberg L.P.
Udita Patel, Amazon.com
Siddhesh Pawar, Google
Baolin Peng, Tencent AI Lab
Wei Peng, Huawei Technologies
Shiva Kumar Pentyala, Salesforce AI
Samrat Phatale, Google Research
Evgeniia Razumovskaia, University of Cambridge
Lina M. Rojas Barahona, Orange Innovation Research
Igor Shalyminov, Amazon AWS

Akshat Shrivastava, Facebook
Shubham Shukla, Independent Researcher
Kai Sun, Meta
Anh Duong Trinh, National College of Ireland
Miroslav Tushev, Amazon
Stefan Ultes, University of Bamberg
David Vandyke, Apple
Nikolas Vitsakis, University of Edinburgh, Heriott-Watt University
Peidong Wang, Microsoft
Peratham Wiriyathammabhum, Self
Chien-Sheng Wu, Salesforce
Hongyuan Zhan, Meta AI
Jianguo Zhang, Salesforce Research
Lukas Zilka, Google

Keynote Talk: Inclusive Conversational AI for Positive Impact

Diyi Yang
Stanford University
2023-07-14 09:10:00 – Room: **Harbour B**

Abstract: Conversational AI has revolutionized the way we interact with technology, holding the potential to create positive impact on a variety of domains. In this talk, we present two studies that develops inclusive conversational AI techniques to empower users in different contexts for social impact. The first one looks at linguistic prejudice with a participatory design approach to develop dialect-inclusive language tools for low-resourced dialects in conversational question answering, together with efficient adaptation of models trained on Standard American English (SAE) to different dialects. The second work introduces CARE, an interactive conversational agent that supports peer counselors by generating personalized suggestions. CARE diagnoses suitable counseling strategies and provides tailored example responses during training, empowering counselors to respond effectively. These works showcase the potential of how inclusive language technologies can address language and communication barriers and foster positive impact.

Bio: Diyi Yang is an assistant professor in the Computer Science Department at Stanford University. Her research goal is to understand the social aspects of language and build socially responsible NLP systems for social impact. Her work has received multiple best paper nominations or awards at top NLP and HCI conferences (e.g., ACL, EMNLP, SIGCHI, and CSCW). She is a recipient of IEEE AI 10 to Watch (2020), the Intel Rising Star Faculty Award (2021), the Samsung AI Researcher of the Year (2021), the Microsoft Research Faculty Fellowship (2021), and the NSF CAREER Award (2022).

Keynote Talk: Build it for One @ Right Place Right Time: Leveraging Context in Conversational Systems

Larry Heck
Georgia Institute of Technology
2023-07-14 09:40:00 – Room: **Harbour B**

Abstract: Recent years have seen significant advances in conversational systems, particularly with the advent of attention-based language models pre-trained on large datasets of unlabeled natural language text. While the breadth of the models has led to fluid and coherent dialogues over a broad range of topics, they can make mistakes when high precision is required. High precision is not only required when specialized skills are involved (legal/medical/tax advice, computations, etc.), but also to avoid seemingly trivial mistakes such as commonsense and other relevant 'in-the-moment' context. Much of this context centers on and should be derived from the user's perspective. This talk will explore prior and current work on leveraging this user-centric context (build it for one) and the user's specific situation (right place right time) to improve the accuracy and utility of conversational systems.

Bio: Larry Heck is a Professor in ECE and Interactive Computing, co-Executive Director of the AI Hub, Farmer Chair of Advanced Computing Concepts, and a GRA Eminent Scholar at Georgia Tech. He is a Fellow of the IEEE, inducted into the Academy of Distinguished Engineers at Georgia Tech, and named a Distinguished Engineer at Texas Tech. After receiving the PhD EE from Georgia Tech, he joined SRI, followed by VP of Research at Nuance, VP of Search and Advertising at Yahoo!, Chief Speech Scientist and Distinguished Engineer at Microsoft, Principal Scientist with Google Research, and CEO of Viv Labs and SVP at Samsung.

Keynote Talk: Building Better Writing Assistants In the Era of Conversational LLMs

Vipul Raheja
Grammarly
2023-07-14 13:30:00 – Room: **Harbour B**

Abstract: Text revision is a complex, iterative process. It is no surprise that human writers are unable to simultaneously comprehend multiple demands and constraints of the task of text revision when producing well-written texts, as they are required to cover the content, follow linguistic norms, set the right tone, follow discourse conventions, etc. This presents a massive challenge and opportunity for intelligent writing assistants, which have undergone an enormous shift in their abilities in the past few years and months via large language models. In addition to the quality of editing suggestions, writing assistance has undergone a monumental shift in terms of being a one-sided, push-based paradigm, to now being a natural language-based, conversational exchange of input and feedback. However, writing assistants still lack in terms of their quality, personalization, and overall usability, limiting the value they provide to users. In this talk, I will present my research, challenges, and insights on building intelligent and interactive writing assistants for effective communication, navigating challenges pertaining to quality, personalization, and usability.

Bio: Vipul Raheja is an Applied Research Scientist at Grammarly. He works on developing robust and scalable approaches centered around improving the quality of written communication, leveraging Natural Language Processing and Machine Learning. His research interests lie at the intersection of large language models and controllable text generation for writing assistance. He also co-organizes the Workshop on Intelligent and Interactive Writing Assistants (In2Writing). He received his Masters in Computer Science from Columbia University and in the past, worked at IBM Research, and x.ai on building conversational scheduling assistants.

Keynote Talk: Dialogue Evaluation via Offline Reinforcement Learning and Emotion Prediction

Nurul Lubis
Heinrich Heine University Düsseldorf
2023-07-14 15:00:00 – Room: **Harbour B**

Abstract: Task-oriented dialogue systems aim to fulfill user goals, such as booking hotels or searching for restaurants, through natural language interactions. They are ideally evaluated through interaction with human users. However, this is unattainable to do at every iteration of the development phase due to time and financial constraints. Therefore, researchers resort to static evaluation on dialogue corpora. Although they are more practical and easily reproducible, they do not fully reflect real performance of dialogue systems. Can we devise an evaluation that keeps the best of both worlds? In this talk I explore the usage of offline reinforcement learning and emotion prediction for dialogue evaluation that is practical, reliable, and strongly correlated with human judgements.

Bio: Nurul Lubis received the B.Eng. degree (cum laude) in 2014 from Bandung Institute of Technology, Bandung, Indonesia and the M.Eng. and Dr.Eng. degrees in 2017 and 2019, respectively, from Nara Institute of Science and Technology (NAIST), Nara, Japan. She received the NAIST Best Student Award in 2019. She was a recipient of the Japanese Ministry of Education, Culture, Sports, Science and Technology (MEXT) scholarship from 2014 to 2019. She was a research intern at Honda Research Institute Japan, Co. Ltd., Saitama, Japan and is currently a postdoctoral researcher at the Heinrich Heine University Düsseldorf, Düsseldorf, Germany. Her research interests include emotion in spoken language, affective dialogue systems, and dialogue policy optimization with reinforcement learning and variational methods.

Keynote Talk: Improving Open Language Models by Learning from Organic Interactions

Jason Weston
Meta AI
2023-07-14 15:50:00 – Room: **Harbour B**

Abstract: We discuss techniques that can be used to learn how to improve AIs (dialogue models) by interacting with organic users "in the wild". Training models with organic data is challenging because interactions with people in the wild include both high quality conversations and feedback, as well as adversarial and toxic behavior. We thus study techniques that enable learning from helpful teachers while avoiding learning from people who are trying to trick the model into unhelpful or toxic responses. We present BlenderBot 3x, an update on the conversational model BlenderBot 3, trained on 6M such interactions from participating users of the system. BlenderBot 3x is both preferred in conversation to BlenderBot 3, and is shown to produce safer responses in challenging situations. We then discuss how we believe continued use of these techniques – and improved variants – can lead to further gains.

Bio: Jason Weston is a research scientist at Meta AI, USA and a Visiting Research Professor at NYU. He earned his PhD in machine learning at Royal Holloway, University of London and AT&T Research in Red Bank, NJ (advisors: Alex Gammerman, Volodya Vovk and Vladimir Vapnik) in 2000. From 2002-2003 he was a research scientist at the Max Planck Institute for Biological Cybernetics, Tuebingen, Germany. From 2003-2009 he was a research staff member at NEC Labs America, Princeton. From 2009-2014 he was a research scientist at Google, NY. Jason's papers include best paper awards at ICML and ECML, and a Test of Time Award for his work A Unified Architecture for Natural Language Processing: Deep Neural Networks with Multitask Learning, ICML 2008 (with Ronan Collobert).

Table of Contents

Program

Friday, July 14, 2023

09:00 - 09:10	*Opening Remarks*
09:10 - 09:40	*Inclusive Conversational AI for Positive Impact (Diyi Yang)*
09:40 - 10:10	*Build it for One @ Right Place Right Time: Leveraging Context in Conversational Systems (Larry Heck)*
10:10 - 10:30	*Generating Video Game Scripts with Style (Best Paper)*
10:30 - 10:50	*Coffee Break*
10:50 - 12:00	*Poster Session*
12:00 - 13:30	*Lunch Break*
13:30 - 14:00	*Building Better Writing Assistants In the Era of Conversational LLMs (Vipul Raheja)*
14:00 - 14:20	*Response Generation in Longitudinal Dialogues: Which Knowledge Representation Helps?*
14:20 - 14:40	*On the Underspecification of Situations in Open-domain Conversational Datasets (Outstanding Paper)*
14:40 - 15:00	*Correcting Semantic Parses with Natural Language through Dynamic Schema Encoding*
15:00 - 15:30	*Dialogue Evaluation via Offline Reinforcement Learning and Emotion Prediction (Nurul Lubis)*
15:30 - 15:50	*Coffee Break*
15:50 - 16:20	*Improving Open Language Models by Learning from Organic Interactions (Jason Weston)*
16:20 - 16:40	*Conversational Recommendation as Retrieval: A Simple, Strong Baseline (Outstanding Paper)*
16:40 - 17:00	*A Survey of Challenges and Methods in the Computational Modeling of Multi-Party Dialog*

Friday, July 14, 2023 (continued)

17:00 - 17:10 *Closing Remarks*

Response Generation in Longitudinal Dialogues: Which Knowledge Representation Helps?

Seyed Mahed Mousavi, Simone Caldarella, Giuseppe Riccardi
Signals and Interactive Systems Lab, University of Trento, Italy
mahed.mousavi@unitn.it, giuseppe.riccardi@unitn.it

Abstract

Longitudinal Dialogues (LD) are the most challenging type of conversation for human-machine dialogue systems. LDs include the recollections of events, personal thoughts, and emotions specific to each individual in a sparse sequence of dialogue sessions. Dialogue systems designed for LDs should uniquely interact with the users over multiple sessions and long periods of time (e.g. weeks), and engage them in personal dialogues to elaborate on their feelings, thoughts, and real-life events. In this paper, we study the task of response generation in LDs. We evaluate whether general-purpose Pre-trained Language Models (PLM) are appropriate for this purpose. We fine-tune two PLMs, GePpeTto (GPT-2) and iT5, using a dataset of LDs. We experiment with different representations of the personal knowledge extracted from LDs for grounded response generation, including the graph representation of the mentioned events and participants. We evaluate the performance of the models via automatic metrics and the contribution of the knowledge via the Integrated Gradients technique. We categorize the natural language generation errors via human evaluations of contextualization, appropriateness and engagement of the user.

1 Introduction

The state-of-the-art dialogue systems are designed for assisting the user to execute a task, holding limited chit-chat conversations with shallow user engagement, or information retrieval over a finite set of topics. The personalization in these systems is limited to a stereotypical user model. This user model is implicitly inferred from conversations with many users, or is limited to a superficial list of persona statements (e.g., "He likes dogs") (Zhang et al., 2018). The dialogue sessions are disconnected and the shared information across sessions is negligible and close to none.

Longitudinal Dialogue (LD) is one of the most challenging types of conversation for human-machine dialogue systems. LDs are multi-session interactions that encompass user-specific situations, thoughts, and emotions. Dialogue systems designed for LDs should interact uniquely with each user about personal life events and emotions over multiple sessions and long periods of time (e.g. weeks). Through each session in LDs, the dialogue system must learn about the user's personal space of events and participants and social interactions, and engage the user in personal dialogues regarding their thoughts, feelings, and personal and world events.

Figure 1 shows an example of three types of human-machine dialogues: task-based, open-domain chit-chat and LD. The user dialogues with the tasked-based dialogue system consists of either independent command-and-control exchanges such as on Day 1, or a task-driven dialogue such as on Day 2. The user model in this system is not personal as it adopts a stereotypical model -implicitly - inferred from dialogue corpora with multiple users. In the open-domain chit-chat dialogue, the dialogue does not include the execution of any explicit task, and the model engages the user in a conversation about movies and news. A common characteristic of task-based and open-domain dialogues is the fact that there is no personal information carried to the next dialogue session. The system does not update/modify the user model with each dialogue session and the level of personalization is intact from one interaction to the other (Personalization in the natural language processing and dialogue models could be added based on the voice user interface requirements and could include the exploitation of personal information such as contact directory, preferences, etc.).

In contrast, the model designed for the LD must account for three main differences compared to the other two systems; A) the contents of the LD are not about general information or knowledge matters as LDs encompass personal emotions, user

Proceedings of the 5th Workshop on NLP for Conversational AI (NLP4ConvAI 2023), pages 1–11
July 14, 2023 ©2023 Association for Computational Linguistics

Time	Task-Based Dialogue	Open-Domain Chit-Chat	Longitudinal Dialogue
Day 1	**User:** Set an alarm for Monday 8 a.m.	**User:** Do you like Shining?	**User:** My boss set a meeting with me tomorrow. I am a bit worried to meet her.
	Machine: I saved the alarm.	**Machine:** *The* Shining? Yes I like most of Kubrick's movies.	**Machine:** Why? Did she say what the meeting is going to be about?
	User: Remind me to call Mike at 5 p.m.	**User:** Cool! I am going to watch the shining for the first time.	**User:** I think she wants to fire me. She has been searching for an other cashier recently.
	Machine: Reminder Saved.	**Machine:** I think you are going to enjoy it.	**Machine:** Uncertainties make us anxious. There may be another explanation.
Day 2	**Machine:** How may I help you?	**Machine:** What's the most interesting thing you've heard recently?	**Machine:** I remember you had a meeting with your boss today. How did it go?
	User: I want an expensive italian restaurant.	**User:** I learned that the Queen of England's last corgi died	**User:** Oh it went well haha! She wants me to train a new cashier. She will be my colleague.
	Machine: I found *Duomo* in the center. Should I book a table?	**Machine:** Wow! Was it a cardigan welsh corgi?	**Machine:** Good! So no bad news! Are you relaxed now?
	User: Yes, for two. Tonight at 8pm.	**User:** No it was pembroke welsh corgi!	**User:** Yeah. They are planning to expand the store. I am not fired! haha!
	Machine: Done! I booked a table for two at *Duomo* for 8 pm.	**Machine:** It was called Candy I think.	**Machine:** I am glad you feel better! Sometimes it's hard to control our emotions.

Figure 1: Examples of a task-based dialogue, a chat-chit, and a Longitudinal Dialogue (LD) in two different sessions. The dialogue system for LDs needs to learn about the user in a timely manner and engage her in a personal conversation encompassing her life events, thoughts, and emotions.

and time-specific situations, and participants; B) the sessions are not disconnected dialogues and we can not model them as stand-alone interactions. In contrast, they belong to a multi-session interaction unique to the individual user, where the information shared in each interaction creates a common ground between the machine and the user. For each interaction, the system must engage the user in a dialogue respecting the common ground based on the information shared in the previous interactions, as well as the novel information in the new dialogue history; C) the machine has to extract the personal information presented in the user responses to construct and update the user model and respond coherently. Similar to a natural interaction between human speakers, the model has to gradually become acquainted with the user throughout the dialogues and not from a superficial list of sentence-based persona descriptions.

There has been limited research on personal conversations with users over a long period of time. Engaging the user to elaborate on personal situations and emotions is a challenging task and designing appropriate collection/elicitation methodologies is not straightforward. As a result, research on multi-session dialogues resorts to crowd-sourcing datasets with superficial persona statements and pretended longitudinality (Xu et al., 2022a,b; Bae et al., 2022). Meanwhile, studies on LDs have been limited to inferring user's attributes such as age and gender (Welch et al., 2019b), or next quick-response selection from a candidate set of "yes," "haha," "okay," "oh," and "nice" (Welch et al., 2019a).

In this work, we study the task of response generation in LDs. Response generation in LDs is subject to appropriateness and accuracy as well as personalization and engagement of the user. The level of personalization in LDs is beyond a set of personal preferences and can not be learned from a limited set of persona statements ("*I like cars*" does not necessarily imply that I like to talk about cars in my interactions). The generated response needs to respect individuals' states, profiles, and experiences that vary among users and dialogue sessions. Therefore, we can not collect a massive knowledge base of user models that can suit all individuals and scenarios. The dialogue system should learn about each user and derive the individual user model through/from the previous dialogue sessions to generate a personal response that is coherent with respect to the dialogue context as well as the previous dialogue sessions.

We investigate the applicability of general-purpose Pre-trained Language Models (PLM) for grounded response generation in LDs. We study whether PLMs can generate a response that is coherent with respect to the dialogue history and grounded on the personal knowledge the user has shared in previous interactions. We conversation-

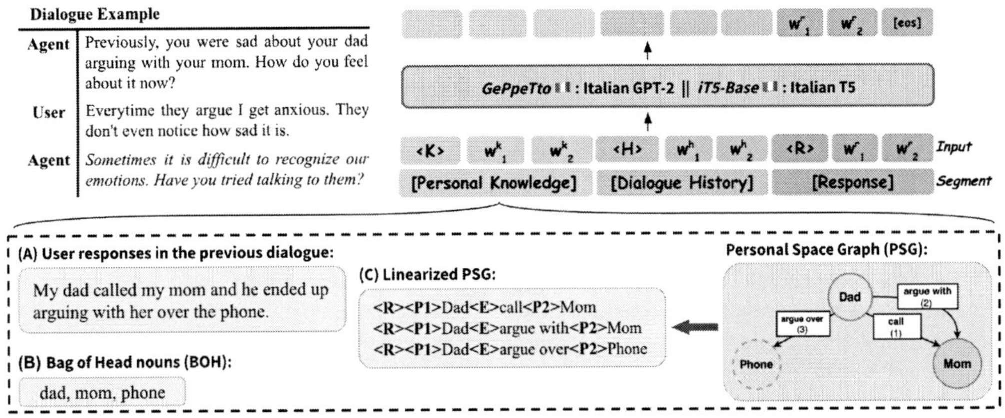

Figure 2: An example of a longitudinal dialogue. The user responses in the previous dialogue session are used as personal knowledge for grounded response generation. The knowledge is presented to the model as A) Unprocessed text (*RAW*); B) Bag of Head nouns (*BOH*); and C) Personal Space Graph (*PSG*) of events and their participants in linearized format. The model then encodes the dialogue history and the knowledge piece and generates a response candidate (the last agent turn in the dialogue example).

ally fine-tuned two recent PLMs, GePpeTto (GPT-2) (De Mattei et al., 2020) and iT5 (Sarti and Nissim, 2022), using a dataset of LDs about real-life events, feelings, and situations that the user has experienced. We use the responses each individual user shared in the previous dialogue sessions with the system as personal knowledge and evaluate whether grounding the generation on such knowledge results in more appropriate and personal responses. In previously published research on grounded generation, the knowledge sequence is provided to the model as-is. In this work, we experiment with three different representations of the knowledge piece; A) *Raw* as unprocessed text, similar to the previously published research; B) bag of head nouns as a distilled syntactic representation of the knowledge; C) graph representation of the events and participants mentioned in the user responses (Mousavi et al., 2021b). An example of a dialogue and different representations of the corresponding personal knowledge is shown in Figure 2.

We evaluate the performance of the models and the impact of different knowledge representations through automatic and human evaluations, as well as explainability studies using the Integrated Gradients technique (Sundararajan et al., 2017). Our contributions can be summarised as follows:

- To the best of our knowledge this is the first study on the task of response generation in LDs.
- We conversationally fine-tune two PLMs with and without grounded response generation on personal knowledge. We study the performance of the models and how different representations of knowledge can affect generation quality.
- We evaluate and compare the performance of the models using automatic evaluation, including explainability studies, and human evaluations, including studying the sub-dimensional errors made by each model.

2 Literature Review

Grounded Response Generation PLMs have achieved comparably well performance for open-domain chit-chats (Zhang et al., 2020), goal-oriented agents (Thulke et al., 2021) and question answering (Zhao et al., 2020). However, such models can generate inappropriate and/or generic responses which can lead to ethical problems and low user engagement (Zhang et al., 2020). Research to address this problem and improve the generation quality includes grounding the generation on external knowledge content. The selection of the knowledge source to ground the generation has been studied as an individual component (Hedayatnia et al., 2020), as well as a joint task along with response generation (Zhao et al., 2020; Huang et al., 2021).

Personal Dialogue Research on personalized response generation has focused on persona descriptions and synthetic sets of user preferences and profiles. Zhang et al. (2018) collected Persona-Chat dataset of open-domain dialogues using crowd workers, where the workers were instructed to impersonate as speakers with synthetic personas of 5 sentences. This dataset has been studied for personal response generation by fine-tuning PLMs (Wolf et al., 2019; Kasahara et al., 2022), by learning the users' persona from the dialogues samples rather than the persona descriptions (Madotto et al., 2019), or investigating different representations of persona statements (Huang et al., 2022). While the mentioned work focused on personalization in open-domain dialogues, Joshi et al. (2017) generated profiles consisting of gender, age, and food preference permutations for the user side in restaurant booking dialogues, which was used in another work (Siddique et al., 2022) to generate personalized responses in a task-based dialogue.

Multi-session Dialogue Studies on multi-session dialogues have been limited to simulated longitudinality and superficial persona. Xu et al. (2022a) extended the Persona-Chat dataset to a multi-session chat dataset with 4 to 5 sessions, by instructing crowd-workers to impersonate the role of returning dialogue partners in the first session (extracted from the Persona-Chat dataset) after a random amount of time. The workers were explicitly asked not to discuss any personal and real-life matters but play the role defined by the persona statements. This approach was further used by Bae et al. (2022) to extend an existing dataset of persona chats in Korean to multi-session dialogues. Xu et al. (2022b) proposed a framework for persona memory in multi-session dialogues and collected a dataset of persona chats in Chinese via crowd workers.

3 Experiments

3.1 Dataset

The dataset of LDs used in this work (Mousavi et al., 2021a) consists of two dialogue sessions for each individual user. The first dialogue session is a set of personal human-machine conversations with real users encompassing their personal life events and emotions. These dialogues are collected from a group of 20 Italian native speakers receiving therapy to handle their distress more effectively. Throughout the interaction, the machine prompts the user to engage her in the recollection of daily life events the user has experienced, while the user shares details about the events and participants that have activated her emotions by answering a set of questions.

For each user, the first session is then followed by a follow-up dialogue. These dialogues were elicited from 4 psychotherapists and 4 trained annotators supervised by the psychotherapists. In the second dialogue session, the user tends to share more details about her feelings and the possible evolution of the previously mentioned events. Meanwhile, the listener provides personal suggestions and asks questions to expand or disambiguate previously stated facts or feelings. A mock-up example of a second dialogue session and the corresponding user response in the previous dialogue is shown in Figure 2. This dataset consists of 800 2-session LDs in the mental health domain with an average of 5 turns per dialogue.

3.2 Models

We fine-tuned two state-of-the-art PLMs using the dataset of LDs.

GePpeTto: Italian GPT-2 The first model we experimented with is GePpeTto (De Mattei et al., 2020), a PLM based on GPT-2 small (12 layers of decoder, 117M parameters) (Radford et al., 2019), trained for the Italian language (13 GB corpus size). We fine-tuned the model using AdamW optimizer (Loshchilov and Hutter, 2017) with an early-stopping wait counter equal to 3 and a history window of 2 last turns.

iT5: Italian T5 The second PLM in our experiments is iT5 (Sarti and Nissim, 2022), a PLM based on T5 (Raffel et al., 2020), trained on the Italian portion of mC4 corpus (275 GB corpus size). We experimented with iT5-Small (12 layers, 60M parameters) and iT5-Base (24 layers, 220M parameters) [1]. We fine-tuned this model class using AdaFactor optimizer (Vaswani et al., 2017) with early stopping wait counter equal to 3 and a history window of 4 last turns.

3.3 Grounded Response Generation

For each user, we extracted her responses in the first dialogue session as personal knowledge to ground the response generation for the second dialogue session. We experimented with three representations of the knowledge piece:

- **(A) RAW**: We provide the responses of the user in the previous dialogue as an unprocessed knowledge piece. The average length of knowledge with this representation is 126.7 tokens.

[1] We were unable to use iT5-Large due to lack of GPU memory

- **(B) Bag of Head nouns (BOH)**: We automatically parse the user responses [2] and extract the head nouns as a distilled syntactic representation of the knowledge.
- **(C) Personal Space Graph (PSG)**: We represent the knowledge by the personal graph of the events and participants mentioned by the user Mousavi et al. (2021b). The predicates in a sentence represent an event, and its corresponding noun dependencies (subject, object) represent the participants. In this graph, the participants are the nodes while the predicates are the relations (edges) among the participants. We obtain a linear representation of the graph using an approach inspired by Ribeiro et al. (2021) in which the authors observed that providing a linearized representation of the graph to the PLMs results in outperforming the models with a graph-specific structural bias for the task of graph-to-text generation.

4 Evaluations

The fine-tuning of the models was done using 80% of the dialogues (640 second-session dialogues, 1284 samples with different turn levels), while the remaining data was split into 10% (80 dialogues, 160 samples with different turn levels) as the validation set for parameter engineering and early-stopping, and 10% as unseen test set. Each split was sampled at the dialogue level to guarantee no history overlap among splits. An example of a second dialogue session and the generated responses are presented in Appendix Table 5.

4.1 Automatic Evaluation

The results of the automatic evaluation of the models is presented in Table 1. The perplexity scores cannot be used to compare the performance between GePpeTto and iT-5 model classes as the vocabulary distributions in the pre-training phase of the two PLMs are not identical. However, the scores are comparable among iT5 variations as the same model class pre-trained using the same data. In fact, the perplexity scores indicate that iT5-Base demonstrates a better performance than iT5-Small in all combinations with knowledge representations. Therefore, we select iT5-Base among the iT5 models and focus the rest of the analysis on GePpeTto and iT5-Base.

[2]the dependency parser used is spaCy: spacy.io

Models	*nll*	*ppl*
GePpeTto	2.76	15.84
+*RAW Knowl.*	2.79	16.33
+*BOH Knowl.*	2.85	17.38
+*PSG Knowl.*	2.77	16.06
iT5-Small	2.18	8.84
+*RAW Knowl.*	2.19	8.95
+*BOH Knowl.*	2.18	8.88
+*PSG Knowl.*	2.19	8.93
iT5-Base	2.05	7.79
+*RAW Knowl.*	2.04	7.70
+*BOH Knowl.*	2.12	8.40
+*PSG Knowl.*	2.09	8.07

Table 1: Automatic evaluation of the models indicates that incorporating the knowledge slightly increases the models' perplexity (Perplexity scores can not be compared among models since the vocabulary distributions of pre-training data are not identical).

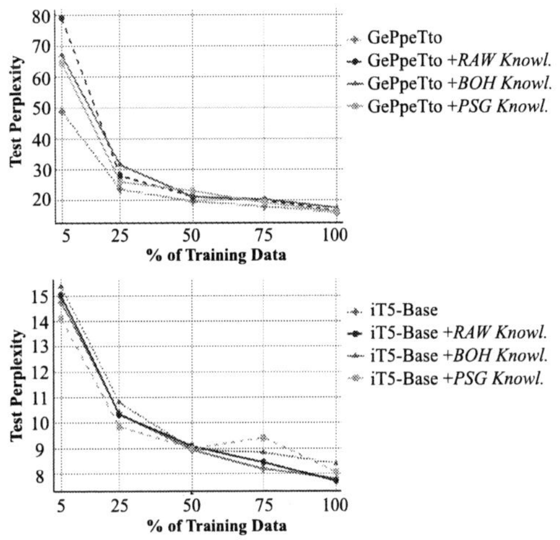

Figure 3: Perplexity score trends of the models over increasing size of the training set. The performance of GePpeTto variations is considerably improved after observing 50% of the fine-tuning training set.

Considering the small size of the LD dataset compared to the data used in the pre-training phase, we studied the impact of fine-tuning the models by optimizing the models over increasing size of the training set. The extension of the training set was gradual (the small portions are subsets of the big portions) and the performance of models was evaluated by measuring the perplexity score on the unseen test set. The results are presented in Figure 3. The performance of both models is improved considerably after observing the first 25% and 50%

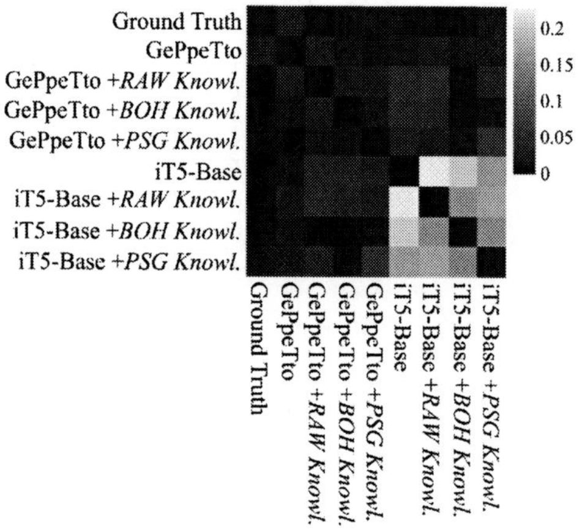

Figure 4: Lexical similarity among generated responses measured by BLEU-4 score. The results indicate a higher similarity among the responses generated by iT5-Base models.

of the train set, thus the fine-tuning has been more effective. However, in the second half of the data, both models show a steady trend while iT5-Base achieves a gradual improvement.

To investigate the impact of grounding on the response lexicalization of the models, we measured the diversity in the generated responses for the test set samples via BLEU-4 score, Figure 4. We observed that there is a higher similarity among responses generated by iT5 models, while the responses generated by GePpeTto variations are more diverse. A similar finding has been observed in the literature about the performance of auto-regressive models compared to encoder-decoder architectures regarding novelty in sequence generation (Tekiroğlu et al., 2022; Bonaldi et al., 2022). Further, responses generated by iT5-Base with *BOH* and *PSG* representations have the lowest lexical similarity. The responses with the highest lexical similarity are generated by iT5-Base with no grounding and *RAW* representation. Nevertheless, there is a negligible lexical similarity between the generated responses and the ground truth.

4.2 Human Evaluation

We sampled 50% of the unseen test set (42 dialogue histories, 80 samples with different turn levels) and evaluated the generated responses via human judges. We evaluated the responses according to four criteria using the protocol proposed by Mousavi et al. (2022):

- ***Correctness***: evaluating grammatical and syntactical structure of the response.
- ***Appropriateness***: evaluating the response to be a proper and coherent continuation with respect to the dialogue history.
- ***Contextualization***: evaluating whether the response refers to the context of the dialogue (not generic) or it consists of non-existing/contradicting information (hallucination cases).
- ***Listening***: whether the generated response shows that the speaker is following the dialogue with attention.

The annotators were asked to evaluate the response candidates and select a decision for each criterion from a 3-point Likert scale as positive (eg. Correct, Appropriate), negative (eg. Not Correct, Not Appropriate), and "I don't know". We recruited 35 native Italian crowd-workers through Prolific crowd-sourcing platform[3]. The workers were asked to perform a qualification task consisting of evaluating 5 samples (sampled from the validation set) in an identical setting to the main task. For the main evaluation, each crowd-worker annotated 3 response candidates for 10 dialogue histories, and each sample was annotated by 7 crowd-workers. We also asked the annotators to motivate their decisions for appropriateness and contextualization criteria by providing an explanation to point out possible errors in the generated response. Moreover, the ground truth was also included in the candidate set to be evaluated.

The Inter Annotator Agreement (IAA) level measured by Fleiss' κ, presented in Appendix Table 4, indicates high levels of subjectivity and complexity in *Contextualization* criterion, suggesting that it has been difficult for the annotators to assess this aspect of the responses.

The results of the human evaluation of responses are presented in Table 2 (the scores are obtained by majority voting). The evaluation of GePpeTto models shows that grounding generally worsens the performance of GePpeTto, regardless of the representation format, as the best performance is achieved by GePpeTto with no knowledge grounding. Nevertheless, *BOH* and *PSG* representations slightly improve the grammatical correctness of this model. The highest level of *Contextualization* among grounded GePpeTto models is achieved by *PSG* representation. Regarding iT5-Base varia-

[3]Prolific: `https://www.prolific.co/`

Models	nll	ppl	Human Evaluation			
			Correctness	**Appropriateness**	**Contextualization**	**Listening**
Ground Truth	-	-	97.62%	100.0%	97.62%	97.62%
GePpeTto	2.76	15.84	83.33%	**66.67%**	**69.05%**	**64.29%**
+*RAW Knowl.*	2.79	16.33	83.33%	59.52%	57.14%	57.14%
+*BOH Knowl.*	2.85	17.38	**92.86%**	45.24%	52.38%	42.86%
+*PSG Knowl.*	2.77	16.06	90.48%	54.76%	64.29%	50.00%
iT5-Base	2.05	7.79	**100.0%**	66.67%	73.81%	66.67%
+*RAW Knowl.*	2.04	7.70	85.71%	80.95%	80.95%	76.19%
+*BOH Knowl.*	2.12	8.40	92.86%	**80.95%**	85.71%	83.33%
+*PSG Knowl.*	2.09	8.07	95.24%	73.81%	**90.48%**	**83.33%**

Table 2: Human Evaluation of the fine-tuned models. The results show the impact of different representations of the knowledge source for grounded response generation in LDs. Refined representations of the knowledge (*BOH* and *PSG*) generally result in better performances than *RAW* representation.

tions, the results indicate that grounding improves the models' performance considerably with respect to *Appropriateness*, *Contextualization*, and *Listening*. However, it decreases the model's *Correctness* with the highest decrease caused by *RAW* representation. *PSG* representation achieves the highest level of *Contextualization* and *Listening* overall, besides the highest level of *Correctness* among grounded models. Therefore, refined representations of the knowledge (*BOH* and *PSG*) generally result in better performances compared to *RAW* representation. Nevertheless, there is still a huge gap between the performance of the best-performing model and the ground truth, suggesting the grounded PLMs are not suitable dialogue models for LDs in the mental health domain.

To gain better insight into the errors made by each model, we investigated the reasons provided by the annotators for their judgments. These results, presented in Figure 5, are complementary to the evaluation decisions, Table 2, and point out the errors that resulted in the negative evaluation of a response by the annotators. The analysis shows that grounding reduces the cases of genericness in rejected responses by GePpeTto, but results in more cases of hallucinations in the outputs of this model. The same trend is observed in iT5-Base with *RAW* representation. Furthermore, refined knowledge representations slightly escalate the genericness issue in rejected responses of iT5-Base. Nevertheless, grounding does have any positive impact on the cases of incoherence in rejected responses of the PLMs.

4.3 Generation Explainability

According to the human evaluation results, iT5-Base with knowledge grounding achieves the best performance among PLMs. We investigated the contribution of personal knowledge and different representations on the model's performance at inference time. We studied the attribution scores of the input tokens using the Integrated Gradients technique (Sundararajan et al., 2017; Sarti et al., 2023) based on backward gradient analysis. We experimented with two thresholds for the attribution scores:

- **Positive Contribution**: Based on the assumption that elements with positive scores have a positive influence on the model's performance, we investigated the tokens with positive attribution scores, However, tokens with small attribution scores have negligible contributions and thus this analysis can be noisy.
- **Significant Contribution**: To identify the tokens with significant contributions to the generation, we selected the top-25% of the tokens in the input sequence (knowledge and history) according to their attribution score. We then investigated what portion of these tokens belong to each segment of the input vector. For a fair comparison, the values are normalized over the segment length.

According to Positive Contribution analysis, 74% of the tokens in the *RAW* representation have a positive contribution to the generation with the majority (30%) of tokens being verbs and nouns. This percentage for *BOH* (Bag of Head Nouns) representation changes to 79.0%. This result suggests the importance of nouns for the model inference.

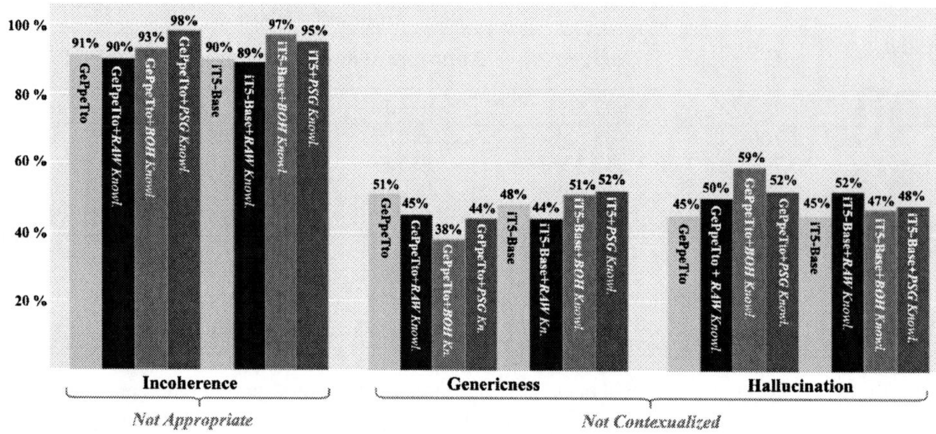

Figure 5: Explanations provided by the crowd-workers to motivate their negative judgments in *Appropriateness* and *Contextualization* criteria, represented by the percentage of the times the error category (x-axis) was selected. The figure is obtained by considering all the votes (i.e. not majority voting). Note that the labels are not mutually exclusive.

Models	*Knowl.*	*History*
iT5-Base		
+*RAW Knowl.*	44.6%	55.4%
+*BOH Knowl.*	39.5%	60.5%
+*PSG Knowl.*	38.7%	61.3%

Table 3: Percentage of tokens with significant contribution to the generation (top-25%) in knowledge and history segments of the input vector for each model.

Regarding the *PSG* representation, 55.6% of the tokens have a positive contribution to the generation (excluding the tags used for linearization), with the majority (68%) of tokens being events rather than participants.

The analysis of the tokens with significant contributions is presented in Table 3. Regarding the model with *RAW* representation, the percentage of tokens with high attribution scores is almost balanced between the knowledge and history segments. However, for the models with refined representations of knowledge (*BOH* and *PSG*), the dialogue history contains moderately more significantly contributing tokens.

5 Conclusion

We studied the task of response generation in Longitudinal Dialogues (LD), where the model should learn about the user's thoughts and emotions from the previous dialogue sessions and generate a personal response that is coherent with respect to the user profile and state, the dialogue context, as well as the previous dialogue sessions. We finetuned two state-of-the-art PLMs for Italian, using a dataset of LDs in the mental health domain. We experimented with grounded generation using user responses in the previous dialogue session as user-specific knowledge. We investigated the impact of different representations of the knowledge, including a graph representation of personal life events and participants mentioned previously by the user.

Our evaluations showed there is still a huge gap between the performance of the general-purpose PLMs with knowledge grounding and the ground truth. Nevertheless, we observed that a) refined representations of the knowledge (such as *BOH* and *PSG*) can be more informative and less noisy for a grounded generation; b) the encoder-decoder model exhibited more diversity in the outputs compared to the auto-regressive model; c) knowledge grounding reduces the cases of genericness in response, though it can result in more hallucinated responses.

Limitations

The dataset used in this work is in Italian and there may be language-specific limitations in the model performance. GePpeTto is the only candidate for auto-regressive models for the Italian language at the time of this research. Therefore, its performance may be limited due to the small number of parameters. We were unable to experiment with iT5-Large model due to computation power limitations.

Acknowledgements

We acknowledge the support of the MUR PNRR project FAIR - Future AI Research (PE00000013) funded by the NextGenerationEU.

References

Sanghwan Bae, Donghyun Kwak, Soyoung Kang, Min Young Lee, Sungdong Kim, Yuin Jeong, Hyeri Kim, Sang-Woo Lee, Woomyoung Park, and Nako Sung. 2022. Keep me updated! memory management in long-term conversations. In *Findings of the Association for Computational Linguistics: EMNLP 2022*, pages 3769–3787, Abu Dhabi, United Arab Emirates. Association for Computational Linguistics.

Helena Bonaldi, Sara Dellantonio, Serra Sinem Tekiroglu, and Marco Guerini. 2022. Human-machine collaboration approaches to build a dialogue dataset for hate speech countering. In *Proceedings of the 2022 Conference on Empirical Methods in Natural Language Processing*, pages 8031–8049. Association for Computational Linguistics.

Lorenzo De Mattei, Michele Cafagna, Felice Dell'Orletta, Malvina Nissim, and Marco Guerini. 2020. Geppetto carves italian into a language model. *arXiv preprint arXiv:2004.14253*.

Behnam Hedayatnia, Karthik Gopalakrishnan, Seokhwan Kim, Yang Liu, Mihail Eric, and Dilek Hakkani-Tur. 2020. Policy-driven neural response generation for knowledge-grounded dialog systems. In *Proceedings of the 13th International Conference on Natural Language Generation*, pages 412–421, Dublin, Ireland. Association for Computational Linguistics.

Qiushi Huang, Yu Zhang, Tom Ko, Xubo Liu, Bo Wu, Wenwu Wang, and Lilian Tang. 2022. Personalized dialogue generation with persona-adaptive attention. *arXiv preprint arXiv:2210.15088*.

Xinxian Huang, Huang He, Siqi Bao, Fan Wang, Hua Wu, and Haifeng Wang. 2021. PLATO-KAG: Unsupervised knowledge-grounded conversation via joint modeling. In *Proceedings of the 3rd Workshop on Natural Language Processing for Conversational AI*, pages 143–154, Online. Association for Computational Linguistics.

Chaitanya K Joshi, Fei Mi, and Boi Faltings. 2017. Personalization in goal-oriented dialog. *arXiv preprint arXiv:1706.07503*.

Tomohito Kasahara, Daisuke Kawahara, Nguyen Tung, Shengzhe Li, Kenta Shinzato, and Toshinori Sato. 2022. Building a personalized dialogue system with prompt-tuning. In *Proceedings of the 2022 Conference of the North American Chapter of the Association for Computational Linguistics: Human Language Technologies: Student Research Workshop*, pages 96–105, Hybrid: Seattle, Washington + Online. Association for Computational Linguistics.

Ilya Loshchilov and Frank Hutter. 2017. Decoupled weight decay regularization. *arXiv preprint arXiv:1711.05101*.

Andrea Madotto, Zhaojiang Lin, Chien-Sheng Wu, and Pascale Fung. 2019. Personalizing dialogue agents via meta-learning. In *Proceedings of the 57th Annual Meeting of the Association for Computational Linguistics*, pages 5454–5459, Florence, Italy. Association for Computational Linguistics.

Seyed Mahed Mousavi, Alessandra Cervone, Morena Danieli, and Giuseppe Riccardi. 2021a. Would you like to tell me more? generating a corpus of psychotherapy dialogues. In *Proceedings of the Second Workshop on Natural Language Processing for Medical Conversations*, pages 1–9, Online. Association for Computational Linguistics.

Seyed Mahed Mousavi, Roberto Negro, and Giuseppe Riccardi. 2021b. An unsupervised approach to extract life-events from personal narratives in the mental health domain. In *CLiC-it*.

Seyed Mahed Mousavi, Gabriel Roccabruna, Michela Lorandi, Simone Caldarella, and Giuseppe Riccardi. 2022. Evaluation of response generation models: Shouldn't it be shareable and replicable? In *Proceedings of the Second Workshop on Natural Language Generation, Evaluation, and Metrics (GEM 2022)*. Association for Computational Linguistics.

Alec Radford, Jeffrey Wu, Rewon Child, David Luan, Dario Amodei, Ilya Sutskever, et al. 2019. Language models are unsupervised multitask learners. *OpenAI blog*, 1(8):9.

Colin Raffel, Noam Shazeer, Adam Roberts, Katherine Lee, Sharan Narang, Michael Matena, Yanqi Zhou, Wei Li, Peter J Liu, et al. 2020. Exploring the limits of transfer learning with a unified text-to-text transformer. *J. Mach. Learn. Res.*, 21(140):1–67.

Leonardo F. R. Ribeiro, Martin Schmitt, Hinrich Schütze, and Iryna Gurevych. 2021. Investigating pretrained language models for graph-to-text generation. In *Proceedings of the 3rd Workshop on Natural Language Processing for Conversational AI*, pages 211–227, Online. Association for Computational Linguistics.

Gabriele Sarti and Malvina Nissim. 2022. It5: Large-scale text-to-text pretraining for italian language understanding and generation. *arXiv preprint arXiv:2203.03759*.

Gabriele Sarti, Ludwig Sickert, Nils Feldhus, and Oskar van der Wal. 2023. Inseq: An interpretability toolkit for sequence generation models.

AB Siddique, MH Maqbool, Kshitija Taywade, and Hassan Foroosh. 2022. Personalizing task-oriented dialog systems via zero-shot generalizable reward function. In *Proceedings of the 31st ACM International Conference on Information & Knowledge Management*, pages 1787–1797.

Mukund Sundararajan, Ankur Taly, and Qiqi Yan. 2017. Axiomatic attribution for deep networks. In *Proceedings of the 34th International Conference on Machine Learning*, volume 70 of *Proceedings of Machine Learning Research*, pages 3319–3328. PMLR.

Serra Sinem Tekiroğlu, Helena Bonaldi, Margherita Fanton, and Marco Guerini. 2022. Using pre-trained language models for producing counter narratives against hate speech: a comparative study. In *Findings of the Association for Computational Linguistics: ACL 2022*, pages 3099–3114, Dublin, Ireland. Association for Computational Linguistics.

David Thulke, Nico Daheim, Christian Dugast, and Hermann Ney. 2021. Adapting document-grounded dialog systems to spoken conversations using data augmentation and a noisy channel model. *arXiv preprint arXiv:2112.08844*.

Ashish Vaswani, Noam Shazeer, Niki Parmar, Jakob Uszkoreit, Llion Jones, Aidan N Gomez, Łukasz Kaiser, and Illia Polosukhin. 2017. Attention is all you need. *Advances in neural information processing systems*, 30.

Charles Welch, Verónica Pérez-Rosas, Jonathan K Kummerfeld, and Rada Mihalcea. 2019a. Learning from personal longitudinal dialog data. *IEEE Intelligent systems*, 34(4):16–23.

Charles Welch, Verónica Pérez-Rosas, Jonathan K Kummerfeld, and Rada Mihalcea. 2019b. Look who's talking: Inferring speaker attributes from personal longitudinal dialog. *arXiv preprint arXiv:1904.11610*.

Thomas Wolf, Victor Sanh, Julien Chaumond, and Clement Delangue. 2019. Transfertransfo: A transfer learning approach for neural network based conversational agents. *arXiv preprint arXiv:1901.08149*.

Jing Xu, Arthur Szlam, and Jason Weston. 2022a. Beyond goldfish memory: Long-term open-domain conversation. In *Proceedings of the 60th Annual Meeting of the Association for Computational Linguistics (Volume 1: Long Papers)*, pages 5180–5197, Dublin, Ireland. Association for Computational Linguistics.

Xinchao Xu, Zhibin Gou, Wenquan Wu, Zheng-Yu Niu, Hua Wu, Haifeng Wang, and Shihang Wang. 2022b. Long time no see! open-domain conversation with long-term persona memory. In *Findings of the Association for Computational Linguistics: ACL 2022*, pages 2639–2650, Dublin, Ireland. Association for Computational Linguistics.

Saizheng Zhang, Emily Dinan, Jack Urbanek, Arthur Szlam, Douwe Kiela, and Jason Weston. 2018. Personalizing dialogue agents: I have a dog, do you have pets too? *arXiv preprint arXiv:1801.07243*.

Yizhe Zhang, Siqi Sun, Michel Galley, Yen-Chun Chen, Chris Brockett, Xiang Gao, Jianfeng Gao, Jingjing Liu, and Bill Dolan. 2020. DIALOGPT : Large-scale generative pre-training for conversational response generation. In *Proceedings of the 58th Annual Meeting of the Association for Computational Linguistics: System Demonstrations*, pages 270–278, Online. Association for Computational Linguistics.

Xueliang Zhao, Wei Wu, Can Xu, Chongyang Tao, Dongyan Zhao, and Rui Yan. 2020. Knowledge-grounded dialogue generation with pre-trained language models. In *Proceedings of the 2020 Conference on Empirical Methods in Natural Language Processing (EMNLP)*, pages 3377–3390, Online. Association for Computational Linguistics.

Appendix

Models	Inter Annotator Agreement Level measured by Fleiss'κ				
	Appropriateness	*Contextualization*	*Correctness*	*Listening*	**IAA per Model**
GePpeTto	0.27	0.14	0.64	0.15	0.32±0.10
+RAW Knowl.	0.42	0.22	0.36	0.27	0.36±0.11
+BOH Knowl.	0.23	0.05	0.31	0.11	0.27±0.05
+PSG Knowl.	0.30	0.39	0.34	0.26	0.42±0.06
iT5-Base	0.24	0.19	0.06	0.18	0.27±0.04
+RAW Knowl.	0.18	0.03	0.30	0.21	0.19±0.06
+BOH Knowl.	0.21	0.17	0.58	0.24	0.26±0.09
+PSG Knowl.	0.17	0.06	0.27	0.14	0.19±0.12
IAA per Dimension	0.31±0.09 Fair	0.20±0.06 Poor	0.43±0.20 Moderate	0.25±0.10 Fair	-

Table 4: Inter-Annotator Agreement (IAA) level calculated by Fleiss' κ for each model and criterion. Low IAA level for *Contextualization* suggests a high level of subjectivity in this criterion.

Dialogue Example		
Knowledge	**User Responses from Previous Dialogue:**	I only worked in the morning, after lunch I went to the bank with Martina to activate her prepaid card since the one she is using now is about to expire. I accompanied Paolo to fix the bike and then I went to the dentist. When I came back, I made sauce for the week and then I ironed. I ran a lot but it was not a very stressful day. I hope to be able to go to bed early to be able to rest!"
Dialogue History	**Dialogue Stimulus:**	I remember you had a positive feeling about what I read in your notes [yesterday] "*I only worked in the morning, after lunch I went to the bank with Martina to activate her prepaid card since the one she is using now is about to expire. I ran a lot but it was not a very stressful day. I hope to be able to go to bed early to be able to rest!*". Do you have any new thoughts on this?"
	User:	I think that working in the morning and in the afternoon was not tiring, actually it was pleasant. I was also able to go to bed early enough, and I am well rested.
Response Candidates	**Ground Truth**	Good! Did you even manage to spend time with your daughter?
	GePpeTto	I see. Do you often find yourself away from each other?
	+RAW Knowl.	I see. Maybe you could try doing more flexible jobs to increase your anxiety.
	+BOH Knowl.	I'm glad to hear that! Have a nice day!
	+PSG Knowl.	Good, it's important to know yourself.
	iT5-Base	I'm glad you feel rested enough. Have you tried any relaxation exercises?
	+RAW Knowl.	I'm glad you were able to go to bed early. If you want to write me about this, we can talk about it anytime.
	+BOH Knowl.	I'm glad you rested well. Did you try any relaxation exercises?
	+PSG Knowl.	I'm happy to you rested well. If you want to write more about this, we can talk about it anytime.

Table 5: Example of a second dialogue session, the corresponding user turns in the first session as personal knowledge, and the generated responses (English translation).

On the Underspecification of Situations in Open-domain Conversational Datasets

Naoki Otani[α*], **Jun Araki**[β], **HyeongSik Kim**[β], **Eduard Hovy**[γ]
[α]Megagon Labs, Mountain View, CA, USA [β]Robert Bosch LLC, Sunnyvale, CA, USA
[γ]University of Melbourne, Melbourne, VIC, Australia
[α]notani@alumni.cmu.edu [β]{jun.araki,hyeongsik.kim}@us.bosch.com
[γ]eduard.hovy@unimelb.edu.au

Abstract

Advances of open-domain conversational systems have been achieved through the creation of numerous conversation datasets. However, many of the commonly used datasets contain little or no information about the conversational situation, such as relevant objects/people, their properties, and relationships. This absence leads to underspecification of the problem space and typically results in undesired dialogue system behavior. This position paper discusses the current state of the field associated with processing situational information. An analysis of response generation using three datasets shows that explicitly provided situational information can improve the coherence and specificity of generated responses, but further experiments reveal that generation systems can be misled by irrelevant information. Our conclusions from this evaluation provide insights into the problem and directions for future research.

1 Introduction

Human communication heavily relies on information about a situation–a set of observable information about relevant objects, their properties, and relationships in the world at a specific time and place. Crucial information can often be implicitly assumed during a conversation, particularly when it can be inferred from co-observed facts (e.g., "they are talking at the front desk in a hotel.") or shared a priori (e.g., "the person was staying in the hotel").

Incorporating such information is essential for both the development and evaluation of conversational technologies. To illustrate this point, we show a conversation example from DailyDialog (Li et al., 2017), along with responses generated by three systems: BlenderBot2 (Komeili et al., 2022; Xu et al., 2022), GPT-3 (Brown et al., 2020), and ChatGPT (GPT-3.5) in Table 1.[1] DailyDialog is a widely used[2] dataset of multi-turn conversations in English. The original example does not describe a surrounding environment explicitly, resulting in ambiguity regarding the situation. Person A could be a traveler leaving a hotel or someone handing over their house key, among other possibilities. The response generated by BlenderBot2 is somewhat relevant to the latter situation but clearly inappropriate in the former. In contrast, the response generated by GPT-3 is appropriate in the former situation but not in other contexts. ChatGPT's response is neutral, though less engaging. This ambiguity underscores the fundamental problem caused by

A:	Hello. I'm leaving. Here is my key.
B:	[Sytem output]

No situational information in input
BlenderBot2: Thank you. It is very kind of you. Do you want me to lock the door?
GPT-3: Thanks. Have a safe trip.
ChatGPT: Okay, take care.

+Situation: They are in a hotel. Person A has a car and is carrying a suitcase. It is raining outside.
BlenderBot2: Sure. Do you want me to load your luggage in the car? It's raining.
GPT-3: Thank you for staying with us. Do you need help with your luggage?
ChatGPT: Okay, thank you. Drive safe and stay dry.

Table 1: Responses from three systems with and without situational information as input. When the situation is unknown, the responses are grounded on their internal assumptions (top). However, when a few situational statements are given, all the systems recognized the same situation *(Person A is checking out of a hotel)* and generated engaging responses (bottom).

*This work was done while the first author was at Carnegie Mellon University.

[1]See Appendix A.2 for the generation setup.
[2]Based on Semantic Scholar, the dataset paper (Li et al., 2017) is cited by over 700 papers as of April 2023.

Proceedings of the 5th Workshop on NLP for Conversational AI (NLP4ConvAI 2023), pages 12–28
July 14, 2023 ©2023 Association for Computational Linguistics

the *underspecification* of the situation. The provision of situational information, such as "they are in a hotel," narrows down the range of ideal behaviors, which helps generation systems produce context-specific responses and establishes a more solid standard for judging quality. This issue is not limited to this particular dataset. Many common open-domain conversational datasets contain little or no additional information besides conversation history (the Twitter dataset (Ritter et al., 2011); DREAM (Sun et al., 2019); MuTual (Cui et al., 2020); *inter alia*). This task setting, which requires systems to infer almost all information solely from previous utterances, poses unnecessary challenges and may lead to undesired system behavior.

In this position paper, we discuss the current state of open-domain conversational datasets concerning how situations are represented (§2). Specifically, we consider situational statements[3] that provide partial information about immediately observable (e.g., today's weather), commonly known (e.g., umbrellas are often used on rainy days), or directly derivable facts related to the task, speaker, and goals (e.g., the hotel's check-out and a guest's required action). Some of these elements have already been effectively integrated into modern conversational systems, particularly for closed-domain, task-oriented dialogues. We argue that open-domain conversational tasks and datasets should be equipped with some form of situational information. Additionally, we conducted case studies on several datasets to explore the potential benefits and challenges associated with situational information (§3). Our analysis indicates that distinguishing between relevant and irrelevant situational information can be challenging for data-driven response engines, offering opportunities for future research.

2 Status Quo

In open-domain response generation tasks, systems generate responses in natural language based on input dialog history (a list of utterances from previous turns). Dialog history often serves as the primary, and sometimes sole, source of context information in many datasets. In this section, we discuss how conventional task design can be improved through the explicit inclusion of situational information.

2.1 Open-domain Conversational Datasets

The recent advancement of open-domain conversational technologies can be largely attributed to the development of large-scale conversation datasets, which facilitate the training of data-driven language generation models. However, many commonly used datasets lack crucial situational information. Below, we provide a brief overview of representative datasets in the field.[4]

Collection of naturally occuering conversation data can be costly (Godfrey et al., 1992). This bottleneck was greatly alleviated by public web resources that contain naturalistic textual conversations. For instance, millions of conversations can be scraped automatically from Twitter (Ritter et al., 2010). Likewise, many large-scale datasets were produced from social media (Wang et al., 2013; Sordoni et al., 2015; Shang et al., 2015; Henderson et al., 2019). While conversations on social media are essentially text chat and do not cover many of the dailylife interactions, online language learning coursewares contain conversation examples in diverse scenarios (Li et al., 2017; Sun et al., 2019; Cui et al., 2020). DailyDialog (Li et al., 2017) is one of the datasets built from English learning materials and 13k multi-turn conversationswe spanning various topics and scenarios. These (semi-)automatically harvested datasets are generally large and effectively used for pre-training language models (Humeau et al., 2019; Shuster et al., 2020). However, they contain only conversation history.

Some prior studies have created conversational datasets enriched with various semantic and pragmatic features. Notably, multi-modal and task-oriented datasets generally allocate dedicated representations for essential situational information such as physical signals (Haber et al., 2019; Moon et al., 2020) and task-specific information or domain knowledge (Budzianowski et al., 2018), but their coverage is limited to one or a few specialized domains. For open-domain conversation systems, the use of focused information has been explored for improving response quality, such as related documents (Zhou et al., 2018; Dinan et al., 2019) and user-based features such as persona (Zhang et al., 2018; Majumder et al., 2020; Dinan et al., 2020b), emotion (Rashkin et al., 2019), social norms (Kim

[3]The situation of a conversation consists of numerous predicates that describe various aspects of surroundings. By *a situational statement*, we mean a single predicate that describes part of a situation.

[4]For a more comprehensive literature review, refer to survey papers on available resources (Serban et al., 2017; Kann et al., 2022).

et al., 2022), and behavior (Ghosal et al., 2022; Zhou et al., 2022). Sato et al. (2017) explored the utilization of time information as well as user types for analyzing conversations on Twitter. Though these studies demonstrate that integrating surrounding information improves response quality in various aspects such as informativeness and engagement, the scope has been limited to specific modalities, domains, and semantic categories. Moreover, detecting certain features, like internal emotion and plans, can be non-trivial in practice. Observable situational information has received little attention. Otani et al. (2023) aimed to represent such information in free-form English texts, but the available resources are limited, and it remains unclear whether existing datasets can be extended to include situational information.

2.2 Necessity of Situational Information

Most importantly, the absence of situational information leads to the underspecification of the problem space. Without knowing the situation in which an utterance is expressed, its interpretation cannot always be determined. For instance, the request "please call Pat" could mean at least two actions: speaking to Pat in person or making a phone call.

Additionally, without sufficient knowledge of the world state, systems may produce meaningless or contradictive responses even if they appear natural. In the research community, the inconsistency within generated responses is recognized to be one of the unsolved problems (Nie et al., 2021; Shuster et al., 2022). This problem may be attributed to the underspecified task setting. As previous examples suggest, the interpretation of human communication often relies on unspoken information. When situational information is absent, systems must assume implicit parameters of the world state on their own, which may not always be correct. For instance, the inconsistency of personality information had been a common challenge for chat bots (Li et al., 2016) and was alleviated by explicitly modeling user-based features (Zhang et al., 2018). Furthermore, training on this problem formulation may force systems to learn superficial patterns.

The challenge of evaluating conversation systems is also compounded by the broadness of the problem space. Previous studies have discredited the use of automatic evaluation methods in response generation tasks (Liu et al., 2016). Although techniques such as considering multiple reference responses may alleviate this problem to some extent (Sai et al., 2020), it remains a significant challenge. Furthermore, even in the task of response selection, reliably evaluating system output is non-trivial due to the potential for false negatives when confusing distractor statements are included in the pool of candidate responses (Hedayatnia et al., 2022).

	Training	Validation	Test	Avg. turn
SUGAR	1,214	102	25	1.0
CICERO	15,171	5,325	25	3.0
ConvAI2	16,878	1,000	25	4.7

Table 2: Datasets used in this study. For manual evaluation, we sampled 25 examples from the test split of each dataset (not presented in this table).

3 Situated Response Generation

In order to analyze the impact of incorporating situational information into response generation, we conducted an empirical analysis using two neural generation models and three English datasets.[5]

3.1 Datasets

We used the following English datasets.

1. SUGAR (Otani et al., 2023): This dataset consists of single-turn conversations in different help-seeking scenarios. Each example includes 12 sentences that describe situational information across six categories, including date, time, location, speaker's behavior, environment, and speaker's possession. Some of the statements are irrelevant and serve as *distractors*. SUGAR represents datasets that provide rich situational information.
2. CICERO (Ghosal et al., 2022): This dataset is a compilation of three datasets, including DailyDialog (Li et al., 2017), MuTual (Cui et al., 2020), and DREAM (Sun et al., 2019). CICERO is an example of conversational datasets that do not explicitly present situational information.[6]
3. ConvAI2 (Zhang et al., 2018; Dinan et al., 2020b): This dataset is designed for persona

[5]The purpose of this analysis is to find out if there are any notable patterns associated with the inclusion of situational statements rather than benchmarking response generation systems.

[6]Although CICERO includes annotations of commonsense reasoning about target utterances, we did not use them as they include unobservable facts. We only used CICERO for the pre-filtering it underwent.

A	Hi, Mike! how are you feeling now?
B	How did you know I was here? is it Tom?
A	I was talking with Bob yesterday and I learnt your right leg had been injured. How did it happen?
B	[System output]
Generated situational statements	
Person B's leg had a surgery last night. It is afternoon now. Person A and Person B are in the hospital. Person B injured his right leg when he was playing baseball. Person A has been informed. Person A has a phone. Person B has a leg brace on. Person B's leg is injured. Person B's leg is getting better. Person A's car is in the parking lot.	

Table 3: An example of generated situational statements. This conversation is taken from the CICERO dataset. These statements represent *an assumption* about the situation. In practice, situational information is *perceived* in some way rather than generated.

chats, with each conversation featuring the speaker's persona information in 4-5 sentences.[7] ConvAI2 is a dataset with user-based features.

We selected 25 test instances for manual evaluation from the test split of each dataset. For CICERO and ConvAI2, which consist of multi-turn conversations, we randomly selected one target turn from each dialogue, and considered its preceeding utterances as conversation history. We chose targets of test instances the second to the fourth turn to reduce the cognitive load during evaluation. As the test split for ConvAI2 is not publicly available, we used its validation split as our test data and selected 1,000 examples for validation from the training split. Table 2 shows the dataset sizes after our filtering process.

3.2 Generating Situational Statements

CICERO and ConvAI2 do not contain descriptions of situational information. We utilized a Transformer-based generation model to automatically generate situational statements for these datasets, which allowed us to analyze how systems could generate situated responses within a specific context (See Appendix A.1 for details). Table 3 shows an example of generated situational statements.

To generate the situational information descriptions, we used the SUGAR dataset to fine-tune $\text{COMET}^{\text{DIS}}_{\text{TIL}}$ (West et al., 2022), which is a GPT-2-XL model (Radford et al., 2019) trained on common-sense knowledge data. We concatenated a previous utterance, a response, and a reference situational statement into one sequence and trained the model to minimize a cross-entropy loss over the situation part. We also fine-tuned another $\text{COMET}^{\text{DIS}}_{\text{TIL}}$ (West et al., 2022) model without reference responses in input to avoid including the gold-standard information in testing instances. In input sequences, each text was headed by special symbols indicating the text type: <utterance> for an utterance, <response> for a response, and <situation category> for a situational statement. The <situation category> symbol is one of date, time, location, behavior, environment, and possession.

Using the fine-tuned model, we added 10 situational statements to each example, including one each for date, time, location, and behavior, and three each for environment and possession. Finally, for quality control, one of the authors manually checked the test samples from CICERO and ConvAI2 (25 for each) and corrected context statements when required (e.g., conflicting facts). The reference responses were hidden during the manual verification to avoid bias. This manual verification process ensures the quality of the test dataset in order to minimize the confusion of annotators in the following manual evaluation of responses.

3.3 Setup

Systems: Considering the reported performance and the availability of implementations, we chose the following baseline systems:

1. BlenderBot2 (BB2): A Transformer-based response generation model that is pre-trained on multiple conversational datasets. We used a distilled 400M-parameters model in the ParlAI library (Miller et al., 2017).
2. GPT-3: A Transformer-based causal language model that is pre-trained on a massive collection of documents. We used GPT-3-DaVinci (175B parameters) through OpenAI API. For each dataset, we manually selected four high-quality training examples and embeded them in a prompt.

We fine-tuned BB2 on the mixture of the aforementioned datasets in a multi-task learning setting. We up-sampled SUGAR and CICERO to balance the data sizes. To alleviate the randomness of system output, we trained two BB2 models with different random seeds, and for each model, we generated one response by beam search with width 2. We obtained top-2 generations from GPT-3 with a beam

[7]We used `revised` persona statements.

width of 4. Appendix A.2 describes implementation details.

Evaluation: We recruited three annotators on Amazon Mechanical Turk to evaluate each response.[8] We employed three criteria: (1) grammaticality (whether the response is grammatically correct), (2) Coherence (whether the response is coherent and contextually appropriate), and (3) context-specificality (whether the response is specifically relevant to the given context.) The latter two criteria were defined based on prior work (Thoppilan et al., 2022; Zhou et al., 2022).[9] Table 4 shows some examples. We collected a total of 1,800 binary judgments for each criterion in our evaluation. The inter-annotator agreement was relatively low, with a Fleiss' kappa of 0.38, likely due to the subjective nature of the quality assessment. The agreement for evaluating BB2 was notably low, possibly because its responses are often not fluent, making it difficult for annotators to rate individual criteria. In contrast, GPT-3's responses were fluent, resulting in a Fleiss' kappa of 0.48. To minimize the impact of this variance, we calculated the final score of each response by averaging the ratings of three annotators and manually reviewed responses with high variance.

3.4 Results

Figure 1 shows the average scores of responses. GPT-3 was highly capable of generating fluent responses based on its internal assumptions about the situations. The annotators was likely inferred the assumed situations to interpret the GPT-3's responses, resulting in higher ratings. In the example below, GPT-3 produced appropriate responses regardless of the presence of situational information.

Example 1
A: "Hi, Mike! how are you feeling now?"
B: "How did you know I was here? is it Tom?"
A: "I was talking with Bob yesterday and I learnt your right leg had been injured. How did it happen?"

GPT-3 (Without situational information in input)
(a) "Yeah, I slipped on the stairs and I sprained my ankle."
(b) "It was a sports accident. I was playing basketball and I sprained my ankle."

GPT-3 (+Situation: "Person A and Person B are in the hospital.", ..., "Person B injured his right leg when he was playing baseball.")
(c) "Yeah, I was playing baseball and I twisted my ankle."
(d) "Yeah, I had a surgery last night. It happened when I was playing baseball. I'm feeling much better now, thanks."

On the other hand, BB2 struggled to identify generalizable patterns through fine-tuning when situational information was not provided. This was evident in SUGAR, where only a single utterance was provided as input to the system. The following example shows responses generated by BB2.

Example 2 *A:* "Could you help me take a bus?"

BB2 (Without situational information in input)
(a) *"Sure. shall I book a taxi as well? I can also book a ride for you to and from work."
(b) "Sure. would you like me to bring your bags, too? they are heavy."

BB2 (+Situation: "The speaker has a bus schedule." ... "There is a backpack near the desk.")
(c) "Sure. shall I pull up your bus schedule? it will show you when the bus is coming."
(d) "Sure. would you like me to get your bag ready? it will go in your backpack."

BB2 produced more coherent and context-specific responses when situational information was explicitly provided. However, as the examples above indicate, BB2's responses were not as fluent as GPT-3's, resulting in lower overall performance.

We observed that in some examples, GPT-3 selected information that was not directly relevant to the immediate previous utterance and returned unnatural responses like the example below.

Example 3 *A:* "Could you help me stretch?"

GPT-3 (Without situational information in input)
"Absolutely. Let me know which muscles you want to focus on and I can show you some stretches."

GPT-3 (+Situation: "The speaker is wearing a jogging suit and running shoes.", ..., "There is a beach ball at home." ... "The nearest beach is open.")
*"Of course! Let's go to the beach and play with the beach ball while we stretch."

[8] Prior work provides multiple empirical results showing that automatic evaluation metrics are not strongly correlated with human judgments (Liu et al., 2016; Deriu et al., 2022). Therefore, we solely rely on manual evaluation in this study. See Appendix B for details.

[9] We adopted the definitions of Zhou et al. with modified terminology.

	Input	Situation	Response	Coh.	Spe.
1	Please start my car.	The speaker's car is functioning.	Sure, I'll do that right now.	✓	
2	Please start my car.	The speaker's car is out of gas.	Sure, I'll do that right now.		
3	Please start my car.	The speaker's car is out of gas.	Sorry, but I'm afraid your car is out of fuel. Would you like me to call a taxi for you instead?	✓	✓
4	Please start my car.	The speaker's car is out of gas.	Sorry, but I can't. Would you like me to call a taxi for you instead?	(*)	✓
5	What is the weather like today?	It's currently raining outside.	It's sunny and warm.		✓
6	Can I get some beer, please?	No beer is left, but wines are available.	Yes, I'll get it right now for you.		
7	Can I get some beer, please?	There are beer and some snacks in the kitchen.	Yes, I'll get it right now for you. Would you also like me to bring some food?	✓	✓

Table 4: Examples for the coherence (denoted as Coh) and context-specificity (denoted as Spe) ratings. ✓ means the criterion is satisfied. (*) The response is not coherent because it does not explain why the car is unavailable.

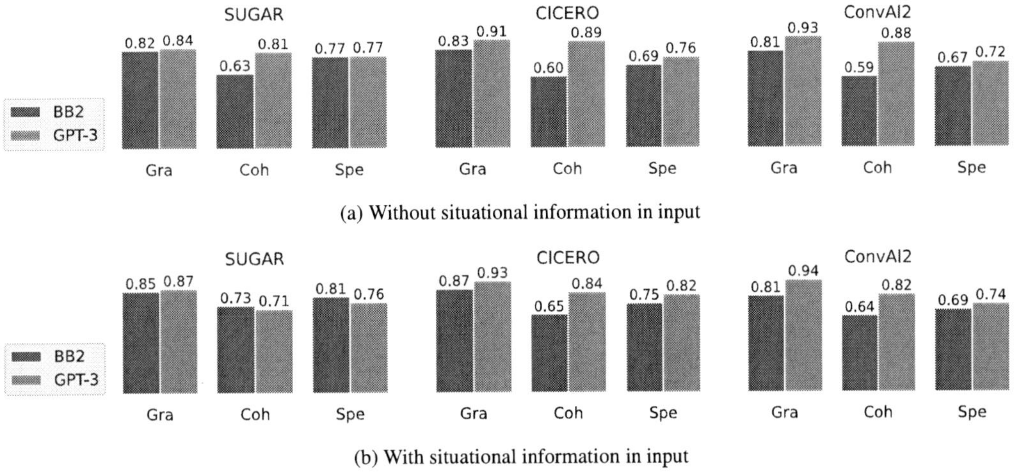

Figure 1: Manual evaluation results. The values displayed represent the average scores of responses in three criteria: (1) grammatical correctness, (2) coherence, and (3) specificity to the context.

Furthermore, as shown in Example 1 and Table 5, semantic consistency within the top-k responses improved when more situational information is given, although this was not evaluated in our experiments. This behavior is fundamentally rooted in the design of the task. Having inconsistent and mutually-exclusive top-k candidates is not a problem when systems need to ground them on nothing.

	[· · ·]
A	I just have my dog, trooper.
B	My wife is thinking about getting our kids a dog. What kind is yours?
A	[System output]
Without context	
1st: I have **a border collie.** He's a great companion.	
2nd: He's **a lab mix.** He's a great companion.	
+A has a pet bulldog named Trooper.	
1st: Trooper is **a bulldog.** He's the best!	
2nd: He's **a bulldog.** He's a great companion!	

Table 5: Top-2 response generation results from GPT-3. The example was taken from CICERO.

3.5 GPT-3's Robustness to Distractors

GPT-3 demonstrated superior performance in response generation, but our observations suggest that it can be misled by irrelevant situational statements (distractors) and return suboptimal responses. To further investigate the model's robustness to distractors, we evaluated GPT-3 on SUGAR with varying numbers of situational statements.

Experimental Setup: We controlled the number of distractors by extending the SUGAR dataset, whose examples have about six distractors. We created instances with 5, 10, and 15 distractors by sampling statements from the whole dataset as necessary. We selected 30 examples at random for this experiment and manually fixed contradictions within situational statements. We generated two responses for each example using GPT-3 through OpenAI's API, employing the same hyperparameter setting used in the previous experiment.

Evaluation: We recruited two annotators on Amazon Mechanical Turk to evaluate each response. Based on previous annotation results, we updated the annotation guidelines and qualification criteria[10], resulting in substantial agreement (Fleiss' kappa of 0.76). We calculated average scores for three dimensions: (1) grammaticality, (2) coherence, and (3) context-specificity.

Results: The evaluation scores of GPT-3 are presented in Figure 2. The grammaticality and context-specificity of responses remained at the same level regardless of the number of distractors, which suggests that GPT-3 is highly capable of integrating provided information into fluent English expressions. On the other hand, the coherence of a response, which requires the model to discern relevant information, exhibits a different trend. The scores are high when no or five distractors were presented (0.86 and 0.90 for 0 and 5 distractors, respectively), but the coherence scores decreased when more distractors were added (0.77 and 0.81 for 10 and 15 distractors, respectively).[11] This is exemplified by the following model outputs.

Example 4 *A:* "Please lock the door."

No distractors ("The speaker is dressed in nice clothing." ..., "The door is unlocked.", ..., "The windows are open.")
"Sure, and do you want me to close the windows too?"

5 distractors (+ "The speaker has a printout titled, Interior design for beginners.", "Person A's doctor told him he should lose weight.", ...)
? "Sure, and do you need any help with the interior design project?"[12]

10 distractors (+ "The speaker has laundry piled up in the room.", "Person A has scissors in the house.", ...)
? "Sure, and should I turn off the windows too?"

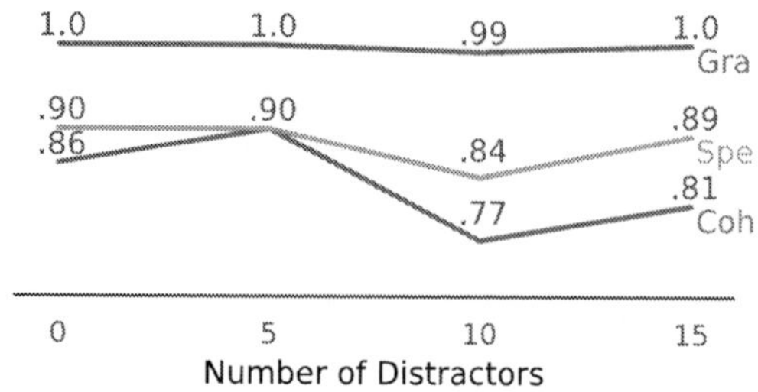

Figure 2: Manual evaluation results with varying number of distractors. Criteria: (1) grammatical correctness, (2) coherence, and (3) specificity to the context.

15 distractors (+ "Person A has a telescope in the house.", "Person A owns an exercise bike.", ...)
*"Sure, and would you like me to help you with the laundry too?"

The coherence score was relatively low (0.86) when no distractors were presented. We conjecture the model may have learned to copy phrases to generate responses instead of reasoning over input texts. We found that the model's responses tended to sound abrupt, as shown in the following example:

Example 5 *Person A:* "Can you assist me with brushing my teeth?"

No distractors ("The speaker has a dental cleaning scheduled.", ..., "There is no more toothpaste in the house.")
*"Sure, I can help you get some toothpaste at the store. Would you like me to come with you?"

4 Discussion

Models' internal assumptions: As discussed in Section 2, the lack of sufficient situational information often makes the interpretation of utterances ambiguous. In such a setting, systems need to learn to make various assumptions about the world state to produce naturally-sounding language, which can be regarded as a form of hallucination. Responses generated in this way can be useless in real applications, where the world state is predetermined. Our empirical analysis also indicates that the systems' consistency can be improved with detailed situational information, which is also aligned with the initial motivation of background-based conversational tasks like persona chat. On the other hand, our results indicates that GPT-3 can generate accurate responses even without the provision of situational information. This observation suggests that

[10] See Appendix B.

[11] There was a minor improvement in performance when the number of distractors rises from 10 to 15. The model might adapt to avoid conflating excessive information when it recognized a majority of the presented situational statements as irrelevant in training examples.

[12] This response might be acceptable given that the speaker has a printout about interior design.

large-scale language models might have already captured information about typical world states and appropriate behavior through pre-training. Nevertheless, there is no guarantee that the model's internal assumption will always align perfectly with the actual world state. Hence, there remains a necessity to provide the model with situational information in some form.

Resource acquisition: Simple collections of textual conversations can be easily obtained at scale from the web, but acquiring their situational information is more difficult. For example, although conversations on Twitter may be grounded in the weather, sport events, and news on a particular day, automatically extracting such alignments may be challenging. The connection between utterances and related information is often obscure, and manual intervention is likely required to obtain high-quality annotations. As a potential remedy for this challenge, we attempted automatic generation of situational information in our case study. The quality of the generated result was fair, but we needed to manually revise the test instances. Recent studies have demonstrated promising results in inducing world knowledge from PLMs (West et al., 2022; Ghosal et al., 2022). The future advancement in this line of work may make it possible to annotate existing open-domain conversation datasets with situational information in a post-hoc manner.

Availability: Different platforms of conversational systems have access to different types of situational information. Smart speakers may be equipped with physical sensors to observe visual and audio information. On the other hand, virtual assistants and text-based chatbots may not have access to such information. However, it is likely that there are some available signals that human communicators and systems could refer to, such as approaching holidays and personal information obtained through previous conversations. Finch et al. (2019) demonstrated that mentioning recent events can improve user engagement in chit-chat. Furthermore, if conversation systems have access to the Internet, which is often the case, they can access diverse kinds of information through external APIs. Access to APIs can also facilitate conversational assistance with task-specific information in various domains (Liang et al., 2023).

Representation: Prior work has demonstrated that a substantial range of surrounding information can be represented and integrated by textual representations (Zhou et al., 2018; Zhang et al., 2018; Rashkin et al., 2019; Kim et al., 2022; Otani et al., 2023), and our study has also shown that textual statements can inform response generation models of situational information. However, it is important to note that certain types of information might be more effectively represented using alternative formats, such as images, audio signals, numerical values, or logical expressions. Future work should explore and develop methods to better represent situational information and incorporate it into computational models.

Adequacy: When situations are taken into account, a different problem arises. Our findings indicate that it is not straightforward to identify relevant situational information and integrate it into a coherent response, even with just 10 situational statements. Additionally, there is a technical limitation on the length of input that a model can handle. situational information can typically be obtained from various sources, and often, an excessive amount of information is present. Humans can quickly focus on crucial information and discard the rest, otherwise, it would take forever to read, process, and reason over surrounding information. Researchers have identified the Frame Problem (McCarthy and Hayes, 1969) that describes the dilemma of a reasoning system in determining which aspects of a situation change and which remain constant after an action. To date, there has been no satisfactory solution to this questions, making the challenge of situated conversation an interesting open challenge.

Common ground: Knowledge about situations is closely related to common ground–the information shared by conversation participants. Without common ground, conversation participants would need to convey every parameter of their message, which is extremely inefficient. The importance of common ground is widely recognized, and decades of dialogue research have been devoted to developing systems that can effectively establish common ground with their interlocutors by inferring, presenting, requesting, accepting, and repairing individual beliefs about various information through conversations (Traum and Allen, 1994; Clark, 1996; Poesio and Rieses, 2010; *inter alia*). In this paper, we did not delve into the problem of common ground, but the consideration of situations, which is our main proposal, is the first step towards computational modeling of grounding.

5 Related Work

Conversation history: There is a rich line of work on how to induce useful contextual information from conversation history, for example, by designing dedicated components for capturing contextual information (Tian et al., 2017; Sankar et al., 2019) and using external knowledge (Young et al., 2018; Wu et al., 2020; *inter alia*). While conversation history contains rich information, we need to also incorporate situational information, which is often unspoken, and to this end, we should think about how to design tasks and datasets.

Prompt design: Our analysis is closely related to work on in-context learning, or prompting, with PLMs. In particular, much attention has been paid to the effective provision of demonstrative examples (Zhao et al., 2021; Liu et al., 2022; Min et al., 2022). This paper discussed the problem from a different perspective, namely what clues should be included in prompts (situations) and how PLMs perform (misleading by distractors). Our observation regarding the latter is consistent with prior work that revealed the vulnerability to perturbations in input (Elazar et al., 2021; Pandia and Ettinger, 2021). Future work should explore ways to robustly identify relevant situational information to generate optimal responses.

6 Conclusion

Our main claim is that situational information, which may or may not be stated explicitly by humans, should be represented and incorporated as input in open-domain conversational tasks and datasets in order to advance the capabilities of conversation systems. We posited that the absence of situational information results in an underspecified problem space, causing a severe problem for both the development and evaluation of conversation systems. Our experiments on three textual datasets highlight the benefits and difficulties of providing explicit and implicit situational information to response generation systems, which motivates future research on situated conversation systems.

Limitations

Firstly, we did not address the fundamental challenge of determining *an adequate amount* of situational information. It is very difficult, if not impossible, to describe *all* the situations required to perform rationale reasoning, so we need to give up somewhere, relying on the reasoning capability of NLP systems.

Secondly, we did not use large-scale data or conduct an extensive search for optimal hyperparameters and prompts (for GPT-3) in our experiments as the primary goal of this study was to raise attentions to potential issues and benefits associated with situational informaiton. The models may have performed better with different configurations. We did not examined the capabilities of larger PLMs in conducting situated conversations at scale. In our empirical analysis, we opted for GPT-3 due to its transparency about technical details compared with later versions of GPT.

Finally, while situational information can aid in the development of truthful and creative response generation systems, it does not address well-known issues associated with conversational technologies, such as safety and bias. In fact, poorly chosen situational information may even amplify undesired bias by linking two irelevant concepts together. To mitigate this problem, researchers and developers should exercise caution when collecting data and carefully monitor system output.

Ethics Statements

The use of crowdsourcing: We recruited human evaluators in Amazon Mechanical Turk. Our evaluation task does not collect any personal information other than anonymized worker IDs and country of residence (due to our location-based worker qualification). We do not plan to release this information to the public. We set the task reward based on trial studies so that the estimated hourly rate would reach at least $9.00.

The risk in the inclusion of situational information: While we believe that incorporating situational information can have a positive impact on conversational technologies in general, as previously mentioned, it is not intended to address well-known issues concerning the toxic behavior of language generation models. Rather, it may introduce another source for models to learn undesirable associations between concepts and language. Therefore, the data and system output should be closely monitored, either manually or through automatic methods such as debiasing techniques (Liu et al., 2020; Dinan et al., 2020a).

Acknowledgments

We thank Yonatan Bisk, Benjamin Van Durme, Lori Levin, and the anonymous reviewers for their feedback.

References

Tom B. Brown, Benjamin Mann, Nick Ryder, Melanie Subbiah, Jared Kaplan, Prafulla Dhariwal, Arvind Neelakantan, Pranav Shyam, Girish Sastry, Amanda Askell, Sandhini Agarwal, Ariel Herbert-Voss, Gretchen Krueger, Tom Henighan, Rewon Child, Aditya Ramesh, Daniel M. Ziegler, Jeffrey Wu, Clemens Winter, Christopher Hesse, Mark Chen, Eric Sigler, Mateusz Litwin, Scott Gray, Benjamin Chess, Jack Clark, Christopher Berner, Sam McCandlish, Alec Radford, Ilya Sutskever, and Dario Amodei. 2020. Language models are few-shot learners. *arXiv*.

Paweł Budzianowski, Tsung-Hsien Wen, Bo-Hsiang Tseng, Iñigo Casanueva, Stefan Ultes, Osman Ramadan, and Milica Gašić. 2018. MultiWOZ - A large-scale multi-domain Wizard-of-Oz dataset for task-oriented dialogue modelling. In *Proceedings of the 2018 Conference on Empirical Methods in Natural Language Processing*, pages 5016–5026, Brussels, Belgium. Association for Computational Linguistics.

Herbert H. Clark. 1996. *Using language*. Cambridge University Press.

Leyang Cui, Yu Wu, Shujie Liu, Yue Zhang, and Ming Zhou. 2020. MuTual: A dataset for multi-turn dialogue reasoning. In *Proceedings of the 58th Annual Meeting of the Association for Computational Linguistics*, pages 1406–1416, Online. Association for Computational Linguistics.

Jan Deriu, Don Tuggener, Pius Von Däniken, and Mark Cieliebak. 2022. Probing the robustness of trained metrics for conversational dialogue systems. In *Proceedings of the 60th Annual Meeting of the Association for Computational Linguistics (Volume 2: Short Papers)*, pages 750–761, Dublin, Ireland. Association for Computational Linguistics.

Emily Dinan, Angela Fan, Adina Williams, Jack Urbanek, Douwe Kiela, and Jason Weston. 2020a. Queens are powerful too: Mitigating gender bias in dialogue generation. In *Proceedings of the 2020 Conference on Empirical Methods in Natural Language Processing*, pages 8173–8188, Online. Association for Computational Linguistics.

Emily Dinan, Varvara Logacheva, Valentin Malykh, Alexander Miller, Kurt Shuster, Jack Urbanek, Douwe Kiela, Arthur Szlam, Iulian Serban, Ryan Lowe, Shrimai Prabhumoye, Alan W. Black, Alexander Rudnicky, Jason Williams, Joelle Pineau, Mikhail Burtsev, and Jason Weston. 2020b. The Second Conversational Intelligence Challenge (ConvAI2). In *The NeurIPS '18 Competition*, The Springer Series on Challenges in Machine Learning, pages 187–208, Cham. Springer International Publishing.

Emily Dinan, Stephen Roller, Kurt Shuster, Angela Fan, Michael Auli, and Jason Weston. 2019. Wizard of Wikipedia: Knowledge-powered conversational agents. In *The Seventh International Conference on Learning Representations*, New Orleans, Louisiana, USA. ArXiv: 1811.01241.

Yanai Elazar, Nora Kassner, Shauli Ravfogel, Abhilasha Ravichander, Eduard Hovy, Hinrich Schütze, and Yoav Goldberg. 2021. Measuring and improving consistency in pretrained language models. *Transactions of the Association for Computational Linguistics*, 9:1012–1031. Place: Cambridge, MA Publisher: MIT Press.

Sarah E. Finch, James D. Finch, Ali Ahmadvand, Choi Ingyu (Jason), Xiangjue Dong, Ruixiang Qi, Harshita Sahijwani, Sergey Volokhin, Zihan Wang, Zihao Wang, and Jinho D. Choi. 2019. Emora: An inquisitive social chatbot who cares for you. In *3rd Proceedings of Alexa Prize*.

Deepanway Ghosal, Siqi Shen, Navonil Majumder, Rada Mihalcea, and Soujanya Poria. 2022. CICERO: A dataset for contextualized commonsense inference in dialogues. In *Proceedings of the 60th Annual Meeting of the Association for Computational Linguistics*, pages 5010–5028, Dublin, Ireland. Association for Computational Linguistics.

J.J. Godfrey, E.C. Holliman, and J. McDaniel. 1992. SWITCHBOARD: telephone speech corpus for research and development. In *[Proceedings] ICASSP-92: 1992 IEEE International Conference on Acoustics, Speech, and Signal Processing*, volume 1, pages 517–520 vol.1. ISSN: 1520-6149.

Janosch Haber, Tim Baumgärtner, Ece Takmaz, Lieke Gelderloos, Elia Bruni, and Raquel Fernández. 2019. The PhotoBook dataset: Building common ground through visually-grounded dialogue. In *Proceedings of the 57th Annual Meeting of the Association for Computational Linguistics*, pages 1895–1910, Florence, Italy. Association for Computational Linguistics.

Behnam Hedayatnia, Di Jin, Yang Liu, and Dilek Hakkani-Tur. 2022. A systematic evaluation of response selection for open domain dialogue. In *Proceedings of the 23rd Annual Meeting of the Special Interest Group on Discourse and Dialogue*, pages 298–311, Edinburgh, UK. Association for Computational Linguistics.

Matthew Henderson, Iñigo Budzianowski Pawełand Casanueva, Sam Coope, Daniela Gerz, Girish Kumar, Nikola Mrkšić, Georgios Spithourakis, Pei-Hao Su, Ivan Vulić, and Tsung-Hsien Wen. 2019. A Repository of Conversational Datasets. In *Proceedings of the First Workshop on NLP for Conversational AI*, pages 1–10, Florence, Italy. Association for Computational Linguistics.

Samuel Humeau, Kurt Shuster, Marie-Anne Lachaux, and Jason Weston. 2019. Poly-encoders: Transformer Architectures and Pre-training Strategies for Fast and Accurate Multi-sentence Scoring. *The Eighth International Conference on Learning Representations*. ArXiv: 1905.01969.

Katharina Kann, Abteen Ebrahimi, Joewie Koh, Shiran Dudy, and Alessandro Roncone. 2022. Open-domain Dialogue Generation: What We Can Do, Cannot Do, And Should Do Next. In *Proceedings of the 4th Workshop on NLP for Conversational AI*, pages 148–165, Dublin, Ireland. Association for Computational Linguistics.

Hyunwoo Kim, Youngjae Yu, Liwei Jiang, Ximing Lu, Daniel Khashabi, Gunhee Kim, Yejin Choi, and Maarten Sap. 2022. ProsocialDialog: A Prosocial Backbone for Conversational Agents. In *Proceedings of the 2022 Conference on Empirical Methods in Natural Language Processing*, pages 4005–4029, Abu Dhabi, United Arab Emirates. Association for Computational Linguistics.

Mojtaba Komeili, Kurt Shuster, and Jason Weston. 2022. Internet-Augmented Dialogue Generation. In *Proceedings of the 60th Annual Meeting of the Association for Computational Linguistics*, pages 8460–8478, Dublin, Ireland. Association for Computational Linguistics.

Jiwei Li, Michel Galley, Chris Brockett, Georgios Spithourakis, Jianfeng Gao, and Bill Dolan. 2016. A persona-based neural conversation model. In *Proceedings of the 54th Annual Meeting of the Association for Computational Linguistics*, pages 994–1003, Berlin, Germany. Association for Computational Linguistics.

Yanran Li, Hui Su, Xiaoyu Shen, Wenjie Li, Ziqiang Cao, and Shuzi Niu. 2017. DailyDialog: A manually labelled multi-turn dialogue dataset. In *Proceedings of the Eighth International Joint Conference on Natural Language Processing*, pages 986–995, Taipei, Taiwan. Asian Federation of Natural Language Processing.

Yaobo Liang, Chenfei Wu, Ting Song, Wenshan Wu, Yan Xia, Yu Liu, Yang Ou, Shuai Lu, Lei Ji, Shaoguang Mao, Yun Wang, Linjun Shou, Ming Gong, and Nan Duan. 2023. TaskMatrix.AI: Completing Tasks by Connecting Foundation Models with Millions of APIs. *arXiv*. ArXiv:2303.16434 [cs].

Chia-Wei Liu, Ryan Lowe, Iulian Serban, Mike Noseworthy, Laurent Charlin, and Joelle Pineau. 2016. How NOT To Evaluate Your Dialogue System: An Empirical Study of Unsupervised Evaluation Metrics for Dialogue Response Generation. In *Proceedings of the 2016 Conference on Empirical Methods in Natural Language Processing*, pages 2122–2132, Austin, Texas. Association for Computational Linguistics.

Haochen Liu, Wentao Wang, Yiqi Wang, Hui Liu, Zitao Liu, and Jiliang Tang. 2020. Mitigating gender bias for neural dialogue generation with adversarial learning. In *Proceedings of the 2020 Conference on Empirical Methods in Natural Language Processing (EMNLP)*, pages 893–903, Online. Association for Computational Linguistics.

Jiachang Liu, Dinghan Shen, Yizhe Zhang, Bill Dolan, Lawrence Carin, and Weizhu Chen. 2022. What Makes Good In-Context Examples for GPT-3? In *Proceedings of Deep Learning Inside Out (DeeLIO 2022): The 3rd Workshop on Knowledge Extraction and Integration for Deep Learning Architectures*, pages 100–114, Dublin, Ireland and Online. Association for Computational Linguistics.

Bodhisattwa Prasad Majumder, Harsh Jhamtani, Taylor Berg-Kirkpatrick, and Julian McAuley. 2020. Like hiking? You probably enjoy nature: Persona-grounded Dialog with Commonsense Expansions. In *Proceedings of the 2020 Conference on Empirical Methods in Natural Language Processing*, pages 9194–9206, Online.

John McCarthy and Patrick J. Hayes. 1969. Some philosophical problems from the standpoint of artificial intelligence. *Machine Intelligence 4*, pages 463—-502.

A. H. Miller, W. Feng, A. Fisch, J. Lu, D. Batra, A. Bordes, D. Parikh, and J. Weston. 2017. ParlAI: A Dialog Research Software Platform. *arXiv preprint arXiv:1705.06476*.

Sewon Min, Xinxi Lyu, Ari Holtzman, Mikel Artetxe, Mike Lewis, Hannaneh Hajishirzi, and Luke Zettlemoyer. 2022. Rethinking the Role of Demonstrations: What Makes In-Context Learning Work? In *Proceedings of the 2022 Conference on Empirical Methods in Natural Language Processing*, pages 11048–11064, Abu Dhabi, United Arab Emirates. Association for Computational Linguistics.

Seungwhan Moon, Satwik Kottur, Paul Crook, Ankita De, Shivani Poddar, Theodore Levin, David Whitney, Daniel Difranco, Ahmad Beirami, Eunjoon Cho, Rajen Subba, and Alborz Geramifard. 2020. Situated and interactive multimodal conversations. In *Proceedings of the 28th International Conference on Computational Linguistics*, pages 1103–1121, Barcelona, Spain (Online). International Committee on Computational Linguistics.

Yixin Nie, Mary Williamson, Mohit Bansal, Douwe Kiela, and Jason Weston. 2021. I like fish, especially dolphins: Addressing contradictions in dialogue modeling. In *Proceedings of the 59th Annual Meeting of the Association for Computational Linguistics and the 11th International Joint Conference on Natural Language Processing*, pages 1699–1713, Online. Association for Computational Linguistics.

Naoki Otani, Jun Araki, HyeongSik Kim, and Eduard Hovy. 2023. A Textual Dataset for Situated Proactive Response Selection. In *Proceedings of the 61st Annual Meeting of the Association for Computational*

Linguistics, Toronto, Canada. Association for Computational Linguistics.

Lalchand Pandia and Allyson Ettinger. 2021. Sorting through the noise: Testing robustness of information processing in pre-trained language models. In *Proceedings of the 2021 Conference on Empirical Methods in Natural Language Processing*, pages 1583–1596, Online and Punta Cana, Dominican Republic. Association for Computational Linguistics.

Adam Paszke, Sam Gross, Francisco Massa, Adam Lerer, James Bradbury, Gregory Chanan, Trevor Killeen, Zeming Lin, Natalia Gimelshein, Luca Antiga, Alban Desmaison, Andreas Kopf, Edward Yang, Zachary DeVito, Martin Raison, Alykhan Tejani, Sasank Chilamkurthy, Benoit Steiner, Lu Fang, Junjie Bai, and Soumith Chintala. 2019. PyTorch: An Imperative Style, High-Performance Deep Learning Library. In *Advances in Neural Information Processing Systems*, volume 32. Curran Associates, Inc.

Massimo Poesio and Hannes Rieses. 2010. Completions, Coordination, and Alignment in Dialogue. *Dialogue & Discourse*, 1(1).

Alec Radford, Jeffrey Wu, Rewon Child, David Luan, Dario Amodei, Ilya Sutskever, et al. 2019. Language models are unsupervised multitask learners. *OpenAI blog*, 1(8):9.

Hannah Rashkin, Eric Michael Smith, Margaret Li, and Y-Lan Boureau. 2019. Towards Empathetic Open-domain Conversation Models: A New Benchmark and Dataset. In *Proceedings of the 57th Annual Meeting of the Association for Computational Linguistics*, pages 5370–5381, Florence, Italy. Association for Computational Linguistics.

Jeff Rasley, Samyam Rajbhandari, Olatunji Ruwase, and Yuxiong He. 2020. DeepSpeed: System Optimizations Enable Training Deep Learning Models with Over 100 Billion Parameters. In *Proceedings of the 26th ACM SIGKDD International Conference on Knowledge Discovery & Data Mining*, page 3505–3506, New York, NY, USA. Association for Computing Machinery.

Alan Ritter, Colin Cherry, and Bill Dolan. 2010. Unsupervised Modeling of Twitter Conversations. In *Human Language Technologies: The 2010 Annual Conference of the North American Chapter of the Association for Computational Linguistics*, pages 172–180, Los Angeles, California. Association for Computational Linguistics.

Alan Ritter, Colin Cherry, and William B Dolan. 2011. Data-Driven Response Generation in Social Media. In *Proceedings of the 2011 Conference on Empirical Methods in Natural Language Processing*, pages 583–593, Edinburgh, Scotland, UK. Association for Computational Linguistics.

Ananya B. Sai, Akash Kumar Mohankumar, Siddhartha Arora, and Mitesh M. Khapra. 2020. Improving Dialog Evaluation with a Multi-reference Adversarial Dataset and Large Scale Pretraining. *Transactions of the Association for Computational Linguistics*, 8:810–827. Place: Cambridge, MA Publisher: MIT Press.

Chinnadhurai Sankar, Sandeep Subramanian, Chris Pal, Sarath Chandar, and Yoshua Bengio. 2019. Do Neural Dialog Systems Use the Conversation History Effectively? An Empirical Study. In *Proceedings of the 57th Annual Meeting of the Association for Computational Linguistics*, pages 32–37, Florence, Italy. Association for Computational Linguistics.

Shoetsu Sato, Naoki Yoshinaga, Masashi Toyoda, and Masaru Kitsuregawa. 2017. Modeling Situations in Neural Chat Bots. In *Proceedings of ACL 2017, Student Research Workshop*, pages 120–127, Vancouver, Canada. Association for Computational Linguistics.

Iulian Vlad Serban, Ryan Lowe, Peter Henderson, Laurent Charlin, and Joelle Pineau. 2017. A Survey of Available Corpora for Building Data-Driven Dialogue Systems. *arXiv*.

Lifeng Shang, Zhengdong Lu, and Hang Li. 2015. Neural Responding Machine for Short-Text Conversation. In *Proceedings of the 53rd Annual Meeting of the Association for Computational Linguistics and the 7th International Joint Conference on Natural Language Processing (Volume 1: Long Papers)*, pages 1577–1586, Beijing, China. Association for Computational Linguistics.

Kurt Shuster, Da Ju, Stephen Roller, Emily Dinan, Y-Lan Boureau, and Jason Weston. 2020. The Dialogue Dodecathlon: Open-Domain Knowledge and Image Grounded Conversational Agents. In *Proceedings of the 58th Annual Meeting of the Association for Computational Linguistics*, pages 2453–2470, Online. Association for Computational Linguistics.

Kurt Shuster, Jack Urbanek, Arthur Szlam, and Jason Weston. 2022. Am I me or you? state-of-the-art dialogue models cannot maintain an identity. In *Findings of the Association for Computational Linguistics: NAACL 2022*, pages 2367–2387, Seattle, United States. Association for Computational Linguistics.

Alessandro Sordoni, Michel Galley, Michael Auli, Chris Brockett, Yangfeng Ji, Margaret Mitchell, Jian-Yun Nie, Jianfeng Gao, and Bill Dolan. 2015. A Neural Network Approach to Context-Sensitive Generation of Conversational Responses. In *Proceedings of the 2015 Conference of the North American Chapter of the Association for Computational Linguistics: Human Language Technologies*, pages 196–205, Denver, Colorado. Association for Computational Linguistics.

Kai Sun, Dian Yu, Jianshu Chen, Dong Yu, Yejin Choi, and Claire Cardie. 2019. DREAM: A Challenge Data Set and Models for Dialogue-Based Reading Comprehension. *Transactions of the Association for Computational Linguistics*, 7:217–231. Place: Cambridge, MA Publisher: MIT Press.

Romal Thoppilan, Daniel De Freitas, Jamie Hall, Noam Shazeer, Apoorv Kulshreshtha, Heng-Tze Cheng, Alicia Jin, Taylor Bos, Leslie Baker, Yu Du, YaGuang Li, Hongrae Lee, Huaixiu Steven Zheng, Amin Ghafouri, Marcelo Menegali, Yanping Huang, Maxim Krikun, Dmitry Lepikhin, James Qin, Dehao Chen, Yuanzhong Xu, Zhifeng Chen, Adam Roberts, Maarten Bosma, Vincent Zhao, Yanqi Zhou, Chung-Ching Chang, Igor Krivokon, Will Rusch, Marc Pickett, Pranesh Srinivasan, Laichee Man, Kathleen Meier-Hellstern, Meredith Ringel Morris, Tulsee Doshi, Renelito Delos Santos, Toju Duke, Johnny Soraker, Ben Zevenbergen, Vinodkumar Prabhakaran, Mark Diaz, Ben Hutchinson, Kristen Olson, Alejandra Molina, Erin Hoffman-John, Josh Lee, Lora Aroyo, Ravi Rajakumar, Alena Butryna, Matthew Lamm, Viktoriya Kuzmina, Joe Fenton, Aaron Cohen, Rachel Bernstein, Ray Kurzweil, Blaise Aguera-Arcas, Claire Cui, Marian Croak, Ed Chi, and Quoc Le. 2022. LaMDA: Language Models for Dialog Applications. *arXiv*.

Zhiliang Tian, Rui Yan, Lili Mou, Yiping Song, Yansong Feng, and Dongyan Zhao. 2017. How to Make Context More Useful? An Empirical Study on Context-Aware Neural Conversational Models. In *Proceedings of the 55th Annual Meeting of the Association for Computational Linguistics (Volume 2: Short Papers)*, pages 231–236, Vancouver, Canada. Association for Computational Linguistics.

David R. Traum and James F. Allen. 1994. Discourse Obligations in Dialogue Processing. In *32nd Annual Meeting of the Association for Computational Linguistics*, pages 1–8, Las Cruces, New Mexico, USA. Association for Computational Linguistics.

Hao Wang, Zhengdong Lu, Hang Li, and Enhong Chen. 2013. A Dataset for Research on Short-Text Conversations. In *Proceedings of the 2013 Conference on Empirical Methods in Natural Language Processing*, pages 935–945, Seattle, Washington, USA. Association for Computational Linguistics.

Peter West, Chandra Bhagavatula, Jack Hessel, Jena Hwang, Liwei Jiang, Ronan Le Bras, Ximing Lu, Sean Welleck, and Yejin Choi. 2022. Symbolic Knowledge Distillation: from General Language Models to Commonsense Models. In *Proceedings of the 2022 Conference of the North American Chapter of the Association for Computational Linguistics: Human Language Technologies*, pages 4602–4625, Seattle, United States. Association for Computational Linguistics.

Thomas Wolf, Lysandre Debut, Victor Sanh, Julien Chaumond, Clement Delangue, Anthony Moi, Pierric Cistac, Tim Rault, Remi Louf, Morgan Funtowicz, Joe Davison, Sam Shleifer, Patrick von Platen, Clara Ma, Yacine Jernite, Julien Plu, Canwen Xu, Teven Le Scao, Sylvain Gugger, Mariama Drame, Quentin Lhoest, and Alexander Rush. 2020. Transformers: State-of-the-Art Natural Language Processing. In *Proceedings of the 2020 Conference on Empirical Methods in Natural Language Processing: System Demonstrations*, pages 38–45, Online. Association for Computational Linguistics.

Sixing Wu, Ying Li, Dawei Zhang, Yang Zhou, and Zhonghai Wu. 2020. Diverse and Informative Dialogue Generation with Context-Specific Commonsense Knowledge Awareness. In *Proceedings of the 58th Annual Meeting of the Association for Computational Linguistics*, pages 5811–5820, Online. Association for Computational Linguistics.

Jing Xu, Arthur Szlam, and Jason Weston. 2022. Beyond Goldfish Memory: Long-Term Open-Domain Conversation. In *Proceedings of the 60th Annual Meeting of the Association for Computational Linguistics*, pages 5180–5197, Dublin, Ireland. Association for Computational Linguistics.

Tom Young, Erik Cambria, Iti Chaturvedi, Hao Zhou, Subham Biswas, and Minlie Huang. 2018. Augmenting End-to-End Dialogue Systems With Commonsense Knowledge. In *Proceedings of the Thirty-Second AAAI Conference on Artificial Intelligence*, pages 4970–4977, New Orleans, LA, USA. AAAI Press.

Saizheng Zhang, Emily Dinan, Jack Urbanek, Arthur Szlam, Douwe Kiela, and Jason Weston. 2018. Personalizing dialogue agents: I have a dog, do you have pets too? In *Proceedings of the 56th Annual Meeting of the Association for Computational Linguistics*, pages 2204–2213, Melbourne, Australia. Association for Computational Linguistics.

Zihao Zhao, Eric Wallace, Shi Feng, Dan Klein, and Sameer Singh. 2021. Calibrate before use: Improving few-shot performance of language models. In *Proceedings of the 38th International Conference on Machine Learning*, pages 12697–12706. PMLR. ISSN: 2640-3498.

Kangyan Zhou, Shrimai Prabhumoye, and Alan W Black. 2018. A Dataset for Document Grounded Conversations. In *Proceedings of the 2018 Conference on Empirical Methods in Natural Language Processing*, pages 708–713, Brussels, Belgium. Association for Computational Linguistics.

Pei Zhou, Hyundong Cho, Pegah Jandaghi, Dong-Ho Lee, Bill Yuchen Lin, Jay Pujara, and Xiang Ren. 2022. Reflect, Not Reflex: Inference-Based Common Ground Improves Dialogue Response Quality. In *Proceedings of the 2022 Conference on Empirical Methods in Natural Language Processing*, pages 10450–10468. Association for Computational Linguistics.

A Implementation Details

Throughout the experiments, we used the models implemented in Python 3.8 with PyTorch v1.13.1 (Paszke et al., 2019) and the Transformers library (Wolf et al., 2020). We preprocessed texts

Max iterations	5,000
Batch size	16
Gradient accumulation	16
Optimizer	Adam
Weight decay	0.01
Gradient clipping	max norm of 1.0
Learning rate (LR)	0.000005
LR warmup (linear)	300 steps
Dropout	0.1

Table 6: Hyperparameters for the $\text{COMET}^{\text{DIS}}_{\text{TIL}}$-based situation generator

Max epochs	10
Batch size	16
Optimizer	Adam
Weight decay	None
Gradient clipping	max norm of 1.0
Learning rate (LR)	0.00001
LR warmup (linear)	100 steps
LR decay (based on validation)	coef. of 0.5
Dropout	0.1

Table 7: Hyperparameters for BlenderBot2

by spaCy[13] (*en-core-web-sm* model) and NLTK[14]. Our tools and resources do not involve license restrictions on the use for research purposes. We will release our code and pre-trained model parameters.

A.1 Situation Generation

We employed $\text{COMET}^{\text{DIS}}_{\text{TIL}}$ (West et al., 2022), which is based on GPT2-XL (Radford et al., 2019) (1.5B parameters), for situation generation. $\text{COMET}^{\text{DIS}}_{\text{TIL}}$is trained on a large-scale collection of event-centric common-sense triples, ATOMIC^{20}_{20}, which may serve as a useful inductive bias for situation generation. The goal of situation generation is to generate statements of observable situational information for a given conversation. Reference responses were added to the input along with an previous utterance for the training and validation data. However, to prevent introducing clues about the reference result, responses were not included in generating situational statements for the test instances in CICERO and ConvAI2.

We fine-tuned a model on the SUGAR dataset using two different input settings. The first setting concatenats a previous utterance, a response, and a reference situational information into one sequence. The second setting concatenated a previous utterance and a reference situational information into one sequence for generating situational statements on test instances, for the aforementioned reason. In both cases, each text was headed by special symbols indicating the text type: <utterance> for an utterance, <response> for a response, and <situation category> for a situational statement. The <situation category> symbol is one of date, time, location, behavior, environment, and possession. The model was optimized to minimize a cross-entropy loss with a label smoothing factor of 0.1 for the tokens in the situational information. Table 6 shows the hyperparameters for the training step. We evaluated the average token-level perplexity on the validation split every 100 steps and terminated training if the value did not improve for 5 consecutive validations. The training process took approximately four hours on an NVIDIA TITAN RTX GPU with the DeepSpeed (Rasley et al., 2020) library.

To generate situations on the CICERO and ConvAI2 datasets, we concatenated a conversation history and a response (for the training and validation splits) followed by one of the situation categories as input. We generated three candidates for each category using nucleus sampling ($p = 0.9$). As the model was trained on SUGAR, which only contains single-turn conversations, we observed that feeding many previous utterances impaired the generation quality. Therefore, we limited the number of previous utterances in the input to 3. Finally, for quality control, one of the authors manually checked the test samples from CICERO and ConvAI2 (25 for each) and corrected situational statements when required (e.g., conflicting facts). The reference responses were hidden during the manual verification to avoid bias. This manual verification process ensures the quality of the test dataset in order to minimize the confusion of annotators in the following manual evaluation of responses.

A.2 Response Generation

BlenderBot2: We used the pre-trained BlenderBot2 model with 400M parameters[15] with web search turned off. We concatenated persona statements (for ConvAI2), situational statements, and a conversation history with newline symbols
n. We denoted text types by dedicated prefixes as practiced in pre-training of BlenderBot2, namely, a persona statement is headed by text `your persona:`, situational statements is headed by `context:`, and each utterance in a conversation history is headed by either <speaker1> or

[13]https://spacy.io/

[14]https://www.nltk.org/

[15]https://parl.ai/projects/blenderbot2/

<speaker2 which corresponds to the speaker of the utterance. a We followed the original configuration of hyperparameters (Table 7). We evaluated a model on the validation set every 1/4 epoch and terminated training if the average token-level perplexity score on the validation set did not improve five times in a row. In our experiments, training finished at around two epochs, taking about 4 hours on one NVIDIA TITAN RTX. For generation, we used nucleus sampling with $p = 0.9$.

GPT-3: We generated responses with GPT-3 with a few-shot learning mannar. We picked four high-quality examples from the training and validation splits for each dataset and provided them with a short instruction in a prompt. Table 8 shows an example of our prompt. We generated responses with top-p=0.9 and temperature=0.7.

ChatGPT: We used the same prompt as that of GPT-3 for generating responses with ChatGPT through OpenAI's interactive demo page [16]. Although the application scope of ChatGPT is highly related to the topic of this paper, ChatGPT is under active development, and there is no established method to reproduce results. Therefore, we only used ChatGPT for performing a few case studies like the example in Table 1.

B Crowdsourced Evaluation

B.1 First Experiment

In the first experiment we rectuited crowd workers on Amazon Mechanical Turk. We set the following qualification requirements for filtering workers: (1) at least 1,000 HITs are approved so far, (2) $\geq$ 99% approval rate, (iii) living in US. Each HIT involves judgment of three response candidates. Workes were paid \$0.30 for each HIT. We used the guidelines and interface developed by (Zhou et al., 2022). Figure 3 shows the annotation guidelines. To monitor the performance of workers, we embedded one dummy response in each HIT. We created the dummy responses to be a clearly bad response.

Initially, we followed Zhou et al. (2022) and also evaluated if the responses are interesting or not, but we found the inter-annotator agreement of this criterion is high enough to draw a reliable conclusion (Fleiss' kappa of 0.2). Therefore, we removed this criterion from our final results.

[16]`https://chat.openai.com/`

B.2 Second Experiment

In the second experiment, we recruited workers who met the following qualifications: (1) The Mechanical Turk *Masters Qualification* has been granted by the platform, (2) Number of HITs approved $\geq$ 1,000, (3) HIT approval rate $\geq$ 95%, (4) Location is US. We increased a reward based on the numbder of distractors. (\$0.35 for 10 distractors and \$0.40 for 15 distractors.)

Three Evaluation Criteria

Please treat each criterion as a separate and independent measure. It is possible for a response to be context-specific or interesting, but still factually incorrect.

1. Is the response grammatically correct?

- As responses are automatically generated by conversation systems, they may contain grammatical errors
- Choose "Yes" if the response is grammatically correct. Otherwise, select "No".

2. Is the response coherent and contextually appropriate?

- Assess whether the response makes sense in the given context using your common sense.
- If the response appears **confusing, out of context, or factually wrong,** then judge it as **"No (Does not make sense.)"** For example, select "No" if
  - The response offers something different from what was asked without mentioning any reasons. ("Please start my car" ➡ "Sure, I'll call a taxi for you.")
  - The response offers something unavailable in the given context. ("Please give me some tea" [Context: no tea left in the house] ➡ "Sure, I'll bring it for you.")
- If the response seems wrong, but you are uncertain, select "No."
- Otherwise, select "Yes".

3. Is the response specifically relevant to the given context?

- Assess if the response is specific to the given context. **Check whether the response is targeted at the given context or could be used in different contexts of various topics.**
  1. If SpeakerA says "I love tennis" and SpeakerB replies "That's nice", then B's response is **not specific ("No.")**This response could occur in many contexts of different topics other than tennis.
  2. If SpeakerB replies, "Me too, I can't get enough of Roger Federer!", then mark this response as **specific ("Yes.")** This response is closely related to the context and is unlikely to occur in other contexts, such as when people are talking about baseball.
- If you are unsure, choose "No."

Figure 3: Evaluation guidelines. We developed the instructions based on the work of Zhou et al. (2022)

Two people are having a conversation in the following examples. Both people are helpful and friendly.

Example 1
Context:
1. Today is Monday.
2. It is afternoon now.
3. <speaker1> and <speaker2> are at school.
4. <speaker2> is studying English.
5. <speaker1> has a phone.
6. <speaker1> has alrady finished lunch.
7. <speaker2> has an English book with her.
8. The nearby restaurant is open.
9. Final exams are coming soon.
10. <speaker2> has not had lunch yet.
Conversation:
<speaker1>: Hi, Lily. Where were you at lunchtime? I was looking for you in the dining hall.
<speaker2>: Oh, sorry, I missed you . My English class ran late again.
<speaker1>: That's been happening quite often recently . Maybe it's because the final exams are coming up.

...

Example 5
Context:
1. Today is Sunday.
2. It is daytime now.
3. <speaker9> and <speaker10> are in the hotel.
4. <speaker10> is working at the hotel.
5. <speaker9> has a car.
6. <speaker9> is carrying a suitcase.
7. <speaker10> has a computer.
8. The door is closed.
9. <speaker9>'s keys are on the desk.
10. It is raining outside.
Conversation:
<speaker9>: Hello. I'm leaving. Here is my key.
<speaker10>:

Table 8: Example of the prompt for GPT-3 and ChatGPT. The examples are taken from CICERO.

Correcting Semantic Parses with Natural Language through Dynamic Schema Encoding

Parker Glenn, Parag Pravin Dakle, Preethi Raghavan
Fidelity Investments, AI Center of Excellence
{parker.glenn, paragpravin.dakle, preethi.raghavan}@fmr.com

Abstract

In addressing the task of converting natural language to SQL queries, there are several semantic and syntactic challenges. It becomes increasingly important to understand and remedy the points of failure as the performance of semantic parsing systems improve. We explore semantic parse correction with natural language feedback, proposing a new solution built on the success of autoregressive decoders in text-to-SQL tasks. By separating the semantic and syntactic difficulties of the task, we show that the accuracy of text-to-SQL parsers can be boosted by up to 26% with only one turn of correction with natural language. Additionally, we show that a T5-base model is capable of correcting the errors of a T5-large model in a zero-shot, cross-parser setting.

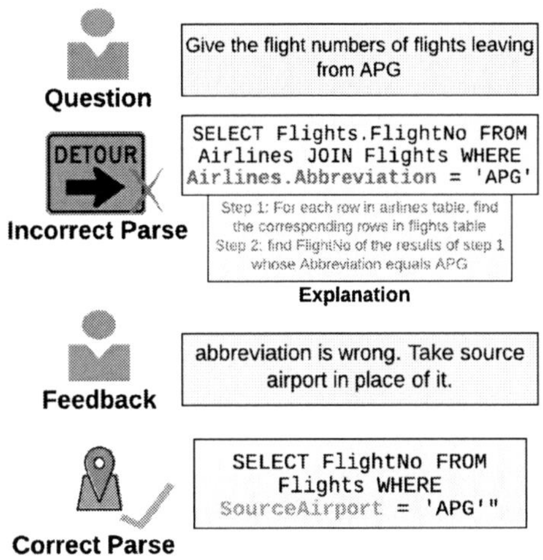

Figure 1: Example item from the SPLASH dataset. An incorrect parse from a neural text-to-SQL model is paired together with natural language feedback commenting on how the parse should be corrected.

1 Introduction

The task of parsing natural language into structured database queries has been a long-standing benchmark in the field of semantic parsing. Success at this task allows individuals without expertise in the downstream query language to retrieve information with ease. This helps to improve data literacy, democratizing accessibility to otherwise opaque public database systems.

Many forms of semantic parsing datasets exist, such as parsing natural language to programming languages (Ling et al., 2016; Oda et al., 2015; Quirk et al., 2015), Prolog assertions for exploring a database of geographical data (Zelle and Mooney, 1996), or SPARQL queries for querying a large knowledge base (Talmor and Berant, 2018). The current work discusses parsing natural language into a structured query language (SQL), perhaps the most well-studied sub-field of semantic parsing.

Most text-to-SQL works frame the task as a one-shot mapping problem. Methods include transition-based parsers (Yin and Neubig, 2018), grammar-based decoding (Guo et al., 2019; Lin et al., 2019), and the most popular approach as of late, sequence to sequence (seq2seq) models (Scholak et al., 2021; Qi et al., 2022; Xie et al., 2022).

In contrast to the one-shot approach, conversational text-to-SQL aims to interpret the natural language to structured representations in the context of a multi-turn dialogue (Yu et al., 2019a,b). It requires some form of state tracking in addition to semantic parsing to handle conversational phenomena like coreference and ellipsis (Rui Zhang, 2019; Hui et al., 2021; Cai et al., 2022).

Interactive semantic parsing frames the task as a multi-turn interaction, but with a different objective than pure conversational text-to-SQL. As a majority of parsing mistakes that neural text-to-SQL parsers make are minor, it is often feasible for humans to suggest fixes for such mistakes using natural language feedback. Displayed in Figure 1, SPLASH (Semantic Parsing with Language

Proceedings of the 5th Workshop on NLP for Conversational AI (NLP4ConvAI 2023), pages 29–38
July 14, 2023 ©2023 Association for Computational Linguistics

Assistance from Humans) is a text-to-SQL dataset containing erroneous parses from a neural text-to-SQL system alongisde human feedback explaining how the interpretation should be corrected (Elgohary et al., 2020). Most similar to SPLASH is the INSPIRED dataset (Mo et al., 2022), which aims to correct errors in SPARQL parses from the ComplexWebQuestions dataset (Talmor and Berant, 2018). While the interactive semantic parsing task evaluates a system's ability to incorporate human feedback, as noted in Elgohary et al. (2020), it targets a different modeling aspect than the traditional conversational paradigm. Hence, good performance on one does not guarantee good performance on the other task.

We make the following contributions: (1) We achieve a new state-of-the-art on the interactive parsing task SPLASH, beating the best published correction accuracy (Elgohary et al., 2021) by 12.33% using DestT5 (Dynamic Encoding of Schemas using T5); (2) We show new evidence that the decoupling of syntactic and semantic tasks improves text-to-SQL results (Li et al., 2023), proposing a novel architecture which leverages a single language model for both tasks; (3) We offer a new small-scale test set for interactive parsing[1], and show that a T5-base interactive model is capable of correcting errors made by a T5-large parser.

2 Dataset

In this work, we evaluate our models on the SPLASH dataset as introduced in Elgohary et al. (2020). It is based on Spider, a large multi-domain and cross-database dataset for text-to-SQL parsing (Yu et al., 2018). Incorrect SQL parses were selected from the output of a Seq2Struct model trained on Spider (Shin, 2019). Seq2Struct achieves an exact set match accuracy of 42.94% on the development set of Spider.

Alongside the incorrect parse, an explanation of the SQL query is generated using a rule-based template. Annotators were then shown the original question q alongside the explanation and asked to provide natural language feedback f such that the incorrect parse p' could be resolved to the final gold parse p.

Each item in the SPLASH dataset is associated with a relational database $\mathcal{D}$. Each database has a schema $\mathcal{S}$ containing tables $T = \{t_1, t_2, ...t_N\}$ and columns $C = \{c_1^1, ..., c_{n_1}^1, c_1^2, ..., c_{n_2}^2, c_1^N, ..., c_{n_N}^N\}$, where N is the number of tables, and n_i is the number of columns in the i-th table. Figure 1 displays an example item from the SPLASH dataset, excluding the full database schema S for brevity.

3 Model

3.1 Dynamic Schema Encoder

In converting natural language to SQL, a parser must handle both the semantic challenges in selecting the correct tables and columns from the database schema, and generate valid SQL syntax. As shown in Li et al. (2023), decoupling the schema linking and skeleton parsing tasks in text-to-SQL improves results when applied to the Spider dataset. We take a similar approach with the SPLASH dataset, separating the semantic and syntactic challenges of text-to-SQL by introducing an auxiliary schema prediction model. This auxiliary model serializes only the most relevant schema items into the input for the final seq2seq text-to-SQL model.

The task of the schema prediction is to output only those schema items (tables, columns, values) that appear in the gold SQL p. The inputs can be represented as follows.

$$d = t_1 : c_1^1, ..., c_{n_1}^1 | ... | t_N : c_1^N, ..., c_{n_N}^N \quad (1)$$

$$x = ([CLS], q, [SEP], d, [SEP], p', [SEP], f) \quad (2)$$

Where d represents a flattened representation of the database schema S, q is the question, p' is the incorrect parse from SPLASH, and f is the natural language feedback. For each schema item, the task is to predict the presence or absence of the item in the final gold SQL parse p.

By introducing this auxiliary schema prediction model, the final text-to-SQL model should only be tasked with stitching together the predicted schema items into valid SQL logic. As shown in the example in Figure 2, the text-to-SQL model is able to filter out the unnecessary "join" clauses from the incorrect parse, given the only table predicted by the schema prediction is "Flights".

This approach was validated by carrying out a simple experiment. We serialize only those "gold" schema items that appear in the translated SQL and fine-tune a T5-base model[2] on the Spider dataset to achieve a best 78.10% execution accuracy. This

[1] https://github.com/parkervg/DestT5

[2] https://huggingface.co/tscholak/t5.1.1.lm100k.base

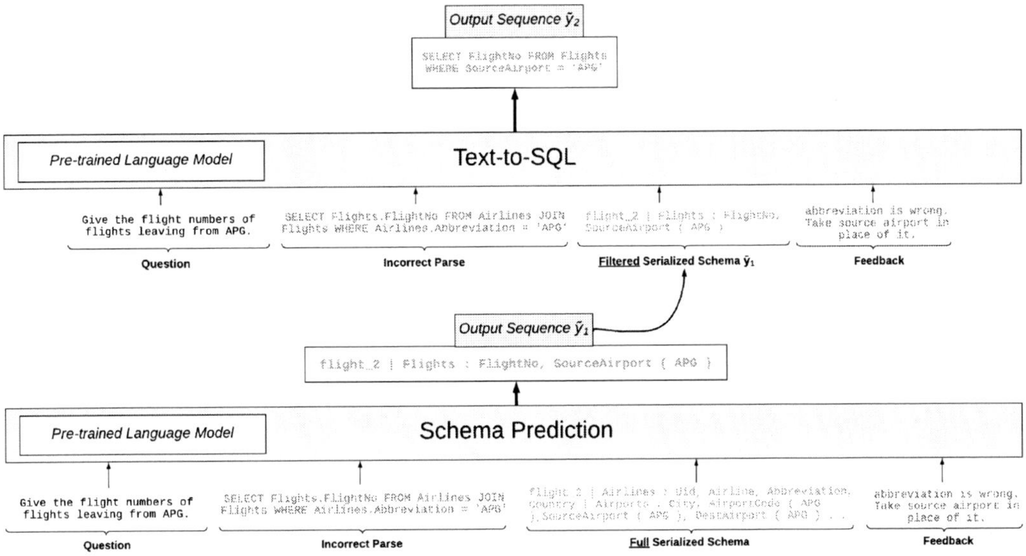

Figure 2: Model architecture. In "Schema Prediction", the database schema is filtered to only the relevant items $\tilde{y}_1$ using a classifier or generator described in Section 3.1. In "Text-to-SQL", the output of the schema prediction model is used to generate the final parse $\tilde{y}_2$.

beats the vanilla T5-base model[3] by 18.7%, demonstrating that successful schema prediction sets up a text-to-SQL model to predict the final query with high accuracy.

Schema Classifier We adopt the RoBERTa-large schema prediction described in Li et al. (2023) for our classification model. To alleviate the label imbalance problem caused by sparse schema targets, focal loss is used as the loss function (Lin et al., 2017). Focal loss adds a factor $(1 - p_t)^\gamma$ to standard cross entropy loss, reducing relative loss for well-classified examples and putting more focus on misclassified examples.

$$\mathcal{L}_2 = \frac{1}{N}\sum_{i=1}^{N} FL(y_i, \hat{y}_i) + \frac{1}{M}\sum_{i=1}^{N}\sum_{k=1}^{n_i} FL(y_k^i, \hat{y}_k^i) \tag{3}$$

Where FL denotes the focal loss function. y_i is the ground truth label of the i-th table, either 0 or 1 indicating the presence or absence, respectively. Similarly, y_k^i is the ground truth label of the k-th column in the i-th table.

Rather than using a hard probability threshold, hyperparameters k_1 and k_2 are introduced. Taking the probabilities from the cross-encoder, only the top-k_1 tables and top-k_2 columns are kept and serialized into a ranked schema serialization, descending by probability.

Schema Generator In addition to the previously discussed RoBERTa-large cross-encoder, we also experiment with a generative schema prediction model. T5 (Text-to-Text Transfer Transformer) is a transformer-based encoder-decoder model that converts all NLP problems into a text-to-text format (Raffel et al., 2020). In our task setup, the encoder applies its bidirectional attention mechanism over the features from SPLASH and the serialized schema items, depicted in Equation 2. The decoder, then, generates the correct SQL parse, employing teacher forcing during the training phase. It is fine-tuned using standard cross-entropy loss.

$$L_1 = -\sum_{i=1}^{M} y_i \log(\hat{y}_i) \tag{4}$$

The target label y_i will always take the form of tokens comprising the gold schema items, i.e., those tables and columns that appear in the correct SQL parse. We format the multi-label targets y as text following the structure shown below. Note that this is the same structure we use to serialize the flattened database schema d in Equation 1.

```
[db_id] | [table] : [column] (...)
```

[3]https://huggingface.co/tscholak/1zha5ono

Schema Model	F1	Precision	Recall
Generator	**88.98**	90.84	89.18
Classifier	34.50	22.12	**94.41**

Table 1: Performance of schema prediction models in predicting gold schema items on the SPLASH test set. Note that the classification-based method of Li et al. (2023) trades low precision for high recall[5].

As the theoretical output space of $\hat{y}$ is the unconstrained vocabulary of the T5 model, schema hallucinations are possible, and column/table pairs may be generated that do not exist in the database context[4]. A trade-off in this approach, however, is that the generation objective allows us to bypass the need for hyperparameters k_1 and k_2, as we simply keep the greedy argmax of $\hat{y}$ directly at each timestep. As shown in Table 1, this optimization objective results in far greater precision than the classification approach but suffers a drop in recall.

3.2 Text-to-SQL Encoder/Decoder

We use a T5-base model to encode the unified input (with schema predictions) and generate the SQL query (Raffel et al., 2020).

3.3 SQL Normalization

We follow the same normalization procedure described in Li et al. (2023). Specifically, we normalize both the incorrect parses and gold SQL queries by (1) replacing table aliases with their original names, (2) adding an *ASC* keyword if *ORDER BY* doesn't already specify, (3) lower-casing all text, and (4) adding spaces around parentheses and replacing double quotes with single quotes.

4 Experiments

4.1 Experimental Setup

We run a series of experiments on the SPLASH dataset to evaluate the robustness of the proposed method. The training set contains 2,775 unique questions from the train split of Spider. SPLASH annotators were also asked to generate paraphrases for a single piece of feedback to improve diversity, resulting in a total of 7,481 items in the train split. The SPLASH test set is based on 506 items from the Spider dev split, coming out to 962 total test items with paraphrasing.

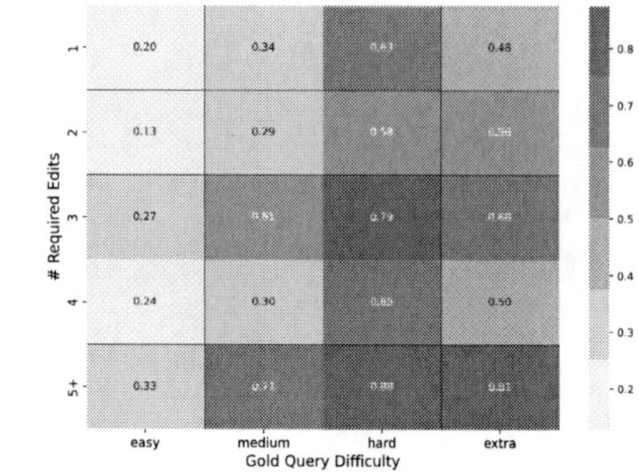

Figure 3: DestT5 error rates on the SPLASH test set, using the Spider exact match metric. As the distance (*# Required Edits*) from the incorrect parse to the gold query increases, error rates also increase.

4.2 Evaluation Metrics

Exact Set Match (EM) This metric evaluates the structural correctness of the predicted SQL. It checks for an orderless set match between each component in the predicted and gold query, ignoring predicted values. Many early text-to-SQL models only report EM accuracy.

Execution Accuracy (EX) Execution accuracy compares the execution results of the predicted SQL query and the gold SQL query. Since two SQL queries that do not have an exact set match may execute to the same results (e.g. "`...ORDER BY val ASC LIMIT 1`" and "`SELECT MAX(val)`"), this metric serves as a performance upper bound. However, this metric can suffer from a high false positive rate. For this reason, we use the test suite execution accuracy with optimized database values described in Zhong et al. (2020).

4.3 Implementation Details

Text-to-SQL All text-to-SQL models use a fine-tuned T5-base. We use the same hyperparameters specified in the PICARD codebase[6]. Models were fine-tuned with Adafactor (Shazeer and Stern, 2018) with a learning rate 1e-4, batch size 16 for 256 epochs. A linear warm-up for the first 10% of training steps is employed, followed by cosine decay.

[4]We note that Scholak et al. (2021) offers a solution for these schema hallucinations, but leave the integration of Picard to future work.

[5]Not considered in this table is the ranking-enhanced nature of the RoBERTa-large method.

[6]`https://github.com/ServiceNow/picard`

	Schema Model	EM%	Shuffled Feature EM% Change: Feedback	Incorrect Parse
All	None	41.17	-	-
	Generator	51.35	-2.17	-28.27
	Classifier	49.79	-2.7	-11.64
- Question	Generator	48.96	-4.47	-30.77
	Classifier	35.97	-11.23	-29.94
- Explanation	**Generator**	**53.43**	-1.77	-18.09
	Classifier	49.27	-2.08	-17.57
- Question - Explanation	Generator	47.00	-5.53	-38.68
	Classifier	38.98	-12.47	-36.9

Table 2: Results on SPLASH test set with various features and schema prediction models. *Generator* refers to the T5-large model, and *Classifier* refers to the RoBERTa-large model of Li et al. (2023). The models are evaluated on the test set with shuffled features to examine the extent to which they utilize the unique interactive components of the parsing task. In bold is DestT5.

Schema Generation T5-large was used for the schema generation model. It was fine-tuned using Adafactor with a constant learning rate of 1e-4 and a batch size of 4 for 512 epochs.

Schema Classification For the schema classification model, we follow the implementation and hyperparameters described in Li et al. (2023). Specifically, we train a cross-encoder based on RoBERTa-large (Liu et al., 2019). AdamW (Loshchilov and Hutter, 2017) with a batch size of 32 and a learning rate of 1e-5 is used for optimization. Focal loss is used to alleviate the label-imbalance problem that comes from sparse schema targets. The threshold hyperparameters k_1 and k_2 are set to 4 and 5, respectively. Specifically, only the top-4 tables and top-5 columns with the highest logits are kept and serialized as a ranked input to the text-to-SQL model.

4.4 Evaluation

Unlike the Spider dataset, performance on the SPLASH dataset is more nuanced and must be viewed holistically. To this end, we plot both "Exact Match %" and "Shuffled Feature Change" in Table 2. The ideal model is one that achieves a competitive exact match metric, while experiencing a large drop in performance with shuffled feedback and incorrect parses[7]. We find the highest exact match accuracy when removing the explanation of the incorrect parse, and by using a T5-based generative schema prediction model. This model, denoted in bold in Table 2, is later referred to as DestT5 (Dynamic Encoding of Schemas using T5). Achieving an EM score of **53.43%**, DestT5 beats the previous best score of NL-EDIT by 12.33% (Elgohary et al., 2021).

Using the scripts provided from Elgohary et al. (2021) to count SQL edits, we plot error rates on the SPLASH test set for both gold query difficulty and the number of edits. "Difficulty" is defined by Yu et al. (2018) and classifies each SQL query into one of four categories depending on the complexity of the query. As seen in the heatmap, error rates share a positive correlation with both SQL difficulty and # edits required to reach the gold parse.

4.5 Generalizing to Other Parsers

In recent years, massive strides have been made in the task of semantic parsing. Since the release of the SPLASH dataset, variations of T5 have largely taken the top spots in the Spider leaderboard. As of April 2023, all 6 models in the top 10 with corresponding publications build off of some T5 model. It is fair, then, to ask if performance on the SPLASH dataset actually corresponds to the ability to fix errors made with modern parsing systems, such as those utilizing T5.

To this end, we evaluate DestT5 on the crowdsourced test sets[9] based on errors made by EditSQL (Rui Zhang, 2019), TaBERT (Yin et al., 2020), and RAT-SQL (Wang et al., 2020). Additionally, we

[7]We note that a T5-base model fine-tuned with the Spider train set achieves 50.00 EM on the SPLASH test set.

[9]https://github.com/MSR-LIT/NLEdit

	Seq2Struct (SPLASH)	EditSQL	TaBERT	RAT-SQL	T5-Large
Spider Dev EM%	41.3	57.6	65.2	69.7	71.2
Spider Dev EX%	-	-	-	-	74.4
NL-EDIT					
SPLASH Test Set EM%	41.1	28	22.7	21.3	-
SPLASH Test Set EX%	-	-	-	-	-
EM Δ w/ Interaction	+20.3	+8.9	+5.9	+4.3	-
EX Δ w/ Interaction	-	-	-	-	-
DESTT5 (OURS)					
SPLASH Test Set EM%	53.43	31.82	31.47	28.37	26.1
SPLASH Test Set EX%	56.86	40.3	28.84	36.53	30.43
EM Δ w/ Interaction	**+26.15**	**+10.16**	**+8.13**	**+5.71**	**+2.83**
EX Δ w/ Interaction	-	-	-	-	+3.3

Table 3: Evaluating zero-shot generalization of DestT5 to other modern parsers. Shown are the scores without interaction on the full Spider dev set, as well as the **Δ w/ Interaction** on the Spider dev set following single-turn corrections with NL-EDIT and DESTT5. This change is a byproduct of the size of the test sets (962, 330, 267, 208, and 112 left-to-right), and it is expected to increase proportional to the reported **Test Set EM%/EX%** as the size of the dataset increases. We indicate instances where the scores are not publicly available for a given model with **-**.

Text-to-SQL Model	Schema F1	# Hallucinated Schema Items
T5-large[8]	79.00	92
T5-base	73.92	121
DestT5	**80.09**	59

Table 4: Analysis of the schema items produced by the final text-to-SQL model. DestT5, with an auxiliary schema prediction model, identifies the presence of gold schema items with a higher F1 than a T5-large text-to-SQL model alone.

compile a new, small-scale test set of errors made by a fine-tuned T5-large model[10] on the Spider dev set. It contains 112 items annotated with feedback referencing the erroneous parse made by the model and is later referred to as the "T5-large Test Set".

Table 3 plots the end-to-end accuracy of DestT5. As mentioned in Elgohary et al. (2021), there is a notable drop in the end-to-end gains as the accuracy of the base parser improves. This is likely due to the fact that as parsers improve, most of the errors are based on very complex gold SQL queries.

4.6 Error Analysis

4.7 Errors on T5-Large Test Set

Figure 4 depicts the outputs of a randomly selected set of interactions from the T5-large test set. We discuss some of the examples below.

[10]https://huggingface.co/tscholak/3vnuv1vf

In Example 1, the original T5-large text-to-SQL model fails to map the phrase "all lines" to both columns *line_1* and *line_2*. However, even with the feedback "Find line_2 as well", the auxiliary schema prediction model fails to select "line_2" as a schema candidate. As a result, the final DestT5 text-to-SQL is not equipped with enough context to generate the correct parse.

In Example 2, an 'easy' gold query (`"SELECT MIN(loser_rank) FROM matches"`) is incorrectly parsed. This is likely due to the same reason described in Lin et al. (2020), characterized by difficulty in mapping "predominantly" to *spoken by the largest percentage of the population*: it remains challenging for large pre-trained models to ground terms like "best rank" to the DB schema. Pre-training tasks have been proposed in attempts to further improve schema grounding in LLMs, but more work can be done to align LLMs with lexical

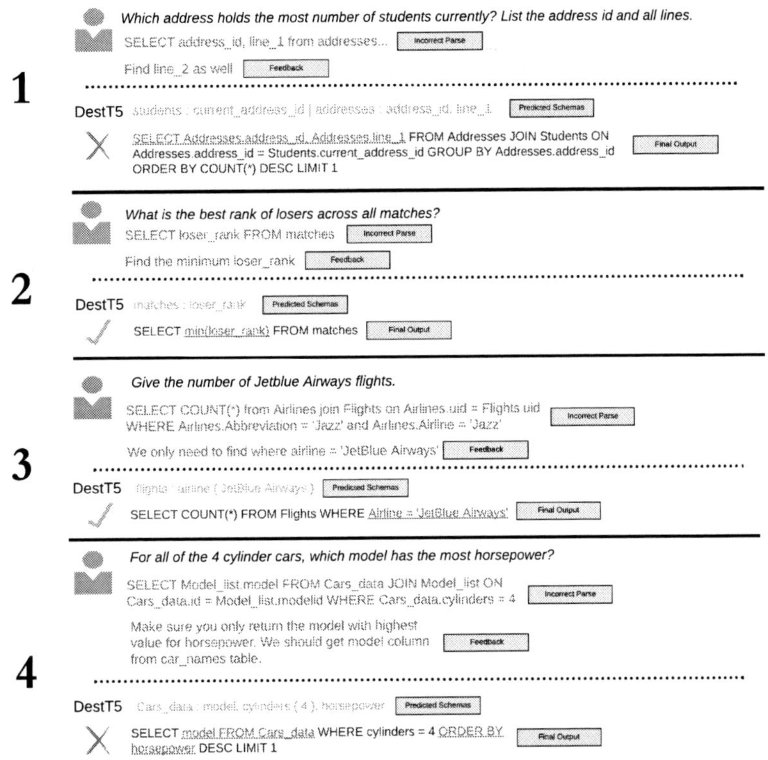

Figure 4: Example outputs of DestT5 on errors made with a T5-large text-to-SQL model. When the schema prediction model fails to identify schema items, the final text-to-SQL output is incorrect. However, when the schema prediction model is correct, it allows the text-to-SQL component to focus its efforts on generating valid SQL syntax, faithful to the feedback. See section 4.7 for more detailed analysis of these examples.

constructs grounded to the syntax of semantic parsing tasks (Deng et al., 2021; Yin et al., 2020). In one turn of interaction with DestT5, this syntax error is corrected.

Example 4 displays an interaction parsing long feedback with mixed success. The interaction allows DestT5 to remedy the missed semantic mapping from "most horsepower" to the "`ORDER BY horsepower`" clause, but it hallucinates the "`Cars_data`" from the "`model`" table, failing to learn from the feedback saying otherwise.

5 Discussion

5.1 Impact of Auxiliary Schema Prediction

Table 2 displays the EM of a standard text-to-SQL model with no auxiliary schema prediction (with all schema items directly serialized as input). As shown, the score drops from 51.35% with an auxiliary generator to 41.17% without. We hypothesize that given the increased number of features in interactive semantic parsing (explanation, feedback, incorrect parse), distilling the role of the text-to-SQL model to primarily handling syntax parsing prevents excessive proliferation of feature interactions.

Table 4 displays the schema F1 scores of various text-to-SQL models. Schema F1 is calculated by comparing those schema items (tables, columns) generated in the predicted parse to the schema items in the gold SQL. As shown, implementing a dedicated schema prediction model into a text-to-SQL pipeline helps identify those gold schema items with a higher F1 score, and minimizes schema hallucinations (i.e. generating tables/columns not present in the database schema).

How often does the text-to-SQL model use the predicted schemas? We evaluate the usage rates of the predicted schema items by the final text-to-SQL model. Specifically, we examine the rate at which DestT5 either predicts a schema item not directly serialized by the schema prediction model, or fails to integrate a schema item that was serialized. We find that on the SPLASH test set, there are 112 instances of overpredictions by the text-to-SQL model and 210 underpredictions. There is an average distance of 0.81 between the serialized schema items and gold schema items, and 0.93 between the schema items predicted by the text-to-SQL model and gold. This indicates that, if the text-to-SQL model were explicitly restricted to use only the schema items generated by the auxiliary schema prediction model, performance will improve. We leave this and other combinations of the two models (such as joint training) to future work.

5.2 Evaluating Interactive Parsing

The goal of interactive semantic parsing is not to parse the most interactions correctly on the SPLASH test set, but more specifically to parse those interactions correctly that the original text-to-SQL model parsed incorrectly. For example, if a hypothetical interactive parsing model A achieves a high EM% on the SPLASH test set, but the "Δ w/ Interaction" metric with modern parsers is small, then the model serves minimal utility in an actual conversational setting. On the other hand, if a model B performs poorly on the SPLASH test set but demonstrates a high "Δ w/ Interaction", we would deem this model as the better interactive semantic parser.

We argue, then, that the "Correction Acc. (%)" metric from SPLASH should be replaced in favor of the end-to-end accuracy, referred to as "Δ w/ Interaction" in Elgohary et al. (2021).

Specifically, future work should include Execution Accuracy (EX%) along with Exact Set Match (EM%). As the set of errors made by modern parsers increasingly drifts towards more difficult gold SQL parses, it becomes more likely that the EM% and EX% scores will be disjoint. Examining the errors by T5-large, it was common for a gold parse to be expressed with an "`EXCEPT SELECT`" clause, whereas the predicted SQL executed identically with a "`NOT IN`" clause.

Additionally, as depicted in Table 3, the EX% score is higher than EM% for all test sets except for TaBERT. This is due to the fact that TaBERT does not predict values. Instead, it uses the placeholder "value" instead of string values, and "LIMIT 0" in limit clauses[11]. Though these instances are not judged as incorrect with EM, they are penalized with EX.

[11] We find this odd, as the feedback provided in the TaBERT test set comments on the values

6 Conclusion

We present a new model, DestT5 (Dynamic Encoding of Schemas using T5), which achieves a new state-of-the-art correction accuracy on the interactive parsing dataset SPLASH. By using T5 as a schema prediction model, we display better performance compared to classification-based methods. We validate our results on a new test set for interactive semantic parsing based on a modern parser, and offer recommendations for evaluating future systems.

Limitations

As mentioned in Table 3, one limitation of the current study is the small scale of the test sets with modern parsers. We encourage future work to emphasize the development and evaluation on these test sets, specifically those which more closely reflect the current SoTA in text-to-SQL (e.g. T5). Additionally, though we have shown using an auxiliary schema prediction model greatly improves the performance of a text-to-SQL system, the addition of a model for the text-to-SQL task is a limitation given the time and training resources required.

References

Zefeng Cai, Xiangyu Li, Binyuan Hui, Min Yang, Bowen Li, Binhua Li, Zheng Cao, Weijie Li, Fei Huang, Luo Si, and Yongbin Li. 2022. STAR: SQL guided pre-training for context-dependent text-to-SQL parsing. In *Findings of the Association for Computational Linguistics: EMNLP 2022*, pages 1235–1247, Abu Dhabi, United Arab Emirates. Association for Computational Linguistics.

Xiang Deng, Ahmed Hassan Awadallah, Christopher Meek, Oleksandr Polozov, Huan Sun, and Matthew Richardson. 2021. Structure-Grounded Pretraining for Text-to-SQL. In *Proceedings of the 2021 Conference of the North American Chapter of the Association for Computational Linguistics: Human Language Technologies*, pages 1337–1350, Online. Association for Computational Linguistics.

Ahmed Elgohary, Saghar Hosseini, and Ahmed Hassan Awadallah. 2020. Speak to your Parser: Interactive Text-to-SQL with Natural Language Feedback. In *Proceedings of the 58th Annual Meeting of the Association for Computational Linguistics*, pages 2065–2077, Online. Association for Computational Linguistics.

Ahmed Elgohary, Christopher Meek, Matthew Richardson, Adam Fourney, Gonzalo Ramos, and Ahmed Hassan Awadallah. 2021. NL-EDIT: Correcting semantic parse errors through natural language interaction. In *Proceedings of the 2021 Conference of the North American Chapter of the Association for Computational Linguistics: Human Language Technologies*, pages 5599–5610, Online. Association for Computational Linguistics.

Jiaqi Guo, Zecheng Zhan, Yan Gao, Yan Xiao, Jian-Guang Lou, Ting Liu, and Dongmei Zhang. 2019. Towards complex text-to-sql in cross-domain database with intermediate representation. In *Proceeding of the 57th Annual Meeting of the Association for Computational Linguistics (ACL)*. Association for Computational Linguistics.

Binyuan Hui, Ruiying Geng, Qiyu Ren, Binhua Li, Yongbin Li, Jian Sun, Fei Huang, Luo Si, Pengfei Zhu, and Xiaodan Zhu. 2021. Dynamic hybrid relation exploration network for cross-domain context-dependent semantic parsing. In *Proceedings of the AAAI Conference on Artificial Intelligence*, volume 35, pages 13116–13124.

Haoyang Li, Jing Zhang, Cuiping Li, and Hong Chen. 2023. Resdsql: Decoupling schema linking and skeleton parsing for text-to-sql. In *AAAI*.

Kevin Lin, Ben Bogin, Mark Neumann, Jonathan Berant, and Matt Gardner. 2019. Grammar-based neural text-to-sql generation. *arXiv preprint arXiv:1905.13326*.

Tsung-Yi Lin, Priya Goyal, Ross Girshick, Kaiming He, and Piotr Dollár. 2017. Focal loss for dense object detection. In *Proceedings of the IEEE international conference on computer vision*, pages 2980–2988.

Xi Victoria Lin, Richard Socher, and Caiming Xiong. 2020. Bridging Textual and Tabular Data for Cross-Domain Text-to-SQL Semantic Parsing. In *Findings of the Association for Computational Linguistics: EMNLP 2020*, pages 4870–4888, Online. Association for Computational Linguistics.

Wang Ling, Phil Blunsom, Edward Grefenstette, Karl Moritz Hermann, Tomáš Kočiský, Fumin Wang, and Andrew Senior. 2016. Latent predictor networks for code generation. In *Proceedings of the 54th Annual Meeting of the Association for Computational Linguistics (Volume 1: Long Papers)*, pages 599–609, Berlin, Germany. Association for Computational Linguistics.

Yinhan Liu, Myle Ott, Naman Goyal, Jingfei Du, Mandar Joshi, Danqi Chen, Omer Levy, Mike Lewis, Luke Zettlemoyer, and Veselin Stoyanov. 2019. Roberta: A robustly optimized bert pretraining approach. *arXiv preprint arXiv:1907.11692*.

Ilya Loshchilov and Frank Hutter. 2017. Decoupled weight decay regularization. *arXiv preprint arXiv:1711.05101*.

Lingbo Mo, Ashley Lewis, Huan Sun, and Michael White. 2022. Towards transparent interactive semantic parsing via step-by-step correction. In *Findings of the Association for Computational Linguistics: ACL 2022*, pages 322–342, Dublin, Ireland. Association for Computational Linguistics.

Yusuke Oda, Hiroyuki Fudaba, Graham Neubig, Hideaki Hata, Sakriani Sakti, Tomoki Toda, and Satoshi Nakamura. 2015. Learning to generate pseudo-code from source code using statistical machine translation. In *2015 30th IEEE/ACM International Conference on Automated Software Engineering (ASE)*, pages 574–584. IEEE.

Jiexing Qi, Jingyao Tang, Ziwei He, Xiangpeng Wan, Yu Cheng, Chenghu Zhou, Xinbing Wang, Quanshi Zhang, and Zhouhan Lin. 2022. RASAT: Integrating Relational Structures into Pretrained Seq2Seq Model for Text-to-SQL. In *Proceedings of the 2022 Conference on Empirical Methods in Natural Language Processing*, pages 3215–3229, Abu Dhabi, United Arab Emirates. Association for Computational Linguistics.

Chris Quirk, Raymond Mooney, and Michel Galley. 2015. Language to code: Learning semantic parsers for if-this-then-that recipes. In *Proceedings of the 53rd Annual Meeting of the Association for Computational Linguistics and the 7th International Joint Conference on Natural Language Processing (Volume 1: Long Papers)*, pages 878–888, Beijing, China. Association for Computational Linguistics.

Colin Raffel, Noam Shazeer, Adam Roberts, Katherine Lee, Sharan Narang, Michael Matena, Yanqi Zhou, Wei Li, and Peter J Liu. 2020. Exploring the limits of transfer learning with a unified text-to-text transformer. *The Journal of Machine Learning Research*, 21(1):5485–5551.

He Yang Er Sungrok Shim Eric Xue Xi Victoria Lin Tianze Shi Caiming Xiong Richard Socher Dragomir Radev Rui Zhang, Tao Yu. 2019. Editing-based sql query generation for cross-domain context-dependent questions. In *Proceedings of the 2019 Conference on Empirical Methods in Natural Language Processing*, Hong Kong, China.

Torsten Scholak, Nathan Schucher, and Dzmitry Bahdanau. 2021. PICARD: Parsing incrementally for constrained auto-regressive decoding from language models. In *Proceedings of the 2021 Conference on Empirical Methods in Natural Language Processing*, pages 9895–9901, Online and Punta Cana, Dominican Republic. Association for Computational Linguistics.

Noam Shazeer and Mitchell Stern. 2018. Adafactor: Adaptive learning rates with sublinear memory cost. In *International Conference on Machine Learning*, pages 4596–4604. PMLR.

Richard Shin. 2019. Encoding Database Schemas with Relation-Aware Self-Attention for Text-to-SQL Parsers. ArXiv:1906.11790 [cs, stat].

Alon Talmor and Jonathan Berant. 2018. The Web as a Knowledge-Base for Answering Complex Questions. In *Proceedings of the 2018 Conference of the North American Chapter of the Association for Computational Linguistics: Human Language Technologies, Volume 1 (Long Papers)*, pages 641–651, New Orleans, Louisiana. Association for Computational Linguistics.

Bailin Wang, Richard Shin, Xiaodong Liu, Oleksandr Polozov, and Matthew Richardson. 2020. RAT-SQL: Relation-aware schema encoding and linking for text-to-SQL parsers. In *Proceedings of the 58th Annual Meeting of the Association for Computational Linguistics*, pages 7567–7578, Online. Association for Computational Linguistics.

Tianbao Xie, Chen Henry Wu, Peng Shi, Ruiqi Zhong, Torsten Scholak, Michihiro Yasunaga, Chien-Sheng Wu, Ming Zhong, Pengcheng Yin, Sida I. Wang, Victor Zhong, Bailin Wang, Chengzu Li, Connor Boyle, Ansong Ni, Ziyu Yao, Dragomir Radev, Caiming Xiong, Lingpeng Kong, Rui Zhang, Noah A. Smith, Luke Zettlemoyer, and Tao Yu. 2022. UnifiedSKG: Unifying and multi-tasking structured knowledge grounding with text-to-text language models. In *Proceedings of the 2022 Conference on Empirical Methods in Natural Language Processing*, pages 602–631, Abu Dhabi, United Arab Emirates. Association for Computational Linguistics.

Pengcheng Yin and Graham Neubig. 2018. TRANX: A transition-based neural abstract syntax parser for semantic parsing and code generation. In *Proceedings of the 2018 Conference on Empirical Methods in Natural Language Processing: System Demonstrations*, pages 7–12, Brussels, Belgium. Association for Computational Linguistics.

Pengcheng Yin, Graham Neubig, Wen-tau Yih, and Sebastian Riedel. 2020. TaBERT: Pretraining for joint understanding of textual and tabular data. In *Proceedings of the 58th Annual Meeting of the Association for Computational Linguistics*, pages 8413–8426, Online. Association for Computational Linguistics.

Tao Yu, Rui Zhang, Heyang Er, Suyi Li, Eric Xue, Bo Pang, Xi Victoria Lin, Yi Chern Tan, Tianze Shi, Zihan Li, Youxuan Jiang, Michihiro Yasunaga, Sungrok Shim, Tao Chen, Alexander Fabbri, Zifan Li, Luyao Chen, Yuwen Zhang, Shreya Dixit, Vincent Zhang, Caiming Xiong, Richard Socher, Walter Lasecki, and Dragomir Radev. 2019a. CoSQL: A Conversational Text-to-SQL Challenge Towards Cross-Domain Natural Language Interfaces to Databases. In *Proceedings of the 2019 Conference on Empirical Methods in Natural Language Processing and the 9th International Joint Conference on Natural Language Processing (EMNLP-IJCNLP)*, pages 1962–1979, Hong Kong, China. Association for Computational Linguistics.

Tao Yu, Rui Zhang, Kai Yang, Michihiro Yasunaga, Dongxu Wang, Zifan Li, James Ma, Irene Li, Qingning Yao, Shanelle Roman, Zilin Zhang, and Dragomir Radev. 2018. Spider: A large-scale human-labeled dataset for complex and cross-domain semantic parsing and text-to-SQL task. In *Proceedings of the 2018 Conference on Empirical Methods in Natural Language Processing*, pages 3911–3921, Brussels, Belgium. Association for Computational Linguistics.

Tao Yu, Rui Zhang, Michihiro Yasunaga, Yi Chern Tan, Xi Victoria Lin, Suyi Li, Heyang Er, Irene Li, Bo Pang, Tao Chen, Emily Ji, Shreya Dixit, David Proctor, Sungrok Shim, Jonathan Kraft, Vincent Zhang, Caiming Xiong, Richard Socher, and Dragomir Radev. 2019b. SParC: Cross-domain semantic parsing in context. In *Proceedings of the 57th Annual Meeting of the Association for Computational Linguistics*, pages 4511–4523, Florence, Italy. Association for Computational Linguistics.

John M Zelle and Raymond J Mooney. 1996. Learning to parse database queries using inductive logic programming. In *Proceedings of the national conference on artificial intelligence*, pages 1050–1055.

Ruiqi Zhong, Tao Yu, and Dan Klein. 2020. Semantic evaluation for text-to-SQL with distilled test suites. In *Proceedings of the 2020 Conference on Empirical Methods in Natural Language Processing (EMNLP)*, pages 396–411, Online. Association for Computational Linguistics.

Dialogue State Tracking with Sparse Local Slot Attention

Longfei Yang[1], **Jiyi Li**[2], **Sheng Li**[3], **Takahiro Shinozaki**[1]
[1]Tokyo Institute of Technology
[2]University of Yamanashi
[3]National Institute of Information and Communications Technology
longfei.yang.cs@gmail.com, jyli@yamanashi.ac.jp, sheng.li@nict.go.jp,
shinot@ict.e.titech.ac.jp

Abstract

Dialogue state tracking (DST) is designed to track the dialogue state during the conversations between users and systems, which is the core of task-oriented dialogue systems. Mainstream models predict the values for each slot with fully token-wise slot attention from dialogue history. However, such operations may result in overlooking the neighboring relationship. Moreover, it may lead the model to assign probability mass to irrelevant parts, while these parts contribute little. It becomes severe with the increase in dialogue length. Therefore, we investigate sparse local slot attention for DST in this work. Slot-specific local semantic information is obtained at a sub-sampled temporal resolution capturing local dependencies for each slot. Then these local representations are attended with sparse attention weights to guide the model to pay attention to relevant parts of local information for subsequent state value prediction. The experimental results on MultiWOZ 2.0 and 2.4 datasets show that the proposed approach effectively improves the performance of ontology-based dialogue state tracking, and performs better than token-wise attention for long dialogues.

1 Introduction

Task-oriented dialogue systems aim to assist users to complete certain tasks and have drawn great attention in both academia and industry (Young et al., 2010, 2013; Chen et al., 2017). As the core of task-oriented dialogue systems, dialogue state tracking (DST) is designed to track the dialogue states during the conversation between users and systems, which is generally expressed as a list of {*(domain, slot, value)*} representing user's goal (Rastogi et al., 2017, 2018). The estimated dialogue states are used for subsequent actions.

To achieve the dialogue state, value prediction is made for each slot given the dialogue history. At each turn, the model inquires of the dialogue history and predicts the state values accordingly (Xu and Hu, 2018; Ren et al., 2018; Wu et al., 2019; Zhang et al., 2019; Heck et al., 2020). With it, how to extract appropriate context information in the noisy dialogue history is crucial and challenging (Hu et al., 2020). Yang et al. (2021) make an empirical study about the effect of different contexts on the performance of DST with several manually designed rules. It indicates that the performance of DST models benefits from selecting appropriate context granularity.

In recent mainstream models, a fully token-wise slot attention mechanism is widely used to capture slot-specific information with dialogue history. The attention assigns an attention weight to each token, measuring the relationship of each token in dialogue history for the specified slot, and then attends them with these weights. Although encouraging results have been achieved, it also brings some risks. First, such operations disperse the distribution of attention, which results in overlooking the neighboring relation (Yang et al., 2018). Some entities (e.g., restaurant and attraction names) in spoken dialogue are generally informal, diverse, and local-compact, where the non-semantic tokens may be included. Moreover, a limitation of the used softmax computation is that the probability distribution in the outputs always has full support (Martins and Astudillo, 2016), i.e., $\text{softmax}(\mathbf{z}) > 0$ for every vector $\mathbf{z}$. It may lead a model to assign probability mass to implausible parts of dialogue history. Involving noise may make the model difficult to focus on the essential parts, and it may be more severe with the increase in dialogue length (Peters et al., 2019).

To tackle this problem, we propose a sparse local slot attention mechanism for this task. In our approach, local semantic information is firstly achieved at a sub-sampled temporal resolution capturing local dependencies for each slot. Then, these local information is attended with sparse attention weights generated by sparsemax function (Martins

Proceedings of the 5th Workshop on NLP for Conversational AI (NLP4ConvAI 2023), pages 39–46
July 14, 2023

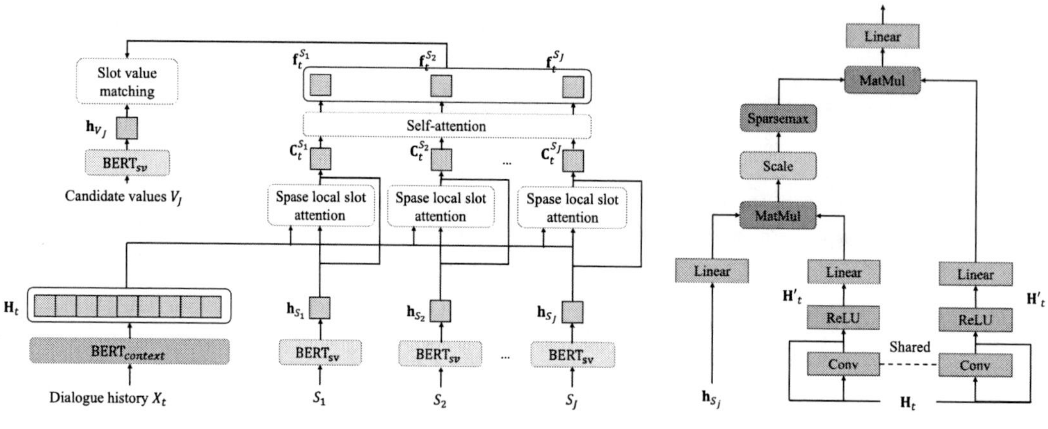

(a) The entire framework of our model.

(b) Sparse local slot attention.

Figure 1: A demonstration of our model: (a) the entire framework, (b) the proposed sparse local slot attention.

and Astudillo, 2016), which outputs sparse posterior distributions by assigning zero probability to irrelevant contents in the dialogue history.

We conduct experiments to verify our approach on MultiWOZ 2.0 and 2.4 datasets. The contributions can be addressed as follows: 1) We propose a sparse local slot attention mechanism to lead the model to focus on relevant local parts to the specific slot for the DST task; 2) We demonstrate that the performance of DST benefits from introducing local information with our proposed approach, and make an empirical study that shows that our model performs better in state prediction for name-related slots and long dialogues than the models based on fully token-wise attention.

2 Related Works

Dialogue state tracking (DST) is the core of task-oriented dialogue systems. In the early years, DST highly relies on hand-crafted semantic features to predict the dialogue states (Williams and Young, 2007; Thomson and Young, 2010; Wang and Lemon, 2013), which is hard to handle lexical and morphological variations in spoken language (Lee et al., 2019). Benefiting from the rapid development of deep learning methods and their successful application in natural language processing, neural method-based DST models have been proposed. (Mrkšić et al., 2017) proposes a novel neural belief tracking (NBT) framework with learning n-gram representation of the utterance. Inspired by it, sorts of neural network-based models have been investigated for DST task (Nouri and Hosseini-Asl, 2018; Ren et al., 2018; Zhong et al., 2018; Hu et al., 2020; Ouyang et al., 2020; Wu et al., 2019) and achieves encouraging results.

Pre-trained models have brought natural language processing to a new era in recent years. Many substantial works have shown that the pre-trained models can learn universal language representations, which are beneficial for downstream tasks (Mikolov et al., 2013; Pennington et al., 2014; McCann et al., 2017; Sarzynska-Wawer et al., 2021; Devlin et al., 2019). More recently, very deep pre-trained language models, such as bidirectional encoder representation from the transformer (BERT) (Devlin et al., 2019) and generative pre-training (GPT) (Radford et al., 2018), trained with an increasing number of self-supervised tasks have been proposed to make the models capturing more knowledge from a large scale of corpora, which have shown their abilities to produce promising results in downstream tasks. In view of it, many pieces of research of DST have explored to establish the models on the basis of pre-trained language models (Hosseini-Asl et al., 2020; Kim et al., 2020; Lee et al., 2019; Zhang et al., 2019; Chen et al., 2020; Chao and Lane, 2019; Ye et al., 2021b; Heck et al., 2020; Lin et al., 2020).

Related to extracting slot-specific information, most of the previous studies rely on dense token-wise attention (Lee et al., 2019; Wang et al., 2020; Ye et al., 2021b). However, several pieces of research have indicated that local information may be missing with it (Yang et al., 2018; Shaw et al., 2018; Sperber et al., 2018; Luong et al., 2015; Yang et al., 2022). Motivated by it, we investigate introducing local modeling in this task. The most relevant research is (Yang et al., 2021), which makes a comprehensive study of how different granularities affect DST. However, this research employs simple hand-crafted rules to neglect several utterances in a dialogue history. Our proposed approach in this work is data-driven.

3 Dialogue State Tracking with Sparse Local Slot Attention

3.1 Encoding

As shown in Figure 1(a), $\text{BERT}_{context}$ is used for encoding the dialogue context, whose parameters are fine-tuned during training. Let's define the dialogue history $D_T = \{R_1, U_1, ..., R_T, U_T\}$ as a set of system responses R and user utterances U in T turns of dialogue, where $R = \{R_t\}_{t=1}^{T}$ and $U = \{U_t\}_{t=1}^{T}$. We define $E_T = \{B_1, ..., B_T\}$ as the dialogue states of T turns, and each E_t is a set of slot value pairs $\{(S_1, V_1), ..., (S_J, V_J)\}$ of J slots. The context encoder accepts the dialogue history till turn t, which can be denoted as $X_t = \{D_t, E'_{t-1}\}$, as the input and generates context vector representations $\mathbf{H}_t = \text{BERT}_{context}(X_t)$.

Another pre-trained BERT_{sv} is employed to encode the slots and candidate values. Its parameters remain frozen during training. For those slots and values containing multiple tokens, the vector corresponding to the [CLS] token is employed to represent them. For each slot S_j and value V_j, $\mathbf{h}_{S_j} = \text{BERT}_{sv}(S_j)$, $\mathbf{h}_{V_j} = \text{BERT}_{sv}(V_j)$.

3.2 Sparse Local Slot Attention

To extract slot-specific information, we propose sparse local slot attention (SLSA). As shown in Figure 1(b), sparse local slot attention accepts the dialogue history $\mathbf{H}_t$ and the representation $\mathbf{h}_{S_j}$ of the specific slot S_j. To obtain local information, we employ a convolutional layer whose kernel has size l and stride m over the context vector representation of dialogue history. The convolutional kernel accepts the local area in the dialogue history representation and multiplies it with the learnable parameters to obtain the local semantic representations.

$$\mathbf{H}'_t = ReLU(Conv(\mathbf{H}_t) + \mathbf{H}_t) \quad (1)$$

After that, multi-head attention with the sparsemax function is employed to retrieve relevant information for each slot. It generates sparse distribution to each local area. The sparsemax function returns the Euclidean projection of the input vector $\mathbf{z}$ onto the probability simplex $\Delta^{K-1} := \{\mathbf{p} \in \mathbb{R}^K | \mathbf{1}^T\mathbf{p} = 1, \mathbf{p} \geq 0\}$. The projection is likely to hit the boundary of the simplex, in which case $sparsemax(\mathbf{z})$ becomes sparse (Martins and Astudillo, 2016).

$$Sparsemax(\mathbf{z}) := \arg\min_{\mathbf{p}\in\Delta^{K-1}} ||\mathbf{p} - \mathbf{z}||^2 \quad (2)$$

Then the output is concatenated with each slot to generate slot-specific representations through a feed-forward layer.

$$\mathbf{Q}_t^{S_j} = \mathbf{h}_{S_j}\mathbf{W}_Q + \mathbf{b}_Q \quad (3)$$

$$\mathbf{K}_t^{S_j} = \mathbf{H}'_t\mathbf{W}_K + \mathbf{b}_K \quad (4)$$

$$\mathbf{V}_t^{S_j} = \mathbf{H}'_t\mathbf{W}_V + \mathbf{b}_V \quad (5)$$

$$\boldsymbol{\alpha}_t^{S_j} = Sparsemax(\frac{\mathbf{Q}_t^{S_j}\mathbf{K}_t^{S_j\,T}}{\sqrt{d_k}})\mathbf{V}_t^{S_j} \quad (6)$$

$$\mathbf{C}_t^{S_j} = \mathbf{W}_2 ReLU(\mathbf{W}_1[\mathbf{h}_{S_j}, \boldsymbol{\alpha}_t^{S_j}] + \mathbf{b}_1) + \mathbf{b}_2 \quad (7)$$

Where $\mathbf{W}_Q, \mathbf{b}_Q, \mathbf{W}_K, \mathbf{b}_K$, $\mathbf{W}_V$, and $\mathbf{b}_V$ are the parameters of the linear layers for projecting query, key, and value respectively. $d_k = d_h/N$ in which d_h is the hidden size of the model, and N is the number of heads.

3.3 Slot Self-Attention

Slot self-attention is introduced to communicate information across different slots. Each sub-layer in the self-attention layer consists of the self-attention block and two fully connected layers of ReLU activation with layer normalization and residual connection. Let $\mathbf{C}_t = [\mathbf{C}_t^{S_1}, ..., \mathbf{C}_t^{S_J}]$ and $\mathbf{F}_t^1 = \mathbf{C}_t$ at the first sub layer, then for the l-th sub-layer,

$$\widetilde{\mathbf{F}}_t^l = LayerNorm(\mathbf{F}_t^l), \quad (8)$$

$$\mathbf{G}_t^l = MultiHead(\widetilde{\mathbf{F}}_t^l, \widetilde{\mathbf{F}}_t^l, \widetilde{\mathbf{F}}_t^l) + \widetilde{\mathbf{F}}_t^l. \quad (9)$$

For the l-th feed forward sub-layer,

$$\widetilde{\mathbf{G}}_t^l = LayerNorm(\mathbf{G}_t^l), \quad (10)$$

$$\mathbf{F}_t^{l+1} = FFN(\widetilde{\mathbf{G}}_t^l) + \widetilde{\mathbf{G}}_t^l. \quad (11)$$

The output of the final layer is regarded as the final slot specific vector $\mathbf{F}_t^{L+1} = [\mathbf{f}_t^{S_1}, ..., \mathbf{f}_t^{S_J}]$.

3.4 Slot Value Matching

A Euclidean distance-based value prediction is performed for each slot, the nearest value is chosen to predict the state value.

$$p(V_t^j|X_t, S_j) = \frac{\exp(-d(\mathbf{h}^{V_j}, \mathbf{f}_t^{S_j}))}{\sum_{V_j' \in \nu_j} \exp(-d(\mathbf{h}^{V_j'}, \mathbf{f}_t^{S_j}))} \quad (12)$$

where $d(\cdot)$ is Euclidean distance function, and ν_j denotes the value space of the slot S_j. The model is trained to maximize the joint probability of all slots. The loss function at each turn t is denoted as the sum of the negative log-likelihood, $\mathcal{L}_t = \sum_{j=1}^{J} -\log(p(V_t^j|X_t, S_j))$.

4 Experiments

4.1 Datasets

We conduct experiments using a couple of mainstream datasets of task-oriented dialogue: MultiWOZ 2.0 and 2.4 datasets. MultiWOZ2.0 (Budzianowski et al., 2018) is currently the largest open-source human-human conversational dataset of multiple domains. MultiWOZ 2.4 is the latest version and fixes the incorrect and inconsistent annotations (Ye et al., 2021a).

4.2 Implementation Details

The BERT$_{context}$ is a pre-trained BERT-base-uncased model, which has 12 layers with 768 hidden units and 12 self-attention heads. Another BERT-base-uncased model is used as the BERT$_{sv}$. For the sparse local slot attention, window size and stride are investigated in the experiment. Padding is added on both sides of the input if needed. The number of attention heads is 4. Adam optimizer is adopted with a batch size of 16, which trains the model with a learning rate of 4e-5 for the encoder and 1e-4 for other parts. The hyper-parameters are selected from the best-performing model over the validation set. We use a dropout with a probability of 0.1 on the dialogue history during training.

4.3 Main Results

The main results are shown in Table 1. As we can see, our model achieves the best performance on all the datasets. We utilize the Wilcoxon signed-rank test, the proposed method is statistically significantly better ($p < 0.05$) than baselines. For the MultiWOZ 2.0 dataset, our proposed SLSA model (window size is 3 and stride is 1) achieves a JGA of 54.83% performing better than STAR with a JGA of 54.53%, which is the previous SOTA. Moreover, on the latest refined version MultiWOZ 2.4 fixing many annotations in the test set, our model obtains a JGA of 77.92%. To sum up, our proposed model achieves a slight improvement on the original MultiWOZ 2.0 dataset, and a significant improvement on the latest refined MultiWOZ 2.4 dataset with a clean test set. We also make an investigation about the effects of local granularities, as shown in Appendix A.1.

Table 1: The joint goal accuracy (JGA) of different models. SLSA denotes our proposed sparse local slot attention.

Model	MW2.0	MW2.4
TRADE (Wu et al., 2019)	48.93	54.97
SOM (Kim et al., 2020)	51.72	66.78
TripPy (Heck et al., 2020)	-	59.62
SimpleTOD (Hosseini-Asl et al., 2020)	-	66.78
SUMBT (Lee et al., 2019)	46.65	61.86
DS-DST (Zhang et al., 2019)	52.24	-
DS-Picklist (Zhang et al., 2019)	54.39	-
SAVN (Wang et al., 2020)	54.52	60.55
SST (Chen et al., 2020)	51.17	-
STAR (Ye et al., 2021b)	54.53	73.62
SLSA	**54.83**	**77.92**

Table 2: The results on the MultiWOZ 2.4 dataset using our model with different settings.

	JGA (%)	SA (%)
SLSA	77.92	99.06
w/o Sparse	75.79	98.96
w/o Local	74.65	98.89
w/o Both	73.88	98.84

4.4 Ablation Study

To further verify the proposed approach, we present some results that show the effectiveness of the components in the proposed approaches. Table 2 presents the joint goal accuracy and slot accuracy obtained when we progressively remove the components in our proposed model on MultiWOZ 2.4 dataset. On one hand, comparing SLSA and "w/o Local" (or "w/o Sparse" and "w/o both"), when the local pattern component is removed, the performance of corresponding model decreases. On the other hand, comparing SLSA and "w/o Sparse" (or "w/o Local" and "w/o both" when the sparse component is removed, the performance of the corresponding model decreases. It shows that the sparse and the local components are effective and important to the proposed model.

4.5 Error Analysis

An error analysis of each slot for the previous SOTA model STAR and our models on MultiWOZ 2.4 is shown in Figure 2, in which the lower the better. The four slots with the highest error rates

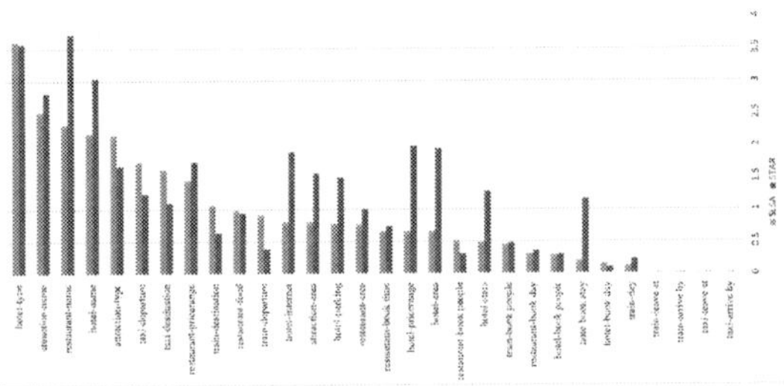

Figure 2: The error rate per slot of STAR and our models on MultiWOZ 2.4 dataset.

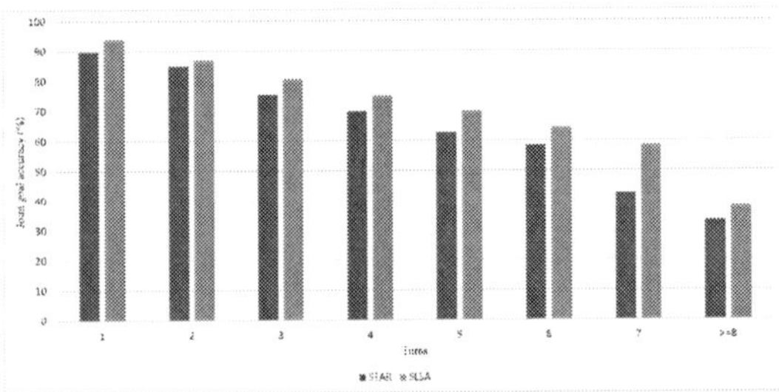

Figure 3: Joint goal accuracy per turn of STAR and our models on MultiWOZ 2.4 dataset.

are *hotel-type* with 3.62%, *attraction-name* with 2.52%, *restaurant-name* with 2.32% and *hotel-name* with 2.17%. It can be noticed that the later three are *name*-related whose values are diverse, local-compact, and may includes several non-semantic tokens. Our proposed models perform better than STAR on these three slots, evidenced by that the error rates are lower. In addition, our model performs better in several categorical slots such as *hotel-internet*, *hotel-parking*, *hotel-stars* and *book stay*. We make a case study shown in Appendix A.2 to have a straightforward understanding of our proposed approach.

4.6 Performance for Long Dialogues

Figure 3 depicts the joint goal accuracy per turn of our models and STAR on MultiWOZ 2.4 dataset. Joint goal accuracy per turn is to measure the performance for long dialogues. It is considered correct if and only all of the values are correctly predicted for each slot until the n-th turn. In the beginning, the performance of these two models for short turns is comparable. Then it decreases as the dialogue length becomes longer since the previous states are employed as part of the input where some mistakes may be included. The trend of our model is a little milder. For very long dialogues whose length is larger than 7, our model performs better than STAR. It shows our model performs better for the long dialogues DST.

5 Conclusion

In his work, we propose a sparse local slot attention for dialogue state tracking to alleviate allocating attention weights to content unrelated to the specific slot of interest. In our approach, local semantic information is firstly achieved at a sub-sampled temporal resolution capturing local dependencies for each slot. Then, these local information is attended with sparse attention weights generated by sparsemax function. The experimental results show that, comparing to several existing models based on dense token-wise attention, our approach effectively improves the performance of ontology-based dialogue state tracking in the state prediction for name-related slots and long dialogues.

Acknowledgement

This work was supported by JSPS KAKENHI Grand Number JP22K12069 and partially supported by JSPS KAKENHI Grant Number 23K11227 and 23H03402.

Limitations

In this work, we propose a sparse local slot attention (SLSA) mechanism to make the model pay attention to slot-specified local areas in dialogue history, and then attend them with sparse distribution generated by sparsemax to neglect some redundant parts. This paper shows the effectiveness of our proposed approaches in state prediction for some specified slots and long dialogues. While we show that the model with SLSA is competitive in dialogue state tracking, there are limitation of that provide avenues for future works. First, it is not as easy to apply SLSA to generation-based dialogue state tracking. Different from ontology-based manners, the condition may be different in the case of generative DST since entire successive information involved in language modeling may be important for language generation. Therefore, how to handle the local and sparse properties for the generative model need to further consider. Second, convolution operation considers a fixed bounded local context. It is a challenge to handle local properties of various lengths.

References

Paweł Budzianowski, Tsung-Hsien Wen, Bo-Hsiang Tseng, Iñigo Casanueva, Stefan Ultes, Osman Ramadan, and Milica Gašić. 2018. MultiWOZ - a large-scale multi-domain Wizard-of-Oz dataset for task-oriented dialogue modelling. In *Proceedings of the 2018 Conference on Empirical Methods in Natural Language Processing*, pages 5016–5026.

Guan-Lin Chao and Ian Lane. 2019. Bert-dst: Scalable end-to-end dialogue state tracking with bidirectional encoder representations from transformer. *arXiv preprint arXiv:1907.03040*.

Hongshen Chen, Xiaorui Liu, Dawei Yin, and Jiliang Tang. 2017. A survey on dialogue systems: Recent advances and new frontiers. *Acm Sigkdd Explorations Newsletter*, 19(2):25–35.

Lu Chen, Boer Lv, Chi Wang, Su Zhu, Bowen Tan, and Kai Yu. 2020. Schema-guided multi-domain dialogue state tracking with graph attention neural networks. In *Proceedings of the AAAI Conference on Artificial Intelligence*, volume 34, pages 7521–7528.

Jacob Devlin, Ming-Wei Chang, Kenton Lee, and Kristina Toutanova. 2019. BERT: Pre-training of deep bidirectional transformers for language understanding. In *Proceedings of the 2019 Conference of the North American Chapter of the Association for Computational Linguistics: Human Language Technologies*, pages 4171–4186.

Michael Heck, Carel van Niekerk, Nurul Lubis, Christian Geishauser, Hsien-Chin Lin, Marco Moresi, and Milica Gasic. 2020. Trippy: A triple copy strategy for value independent neural dialog state tracking. In *Proceedings of the 21th Annual Meeting of the Special Interest Group on Discourse and Dialogue*, pages 35–44.

Ehsan Hosseini-Asl, Bryan McCann, Chien-Sheng Wu, Semih Yavuz, and Richard Socher. 2020. A Simple Language Model for Task-Oriented Dialogue. In *Advances in Neural Information Processing Systems*, volume 33, pages 20179–20191.

Jiaying Hu, Yan Yang, Chencai Chen, Liang He, and Zhou Yu. 2020. SAS: Dialogue state tracking via slot attention and slot information sharing. In *Proceedings of the 58th Annual Meeting of the Association for Computational Linguistics*, pages 6366–6375.

Sungdong Kim, Sohee Yang, Gyuwan Kim, and Sang-Woo Lee. 2020. Efficient dialogue state tracking by selectively overwriting memory. In *Proceedings of the 58th Annual Meeting of the Association for Computational Linguistics*, pages 567–582.

Hwaran Lee, Jinsik Lee, and Tae-Yoon Kim. 2019. SUMBT: Slot-utterance matching for universal and scalable belief tracking. In *Proceedings of the 57th Annual Meeting of the Association for Computational Linguistics*, pages 5478–5483.

Zhaojiang Lin, Andrea Madotto, Genta Indra Winata, and Pascale Fung. 2020. Mintl: Minimalist transfer learning for task-oriented dialogue systems. In *Proceedings of the 2020 Conference on Empirical Methods in Natural Language Processing*, pages 3391–3405.

Thang Luong, Hieu Pham, and Christopher D. Manning. 2015. Effective approaches to attention-based neural machine translation. In *Proceedings of the 2015 Conference on Empirical Methods in Natural Language Processing*, pages 1412–1421.

Andre Martins and Ramon Astudillo. 2016. From softmax to sparsemax: A sparse model of attention and multi-label classification. In *International conference on machine learning*, pages 1614–1623.

Bryan McCann, James Bradbury, Caiming Xiong, and Richard Socher. 2017. Learned in translation: Contextualized word vectors. *arXiv preprint arXiv:1708.00107*.

Tomas Mikolov, Ilya Sutskever, Kai Chen, Greg S Corrado, and Jeff Dean. 2013. Distributed representations of words and phrases and their compositionality. In *Advances in neural information processing systems*, pages 3111–3119.

Nikola Mrkšić, Diarmuid Ó Séaghdha, Tsung-Hsien Wen, Blaise Thomson, and Steve Young. 2017. Neural belief tracker: Data-driven dialogue state tracking. In *Proceedings of the 55th Annual Meeting of the Association for Computational Linguistics*, pages 1777–1788.

Elnaz Nouri and Ehsan Hosseini-Asl. 2018. Toward scalable neural dialogue state tracking. In *NeurIPS 2018, 2nd Conversational AI workshop*.

Yawen Ouyang, Moxin Chen, Xinyu Dai, Yinggong Zhao, Shujian Huang, and Jiajun Chen. 2020. Dialogue state tracking with explicit slot connection modeling. In *Proceedings of the 58th Annual Meeting of the Association for Computational Linguistics*, pages 34–40.

Jeffrey Pennington, Richard Socher, and Christopher D. Manning. 2014. Glove: Global vectors for word representation. In *Empirical Methods in Natural Language Processing (EMNLP)*, pages 1532–1543.

Ben Peters, Vlad Niculae, and André FT Martins. 2019. Sparse sequence-to-sequence models. *arXiv preprint arXiv:1905.05702*.

Alec Radford, Karthik Narasimhan, Tim Salimans, and Ilya Sutskever. 2018. Improving language understanding by generative pre-training.

Abhinav Rastogi, Raghav Gupta, and Dilek Hakkani-Tur. 2018. Multi-task learning for joint language understanding and dialogue state tracking. *arXiv preprint arXiv:1811.05408*.

Abhinav Rastogi, Dilek Hakkani-Tür, and Larry Heck. 2017. Scalable multi-domain dialogue state tracking. In *2017 IEEE Automatic Speech Recognition and Understanding Workshop (ASRU)*, pages 561–568.

Liliang Ren, Kaige Xie, Lu Chen, and Kai Yu. 2018. Towards universal dialogue state tracking. In *Proceedings of the 2018 Conference on Empirical Methods in Natural Language Processing*, pages 2780–2786.

Justyna Sarzynska-Wawer, Aleksander Wawer, Aleksandra Pawlak, Julia Szymanowska, Izabela Stefaniak, Michal Jarkiewicz, and Lukasz Okruszek. 2021. Detecting formal thought disorder by deep contextualized word representations. *Psychiatry Research*, 304:114135.

Peter Shaw, Jakob Uszkoreit, and Ashish Vaswani. 2018. Self-attention with relative position representations. In *Proceedings of the 2018 Conference of the North American Chapter of the Association for Computational Linguistics: Human Language Technologies*, pages 464–468.

Matthias Sperber, Jan Niehues, Graham Neubig, Sebastian Stüker, and Alex Waibel. 2018. Self-attentional acoustic models. *arXiv preprint arXiv:1803.09519*.

Blaise Thomson and Steve Young. 2010. Bayesian update of dialogue state: A pomdp framework for spoken dialogue systems. *Computer Speech & Language*, 24(4):562–588.

Yexiang Wang, Yi Guo, and Siqi Zhu. 2020. Slot attention with value normalization for multi-domain dialogue state tracking. In *Proceedings of the 2020 Conference on Empirical Methods in Natural Language Processing*, pages 3019–3028.

Zhuoran Wang and Oliver Lemon. 2013. A simple and generic belief tracking mechanism for the dialog state tracking challenge: On the believability of observed information. In *Proceedings of the SIGDIAL 2013 Conference*, pages 423–432.

Jason D. Williams and Steve Young. 2007. Partially observable markov decision processes for spoken dialog systems. *Computer Speech & Language*, 21(2):393–422.

Chien-Sheng Wu, Andrea Madotto, Ehsan Hosseini-Asl, Caiming Xiong, Richard Socher, and Pascale Fung. 2019. Transferable multi-domain state generator for task-oriented dialogue systems. In *Proceedings of the 57th Annual Meeting of the Association for Computational Linguistics*, pages 808–819.

Puyang Xu and Qi Hu. 2018. An end-to-end approach for handling unknown slot values in dialogue state tracking. In *Proceedings of the 56th Annual Meeting of the Association for Computational Linguistics*, pages 1448–1457.

Baosong Yang, Zhaopeng Tu, Derek F Wong, Fandong Meng, Lidia S Chao, and Tong Zhang. 2018. Modeling localness for self-attention networks. In *Proceedings of the 2018 Conference on Empirical Methods in Natural Language Processing*, pages 4449–4458.

Longfei Yang, Jiyi Li, Sheng Li, and Takahiro Shinozaki. 2022. Multi-domain dialogue state tracking with top-k slot self attention. In *Proceedings of the 23rd Annual Meeting of the Special Interest Group on Discourse and Dialogue*, pages 231–236.

Puhai Yang, Heyan Huang, and Xian-Ling Mao. 2021. Comprehensive study: How the context information of different granularity affects dialogue state tracking? *arXiv preprint arXiv:2105.03571*.

Fanghua Ye, Jarana Manotumruksa, and Emine Yilmaz. 2021a. Multiwoz 2.4: A multi-domain task-oriented dialogue dataset with essential annotation corrections to improve state tracking evaluation. *arXiv preprint arXiv:2104.00773*.

Fanghua Ye, Jarana Manotumruksa, Qiang Zhang, Shenghui Li, and Emine Yilmaz. 2021b. Slot self-attentive dialogue state tracking. In *Proceedings of the Web Conference 2021*, pages 1598–1608.

Steve Young, Milica Gašić, Simon Keizer, François Mairesse, Jost Schatzmann, Blaise Thomson, and Kai Yu. 2010. The hidden information state model: A practical framework for pomdp-based spoken dialogue management. *Computer Speech & Language*, 24(2):150–174.

Steve Young, Milica Gašić, Blaise Thomson, and Jason D Williams. 2013. Pomdp-based statistical spoken dialog systems: A review. *Proceedings of the IEEE*, 101(5):1160–1179.

Jian-Guo Zhang, Kazuma Hashimoto, Chien-Sheng Wu, Yao Wan, Philip S Yu, Richard Socher, and Caiming Xiong. 2019. Find or classify? dual strategy for slot-value predictions on multi-domain dialog state tracking. *arXiv preprint arXiv:1910.03544*.

Victor Zhong, Caiming Xiong, and Richard Socher. 2018. Global-locally self-attentive encoder for dialogue state tracking. In *Proceedings of the 56th Annual Meeting of the Association for Computational Linguistics*, pages 1458–1467.

Table 3: The results with different sizes ls and strides ms of the local window in our model.

Setup	SLSA_{conv}
$l = 1, m = 1$	74.82
$l = 3, m = 1$	77.92
$l = 3, m = 2$	76.45
$l = 3, m = 3$	76.87
$l = 5, m = 1$	74.89
$l = 5, m = 3$	74.46
$l = 5, m = 5$	73.44

A Appendix

A.1 Effects of Different Locality Granularities

We compare our model with different sizes and strides of the window of the local pattern to see how different granularities affect the performance on MultiWOZ 2.4 dataset, as shown in Table 3.

It shows that the best result is achieved when the size of 3 and the stride of 1, while the performance is not improved by enlarging the size of the local window or decreasing it. Note that, as mentioned in the experimental settings, in the main results, the hyperparameters of window size and stride are selected by tuning on the validation set.

A.2 Case Study

Figure 4 and 5 demonstrate the predicted states of STAR and our model on two pieces of dialogues from the MultiWOZ 2.4 dataset. We color the input with the weights generated by sparse local slot attention in our model and the dense token-wise attention used in STAR. Note that in our model, one position with a dark background means the local area around this position is focused. It is different from STAR, in which one position denotes a token.

As shown in Figure 4, although STAR captures the relevant information for *attraction-name* but not the best. Our models are able to focus on the local area covering the entity. As shown in Figure 5, the user says "nothing in particular" indicating he/him does not prefer "a certain area". STAR fails to capture this information, and its attention is scattered. Our model realizes this and successfully gets the user's point. Although the values "none" and "do not care" indicate the *attraction-area* does not need concrete values, they denote the user's different intentions.

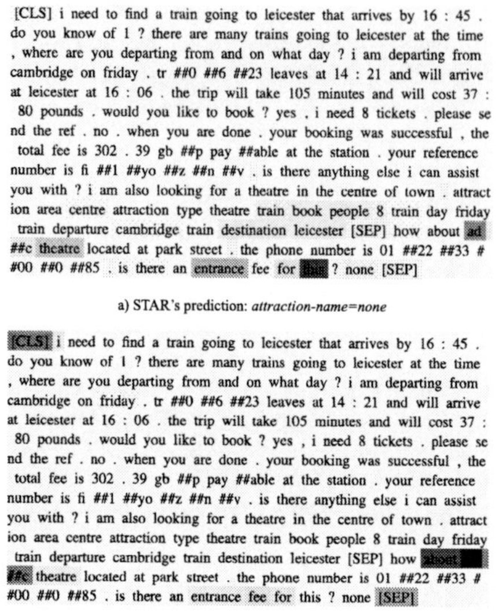

Figure 4: The predicted dialogue states for slot $attraction - name$ with STAR and our model on dialogue PMUL1424.

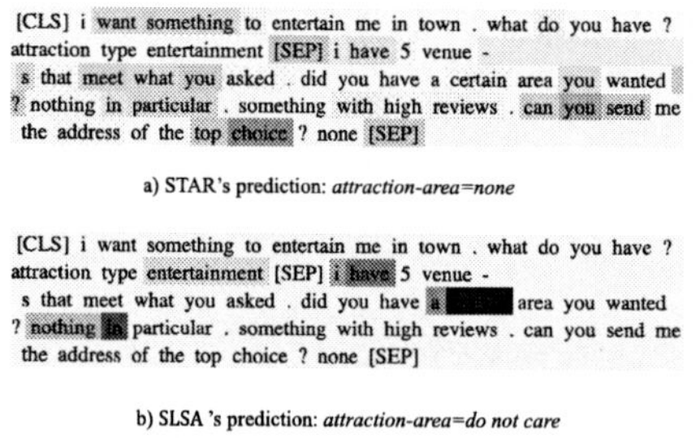

Figure 5: The predicted dialogue states for slot $attraction - area$ with STAR and our model on dialogue PMUL2415.

LLM-EVAL: Unified Multi-Dimensional Automatic Evaluation for Open-Domain Conversations with Large Language Models

Yen-Ting Lin Yun-Nung Chen
National Taiwan University, Taipei, Taiwan
{ytl, y.v.chen}@ieee.org

Abstract

We propose LLM-EVAL, a unified multi-dimensional automatic evaluation method for open-domain conversations with large language models (LLMs). Existing evaluation methods often rely on human annotations, ground-truth responses, or multiple LLM prompts, which can be expensive and time-consuming. To address these issues, we design a single prompt-based evaluation method that leverages a unified evaluation schema to cover multiple dimensions of conversation quality in a single model call. We extensively evaluate the performance of LLM-EVAL on various benchmark datasets, demonstrating its effectiveness, efficiency, and adaptability compared to state-of-the-art evaluation methods. Our analysis also highlights the importance of choosing suitable LLMs and decoding strategies for accurate evaluation results. LLM-EVAL offers a versatile and robust solution for evaluating open-domain conversation systems, streamlining the evaluation process and providing consistent performance across diverse scenarios.

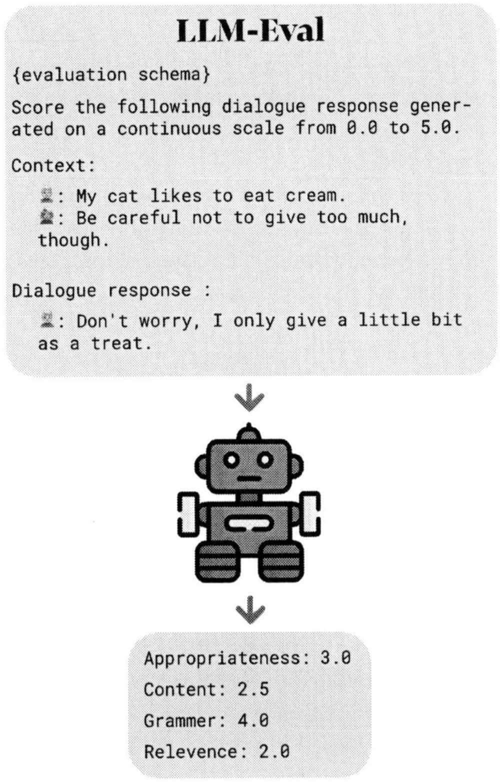

Figure 1: An illustration of our proposed LLM-EVAL framework, which leverages a unified multi-dimensional evaluation schema and a single prompt to efficiently evaluate open-domain conversations with large language models.

1 Introduction

Effective evaluation of open-domain conversation systems is a critical yet challenging problem in natural language processing research (Smith et al., 2022). Accurate and consistent evaluation methods are essential for understanding and improving the performance of dialogue systems. Traditional automatic evaluation metrics, such as BLEU (Papineni et al., 2002) and ROUGE (Lin, 2004), are insufficient for capturing the nuances of natural language conversations (Liu et al., 2016; Deriu et al., 2021), leading to the development of various advanced metrics (Tao et al., 2018; Ghazarian et al., 2019; Sai et al., 2020; Huang et al., 2020; Mehri and Eskenazi, 2020b; Phy et al., 2020; Zhang et al., 2021a; Li et al., 2021; Fu et al., 2023; Liu et al., 2023). However, most existing methods require annotation data , human references, or multiple prompts, which could be expensive, time-consuming, or prone to errors.

In this paper, we address the problem of evaluating open-domain conversation systems with a focus on large language models (LLMs) (Figure 1). Our goal is to develop an efficient and accurate evaluation method that covers multiple dimensions of conversation quality, such as content, grammar, relevance, and appropriateness, without requiring human references or multiple prompts. We build upon recent advances in LLMs (Brown et al., 2020;

Proceedings of the 5th Workshop on NLP for Conversational AI (NLP4ConvAI 2023), pages 47–58
July 14, 2023

Bai et al., 2022; OpenAI, 2023), and propose a unified multi-dimensional evaluation method called LLM-EVAL.

Existing evaluation methods have demonstrated promising results in various aspects of dialogue evaluation. However, they often rely on human annotations (Mehri and Eskenazi, 2020b; Phy et al., 2020), ground-truth responses (Ghazarian et al., 2020; Zhang et al., 2020a), or multiple LLM inferences (Fu et al., 2023; Liu et al., 2023), limiting their efficiency and adaptability in practical scenarios. We aim to bridge this gap by proposing LLM-EVAL, a single-prompt-based evaluation method that leverages a unified evaluation schema to cover multiple dimensions of conversation quality in a single model call.

In LLM-EVAL, we design a natural language instruction that defines the evaluation task and desired criteria, as well as a format instruction that specifies the structure and range of scores for each dimension. The single prompt is created by concatenating the dialogue context, reference (if available), and generated response, and then fed to a large language model, which outputs scores for each dimension based on the defined schema.

We extensively evaluate the performance of LLM-EVAL on a variety of benchmark datasets, covering diverse dialogue systems and evaluation dimensions. Our experiments demonstrate that LLM-EVAL consistently outperforms most baselines and state-of-the-art evaluation methods in terms of correlation with human judgments. The proposed method is also robust and versatile, adapting to different scoring ranges and evaluation scenarios.

In summary, our main contributions are 3-fold:

- We propose LLM-EVAL, a unified multi-dimensional automatic evaluation method for open-domain conversations with large language models, which streamlines the evaluation process by using a single prompt and a unified evaluation schema.
- We extensively evaluate the performance of LLM-EVAL on a variety of benchmark datasets, demonstrating its effectiveness and efficiency in comparison with state-of-the-art evaluation methods.
- We provide an in-depth analysis of the impact of different LLMs and decoding methods on the performance of LLM-EVAL, highlighting the importance of choosing suitable LLMs and decoding strategies for accurate evaluation results.

2 Related Work

Multi-Dimensional Metrics Multi-dimensional evaluation metrics have been proposed to assess various aspects of dialogue quality, such as content, grammar, relevance, and appropriateness. Examples include USR (Mehri and Eskenazi, 2020b), which trains multiple models to measure qualities like fluency, relevance, and knowledge conditioning, and GRADE (Huang et al., 2020), which models topic transition dynamics in dialogue history using a graph representation. FlowScore (Li et al., 2021) leverages dynamic information flow in dialog history to measure dialogue quality. Unlike these approaches, LLM-EVAL employs a single prompt-based evaluation method that leverages a unified evaluation schema, streamlining the evaluation process and providing a more efficient and adaptable solution.

Unsupervised Metrics Unsupervised evaluation metrics aim to assess the quality of dialogue responses without requiring human annotations. Notable unsupervised methods include DEB (Sai et al., 2020), which fine-tunes BERT with an NSP objective on a dataset with relevant and adversarial irrelevant responses, and FED (Mehri and Eskenazi, 2020a), an unsupervised method that measures dialogue quality using features derived from response embeddings and language model probabilities. In contrast, LLM-EVAL leverages the power of large language models to provide a unified multi-dimensional evaluation, achieving better performance and adaptability compared to existing unsupervised methods.

Large Language Models for Evaluation Recent works have explored using large language models for dialogue evaluation. GPTScore (Fu et al., 2023) employs models like GPT-3 to assign higher probabilities to quality content, using multiple prompts for a multi-dimensional assessment. Chen et al. (2023) explores using ChatGPT and InstructGPT to evaluate text quality without references, and compares different paradigms of using LLMs, including generating explicit scores, using model confidence to determine implicit scores, and directly comparing pairs of texts. G-EVAL (Liu et al., 2023), a framework that leverages LLMs with chain-of-thoughts (CoT)(Wei et al., 2022) and a form-filling paradigm. G-EVAL with GPT-4 as the backbone model achieves a high correlation with human judgments on a summarization task. However, both GPTScore and G-EVAL require multiple prompts or complex scoring functions that use probabilities of output tokens and their weighted summation as the final score, which can be inefficient or time-consuming. LLM-EVAL addresses these issues by using a single prompt and a unified evaluation schema, offering a more efficient and adaptable evaluation method for open-domain conversations. Additionally, LLM-EVAL provides multi-dimensional evaluation scores in a single model call, further streamlining the evaluation process.

3 Methodology

LLM-EVAL is an efficient prompt-based evaluator tailored for open-domain conversations with large language models. It encompasses a single prompt that addresses the evaluation task, desired evaluation criteria, and a unified multi-dimensional evaluation schema. This method eradicates the necessity for numerous LLMs inferences or intricate scoring functions (Fu et al., 2023; Liu et al., 2023), while still delivering a comprehensive assessment of the generated text.

Unified Evaluation Schema The evaluation schema is a natural language instruction that defines the task and the desired evaluation criteria. It is designed to cover multiple dimensions of the evaluation, such as content, grammar, relevance, and appropriateness. The schema is provided as a format instruction, which specifies the structure and the range of the scores for each dimension. For example, the evaluation schema can be:

> *Human: The output should be formatted as a JSON instance that conforms to the JSON schema below. ... Here is the output schema: {"properties": {"content": {"title": "Content", "description": "content score in the range of 0 to 100", "type": "integer"*, "grammar": ...}

Single Prompt for Evaluation The single prompt is designed to include the necessary dialogue context and the target response that needs to be evaluated, along with the evaluation schema. The prompt is concatenated with the dialogue context, the reference (if available), and the generated response, and then fed to the large language model to output a score for each evaluation dimension, based on the defined schema. For example, the prompt for evaluating a dialogue response with human reference can be:

> *Context: {context}*
> *Reference: {reference}*
> *Dialogue response: {response}*

Efficient Evaluation By using a single prompt with a unified evaluation schema, LLM-EVAL can efficiently obtain multi-dimensional scores for the responses without the need for multiple prompts. The large language model is called only once, and it directly provides the evaluation scores for each dimension based on the defined schema. For instance, given a dialogue context, reference, and generated response, the LLM-EVAL method would produce an example output that looks like this:

> *Output: {"appropriateness": 3.0, "content": 2.5, "grammar": 4.0, "relevance": 2.0}*

This output showcases the multi-dimensional evaluation of the generated response, with each dimension receiving a score based on the predefined schema. The scores help in understanding the quality of the response in terms of appropriateness, content, grammar, and relevance, while still maintaining the efficiency of the evaluation process by requiring just a single call to the large language model. For a detailed description of the prompt templates used in our experiments with LLM-EVAL, please refer to Appendix A.

4 Experiments

4.1 Datasets and Benchmarks

Our proposed LLM-EVAL method is assessed on an array of datasets spanning diverse dialogue systems and evaluation dimensions. We provide a concise overview of the datasets and their features in this section. The datasets include human annotations, where each entry comprises a dialogue context, a generated response, and associated scores. A ground-truth human reference may also be present. For data lacking human reference, we only evaluate reference-free metrics.

DSTC10 Hidden Set The DSTC10 hidden set (Zhang et al., 2021b) is a multi-dimensional evaluation dataset that includes JSALT (Kong-Vega et al.,

2018), NCM, ESL (Vinyals and Le, 2015; Sedoc et al., 2019; Lee et al., 2020), Topical-DSTC10 (Gopalakrishnan et al., 2019) and Persona-DSTC10 (Zhang et al., 2018). JSALT contains human-generated dialogue segments from EmpatheticDialogues (Rashkin et al., 2019) and TopicalChat (Gopalakrishnan et al., 2019). NCM and ESL are datasets with pairwise comparisons between system responses, collected from an English learning website and hand-crafted prompts. Topical-DSTC10 and Persona-DSTC10 are newly created datasets that include responses from various dialogue systems, such as LSTM Seq2Seq, HRED, VHRED, BlenderBot, DialoGPT, T5, and GPT-3.

Overall Scores with Human Reference TopicalChat-USR evaluates response quality in knowledge-grounded dialogues, emphasizing topical understanding. PersonaChat-USR measures response quality in personalized conversations, highlighting the incorporation of speaker personas (Mehri and Eskenazi, 2020b). ConvAI2-GRADE examines the quality of chit-chat dialogue systems, focusing on engaging and contextually relevant responses. DailyDialog-GRADE investigates response quality in everyday conversational contexts. EmpatheticDialogue-GRADE assesses the quality of empathetic responses in dialogue systems (Huang et al., 2020). DSTC6 evaluates end-to-end conversation modeling with human-generated responses (Hori and Hori, 2017).

Overall Scores without Human Reference DailyDialog-PredictiveEngagement evaluates engagement in dialogue systems without relying on human references (Ghazarian et al., 2020). FED is an unsupervised method that measures the quality of dialogue responses without using human references (Mehri and Eskenazi, 2020a). DSTC9 focuses on the end-to-end evaluation of context-aware dialogue systems without human references (Mehri et al., 2022).

We compare the performance of LLM-EVAL with existing evaluation methods on these datasets to demonstrate its effectiveness and efficiency in evaluating open-domain conversations. The evaluation results are presented in terms of correlation with human judgments, using Pearson's correlation coefficient (r) and Spearman's correlation coefficient (ρ).

4.2 LLM-EVAL Configurations

We evaluate LLM-EVAL under different settings to demonstrate its effectiveness and adaptability. The configurations are as follows:

LLM-EVAL 0-5 The evaluation scores for each dimension are in the range of 0 to 5 with one decimal place, which is more close to common 1-5 Likert scale used in human evaluation.

LLM-EVAL 0-100 The evaluation scores for each dimension are in the range of 0 to 100 as integers, providing a finer-grained scale for evaluation.

The evaluation schema prompt for both configurations remains the same, with only the range of scores differing between them. We test the LLM-EVAL method with and without human references for each configuration if applicable.

Unless specified otherwise, throughout our experiments and evaluations, we employ the Anthropic Claude API with the `claude-v1.3` model and use greedy decoding, which selects the token with the highest probability at each time step during the generation process.

4.3 Baseline Evaluation Metrics

We compare LLM-EVAL with several state-of-the-art evaluation metrics, including both traditional and LLM-based approaches.

- **Deep-AM-FM** measures dialog quality with Adequacy Metric (AM) and Fluency Metric (FM), utilizing BERT embeddings and language model probabilities (Zhang et al., 2020a).
- **DSTC10 Team 1** boosted DyanEval's (Zhang et al., 2021a) turn-level evaluation performance by integrating auxiliary objectives and combining USL-H(Phy et al., 2020), DEB (Sai et al., 2020), and an improved DyanEval, with weights based on input dialogue data characteristics (Zhang et al., 2021b).
- **MME-CRS** introduces the Multi-Metric Evaluation, consisting of 5 parallel sub-metrics to assess dialogue quality across fluency, relevance, engagement, specificity, and topic coherence. The approach utilizes Correlation Re-Scaling to model sub-metric relationships (Zhang et al., 2022).
- **BERTScore** computes the F1 score by matching token embeddings in human references and system responses (Zhang et al., 2020b).

Spearman ρ (%)	JSALT APP	ESL APP	NCM APP	TopicalChat-DSTC10 APP	CON	GRA	REL	PersonaChat-DSTC10 APP	CON	GRA	REL	Avg
Deep-AM-FM	5.1	32.3	16.5	18.2	9.4	17.9	26.2	21.0	14.7	19.1	24.1	18.4
DSTC10 Team 1	**27.7**	42.0	29.9	29.7	7.0	11.6	37.0	38.6	19.3	18.6	44.5	30.2
MME-CRS	11.7	41.4	29.9	32.6	17.2	9.0	**44.8**	45.6	32.5	22.0	**54.8**	31.0
without human reference												
LLM-EVAL$_{0-5}$	23.2	51.8	**34.4**	**38.6**	20.6	**33.2**	42.8	**48.2**	36.9	**34.5**	52.1	**37.8**
LLM-EVAL$_{0-100}$	27.3	50.5	34.2	**38.6**	21.3	32.7	41.1	47.6	**37.8**	30.2	51.9	37.6
with human reference												
LLM-EVAL$_{0-5}$	25.4	51.8	32.5	38.0	21.5	31.2	42.2	47.9	36.0	30.6	49.1	36.9
LLM-EVAL$_{0-100}$	25.7	**51.9**	30.8	38.2	**21.6**	30.0	40.2	45.4	34.8	28.6	49.3	36.0

Table 1: Spearman correlation coefficients between human ratings and automatic metrics across multiple dimensions (*APP* for Appropriateness, *CON* for Content, *GRA* for Grammar, and *REL* for Relevance) for DSTC10 hidden test datasets with human reference. Each team is represented by the best submission on 5 test datasets. The best score for each column is highlighted in bold. The second best is underlined. Note that the last column is averaged over 11 dimension-wise correlation scores of all five datasets.

r / ρ (%)	TopicalChat	PersonaChat	ConvAI2	DD	ED	DSTC6	Average
BLEU-4	21.6 / 29.6	13.5 / 9.0	0.3 / 12.8	7.5 / 18.4	-5.1 / 0.2	13.1 / 29.8	8.5 / 16.6
ROUGE-L	27.5 / 28.7	6.6 / 3.8	13.6 / 14.0	15.4 / 14.7	2.9 / -1.3	33.2 / 32.6	16.5 / 15.4
BERTScore	29.8 / 32.5	15.2 / 12.2	22.5 / 22.4	12.9 / 10.0	4.6 / 3.3	36.9 / 33.7	20.3 / 19.0
DEB	18.0 / 11.6	29.1 / 37.3	42.6 / 50.4	33.7 / **36.3**	35.6 / 39.5	21.1 / 21.4	30.0 / 32.8
GRADE	20.0 / 21.7	35.8 / 35.2	56.6 / 57.1	27.8 / 25.3	33.0 / 29.7	11.9 / 12.2	30.9 / 30.2
USR	41.2 / 42.3	44.0 / 41.8	50.1 / 50.0	5.7 / 5.7	26.4 / 25.5	18.4 / 16.6	31.0 / 30.3
USL-H	32.2 / 34.0	49.5 / 52.3	44.3 / 45.7	10.8 / 9.3	29.3 / 23.5	21.7 / 17.9	31.3 / 30.5
without human reference							
LLM-EVAL$_{0-5}$	55.7 / 58.3	51.0 / 48.0	59.3 / 59.6	31.8 / 32.2	42.1 / 41.4	43.3 / 41.1	47.2 / 46.8
LLM-EVAL$_{0-100}$	49.0 / 49.9	53.3 / 51.5	**61.3 / 61.8**	**34.6** / 34.9	43.2 / 42.3	44.0 / 41.8	**47.6** / 47.0
with human reference							
LLM-EVAL$_{0-5}$	**56.5 / 59.4**	**55.4 / 53.1**	43.1 / 43.8	32.0 / 32.2	40.0 / 40.1	47.0 / 45.5	45.7 / 45.7
LLM-EVAL$_{0-100}$	55.6 / 57.1	53.8 / 52.7	45.6 / 45.9	33.4 / 34.0	**43.5 / 43.2**	**49.8 / 49.9**	47.0 / **47.1**

Table 2: Correlation coefficients (Pearson r and Spearman ρ) between human ratings and automatic metrics in terms of overall scores for datasets with human reference. We use the following abbreviations: TopicalChat (TopicalChat-USR), PersonaChat (PersonaChat-USR), ConvAI2 (ConvAI2-GRADE), DD (DailyDialog-GRADE), ED (EmpatheticDialogue-GRADE). The best score for each column is highlighted in bold. The second best is underlined.

- **DEB** constructs a dialog dataset with relevant and adversarial irrelevant responses, then fine-tunes BERT with an NSP objective (Sai et al., 2020).
- **GRADE** models topic transition dynamics in dialog using a graph representation of the dialog history (Huang et al., 2020).
- **USR** trains several models to measure different qualities of dialogs, including fluency, relevance, and knowledge conditioning (Mehri and Eskenazi, 2020b).
- **USL-H** combines three models trained with different objectives (VUP, NSP, MLM) to evaluate response validity, sensibleness, and likelihood (Phy et al., 2020).
- **DynaEval** leverages a graph structure to model dialog-level interactions between user and system (Zhang et al., 2021a).
- **FlowScore** models dynamic information flow in dialog history and measures dialog quality using DialoFlow representations (Li et al., 2021).
- **GPTScore** evaluates text using models like GPT-3, assigning higher probabilities to quality content through multiple prompts for a multi-dimensional assessment. However, it may not be as effective as LLM-EVAL, which only requires a single prompt (Fu et al., 2023).
- **Traditional Metrics**: We also include classic metrics such as BLEU (Papineni et al., 2002) and ROUGE (Lin, 2004), which have known limitations in dialogue evaluation.

4.4 Results of DSTC10 Hidden Set

The results of our proposed LLM-EVAL method on the DSTC10 hidden set are presented in Table

r / ρ (%)	DailyDialog-PE Turn-Level	FED Turn-Level	FED Dialog-Level	DSTC9 Dialog-Level	Average
DynaEval	16.7 / 16.0	31.9 / 32.3	50.3 / 54.7	9.3 / 10.1	27.1 / 28.3
USL-H	68.8 / 69.9	20.1 / 18.9	7.3 / 15.2	10.5 / 10.5	26.7 / 28.6
FlowScore	-	-6.5 / -5.5	-7.3 / -0.3	14.7 / 14.0	0.3 / 2.7
GPTScore	-	- / 38.3	- / 54.3	-	- / 46.3
LLM-EVAL *0-5*	71.0 / **71.3**	**60.4 / 50.9**	**67.6 / 71.4**	15.9 / 16.5	**53.7 / 52.5**
LLM-EVAL *0-100*	**71.4** / 71.0	59.7 / 49.9	64.4 / 70.4	**16.1 / 18.6**	52.9 / 52.5

Table 3: Correlation coefficients (Pearson r and Spearman ρ) between human ratings and automatic metrics in terms of overall scores for datasets without human reference. The best score for each column is highlighted in bold. The second best is underlined.

1. We compare the performance of LLM-EVAL with other participating teams and baselines in the DSTC10 challenge. The evaluation is performed in terms of Spearman correlation coefficients between human ratings and automatic metrics across multiple dimensions, including Appropriateness (APP), Content (CON), Grammar (GRA), and Relevance (REL).

The results show that LLM-EVAL consistently outperforms most of the baselines and even the best performing team in DSTC10 across different dimensions and datasets. In particular, LLM-EVAL with a 0-5 score range achieves the highest average Spearman correlation coefficient of 0.378 among all the methods without human reference.

When comparing the two LLM-EVAL configurations, both 0-5 and 0-100 settings demonstrate competitive performance, with the 0-5 configuration slightly outperforming the 0-100 configuration in both cases with or without human reference. This indicates that the LLM-EVAL method is robust and versatile in evaluating open-domain conversations, as it can adapt to different scoring ranges and consistently outperform all baselines and the best performing team in DSTC10 across various dimensions and datasets.

4.5 Overall Scores with Human Reference

The results of LLM-EVAL on datasets with overall scores and human references are presented in Table 2. We compare the performance of LLM-EVAL with other top-performing evaluation methods (Yeh et al., 2021), such as BLEU, ROUGE, BERTScore, DEB, GRADE, USR, and USL-H. The meta-evaluation is performed in terms of Pearson correlation coefficient (r) and Spearman correlation coefficient (ρ) between human ratings and automatic metrics.

For the DailyDialog-GRADE, ConvAI2-GRADE, and EmpatheticDialogue-GRADE datasets, we use the *"Relevance"* dimension for evaluation, while for the DSTC6 dataset, we use the *"Overall"* score. For TopicalChat-USR and PersonaChat-USR, we predict all the *"Engaging, Maintains Context, Natural, Overall, Understandable, Uses Knowledge"* dimensions in the original annotations but only use the *"Overall"* score for meta-evaluation.

LLM-EVAL consistently outperforms most of the baselines across the datasets and correlation coefficients, with LLM-Eval 0-100 configuration achieving the highest average correlation coefficient across all datasets.

The consistent performance of both configurations across different datasets and dimensions indicates that LLM-EVAL is a reliable and effective evaluation tool for open-domain conversations with human references. Its ability to adapt to different scoring ranges while maintaining competitive performance against state-of-the-art evaluation methods showcases the versatility and robustness of the LLM-EVAL approach.

4.6 Overall Scores without Human Reference

Table 3 presents the performance of LLM-EVAL on datasets without human references, comparing it with other high-performing evaluation methods such as DynaEval, USL-H, and FlowScore.

For the evaluation of DailyDialog-PredictiveEngagement and DSTC9 datasets, we utilize the *"Overall"* score. In the FED dataset, we predict *"Correctness, Engagement, Fluency, Interestingness, Overall, Relevance, Semantically Appropriateness, Specificity, and*

Spearman ρ (%)	Topical-DSTC10 APP	CON	GRA	REL	Persona-DSTC10 APP	CON	GRA	REL	Average
Deep-AM-FM	18.2	9.4	17.9	26.2	21.0	14.7	19.1	24.1	18.9
DSTC10 Team 1	29.7	7.0	11.6	37.0	38.6	19.3	18.6	44.5	25.8
MME-CRS	32.6	17.2	9.0	**44.8**	45.6	32.5	22.0	**54.8**	32.3
without human reference									
LLM-EVAL *0-5*									
`Anthropic Claude`	**38.6**	20.6	33.2	42.8	**48.2**	36.9	**34.5**	52.1	**38.4**
`Anthropic Claude` $top\_p = 0.9$	31.9	16.9	30.2	38.5	39.4	30.2	28.9	46.3	32.8
`OpenAI ChatGPT`	35.7	18.4	33.1	37.3	43.5	33.4	30.1	48.8	35.0
`OpenAI GPT-3.5`	29.3	16.9	20.9	37.1	36.5	30.2	21.7	45.2	29.7
LLM-EVAL *0-100*									
`Anthropic Claude`	**38.6**	21.3	32.7	41.1	47.6	**37.8**	30.2	51.9	37.7
`Anthropic Claude` $top\_p = 0.9$	30.1	15.6	27.3	37.7	36.2	27.9	25.9	45.4	30.8
`OpenAI ChatGPT`	36.2	16.7	**33.4**	36.0	44.0	31.7	31.4	48.1	34.7
`OpenAI GPT-3.5`	28.2	13.9	23.5	34.0	34.8	24.7	21.7	42.9	28.0
with human reference									
LLM-EVAL *0-5*									
`Anthropic Claude`	38.0	21.5	31.2	42.2	47.9	36.0	30.6	49.1	37.1
`Anthropic Claude-instant`	26.5	14.3	30.1	27.0	33.4	30.5	25.8	35.2	27.9
`OpenAI ChatGPT`	34.0	18.9	30.3	35.1	39.4	30.0	25.6	40.9	31.8
`OpenAI GPT-3.5`	30.0	17.3	21.2	38.8	37.9	28.8	20.8	45.1	30.0
LLM-EVAL *0-100*									
`Anthropic Claude`	38.2	**21.6**	30.0	40.2	45.4	34.8	28.6	49.3	36.0
`Anthropic Claude-instant`	28.0	14.3	32.1	34.0	37.5	31.1	32.0	40.8	31.2
`OpenAI ChatGPT`	34.6	20.6	31.1	35.4	39.7	31.3	23.8	44.1	32.6
`OpenAI GPT-3.5`	12.4	20.8	30.5	37.8	26.6	20.7	24.0	40.0	26.6

Table 4: Spearman correlation coefficients between human ratings and LLM-EVAL with different configurations across multiple dimensions (*APP* for Appropriateness, *CON* for Content, *GRA* for Grammar, and *REL* for Relevance) for Topical-DSTC10 and Persona-DSTC10. The best score for each column is highlighted in bold. The second best is underlined.

Understandability" dimensions for turn-based evaluation, and *"Coherence, Consistency, Topic Depth, Diversity, Error Recovery, Flexibility, Informativeness, Inquisitiveness, Likability, Overall, and Understandability"* dimensions for dialogue-based evaluation. Nonetheless, only the "Overall" score is used for meta-evaluation in each scenario.

Both LLM-EVAL configurations, 0-5 and 0-100, consistently display strong performance across the datasets, highlighting their resilience and flexibility. The method's capacity to accommodate different scoring ranges while maintaining competitiveness against state-of-the-art evaluation techniques demonstrates LLM-EVAL's adaptability and robustness. This establishes its value as an efficient and versatile evaluation solution in reference-free settings.

5 Analysis

5.1 Different LLMs

In this section, we analyze the performance of LLM-EVAL when using different large language models for evaluation. Table 4 presents the Spearman correlation coefficients between human ratings and LLM-EVAL with various model configurations and scoring ranges for the Topical-DSTC10 and Persona-DSTC10 datasets. We compare the performance of LLM-EVAL when using different LLMs, such as `Anthropic Claude`, `OpenAI ChatGPT`, `Anthropic Claude-instant`, and `OpenAI GPT-3.5` [1].

Among these models, `Claude` and `ChatGPT` are optimized for chat applications, while `GPT-3.5` is not. We observe that both `Claude` and `ChatGPT` generally achieve better performance across all dimensions when compared to `GPT-3.5`. This suggests that using dialogue-optimized LLMs in the LLM-EVAL method leads to more accurate evaluation results in the context of open-domain conversations.

Moreover, when comparing the `Claude` and `ChatGPT` models, both models demonstrate competitive performance across different evaluation dimensions, with `Claude` slightly outperforming `ChatGPT` in certain configurations.

[1] Anthropic Claude (claude-v1.3), OpenAI ChatGPT (gpt-3.5-turbo-0301), Anthropic Claude-instant (claude-instantv1.0), and OpenAI GPT-3.5 (text-davinci-003).

We also analyze the performance of `Claude-instant`, a smaller version of `Claude`. Although it is not as competitive as its larger counterpart, it still achieves reasonable performance in some cases. This implies that smaller models, while not optimal, can still be employed for LLM-EVAL to a certain extent, possibly providing a more resource-efficient option in specific scenarios.

In conclusion, our analysis demonstrates that dialogue-optimized LLMs, such as `Claude` and `ChatGPT`, yield better performance in the LLM-EVAL method for open-domain conversation evaluation. Although smaller models like `Anthropic Claude-instant` may not achieve the best performance, they can still be considered for resource-limited scenarios. Overall, the choice of LLMs in LLM-EVAL plays a crucial role in obtaining accurate evaluation results.

5.2 Decoding Methods

In our experiments, we employ greedy decoding for generating responses using the Anthropic API with the `claude-v1.3` model. Greedy decoding selects the token with the highest probability at each time step during the generation process. However, other decoding methods, such as nucleus sampling could be employed in the LLM-EVAL method to explore their impact on the evaluation results.

Nucleus sampling, also known as top-p sampling, samples tokens from the top-p most probable tokens at each time step, where p is a predefined probability threshold. This method introduces some randomness into the generation process and could lead to more diverse and creative responses.

Comparing the performance of `Claude` and `Claude` $top\_p = 0.9$ in Table 4, we observe that greedy decoding generally achieves better performance across all evaluation dimensions. This finding suggests that using greedy decoding with the LLM-EVAL method provides more accurate and consistent evaluation results compared to nucleus sampling.

One possible reason for this difference in performance is that greedy decoding tends to generate more coherent and focused responses due to its deterministic nature. In contrast, nucleus sampling introduces randomness into the generation process, which may result in less focused or less relevant responses, affecting the evaluation scores. Consequently, greedy decoding appears to be a more suitable choice for the LLM-EVAL method.

6 Conclusion

In this paper, we introduced LLM-EVAL, a unified multi-dimensional automatic evaluation method for open-domain conversations with large language models. The proposed method employs a single prompt along with a unified evaluation schema that covers multiple dimensions of evaluation, such as content, grammar, relevance, and appropriateness. This approach streamlines the evaluation process and eliminates the need for multiple prompts. Experiments on various datasets demonstrated the effectiveness and efficiency of LLM-EVAL, consistently outperforming most baselines and state-of-the-art evaluation methods.

As future work, we plan to explore reinforcement learning from LLMs feedback and investigate LLM-in-the-loop evaluation strategies as an alternative to human-in-the-loop methods. This will further enhance the applicability and performance of the LLM-EVAL method in various dialogue system evaluation scenarios.

Limitations

Although LLM-EVAL has shown promising results in assessing open-domain conversations, it is crucial to acknowledge its limitations.

Firstly, the performance of our method relies heavily on the large language models underlying it, which may exhibit biases or generate unexpected outputs. If the language model misinterprets the evaluation schema or prompt instructions, it could lead to inaccurate evaluation scores.

Secondly, the choice of LLM significantly influences the evaluation results, as demonstrated in our analysis. While dialogue-optimized LLMs produce better performance, this selection may limit LLM-EVAL's applicability for particular tasks or dialogue systems.

Thirdly, our approach employs single-number scoring for each evaluation dimension, which may fail to capture the subtleties of human judgments, particularly for subjective aspects like engagement, creativity, or humor.

Lastly, the effectiveness of LLM-EVAL hinges on the quality and clarity of the prompts and evaluation schemas. Creating such prompts and schemas may require domain expertise and knowledge of LLM behavior, posing challenges for non-experts.

To overcome these limitations, future research can focus on exploring alternative prompt designs, refining evaluation schemas, and expanding the method to cover a wider range of evaluation dimensions and dialogue system types.

Ethics Statement

We acknowledge that there are potential ethical concerns associated with the use of large language models in our evaluation method.

A primary concern is the biases present in large language models. These biases are introduced during training, as the models learn from textual data that may contain biased information, stereotypes, or misinformation. When using these biased models for evaluation, it is possible that the evaluation scores produced by LLM-EVAL may reflect and perpetuate these biases, potentially leading to biased evaluations of dialogue system outputs. This could, in turn, affect the development of future dialogue systems by encouraging biased behavior.

To mitigate this concern, researchers and developers should be cautious when interpreting the evaluation results obtained through LLM-EVAL and consider potential biases in the large language models used. Moreover, future work could explore techniques to debias language models or employ alternative evaluation schemas that actively account for biases in the evaluation process.

Acknowledgements

We thank the reviewers for their insightful comments. This work was financially supported by the Young Scholar Fellowship Program by the National Science and Technology Council (NSTC) in Taiwan, under Grants 111-2222-E-002-013-MY3 and 111-2628-E-002-016.

References

Yuntao Bai, Andy Jones, Kamal Ndousse, Amanda Askell, Anna Chen, Nova DasSarma, Dawn Drain, Stanislav Fort, Deep Ganguli, Tom Henighan, Nicholas Joseph, Saurav Kadavath, Jackson Kernion, Tom Conerly, Sheer El Showk, Nelson Elhage, Zac Hatfield-Dodds, Danny Hernandez, Tristan Hume, Scott Johnston, Shauna Kravec, Liane Lovitt, Neel Nanda, Catherine Olsson, Dario Amodei, Tom B. Brown, Jack Clark, Sam McCandlish, Chris Olah, Benjamin Mann, and Jared Kaplan. 2022. Training a helpful and harmless assistant with reinforcement learning from human feedback. *CoRR*, abs/2204.05862.

Tom B. Brown, Benjamin Mann, Nick Ryder, Melanie Subbiah, Jared Kaplan, Prafulla Dhariwal, Arvind Neelakantan, Pranav Shyam, Girish Sastry, Amanda Askell, Sandhini Agarwal, Ariel Herbert-Voss, Gretchen Krueger, Tom Henighan, Rewon Child, Aditya Ramesh, Daniel M. Ziegler, Jeffrey Wu, Clemens Winter, Christopher Hesse, Mark Chen, Eric Sigler, Mateusz Litwin, Scott Gray, Benjamin Chess, Jack Clark, Christopher Berner, Sam McCandlish, Alec Radford, Ilya Sutskever, and Dario Amodei. 2020. Language models are few-shot learners. In *Advances in Neural Information Processing Systems 33: Annual Conference on Neural Information Processing Systems 2020, NeurIPS 2020, December 6-12, 2020, virtual.*

Yi Chen, Rui Wang, Haiyun Jiang, Shuming Shi, and Ruifeng Xu. 2023. Exploring the use of large language models for reference-free text quality evaluation: A preliminary empirical study. *CoRR*, abs/2304.00723.

Jan Deriu, Álvaro Rodrigo, Arantxa Otegi, Guillermo Echegoyen, Sophie Rosset, Eneko Agirre, and Mark Cieliebak. 2021. Survey on evaluation methods for dialogue systems. *Artif. Intell. Rev.*, 54(1):755–810.

Jinlan Fu, See-Kiong Ng, Zhengbao Jiang, and Pengfei Liu. 2023. Gptscore: Evaluate as you desire. *CoRR*, abs/2302.04166.

Sarik Ghazarian, Johnny Wei, Aram Galstyan, and Nanyun Peng. 2019. Better automatic evaluation of open-domain dialogue systems with contextualized embeddings. In *Proceedings of the Workshop on Methods for Optimizing and Evaluating Neural Language Generation*, pages 82–89, Minneapolis, Minnesota. Association for Computational Linguistics.

Sarik Ghazarian, Ralph M. Weischedel, Aram Galstyan, and Nanyun Peng. 2020. Predictive engagement: An efficient metric for automatic evaluation of open-domain dialogue systems. In *The Thirty-Fourth AAAI Conference on Artificial Intelligence, AAAI 2020, The Thirty-Second Innovative Applications of Artificial Intelligence Conference, IAAI 2020, The Tenth AAAI Symposium on Educational Advances in Artificial Intelligence, EAAI 2020, New York, NY, USA, February 7-12, 2020*, pages 7789–7796. AAAI Press.

Karthik Gopalakrishnan, Behnam Hedayatnia, Qinglang Chen, Anna Gottardi, Sanjeev Kwatra, Anu Venkatesh, Raefer Gabriel, and Dilek Hakkani-Tür. 2019. Topical-chat: Towards knowledge-grounded open-domain conversations. In *Interspeech 2019, 20th Annual Conference of the International Speech Communication Association, Graz, Austria, 15-19 September 2019*, pages 1891–1895. ISCA.

Chiori Hori and Takaaki Hori. 2017. End-to-end conversation modeling track in DSTC6. *CoRR*, abs/1706.07440.

Lishan Huang, Zheng Ye, Jinghui Qin, Liang Lin, and Xiaodan Liang. 2020. GRADE: Automatic graph-enhanced coherence metric for evaluating open-domain dialogue systems. In *Proceedings of the 2020 Conference on Empirical Methods in Natural Language Processing (EMNLP)*, pages 9230–9240, Online. Association for Computational Linguistics.

Naomi Kong-Vega, Mingxin Shen, Mo Wang, and Luis Fernando D'Haro. 2018. Subjective annotation and evaluation of three different chatbots WOCHAT: shared task report. In *9th International Workshop on Spoken Dialogue System Technology, IWSDS 2018, Singapore, April 18-20, 2018*, volume 579 of *Lecture Notes in Electrical Engineering*, pages 371–378. Springer.

Seolhwa Lee, Heuiseok Lim, and João Sedoc. 2020. An evaluation protocol for generative conversational systems. *CoRR*, abs/2010.12741.

Zekang Li, Jinchao Zhang, Zhengcong Fei, Yang Feng, and Jie Zhou. 2021. Conversations are not flat: Modeling the dynamic information flow across dialogue utterances. In *Proceedings of the 59th Annual Meeting of the Association for Computational Linguistics and the 11th International Joint Conference on Natural Language Processing (Volume 1: Long Papers)*, pages 128–138, Online. Association for Computational Linguistics.

Chin-Yew Lin. 2004. ROUGE: A package for automatic evaluation of summaries. In *Text Summarization Branches Out*, pages 74–81, Barcelona, Spain. Association for Computational Linguistics.

Chia-Wei Liu, Ryan Lowe, Iulian Serban, Mike Noseworthy, Laurent Charlin, and Joelle Pineau. 2016. How NOT to evaluate your dialogue system: An empirical study of unsupervised evaluation metrics for dialogue response generation. In *Proceedings of the 2016 Conference on Empirical Methods in Natural Language Processing*, pages 2122–2132, Austin, Texas. Association for Computational Linguistics.

Yang Liu, Dan Iter, Yichong Xu, Shuohang Wang, Ruochen Xu, and Chenguang Zhu. 2023. G-eval: NLG evaluation using GPT-4 with better human alignment. *CoRR*, abs/2303.16634.

Shikib Mehri and Maxine Eskenazi. 2020a. Unsupervised evaluation of interactive dialog with DialoGPT. In *Proceedings of the 21th Annual Meeting of the Special Interest Group on Discourse and Dialogue*, pages 225–235, 1st virtual meeting. Association for Computational Linguistics.

Shikib Mehri and Maxine Eskenazi. 2020b. USR: An unsupervised and reference free evaluation metric for dialog generation. In *Proceedings of the 58th Annual Meeting of the Association for Computational Linguistics*, pages 681–707, Online. Association for Computational Linguistics.

Shikib Mehri, Yulan Feng, Carla Gordon, Seyed Hossein Alavi, David Traum, and Maxine Eskenazi. 2022. Interactive evaluation of dialog track at DSTC9. In *Proceedings of the Thirteenth Language Resources and Evaluation Conference*, pages 5731–5738, Marseille, France. European Language Resources Association.

OpenAI. 2023. GPT-4 technical report. *CoRR*, abs/2303.08774.

Kishore Papineni, Salim Roukos, Todd Ward, and Wei-Jing Zhu. 2002. Bleu: a method for automatic evaluation of machine translation. In *Proceedings of the 40th Annual Meeting of the Association for Computational Linguistics*, pages 311–318, Philadelphia, Pennsylvania, USA. Association for Computational Linguistics.

Vitou Phy, Yang Zhao, and Akiko Aizawa. 2020. Deconstruct to reconstruct a configurable evaluation metric for open-domain dialogue systems. In *Proceedings of the 28th International Conference on Computational Linguistics*, pages 4164–4178, Barcelona, Spain (Online). International Committee on Computational Linguistics.

Hannah Rashkin, Eric Michael Smith, Margaret Li, and Y-Lan Boureau. 2019. Towards empathetic open-domain conversation models: A new benchmark and dataset. In *Proceedings of the 57th Annual Meeting of the Association for Computational Linguistics*, pages 5370–5381, Florence, Italy. Association for Computational Linguistics.

Ananya B. Sai, Akash Kumar Mohankumar, Siddhartha Arora, and Mitesh M. Khapra. 2020. Improving dialog evaluation with a multi-reference adversarial dataset and large scale pretraining. *Transactions of the Association for Computational Linguistics*, 8:810–827.

João Sedoc, Daphne Ippolito, Arun Kirubarajan, Jai Thirani, Lyle Ungar, and Chris Callison-Burch. 2019. ChatEval: A tool for chatbot evaluation. In *Proceedings of the 2019 Conference of the North American Chapter of the Association for Computational Linguistics (Demonstrations)*, pages 60–65, Minneapolis, Minnesota. Association for Computational Linguistics.

Eric Smith, Orion Hsu, Rebecca Qian, Stephen Roller, Y-Lan Boureau, and Jason Weston. 2022. Human evaluation of conversations is an open problem: comparing the sensitivity of various methods for evaluating dialogue agents. In *Proceedings of the 4th Workshop on NLP for Conversational AI*, pages 77–97, Dublin, Ireland. Association for Computational Linguistics.

Chongyang Tao, Lili Mou, Dongyan Zhao, and Rui Yan. 2018. RUBER: an unsupervised method for automatic evaluation of open-domain dialog systems. In *Proceedings of the Thirty-Second AAAI Conference* on Artificial Intelligence, (AAAI-18), the 30th innovative Applications of Artificial Intelligence (IAAI-18), and the 8th AAAI Symposium on Educational Advances in Artificial Intelligence (EAAI-18), New Orleans, Louisiana, USA, February 2-7, 2018, pages 722–729. AAAI Press.

Oriol Vinyals and Quoc V. Le. 2015. A neural conversational model. *CoRR*, abs/1506.05869.

Jason Wei, Xuezhi Wang, Dale Schuurmans, Maarten Bosma, Brian Ichter, Fei Xia, Ed H. Chi, Quoc V. Le, and Denny Zhou. 2022. Chain-of-thought prompting elicits reasoning in large language models. In *NeurIPS*.

Yi-Ting Yeh, Maxine Eskenazi, and Shikib Mehri. 2021. A comprehensive assessment of dialog evaluation metrics. In *The First Workshop on Evaluations and Assessments of Neural Conversation Systems*, pages 15–33, Online. Association for Computational Linguistics.

Chen Zhang, Yiming Chen, Luis Fernando D'Haro, Yan Zhang, Thomas Friedrichs, Grandee Lee, and Haizhou Li. 2021a. DynaEval: Unifying turn and dialogue level evaluation. In *Proceedings of the 59th Annual Meeting of the Association for Computational Linguistics and the 11th International Joint Conference on Natural Language Processing (Volume 1: Long Papers)*, pages 5676–5689, Online. Association for Computational Linguistics.

Chen Zhang, Luis Fernando D'Haro, Rafael E. Banchs, Thomas Friedrichs, and Haizhou Li. 2020a. Deep AM-FM: toolkit for automatic dialogue evaluation. In *Conversational Dialogue Systems for the Next Decade - 11th International Workshop on Spoken Dialogue Systems, IWSDS 2020, Madrid, Spain, 21-23 September, 2020*, volume 704 of *Lecture Notes in Electrical Engineering*, pages 53–69. Springer.

Chen Zhang, João Sedoc, Luis Fernando D'Haro, Rafael E. Banchs, and Alexander Rudnicky. 2021b. Automatic evaluation and moderation of open-domain dialogue systems. *CoRR*, abs/2111.02110.

Pengfei Zhang, Xiaohui Hu, Kaidong Yu, Jian Wang, Song Han, Cao Liu, and Chunyang Yuan. 2022. MME-CRS: multi-metric evaluation based on correlation re-scaling for evaluating open-domain dialogue. *CoRR*, abs/2206.09403.

Saizheng Zhang, Emily Dinan, Jack Urbanek, Arthur Szlam, Douwe Kiela, and Jason Weston. 2018. Personalizing dialogue agents: I have a dog, do you have pets too? In *Proceedings of the 56th Annual Meeting of the Association for Computational Linguistics (Volume 1: Long Papers)*, pages 2204–2213, Melbourne, Australia. Association for Computational Linguistics.

Tianyi Zhang, Varsha Kishore, Felix Wu, Kilian Q. Weinberger, and Yoav Artzi. 2020b. Bertscore: Evaluating text generation with BERT. In *8th International Conference on Learning Representations, ICLR 2020, Addis Ababa, Ethiopia, April 26-30, 2020*. OpenReview.net.

A Prompt Templates

Below are the prompt templates used in our experiments with LLM-EVAL. They provide examples of the natural language instructions used to define the evaluation task and desired criteria, as well as the format instructions that specify the structure and range of scores for each dimension.

A.1 Evaluation Schema

The evaluation schema used in LLM-EVAL is a natural language instruction that defines the task and the desired evaluation criteria. It covers multiple dimensions of evaluation, such as content, grammar, relevance, and appropriateness. An example of the format instruction specifying the structure and range of scores for each dimension is as follows:

```
Human: The output should be formatted as a
JSON instance that conforms to the JSON
schema below.

As an example, for the schema {"properties":
{"foo": {"title": "Foo", "description": "a
list of strings", "type": "array", "items":
{"type": "string"}}}, "required": ["foo"]}}
the object {"foo": ["bar", "baz"]} is a
well-formatted instance of the schema.
The object {"properties": {"foo": ["bar",
"baz"]}} is not well-formatted.

Here is the output schema:
{"properties": {"content": {"title":
"Content", "description": "content score
in the range of 0 to 100", "type":
"integer"}, "grammar": {"title": "Grammar",
"description": "grammar score in the range
of 0 to 100", "type": "integer"}, "relevance":
{"title": "Relevance", "description":
"relevance score in the range of 0 to 100",
"type": "integer"}, "appropriateness":
{"title": "Appropriateness", "description":
"appropriateness score in the range of 0 to
100", "type": "integer"}}, "required":
["content", "grammar", "relevance",
"appropriateness"]}
```

A.2 Reference-based Turn-level Evaluation

For reference-based turn-level evaluation, the single prompt is designed to include the necessary dialogue context, the reference, and the target response that needs to be evaluated, along with the evaluation schema. An example prompt template for evaluating a dialogue response with a human reference is:

```
{evaluation_schema}

Score the following dialogue response
generated on a continuous scale from
{score_min} to {score_max}.

Context: {context}
Reference: {reference}
Dialogue response: {response}
```

A.3 Reference-free Turn-level Evaluation

For reference-free turn-level evaluation, the single prompt includes the dialogue context and the target response that needs to be evaluated, without requiring a human reference. The evaluation schema is also included in the prompt. An example prompt template for evaluating a dialogue response without a human reference is:

```
{evaluation_schema}

Score the following dialogue response
generated on a continuous scale from
{score_min} to {score_max}.

Context: {context}
Dialogue response: {response}
```

A.4 Dialogue-level Evaluation

For dialogue-level evaluation, the single prompt is designed to cover the entire dialogue instead of individual turns. The evaluation schema is also included in the prompt. An example prompt template for evaluating a dialogue is:

```
{evaluation_schema}

Score the following dialogue generated
on a continuous scale from {score_min}
to {score_max}.

Dialogue: {dialog}
```

cTBLS: Augmenting Large Language Models with Conversational Tables

Anirudh S Sundar, Larry Heck
AI Virtual Assistant (AVA) Lab
The Georgia Institute of Technology
{asundar34,larryheck}@gatech.edu

Abstract

Optimizing accuracy and performance while eliminating hallucinations of open-domain conversational large language models (LLMs) is an open research challenge. A particularly promising direction is to augment and ground LLMs with information from structured sources. This paper introduces Conversational Tables (cTBLS), a three-step architecture to retrieve and generate dialogue responses grounded on retrieved tabular information. cTBLS uses Transformer encoder embeddings for Dense Table Retrieval and obtains up to 125% relative improvement over the retriever in the previous state-of-the-art system on the HYRBIDIALOGUE dataset. cTBLS then uses a shared process between encoder and decoder models to perform a coarse+fine tabular knowledge (e.g., cell) ranking combined with a GPT-3.5 LLM response generator to yield a 2x relative improvement in ROUGE scores. Finally, human evaluators prefer cTBLs +80% of the time (coherency, fluency) and judge informativeness to be 4x better than the previous state-of-the-art.

1 Introduction

Equipping conversational AI with multimodal capabilities broadens the range of dialogues that humans have with such systems. A persisting challenge in multimodal conversational AI is the development of systems that produce conversationally coherent responses grounded in textual and non-textual modalities (Sundar and Heck, 2022).

It is well-established that large language models (LLMs) possess real-world knowledge stored within their parameters, as demonstrated by recent research (Roberts et al., 2020; Heinzerling and Inui, 2021). Nevertheless, the incorporation of conversation-specific extrinsic knowledge into these models to yield precise responses remains an active area of investigation. While humans can easily retrieve contextual information from tables by examining rows and columns, LLMs often struggle to identify relevant information amidst conversational distractions.

HYBRIDIALOGUE (Nakamura et al., 2022), a dataset of conversations grounded on structured and unstructured knowledge from tables and text, introduces the task of responding to messages by utilizing information from external knowledge and prior dialogue turns. The authors also present an approach and experimental results on HYBRIDIALOGUE that represents the current state-of-the-art (SoTA).

This paper proposes an extension to the SoTA approach of HYBRIDIALOGUE in the form of Conversational Tables (cTBLS) [1], a novel three-step encoder-decoder architecture designed to augment LLMs with tabular data in conversational settings. In the first step, cTBLS uses a dual-encoder Transformer-based (Vaswani et al., 2017) Dense Table Retriever (DTR) to retrieve the correct table from the entire corpus based on the user's query. The second step employs a fine-tuned dual-encoder Transformer to track system state and rank cells in the retrieved table according to their relevance to the conversation. Finally, cTBLS utilizes GPT-3.5 to generate a natural language response by prompting it with the ranked cells.

While previous research separated knowledge retrieval and response generation between encoder and decoder models, this paper demonstrates that LLM decoders can perform these tasks jointly when prompted with knowledge sources ranked by language model encoders. Furthermore, by pre-training the Dense Table Retriever to perform retrieval over a corpus of tables, cTBLS can be extended to new knowledge sources without retraining, by appending additional knowledge to the corpus.

Compared to the previous SoTA, experiments

[1] Our code will be available at https://github.com/avalab-gt/cTBLS

Proceedings of the 5th Workshop on NLP for Conversational AI (NLP4ConvAI 2023), pages 59–70
July 14, 2023

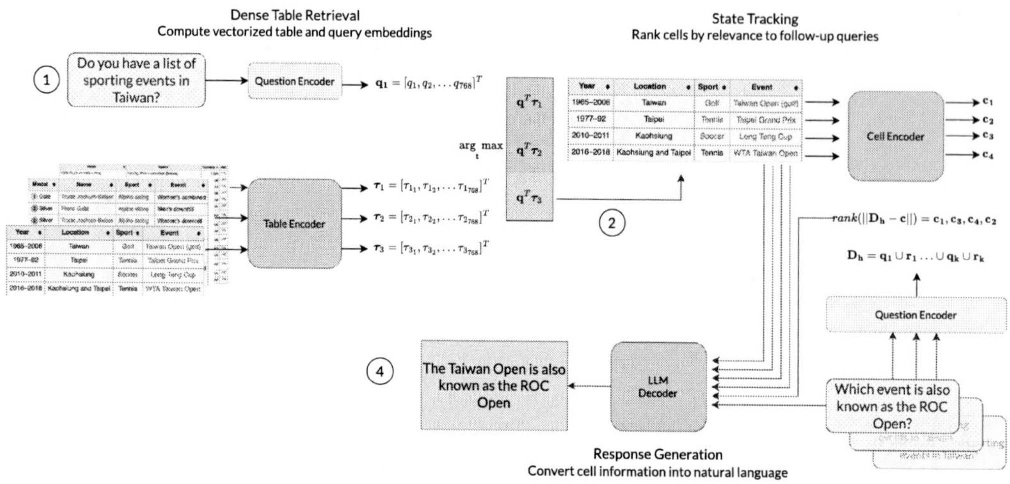

Figure 1: cTBLS for conversations on HYBRIDIALOGUE. Dense Table Retrieval identifies the table most relevant to the initial query. The retrieved table is provided to the state tracker for follow-up queries. State Tracking ranks cells in the table based on their ability to answer a follow-up query. Response Generation utilizes a LLM Decoder provided with the ranked cell information and the follow-up query to convert tabular data into a natural language response and continue the conversation. Details on individual components are provided in Section 3.

on cTBLS show up to 125% relative improvement in table retrieval and a 2x relative improvement in ROUGE scores. In addition, human evaluators prefer cTBLs +80% of the time (coherency, fluency) and judge informativeness to be 4x better than the previous SoTA.

Our contributions are as follows:

1. The introduction of Conversational Tables (cTBLS), a novel three-step encoder-decoder architecture designed to augment LLMs with tabular data in conversational settings.

2. Experimental results demonstrating that Dense Table Retrieval, which utilizes neural models fine-tuned with a summary of tabular information, outperforms sparse techniques based on keyword matching for table retrieval.

3. The presentation of evidence that augmenting state-of-the-art LLM decoders using knowledge sources ranked by encoder language models leads to better results on automatic (ROUGE-Precision) and human (Coherence, Fluency, and Informativeness) evaluation for knowledge-grounded response generation while limiting the number of API calls to these models.

This paper presents the cTBLS system and demonstrates its application to the HYBRIDIALOGUE dataset. In Section 2, we review the existing literature in the fields of Table Question Answering and Knowledge Grounded Response Generation. Section 3 describes the various components of cTBLS as presented in Figure 1. In Section 4, we evaluate the performance of cTBLS against previous methods for conversations over tables and report experimental results from automatic and human evaluations. Finally, Section 5 concludes the paper and outlines potential directions for future research.

2 Related Work

2.1 Table Question Answering

Table Question Answering is a well-researched precursor to conversations over tables. In WIKITABLEQUESTIONS, Pasupat and Liang (2015) transform HTML tables into a knowledge graph and retrieve the correct answer by converting natural language questions into graph queries. FRETS (Jauhar et al., 2016) uses a log-linear model conditioned on alignment scores between cells in tables and individual QA pairs in the training set. Cho et al. (2018) introduce NEOP, a multi-layer sequential network with attention supervision to answer queries conditioned on tables. Hannan et al. (2020) propose MANYMODALQA, which uses a modality selection network and pre-trained text-based QA, Table-based QA, and Image-based QA models to jointly answer questions over text, tables, and images. Chen et al. (2020c) present HYBRIDER, which performs multi-hop QA over tables using keyword-matching for cell linking followed by BERT (Devlin et al., 2019) for reasoning. Chen et al. (2020a) propose OTT-QA, which uses a fusion retriever to identify relevant tables and text and a cross-block reader based on a long-range Sparse Attention Transformer (Ainslie et al., 2020) to choose the correct answer. Heck and Heck (2020) perform multi-task fine-tuning of Transformer encoders by modeling slot filling as question answering over tabular and visual information in Visual Slot. Herzig et al. (2020) and Yin et al. (2020) extend BERT for Table Question Answering by pre-training a masked language model over text-table pairs in TAPAS and TaBERT, respectively. Recent work building off the Transformer architecture for Table Question Answering includes (Eisenschlos et al., 2021; Li et al., 2021; Herzig et al., 2021; Zayats et al., 2021; Zhao et al., 2022; Huang et al., 2022; Yang et al., 2022; Chen, 2022). Jin et al. (2022) provide a comprehensive survey of advancements in Table Question Answering.

2.2 Knowledge Grounded Response Generation

Early work related to grounding responses generated by language models in real-world knowledge was motivated by the need to improve prior information for open-domain dialogue (Heck et al., 2013; Hakkani-Tür et al., 2014; Hakkani-Tür et al., 2014; Huang et al., 2015; Jia et al., 2017). More recently, knowledge grounded response generation has been applied to mitigate the hallucination problem (Maynez et al., 2020; Shuster et al., 2021) in LLMs. RAG (Lewis et al., 2020) fine-tunes LLMs using Dense Passage Retrieval (Karpukhin et al., 2020) over a Wikipedia dump to ground responses for Open Domain Question Answering. KGPT (Chen et al., 2020b) and SKILL (Moiseev et al., 2022) pre-train a Transformer encoder (Vaswani et al., 2017) with English Wikidump for Natural Language Generation. Fusion-in-Decoder (Izacard and Grave, 2021) fine-tunes decoder models using evidence acquired through Dense Passage Retrieval.

Recent research also includes a dual-stage approach where LLMs generate knowledge sources based on prompts (Yu et al., 2022; Bonifacio et al., 2022; Jeronymo et al., 2023). Closest to our work, Wizard of Wikipedia (Dinan et al., 2018) jointly optimizes an encoder-decoder Transformer to produce dialogue responses conditioned on retrieved knowledge and dialogue context but does not extend their approach to the multiple modalities. REPLUG (Shi et al., 2023) ensembles output responses generated by prompting large language models with inputs from a dense retriever in a zero-shot setting. However, this requires multiple API calls to state-of-the-art LLMs. LLM-AUGMENTER (Peng et al., 2023) incorporates external knowledge in LLM responses by matching keywords in dialogue state to candidate knowledge sources obtained through web-search. A survey of knowledge fusion in LLMs is available in Colon-Hernandez et al. (2021) and Richardson and Heck (2023).

In contrast to prior research that focuses on either Table Question Answering or Knowledge Grounded Response Generation, our work, cTBLS, addresses the challenge of generating responses grounded on tabular knowledge. Moreover, while cTBLS is fine-tuned to retrieve tables and filter out incorrect references, it leverages the power of SoTA pre-trained LLMs for response generation. Furthermore, by fine-tuning open-source table and knowledge retrievers to remove inaccurate references, cTBLS reduces the number of API calls to the SoTA LLMs.

3 Method

The challenge of developing conversational systems grounded in tabular information consists of three tasks, namely table retrieval, system state tracking, and response generation. Table retrieval requires identifying the most relevant table in the dataset based on a given natural language query. System state tracking is responsible for ranking the cells in the table, enabling the system to provide responses to follow-up queries about the table. Finally, response generation involves converting the ranked cells into a natural language response.

3.1 Table Retrieval

Table retrieval is a prerequisite to answering queries when the exact table to converse over is unspecified. The objective is to identify the correct table from a vast corpus. cTBLS proposes formulating table retrieval as document retrieval by assigning a relevance score to each table based on its relevance to the natural language query. Inspired by Karpukhin et al. (2020) and Huang et al. (2013), cTBLS uses a dual-encoder-based Dense Table Retrieval (DTR) model. The DTR model pre-computes a vectorized embedding of all tables in the corpus. Given a

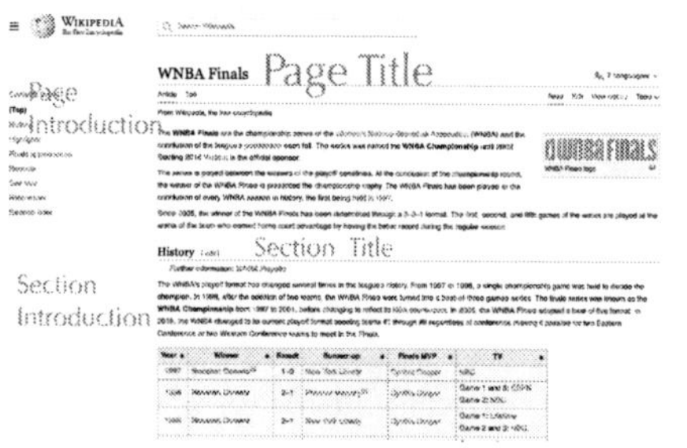

Figure 2: An example of table-associated text in the context of Wikipedia, where the input to the DTR text-encoder includes the page title, the introduction to the article, the section title, and the introduction paragraph.

query at inference, the retrieved table is closest to the query in the embedded space, indicated by the upper-left portion of Figure 1.

The DTR model consists of a table encoder and a question encoder, initialized from RoBERTa-base (Liu et al., 2019). The input to the table encoder comprises the table's title and, if available, textual information associated with the table. Figure 2 presents an example of table-associated text in the context of Wikipedia, where introductions from the page and section provide additional grounding. The input to the question encoder is the current query to be answered. Taking the average over the sequence of the last hidden state at the table and question encoder results in 768-dimensional embeddings of the table information and the query.

The DTR model is optimized through a contrastive prediction task, which aims to maximize the similarity between embeddings of a given query q and the table to be retrieved τ while minimizing the similarity to other incorrect tables τ_{n_i} for $i = 1, \ldots, N$. As per (Karpukhin et al., 2020), normalized embedding vectors are utilized to optimize the objective in Equation 1:

$$\arg\min_{\tau} \left(-\log \frac{e^{q \cdot \tau}}{e^{q \cdot \tau} + \sum_{i=1}^{N} e^{q \cdot \tau_{n_i}}} \right) \quad (1)$$

Given a batch B of d-dimensional query embeddings $\mathbf{Q}$ and table embeddings $\mathbf{T}$, the DTR model computes the similarity $\mathbf{QT}^T (\in \mathbb{R}^{B \times B})$ between every query and table in the batch. This similarity computation enables the sampling of negatives from other query-table pairs, resulting in B^2 training samples in each batch, consisting of B positive pairs along the diagonal and $B^2 - B$ negatives.

3.2 Coarse System State Tracking

Given a table, system state tracking involves ranking cells in the table by their relevance to conversational queries. In contrast to quesiton-answering, conversational queries require leveraging information from external modalities in conjunction with prior dialogue turns to generate coherent responses (Sundar and Heck, 2022). cTBLS addresses system state tracking through two sub-tasks - coarse and fine system state tracking. Coarse system state tracking ranks cells in the table, while fine system state tracking identifies fine-grained information in the most relevant cell to answer the query.

cTBLS uses a RoBERTa-base dual-encoder architecture for coarse system state tracking. The cell encoder embeds all cells and associated hyperlinked information, and the question encoder generates embeddings for the dialogue history ($\mathbf{D_h}$) that includes the current turn's query as well as previous queries and responses.

To rank cells based on their relevance to the follow-up query, as illustrated in the upper-right section of Figure 1, the question and cell encoders are optimized using a triplet loss configuration. This optimization aims to minimize the distance between the anchor $\mathbf{D_h}$ and the positive cell c, while pushing the negative cell $\overline{c}$ further away from $\mathbf{D_h}$ by a margin m (Equation 2).

$$\arg\min_{c_i} \left(\max\{d(\mathbf{D_h}, c) - d(\mathbf{D_h}, \overline{c}) + m, 0\}\right) \quad (2)$$

$$d(x, y) = ||x - y||_2 \quad (3)$$

For our approach, we utilize an anchor-positive-negative triplet consisting of the complete dialogue history (including queries and responses from previous turns) concatenated with the current query as the anchor, the correct cell as the positive, and other cells from the same table that are not relevant to the query as negatives. We measure the distance between the anchor and the positive and between the anchor and the negatives using the 2-norm distance function $d(\cdot)$.

3.3 Fine System State Tracking and Response Generation

In contrast to coarse system state tracking, fine system state tracking involves identifying the exact phrase that answers the query from a ranked subset. The extracted phrase is converted into a natural language response that is coherent within the context of the conversation.

cTBLS employs GPT-3.5 (Brown et al., 2020) to perform fine system state tracking and response generation jointly. GPT-3.5 is prompted to generate a natural language response to a follow-up query conditioned on cells of the table ranked by their relevance to the query as obtained from the coarse state tracker. The prompt includes the dialogue history, ranked knowledge sources, and the query to be answered. The bottom-right section of Figure 1 outlines this process.

4 Experiments

4.1 HYBRIDIALOGUE

The HYBRIDIALOGUE dataset (Nakamura et al., 2022) comprises 4800 natural language conversations grounded in text and tabular information from Wikipedia. Crowdsourced workers break down multi-hop questions from the OTT-QA dataset (Chen et al., 2020a) into natural questions and conversational responses related to tabular data. On average, dialogues in the dataset consist of 4-5 conversation turns, with a total of 21,070 turns available in the dataset. Examples of conversations can be found in Figures 3 and 4.

4.2 Table Retrieval

The first conversation turn of HYBRIDIALOGUE requires selecting the correct table based on the input query for which we use the Dense Table Retriever outlined in Section 3.1. The Dense Table Retriever is fine-tuned for 20 epochs using Adam (Kingma and Ba, 2014) with a learning rate of 1e-6 and a linear learning schedule with five warmup steps. The loss function is a modification of the contrastive loss implementation from ConVIRT (Zhang et al., 2022), with image embeddings replaced by table embeddings. The table retriever used in the HYBRIDIALOGUE paper (Nakamura et al., 2022) was the BM25Okapi Retriever (Trotman et al., 2014) from rank-bm25. According to the results presented in Table 1, cTBLS-DTR outperforms BM25 in terms of Mean Reciprocal Rank (MRR), Top-1 Accuracy, and Top-3 Accuracy on HYBRIDIALOGUE.

4.3 Coarse State Tracking

Coarse state tracking ranks cells from a table based on their relevance to a query. As before, the dual-encoder coarse state tracker of cTBLS consists of RoBERTa-base fine-tuned using Adam with a learning rate of 1e-6 and a linear learning schedule with five warmup steps. In contrast to table retrieval, the state tracker uses triplet margin loss with a margin of 1.0 (Equation 2) instead of contrastive loss (Equation 1). The results, as demonstrated in Table 2, show that fine-tuning RoBERTa-base solely on HYBRIDIALOGUE surpasses the performance of SentenceBERT (Reimers and Gurevych, 2019). Furthermore, it nearly attains the same MRR @10 as TaPas (Herzig et al., 2020), even without additional table pre-training on the SQA dataset (Iyyer et al., 2017).

	MRR @10	Top 1 Acc	Top 3 Acc
BM25	0.491	0.345	0.460
cTBLS-DTR	**0.846**	**0.777**	**0.901**

Table 1: BM25 vs cTBLS-DTR for retrieval on first turn of conversation, results on HYBRIDIALOGUE testing dataset. cTBLS-DTR obtains up to 125% relative improvement over sparse table retrieval

	MRR@10
SentenceBERT (Reimers and Gurevych, 2019)	0.603
TaPas (Herzig et al., 2020)	**0.689**
cTBLS - RoBERTa-base	0.683

Table 2: System state tracking results on HYBRIDIALOGUE. cTBLS achieves nearly the same Mean Reciprocal Rank (MRR) @ 10 as TaPaS, without additional table pre-training on SQA (Iyyer et al., 2017)

4.4 Fine State Tracking and Response Generation

cTBLS uses GPT-3.5 (text-davinci-003) with the existing dialogue context, the current query, and the retrieved references from coarse state tracking to obtain a natural language response. Since fine-tuning the best available version of the model is cost prohibitive, we opt to prompt GPT-3.5 to generate responses instead.

	Top-1	Top-3	Top-10
cTBLS - RoBERTa-base	0.559	0.778	0.925

Table 3: Top-k accuracy for cTBLS on coarse system state tracking. cTBLS ranks the correct cell as the top reference in 56% of follow-up queries on HYBRIDIALOGUE. The correct cell is ranked in the Top-3 and Top-10 retrievals in approximately 78% and 93% of conversations, respectively.

Model	TR	KR	RG	ROUGE-1	ROUGE-2	ROUGE-L
-	BM25	Top-1	DialoGPT	0.207	0.042	0.181
-	BM25	Top-3	DialoGPT	0.212	0.045	0.186
-	BM25	Top-1	GPT3.5	0.428	0.207	0.369
-	BM25	Top-3	GPT3.5	0.475	0.242	0.413
-	DTR	Top-1	DialoGPT	0.222	0.051	0.195
-	DTR	Top-3	DialoGPT	0.226	0.059	0.199
-	DTR	Top-1	GPT3.5	0.494	0.255	0.424
-	DTR	Top-3	GPT3.5	0.560	0.295	0.479
HYBRIDIALOGUE	Gold	Top-1	DialoGPT	0.438	0.212	0.375
cTBLS NoK	Gold	-	GPT3.5	0.487	0.229	0.422
cTBLS Top-1	Gold	Top-1	GPT3.5	0.603	0.304	0.517
cTBLS Top-3	Gold	Top-3	GPT3.5	**0.642**	**0.322**	**0.548**

Table 4: Ablation study on automatic evaluation metrics ROUGE-1, ROUGE-2, and ROUGE-L Precision. Using Dense Table Retrieval (DTR) improves results over BM25 across Top-1 and Top-3 knowledge for DialoGPT and GPT3.5. Furthermore, using Top-3 knowledge sources results in better results than using only Top-1 knowledge sources for DialoGPT and GPT3.5 using both table retrieval methods. cTBLS No Knowledge (NoK), Top-1 Knowledge, Top-3 Knowledge, and HYBRIDIALOGUE use ground truth table retrieval. cTBLS exhibits a 2x relative improvement in ROUGE Precision over HYBRIDIALOGUE. TR: Table Retrieval, KR: Knowledge Retrieval, RG: Response Generation

The results presented in Table 3 demonstrate that the coarse state tracker successfully retrieves the correct cell in approximately 56% of conversations during inference. Furthermore, it achieves Top-3 and Top-10 retrievals in approximately 78% and 93% of conversations, respectively. Motivated by these results, the fine state tracker of cTBLS is evaluated in two different configurations by prompting GPT-3.5 augmented with the Top-1 and Top-3 knowledge references (cTBLS Top-1 and cTBLS Top-3). Due to limits on token length associated with the OpenAI API, we remove stopwords from the knowledge provided in the prompt and do not experiment with Top-10 knowledge augmentation.

Since LLMs store factual information in their weights (Roberts et al., 2020; Heinzerling and Inui, 2021), we compare to few-shot prompting (using two examples) with no knowledge sources (cTBLS-NoK). Furthermore, to enable a meaningful comparison with existing research (Nakamura et al., 2022), we measure cTBLS against the system proposed by HYBRIDIALOGUE that utilizes a fine-tuned DialoGPT-medium (Zhang et al., 2019) model augmented with Top-1 knowledge.

Table 4 presents ROUGE-1, ROUGE-2, and ROUGE-L precision (Lin, 2004) for all models assessed. The results demonstrate that superior downstream performance can be achieved through improvements in table retrieval. Specifically, when keeping the number of knowledge sources constant, we observe an improvement in ROUGE precision scores when transitioning from BM25 to DTR, and from DTR to gold table retrieval. The inclusion of additional knowledge sources leads to an improved n-gram overlap with the ground truth reference, as evidenced by the Top-3 knowledge augmented models outperforming their Top-1 counterparts utilizing the same table retriever, and cTBLS Top-1 outperforming the baseline model cTBLS NoK. Moreover, cTBLS Top-3 achieves the best performance across all automatic metrics, suggesting the benefits of splitting knowledge retrieval into coarse and fine state tracking, and utilizing additional knowledge sources. Finally, all three configurations of cTBLS demonstrate superior performance to HYBRIDIALOGUE.

4.5 Human Evaluation

To gain a deeper understanding of cTBLS, we conducted human evaluation using the metrics outlined by Nakamura et al. (2022), namely Coherence, Fluency, and Informativeness. For the evaluation of these metrics, we enlisted crowd workers from Amazon Mechanical Turk (AMT) to assess 50% of the test data. The evaluation process involved a comparison between the responses generated by HYBRIDIALOGUE and cTBLS Top-3.

	cTBLS Top-3 vs HYBRIDIALOGUE
Coherence	0.842
Fluency	0.827

Table 5: Coherence and Fluency - cTBLS Top-3 is more conversationally coherent than the best performing HYBRIDIALOGUE system 84.2% of the time and is more fluent 82.7% of the time.

In accordance with the methodology delineated in Nakamura et al. (2022), Coherence was defined as the degree to which a response continued the conversation in a logically coherent manner based on prior context. Fluency, conversely, was determined by evaluating absence of grammatical and spelling errors, and appropriate use of parts of speech.

To ensure the quality of the evaluated responses, we engaged crowd workers possessing a Masters qualification on AMT and originating from English-speaking countries (USA, Canada, Australia, New Zealand, or Great Britain). Each task required approximately 30 seconds to complete, and workers were remunerated at a rate of $0.05 per task. Moreover, to minimize bias and guarantee the dependability of the evaluations, we assigned two crowd workers to assess each response, with a response deemed more coherent or fluent only if both evaluations concurred.

The results presented in Table 5 reveal that the responses generated by cTBLS Top-3 were more coherent than those produced by HYBRIDIALOGUE in 84.2% of cases and exhibited greater fluency 82.7% of the time, suggesting that improvements in table retrieval, knowledge retrieval, and response generation lead to better downstream performance.

Informativeness represents the accuracy of machine-generated responses when compared to the ground-truth (Nakamura et al., 2022) and serves as a measure of hallucination in LLMs. Hallucinated responses tend to be less informative, deviating significantly from the ground-truth.

To evaluate informativeness, crowd workers determined whether generated responses were semantically equivalent to the ground truth response. Each response was assessed by two Turkers, and a response was deemed more informative only if there was inter-annotator agreement. The absence of illustrative examples in the prompting process resulted in responses generated by cTBLS Top-1 and cTBLS Top-3 being longer than the ground truth response. Consequently, the knowledge-augmented

	Informativeness
HYBRIDIALOGUE	0.124
cTBLS - NoK	0.306
cTBLS Top-1	0.456
cTBLS Top-3	**0.500**

Table 6: Human Evaluation Metrics - Fraction of cases where model response is semantically equivalent to ground truth response. Using more knowledge sources results in responses that are more informative, helping reduce hallucination.

cTBLS responses were considered informative if all the information provided in the ground truth was encapsulated in the model response, even if cTBLS included supplementary information.

The data in Table 6 indicate that cTBLS Top-3 encompasses the same information as the ground truth response 50% of the time, a higher rate than cTBLS Top-1 at 45.6%, exemplifying the benefits of partitioning retrieval into coarse and fine state tracking and augmenting with additional knowledge. Based on these findings, we hypothesize that the attention mechanism in decoder models facilitates additional knowledge retrieval. cTBLS NoK generates the correct response 30.6% of the time, suggesting that HYBRIDIALOGUE comprises questions and answers predicated on general world knowledge embedded in the weights of LLMs. Responses produced by HYBRIDIALOGUE are informative in merely 12.4% of instances.

Figure 3 presents a comparison of responses generated by various configurations of cTBLS on the HYBRIDIALOGUE dataset. The entire dialogue history constitutes the context and is depicted as an exchange between the user (in blue) and the system (in yellow). The final question box represents the follow-up query to be addressed, while the last answer chat box indicates the ground truth response. Knowledge K1, K2, and K3 correspond to cells of the table retrieved during state tracking, based on which responses are produced. cTBLS NoK generates a response solely relying on the context, cTBLS Top-1 formulates a response conditioned on K1, and cTBLS Top-3 devises a response based on K1, K2, and K3.

cTBLS NoK creates a hallucinated response, answering with the random Faroese club B68 Toftir. Similarly, cTBLS Top-1 hallucinates a response, opting for B36 Tórshavn, as K1 refers to the stadium Viò Margáir rather than the correct club's

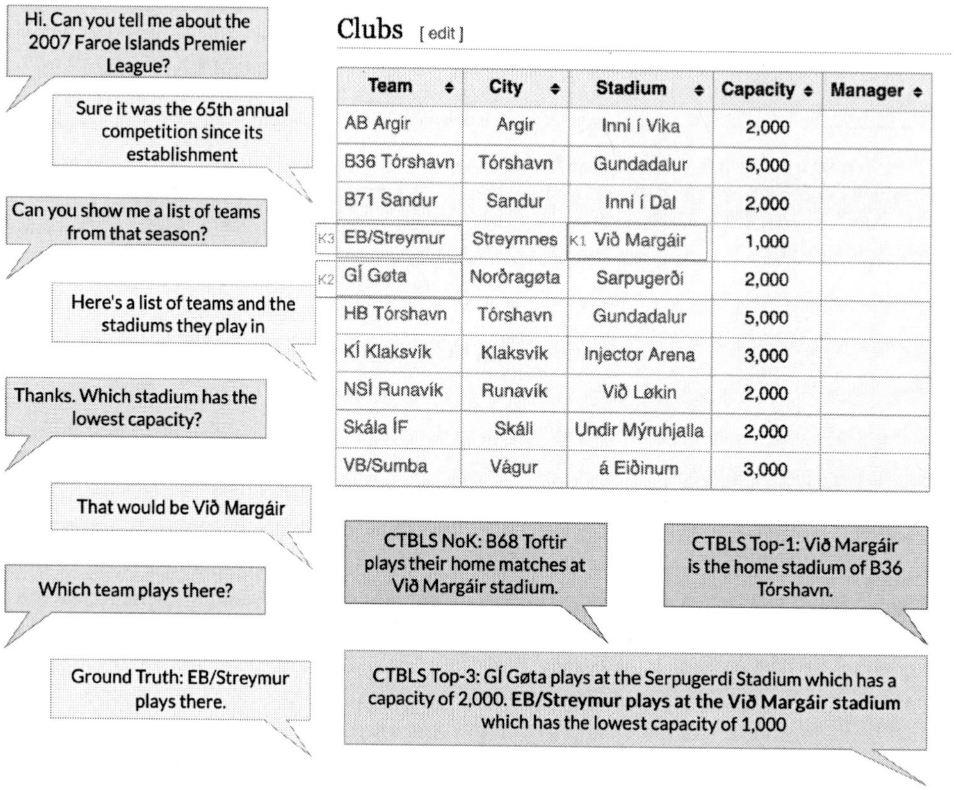

Figure 3: Generated responses vs Ground Truth on HYBRIDIALOGUE test set. Questions are in blue and responses in yellow. K1, K2, and K3 represent the Top 3 knowledge sources ranked by relevance to the query "Which team plays there?". cTBLS Top-3 is able to leverage K3 to generate the correct response while cTBLS NoK hallucinates a response and cTBLS Top-1 generates an incorrect response based on K1. Table obtained from Wikipedia available here

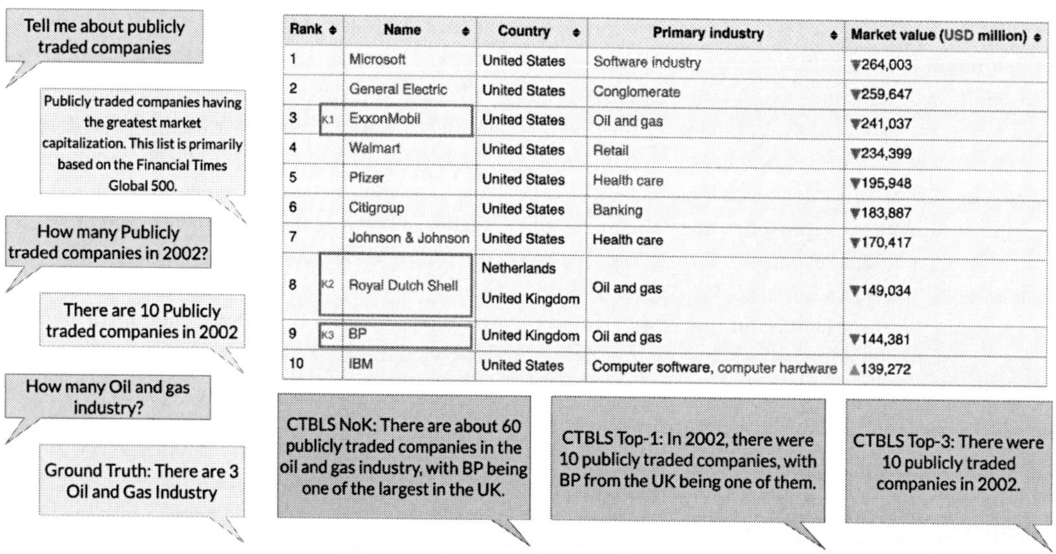

Figure 4: Generated responses vs Ground Truth on HYBRIDIALOGUE test set. Despite selecting the rows of the table corresponding to Oil and gas industries, cTBLS NoK, Top-1, and Top-3 struggle with counting and hallucinate a response. Table obtained from Wikipedia available here

name. In contrast, cTBLS Top-3 produces the accurate response, EB/Streymur, since K3 contains the necessary information. This example demonstrates the benefits of augmenting response generation with additional pertinent knowledge, which aids in mitigating the hallucination problem (Maynez et al., 2020).

5 Conclusion

In this paper, we introduce Conversational Tables (cTBLS), a system designed to address multi-turn dialogues that are grounded in tabular data. cTBLS separates tabular dialogue into three distinct tasks, specifically table retrieval, system state tracking, and response generation. The dense table retrieval system of cTBLS yields an enhancement of up to 125% relative to keyword-matching based techniques on the HYBRIDIALOGUE dataset, with regard to Top-1 Accuracy and Mean Reciprocal Rank @ 10. Furthermore, cTBLS conducts system state tracking utilizing a two-step process shared between encoder and decoder models. This methodology results in natural language responses exhibiting a 2x relative improvement in ROUGE scores. Human evaluators favor cTBLS +80% of the time (coherency and fluency) and judge informativeness to be 4x better than the previous state-of-the-art.

6 Limitations

Although cTBLS enhances LLMs with tabular knowledge to generate grounded responses, certain limitations remain to be addressed.

Firstly, the efficacy of cTBLS is constrained by the total number of knowledge sources employed during the augmentation process. Token length restrictions in the OpenAI API limit the knowledge augmentation to the top three cells of the table. Another limitation is the incapacity of cTBLS to handle queries pertaining to the entire table. Figure 4 demonstrates one such instance in which the state tracker module accurately retrieves three rows of the table corresponding to oil and gas industries, yet the response generation module fails to utilize this information when transforming the retrieved state into a response. Generally, cTBLS encounters difficulties with counting, comparing the values of cells, and other mathematical operations, an issue we aim to address in future research.

7 Acknowledgements

We would like to thank Christopher Richardson, Benjamin Z Reichman, Atishay Jain, and Srikar Bhumireddy for their contributions. We would also like to thank the review committee for their feedback. This work was supported by NSF IIS-2112633 and by CoCoSys, one of seven centers in JUMP 2.0, a Semiconductor Research Corporation (SRC) program sponsored by DARPA.

References

Joshua Ainslie, Santiago Ontanon, Chris Alberti, Vaclav Cvicek, Zachary Fisher, Philip Pham, Anirudh Ravula, Sumit Sanghai, Qifan Wang, and Li Yang. 2020. ETC: Encoding long and structured inputs in transformers. In *Proceedings of the 2020 Conference on Empirical Methods in Natural Language Processing (EMNLP)*, pages 268–284, Online. Association for Computational Linguistics.

Luiz Bonifacio, Hugo Abonizio, Marzieh Fadaee, and Rodrigo Nogueira. 2022. Inpars: Data augmentation for information retrieval using large language models. *arXiv preprint arXiv:2202.05144*.

Tom Brown, Benjamin Mann, Nick Ryder, Melanie Subbiah, Jared D Kaplan, Prafulla Dhariwal, Arvind Neelakantan, Pranav Shyam, Girish Sastry, Amanda Askell, et al. 2020. Language models are few-shot learners. *Advances in neural information processing systems*, 33:1877–1901.

Wenhu Chen. 2022. Large language models are few (1)-shot table reasoners. *arXiv preprint arXiv:2210.06710*.

Wenhu Chen, Ming-Wei Chang, Eva Schlinger, William Wang, and William W Cohen. 2020a. Open question answering over tables and text. *arXiv preprint arXiv:2010.10439*.

Wenhu Chen, Yu Su, Xifeng Yan, and William Yang Wang. 2020b. Kgpt: Knowledge-grounded pretraining for data-to-text generation. *arXiv preprint arXiv:2010.02307*.

Wenhu Chen, Hanwen Zha, Zhiyu Chen, Wenhan Xiong, Hong Wang, and William Yang Wang. 2020c. HybridQA: A dataset of multi-hop question answering over tabular and textual data. In *Findings of the Association for Computational Linguistics: EMNLP 2020*, pages 1026–1036, Online. Association for Computational Linguistics.

Minseok Cho, Reinald Kim Amplayo, Seung-won Hwang, and Jonghyuck Park. 2018. Adversarial tableqa: Attention supervision for question answering on tables. In *Asian Conference on Machine Learning*, pages 391–406. PMLR.

Pedro Colon-Hernandez, Catherine Havasi, Jason Alonso, Matthew Huggins, and Cynthia Breazeal. 2021. Combining pre-trained language models and structured knowledge. *arXiv preprint arXiv:2101.12294*.

Jacob Devlin, Ming-Wei Chang, Kenton Lee, and Kristina Toutanova. 2019. BERT: Pre-training of deep bidirectional transformers for language understanding. In *Proceedings of the 2019 Conference of the North American Chapter of the Association for Computational Linguistics: Human Language Technologies, Volume 1 (Long and Short Papers)*, pages 4171–4186, Minneapolis, Minnesota. Association for Computational Linguistics.

Emily Dinan, Stephen Roller, Kurt Shuster, Angela Fan, Michael Auli, and Jason Weston. 2018. Wizard of wikipedia: Knowledge-powered conversational agents. *arXiv preprint arXiv:1811.01241*.

Julian Martin Eisenschlos, Maharshi Gor, Thomas Müller, and William W Cohen. 2021. Mate: multi-view attention for table transformer efficiency. *arXiv preprint arXiv:2109.04312*.

Dilek Hakkani-Tür, Malcolm Slaney, Asli Celikyilmaz, and Larry Heck. 2014. Eye gaze for spoken language understanding in multi-modal conversational interactions. In *Proceedings of the 16th International Conference on Multimodal Interaction*, ICMI '14, page 263–266, New York, NY, USA. Association for Computing Machinery.

Dilek Hakkani-Tür, Asli Celikyilmaz, Larry Heck, Gokhan Tur, and Geoff Zweig. 2014. Probabilistic enrichment of knowledge graph entities for relation detection in conversational understanding. In *Proceedings of Interspeech*.

Darryl Hannan, Akshay Jain, and Mohit Bansal. 2020. Manymodalqa: Modality disambiguation and qa over diverse inputs. In *Proceedings of the AAAI Conference on Artificial Intelligence*, volume 34, pages 7879–7886.

Larry Heck, Dilek Hakkani-Tür, Madhu Chinthakunta, Gokhan Tur, Rukmini Iyer, Partha Parthasacarthy, Lisa Stifelman, Elizabeth Shriberg, and Ashley Fidler. 2013. Multimodal conversational search and browse. *First Workshop on Speech, Language and Audio in Multimedia Marseille, France*.

Larry Heck and Simon Heck. 2020. Zero-shot visual slot filling as question answering. *arXiv preprint arXiv:2011.12340*.

Benjamin Heinzerling and Kentaro Inui. 2021. Language models as knowledge bases: On entity representations, storage capacity, and paraphrased queries. In *Proceedings of the 16th Conference of the European Chapter of the Association for Computational Linguistics: Main Volume*, pages 1772–1791, Online. Association for Computational Linguistics.

Jonathan Herzig, Thomas Müller, Syrine Krichene, and Julian Eisenschlos. 2021. Open domain question answering over tables via dense retrieval. In *Proceedings of the 2021 Conference of the North American Chapter of the Association for Computational Linguistics: Human Language Technologies*, pages 512–519, Online. Association for Computational Linguistics.

Jonathan Herzig, Pawel Krzysztof Nowak, Thomas Müller, Francesco Piccinno, and Julian Eisenschlos. 2020. TaPas: Weakly supervised table parsing via pre-training. In *Proceedings of the 58th Annual Meeting of the Association for Computational Linguistics*, pages 4320–4333, Online. Association for Computational Linguistics.

Hongzhao Huang, Larry Heck, and Heng Ji. 2015. Leveraging deep neural networks and knowledge graphs for entity disambiguation. *arXiv preprint arXiv:1504.07678*.

Junjie Huang, Wanjun Zhong, Qian Liu, Ming Gong, Daxin Jiang, and Nan Duan. 2022. Mixed-modality representation learning and pre-training for joint table-and-text retrieval in openqa. *arXiv preprint arXiv:2210.05197*.

Po-Sen Huang, Xiaodong He, Jianfeng Gao, Li Deng, Alex Acero, and Larry Heck. 2013. Learning deep structured semantic models for web search using clickthrough data. In *Proceedings of the 22nd ACM international conference on Information & Knowledge Management*, pages 2333–2338. ACM.

Mohit Iyyer, Wen-tau Yih, and Ming-Wei Chang. 2017. Search-based neural structured learning for sequential question answering. In *Proceedings of the 55th Annual Meeting of the Association for Computational Linguistics (Volume 1: Long Papers)*, pages 1821–1831, Vancouver, Canada. Association for Computational Linguistics.

Gautier Izacard and Edouard Grave. 2021. Leveraging passage retrieval with generative models for open domain question answering. In *Proceedings of the 16th Conference of the European Chapter of the Association for Computational Linguistics: Main Volume*, pages 874–880, Online. Association for Computational Linguistics.

Sujay Kumar Jauhar, Peter Turney, and Eduard Hovy. 2016. Tables as semi-structured knowledge for question answering. In *Proceedings of the 54th Annual Meeting of the Association for Computational Linguistics (Volume 1: Long Papers)*, pages 474–483, Berlin, Germany. Association for Computational Linguistics.

Vitor Jeronymo, Luiz Bonifacio, Hugo Abonizio, Marzieh Fadaee, Roberto Lotufo, Jakub Zavrel, and Rodrigo Nogueira. 2023. Inpars-v2: Large language models as efficient dataset generators for information retrieval. *arXiv preprint arXiv:2301.01820*.

Robin Jia, Larry Heck, Dilek Hakkani-Tür, and Georgi Nikolov. 2017. Learning concepts through conversations in spoken dialogue systems. In *2017 IEEE International Conference on Acoustics, Speech and Signal Processing (ICASSP)*, pages 5725–5729.

Nengzheng Jin, Joanna Siebert, Dongfang Li, and Qingcai Chen. 2022. A survey on table question answering: Recent advances. In *Knowledge Graph and Semantic Computing: Knowledge Graph Empowers the Digital Economy*, pages 174–186, Singapore. Springer Nature Singapore.

Vladimir Karpukhin, Barlas Oguz, Sewon Min, Patrick Lewis, Ledell Wu, Sergey Edunov, Danqi Chen, and Wen-tau Yih. 2020. Dense passage retrieval for open-domain question answering. In *Proceedings of the 2020 Conference on Empirical Methods in Natural Language Processing (EMNLP)*, pages 6769–6781, Online. Association for Computational Linguistics.

Diederik P Kingma and Jimmy Ba. 2014. Adam: A method for stochastic optimization. *arXiv preprint arXiv:1412.6980*.

Patrick Lewis, Ethan Perez, Aleksandra Piktus, Fabio Petroni, Vladimir Karpukhin, Naman Goyal, Heinrich Küttler, Mike Lewis, Wen-tau Yih, Tim Rocktäschel, Sebastian Riedel, and Douwe Kiela. 2020. Retrieval-augmented generation for knowledge-intensive nlp tasks. In *Advances in Neural Information Processing Systems*, volume 33, pages 9459–9474. Curran Associates, Inc.

Alexander Hanbo Li, Patrick Ng, Peng Xu, Henghui Zhu, Zhiguo Wang, and Bing Xiang. 2021. Dual reader-parser on hybrid textual and tabular evidence for open domain question answering. In *Proceedings of the 59th Annual Meeting of the Association for Computational Linguistics and the 11th International Joint Conference on Natural Language Processing (Volume 1: Long Papers)*, pages 4078–4088, Online. Association for Computational Linguistics.

Chin-Yew Lin. 2004. ROUGE: A package for automatic evaluation of summaries. In *Text Summarization Branches Out*, pages 74–81, Barcelona, Spain. Association for Computational Linguistics.

Yinhan Liu, Myle Ott, Naman Goyal, Jingfei Du, Mandar Joshi, Danqi Chen, Omer Levy, Mike Lewis, Luke Zettlemoyer, and Veselin Stoyanov. 2019. Roberta: A robustly optimized bert pretraining approach. *arXiv preprint arXiv:1907.11692*.

Joshua Maynez, Shashi Narayan, Bernd Bohnet, and Ryan McDonald. 2020. On faithfulness and factuality in abstractive summarization. In *Proceedings of the 58th Annual Meeting of the Association for Computational Linguistics*, pages 1906–1919, Online. Association for Computational Linguistics.

Fedor Moiseev, Zhe Dong, Enrique Alfonseca, and Martin Jaggi. 2022. SKILL: Structured knowledge infusion for large language models. In *Proceedings of the 2022 Conference of the North American Chapter of the Association for Computational Linguistics: Human Language Technologies*, pages 1581–1588, Seattle, United States. Association for Computational Linguistics.

Kai Nakamura, Sharon Levy, Yi-Lin Tuan, Wenhu Chen, and William Yang Wang. 2022. HybriDialogue: An information-seeking dialogue dataset grounded on tabular and textual data. In *Findings of the Association for Computational Linguistics: ACL 2022*, pages 481–492, Dublin, Ireland. Association for Computational Linguistics.

Panupong Pasupat and Percy Liang. 2015. Compositional semantic parsing on semi-structured tables. In *Proceedings of the 53rd Annual Meeting of the Association for Computational Linguistics and the 7th International Joint Conference on Natural Language Processing (Volume 1: Long Papers)*, pages 1470–1480, Beijing, China. Association for Computational Linguistics.

Baolin Peng, Michel Galley, Pengcheng He, Hao Cheng, Yujia Xie, Yu Hu, Qiuyuan Huang, Lars Liden, Zhou Yu, Weizhu Chen, and Jianfeng Gao. 2023. Check your facts and try again: Improving large language models with external knowledge and automated feedback.

Nils Reimers and Iryna Gurevych. 2019. Sentence-BERT: Sentence embeddings using Siamese BERT-networks. In *Proceedings of the 2019 Conference on Empirical Methods in Natural Language Processing and the 9th International Joint Conference on Natural Language Processing (EMNLP-IJCNLP)*, pages 3982–3992, Hong Kong, China. Association for Computational Linguistics.

Christopher Richardson and Larry Heck. 2023. Commonsense reasoning for conversational ai: A survey of the state of the art. *Workshop on Knowledge Augmented Methods for NLP, (KnowledgeNLP-AAAI'23)*.

Adam Roberts, Colin Raffel, and Noam Shazeer. 2020. How much knowledge can you pack into the parameters of a language model? In *Proceedings of the 2020 Conference on Empirical Methods in Natural Language Processing (EMNLP)*, pages 5418–5426, Online. Association for Computational Linguistics.

Weijia Shi, Sewon Min, Michihiro Yasunaga, Minjoon Seo, Rich James, Mike Lewis, Luke Zettlemoyer, and Wen-tau Yih. 2023. Replug: Retrieval-augmented black-box language models. *arXiv preprint arXiv:2301.12652*.

Kurt Shuster, Spencer Poff, Moya Chen, Douwe Kiela, and Jason Weston. 2021. Retrieval augmentation reduces hallucination in conversation. In *Findings of the Association for Computational Linguistics: EMNLP 2021*, pages 3784–3803, Punta Cana, Dominican Republic. Association for Computational Linguistics.

Anirudh Sundar and Larry Heck. 2022. Multimodal conversational AI: A survey of datasets and approaches. In *Proceedings of the 4th Workshop on NLP for Conversational AI*, pages 131–147, Dublin, Ireland. Association for Computational Linguistics.

Andrew Trotman, Antti Puurula, and Blake Burgess. 2014. Improvements to bm25 and language models examined. In *Proceedings of the 2014 Australasian Document Computing Symposium*, ADCS '14, page 58–65, New York, NY, USA. Association for Computing Machinery.

Ashish Vaswani, Noam Shazeer, Niki Parmar, Jakob Uszkoreit, Llion Jones, Aidan N Gomez, Łukasz Kaiser, and Illia Polosukhin. 2017. Attention is all you need. *Advances in neural information processing systems*, 30.

Jingfeng Yang, Aditya Gupta, Shyam Upadhyay, Luheng He, Rahul Goel, and Shachi Paul. 2022. Tableformer: Robust transformer modeling for table-text encoding. *arXiv preprint arXiv:2203.00274*.

Pengcheng Yin, Graham Neubig, Wen-tau Yih, and Sebastian Riedel. 2020. TaBERT: Pretraining for joint understanding of textual and tabular data. In *Proceedings of the 58th Annual Meeting of the Association for Computational Linguistics*, pages 8413–8426, Online. Association for Computational Linguistics.

Wenhao Yu, Dan Iter, Shuohang Wang, Yichong Xu, Mingxuan Ju, Soumya Sanyal, Chenguang Zhu, Michael Zeng, and Meng Jiang. 2022. Generate rather than retrieve: Large language models are strong context generators. *arXiv preprint arXiv:2209.10063*.

Vicky Zayats, Kristina Toutanova, and Mari Ostendorf. 2021. Representations for question answering from documents with tables and text. In *Proceedings of the 16th Conference of the European Chapter of the Association for Computational Linguistics: Main Volume*, pages 2895–2906, Online. Association for Computational Linguistics.

Yizhe Zhang, Siqi Sun, Michel Galley, Yen-Chun Chen, Chris Brockett, Xiang Gao, Jianfeng Gao, JJ (Jingjing) Liu, and Bill Dolan. 2019. Dialogpt: Large-scale generative pre-training for conversational response generation. In *arXiv:1911.00536*.

Yuhao Zhang, Hang Jiang, Yasuhide Miura, Christopher D Manning, and Curtis P Langlotz. 2022. Contrastive learning of medical visual representations from paired images and text. In *Machine Learning for Healthcare Conference*, pages 2–25. PMLR.

Yilun Zhao, Yunxiang Li, Chenying Li, and Rui Zhang. 2022. MultiHiertt: Numerical reasoning over multi hierarchical tabular and textual data. In *Proceedings of the 60th Annual Meeting of the Association for Computational Linguistics (Volume 1: Long Papers)*, pages 6588–6600, Dublin, Ireland. Association for Computational Linguistics.

IDAS: Intent Discovery with Abstractive Summarization

Maarten De Raedt[◇♣] **Fréderic Godin**[◇] **Thomas Demeester**[♣] **Chris Develder**[♣]
[◇] Sinch Chatlayer [♣] Ghent University
{maarten.deraedt, thomas.demeester, chris.develder}@ugent.be
frederic.godin@sinch.com

Abstract

Intent discovery is the task of inferring latent intents from a set of unlabeled utterances, and is a useful step towards the efficient creation of new conversational agents. We show that recent competitive methods in intent discovery can be outperformed by clustering utterances based on *abstractive summaries*, i.e., "labels", that retain the core elements while removing non-essential information. We contribute the IDAS approach, which collects a set of descriptive utterance labels by prompting a Large Language Model, starting from a well-chosen seed set of prototypical utterances, to bootstrap an In-Context Learning procedure to generate labels for non-prototypical utterances. The utterances and their resulting noisy labels are then encoded by a *frozen* pre-trained encoder, and subsequently clustered to recover the latent intents. For the *unsupervised* task (without any intent labels) IDAS outperforms the state-of-the-art by up to +7.42% in standard cluster metrics for the Banking, StackOverflow, and Transport datasets. For the *semi-supervised* task (with labels for a subset of intents) IDAS surpasses 2 recent methods on the CLINC benchmark without even using labeled data.

Utterance	Generated label
find out when my next upcoming payday will be	when is next payday
my next paycheck is available when	when is next payday
what is the date of my last paycheck	when was last payday
i want to know how to change my oil	how to change oil
what is the way to change motor oil	how to change oil
how easy is it to change your own oil	DIY oil change
can you tell me the *apr* on my visa card	*interest rate inquiry*
what's the annual rate on my discover card	interest rate inquiry

Table 1: *Illustration* based on GPT-3 and CLINC (Larson et al., 2019), demonstrating how *abstractly* summarizing utterances retains the core elements while removing non-intent related information. The example in the bottom block, where *apr* is labeled as *interest rate inquiry*, exemplifies the broad domain knowledge captured by LLMs.

1 Introduction

Intent classification is ubiquitous in conversational modelling. To that end, finetuning Large Language Models (LLMs) on task-specific intent data has been proven very effective (Casanueva et al., 2020; Zhang et al., 2021d). However, such finetuning requires manually annotated (utterance, intent) pairs as training data, which are time-consuming and thus expensive to acquire. Companies often have an abundance of utterances relevant to the application area of their interest, e.g., those exchanged between customers and support agents, but manually annotating them remains costly. Consequently, intent discovery aims to recover latent intents without using any such manually annotated utterances, by partitioning a given set of (unlabeled) utterances into clusters, where utterances within a cluster should share the same *conversational goal* or *intent*.

Prior works typically (i) train an unsupervised sentence encoder to map utterances to vectors, after which these are (ii) clustered to infer latent intents. Such unsupervised encoder training is achieved largely under the assumption that utterances with similar encodings convey the same intent. For instance, by iteratively clustering and updating the encoder with supervision from the cluster assignments (Xie et al., 2016a; Caron et al., 2018a; Hadifar et al., 2019; Zhang et al., 2021c), or by retrieving utterances with similar encodings and using them as positive pairs to train the encoder with contrastive learning (Zhang et al., 2021a, 2022).

Yet, it remains unclear which particular features cause utterance representations to be similar. Various noisy features unrelated to the underlying intents, e.g., *syntax*, *n-gram overlap*, *nouns*, etc. may contribute in making utterances similar, leading to sentence encoders whose vector encodings may inadequately represent the underlying intents.

Different from prior works that train unsupervised encoders, we use a pre-trained encoder without requiring any further finetuning, since we pro-

Proceedings of the 5th Workshop on NLP for Conversational AI (NLP4ConvAI 2023), pages 71–88
July 14, 2023 ©2023 Association for Computational Linguistics

pose making utterances more (dis)similar in the textual space by *abstractly* summarizing them into concise descriptions, i.e., "labels", that preserve their core elements while removing non-essential information. We hypothesize that these core elements better represent intents and prevent non-intent related information from influencing the vector similarity. Table 1 illustrates how labels retain the intent-related information by discarding irrelevant aspects such as syntax and nouns.

This paper introduces Intent Discovery with Abstractive Summarization (IDAS in short), whereby the label generation process builds upon recent advancements of In-Context Learning (ICL) (Brown et al., 2020). In ICL, an LLM is prompted with an instruction including a small number of (input, output) demonstrations of the task at hand. ICL has shown to be effective at few-shot learning without additional LLM finetuning (Min et al., 2022a,b). However, intent discovery is unsupervised and therefore lacks the annotated (utterance, label) demonstrations required for ICL. To overcome this limitation, our proposed IDAS proceeds in four steps. First, a subset of diverse *prototypical* utterances representative of distinct latent intents are identified by performing an initial clustering and selecting those utterances closest to each cluster's centroid, for which an LLM is then prompted to generate a short descriptive label. Second, labels for the remaining *non-prototypical* utterances are obtained by retrieving the subset of the n utterances most similar to the input utterance, from the continually expanding set of utterances with already generated labels (initialized with just the prototypes), and using those n neighbors as ICL-demonstrations to generate the input utterance's label. Third, as the generated labels may still turn out too general or noisy, utterances with their labels are combined into a single vector representation using a *frozen* pre-trained encoder. Finally, K-means clusters the combined encodings to infer latent intents.

We compare our IDAS approach with the state-of-the-art in unsupervised intent discovery on Banking (Casanueva et al., 2020), StackOverflow (Xu et al., 2015), and a private dataset from a transport company, to assess IDAS's effectiveness in practice. We show that IDAS substantially outperforms the state-of-the-art, with average improvements in cluster metrics of +3.94%, +2.86%, and +3.34% in Adjusted Rand Index, Normalized Mutual Information, and Cluster Accuracy, respectively. Further, IDAS surpasses two *semi-supervised* intent discovery methods on CLINC (Larson et al., 2019) despite not using any ground truth annotations.

2 Related Work

Statistical approaches: Early, more general short text clustering methods employ statistical methods such as tf-idf (Sparck Jones, 1972), to map text to vectors. Yet, the sparsity of these encodings prevents similar texts, but phrased with different synonyms, from being assigned to the same cluster. To specifically mitigate this synonym effect, external features have been used to enrich such *sparse* vectors, e.g., with WordNet (Miller, 1995) synonyms or lexical chains (Hotho et al., 2003; Wei et al., 2015), or Wikipedia titles or categories (Banerjee et al., 2007; Hu et al., 2009).

Neural sentence encoders: Rather than relying on external knowledge sources, neural approaches pre-train sentence encoders in a self-supervised way (Kiros et al., 2015; Gao et al., 2021), or with supervision (Conneau et al., 2017; Reimers and Gurevych, 2019; Gao et al., 2021), to produce *dense* general-purpose vectors that better capture synonymy and semantic relatedness.

Unsupervised intent discovery: Since general-purpose neural encoders may fail to capture domain-specific intent information, intent discovery solutions have shifted towards unsupervised sentence encoders specifically trained on the domain data at hand. For instance, Xu et al. (2015) train a self-supervised Convolutional Neural Network, and use it to encode and cluster utterances with K-means. Zhang et al. (2022) adopt the same 2-step approach, but instead pre-train the encoder with contrastive learning, where utterances with similar vector encodings are retrieved to serve as positive pairs. A more common strategy is to cluster and train the encoder end-to-end, either by (i) *iteratively* clustering utterances and updating the encoder with supervision from the cluster assignments (Xie et al., 2016a; Caron et al., 2018b; Hadifar et al., 2019), or (ii) *simultaneously* clustering utterances and updating the encoder's weights with a joint loss criterion (Yang et al., 2017a; Zhang et al., 2021a).

As an alternative strategy to make utterances more (dis)similar based on the intents they convey, we employ an LLM to summarize utterances into labels that retain both the utterances' core ele-

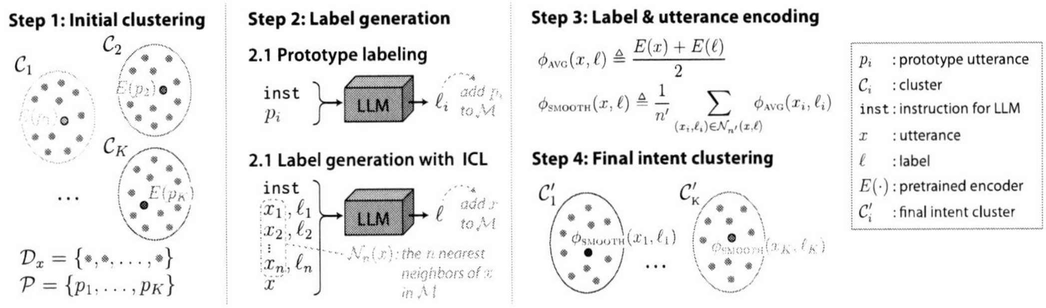

Fig. 1: Overview of our IDAS approach.

ments and domain-specific information as encoded in the LLM's weights. Since our generated labels should increase the (dis)similarity of (un)related utterances in the input space, rather than directly in the vector space, we use a *frozen* pre-trained encoder, thus deviating from the above methods that *train* unsupervised encoders.

Semi-supervised intent discovery: Similar to our current work, the aforementioned methods focus on *unsupervised* intent discovery. In the related but different *semi-supervised* intent discovery task, a fraction of the latent intents is assumed to be known, i.e., the "Known Class Ratio". Annotated data from these known intents is exploited to improve the detection of both known and unknown intent utterances, e.g., by optimizing a cluster loss with pairwise constraints derived from utterances of the same known intent (Lin et al., 2020). Alternative 2-step approaches first pre-train encoders with supervision from known intent utterances, then either directly encode and cluster utterances with K-means (Shen et al., 2021), or further refine the encoder on the unlabeled utterances. The latter refinement can be achieved through contrastive learning (Zhang et al., 2022) or by iteratively clustering and updating the encoder (Zhang et al., 2021b,c).

In-context learning: The core idea of ICL (Brown et al., 2020) is to perform tasks through inference, i.e., without updating parameters, by prompting an LLM with the string concatenation comprising (i) a task instruction, (ii) a small set of (input, output) demonstrations, and (iii) the input. We implement IDAS's label generation process with ICL, as it has shown to substantially outperform zero-shot approaches *without* demonstrations (Min et al., 2022a,b; Chen et al., 2022). However, since we focus on unsupervised intent discovery and thus lack annotated (utterance, label) demonstrations, we bootstrap the set of demonstrations with automatically retrieved "prototypes". Rather than selecting demonstrations randomly, Liu et al. (2022) found that it is more effective to pick demonstrations similar to the input utterance, which we thus do. Note that alternative methods are possible (Rubin et al., 2022; Sorensen et al., 2022).

3 Methodology

Task formulation: Let $\{(x_i, y_i)|i = 1 \dots N\}$ be a dataset of N utterances $x \in \mathcal{X}$ from the set of natural language expressions $\mathcal{X}$, with corresponding intents y chosen from a set of K possible intents $\mathcal{Y} = \{y_i|i = 1 \dots K\}$. Given the utterances without the intents, $\mathcal{D}_x = \{x_i|i = 1 \dots N\}$, intent discovery aims to infer $\mathcal{Y}$ from $\mathcal{D}_x$ by mapping utterances x_i to vectors $E(x_i)$ with encoder $E : \mathcal{X} \to \mathbb{R}^d$, based on which the utterances are partitioned into clusters $\{\mathcal{C}_i|i = 1 \dots K\}$, such that clustered utterances (e.g., $x_{i,j}, x_{k,j} \in \mathcal{C}_j$) share the same intent ($y_{i,j} = y_{k,j}$), while utterances from different clusters (e.g., $x_{i,j} \in \mathcal{C}_j$ and $x_{k,l} \in \mathcal{C}_l$, $\mathcal{C}_l \neq \mathcal{C}_k$) have distinct intents ($y_{i,j} \neq y_{k,l}$).

Overview: As summarized in Fig. 1, to infer latent intents IDAS (1) identifies a subset of diverse "prototypes", $\mathcal{P} \subset \mathcal{D}_x$, representative of the latent intents (§3.1); then (2) independently summarizes them into labels, which are further used to also generate labels for the remaining non-prototypical utterances $x \in \mathcal{D}_x \setminus \mathcal{P}$, by retrieving from the subset $\mathcal{M}$ of utterances that already have labels (initially $\mathcal{P}$) the set $\mathcal{N}_n(x)$ of n utterances most similar to x as ICL-demonstrations for generating the label of x (§3.2); further (3) encodes utterances and their labels into a single vector representation with a *frozen* pre-trained encoder (§3.3); and finally (4) infers the latent intents by performing K-means on the combined representations (§3.4).

3.1 Step 1: Initial Clustering

The objective of this step is to identify a diverse set of prototypes, $\mathcal{P} \subset \mathcal{D}_x$, that in Step 2 will be automatically labeled by an LLM and serve as initial demonstrations for generating the labels of non-prototypical utterances. It is therefore important to choose prototypes $p \in \mathcal{P}$ that each represent a distinct latent intent $y \in \mathcal{Y}$, and collectively cover as many as possible of all latent intents. We assume a similarity function between two vector representations of utterances by $s : \mathbb{R}^d \times \mathbb{R}^d \rightarrow \mathbb{R}$, and use it to retrieve prototypes by performing an initial clustering on the utterances in $\mathcal{D}_x$, in the vector representation space induced by encoder E. Then we select a prototype from each identified cluster, as the utterance in that cluster whose vector representation is closest to the cluster's centroid.

Formally, the utterances in $\mathcal{D}_x$ are first encoded with E and then partitioned into K (=$|\mathcal{Y}|$) clusters

$$\mathcal{C}_1, \ldots, \mathcal{C}_K = K\text{-means}(\mathcal{D}_x),$$

for which the respective centroids $c_i \in \mathbb{R}^d$ and prototypes $p_i \in \mathcal{D}_x$ are calculated as

$$c_i = \frac{1}{|\mathcal{C}_i|} \sum_{x \in \mathcal{C}_i} E(x), \quad p_i = \operatorname*{argmax}_{x \in \mathcal{C}_i} s(E(x), c_i).$$

3.2 Step 2: Label Generation

Step 2.1: Prototype Labeling To generate label ℓ_i for prototype p_i, we employ an LLM and provide it with an instruction (`inst`) such as "`describe the question in a maximum of 5 words`". The LLM then generates a concise description of the prototype p_i, which we use as its label ℓ_i. Mathematically, this is represented as

$$\ell_i = \operatorname*{argmax}_{\ell \in \mathcal{X}} P(\ell | \, \texttt{inst}, p_i),$$

where P denotes the probability distribution of the LLM, and ℓ_i represents the token sequence $t_{1_i}, \ldots, t_{l_i}$ output by the LLM.

Step 2.2: Label Generation with ICL To generate label ℓ for the non-prototypical utterance $x \in \mathcal{D}_x \setminus \mathcal{P}$, `IDAS` utilizes ICL by conditioning an LLM on the prompt, i.e., the string concatenation of (i) an instruction `inst`, e.g., "`classify the question into one of the labels`", (ii) the set of n demonstrations of (utterance, label) pairs $\{(x_i, \ell_i) | i = 1 \ldots n\}$, and (iii) the utterance x itself. Formally, the label is the token sequence generated by the LLM that maximizes the probability given the prompt:

$$\ell = \operatorname*{argmax}_{\ell \in \mathcal{X}} P(\ell | \, \texttt{inst}, x_1, \ell_1, \ldots, x_n, \ell_n, x).$$

Since unsupervised intent discovery lacks manually annotated demonstrations, `IDAS` uses a continually expanding set of utterances with *automatically* generated labels, denoted by $\mathcal{M}$. Initially, $\mathcal{M} = \mathcal{P}$, with $\mathcal{P}$ the set of prototypes from Step 2.1. An utterance x with newly generated label ℓ is added to $\mathcal{M}$, such that it can serve as a demonstration for remaining unlabeled utterances.

Typically, ICL uses a small set of n demonstrations (i) due to the limit on the number of input tokens of LLMs, and (ii) because performance does not improve for larger number of demonstrations (Min et al., 2022c). Moreover, Liu et al. (2022) found that selecting demonstrations as samples similar to the test input, rather than choosing them randomly, substantially boosts ICL's performance. Therefore, `IDAS` adopts KATE (Liu et al., 2022) by first mapping utterances in $\mathcal{M}$ to vectors with encoder E, and then using the similarity function s to select the set of the n most similar utterances[1] from $\mathcal{M}$ to $E(x)$, denoted by $\mathcal{N}_n(x) \subset \mathcal{M}$, as demonstrations for input utterance x.

Note that while we use "`classify`" in the instruction, we do not consider the prototypical labels generated in Step 1 as a fixed label set (i.e., *verbalizers*). Rather, label ℓ for non-prototypical utterance x is the token sequence as generated directly by the LLM. As a result, labels for non-prototypical utterances may still differ from those generated for the prototypes. Particularly, the LLM can generate new labels for input utterances that represent intents for which no prototypes have been identified yet, and thus have no ICL demonstrations of the latent intent. Thus, we minimize error propagation from Step 1. On the other hand, when the LLM considers that a demonstration likely shares the same latent intent with the input utterance, the "`classify`" instruction should encourage the LLM to generate a copy of that demonstration's label, which in turn minimizes variation among generated labels of utterances with the same latent intent.

3.3 Step 3: Encoding Utterances and Labels

After Step 2, each utterance $x \in \mathcal{D}_x$ has an associated generated label $\ell \in \mathcal{M}$. We use the pre-trained

[1]We set hyperparameter n to 8, based on the findings of Min et al. (2022c); Lyu et al. (2022). Ablations for different n values are presented in §5.2.

encoder E to respectively encode the utterances and their corresponding labels into separate vectors $E(x)$ and $E(\ell)$, after which these are averaged into the combined representation:

$$\phi_{\text{AVG}}(x, \ell) \triangleq \frac{E(x) + E(\ell)}{2}. \quad (1)$$

(Note that utterances could also be represented just by their label encoding $E(\ell)$, yet such generated labels could be noisy or overly general.)

We further contribute a non-parametric smoothing method that (i) aims to suppress features that are specific to individual utterances and thus potentially less representative of the underlying intents, while (ii) enhancing those features that are shared across utterances and thus more likely to be representative of the latent intents. We therefore represent utterance x as the average of the vector encodings of the n' most similar utterances $\mathcal{N}_{n'}(x, \ell)$ to x, including x itself:

$$\phi_{\text{SMOOTH}}(x, \ell) \triangleq \frac{1}{n'} \sum_{(x_i, \ell_i) \in \mathcal{N}_{n'}(x, \ell)} \phi_{\text{AVG}}(x_i, \ell_i). \quad (2)$$

We automatically determine the value of n' as the value that maximizes the average silhouette score (Rousseeuw, 1987) among all samples, which for sample i is given by

$$\text{silhouette-score}(i) = \frac{b(i) - a(i)}{\max(a(i), b(i))},$$

where $a(i)$ is the average distance of sample i to all other samples in its cluster, and $b(i)$ is the average distance of sample i to all samples in the neighboring cluster nearest to i.

3.4 Step 4: Final intent discovery

To finally infer the latent intents, we represent each utterance $x \in \mathcal{D}_x$ with its label ℓ as $\phi_{\text{SMOOTH}}(x, \ell)$, and apply K-means clustering, setting K to the ground truth number of latent intents $|\mathcal{Y}|$, following Hadifar et al. (2019); Zhang et al. (2021a,c, 2022).

4 Experimental Setup

4.1 Datasets

We evaluate our IDAS approach on two widely adopted intent classification datasets, CLINC (Larson et al., 2019) and Banking (Casanueva et al., 2020), as well as the StackOverflow topic classification dataset (Xu et al., 2015). We also use a private dataset from a transportation company. Table 2 summarizes dataset statistics.

Dataset	# Train	# Test	# Intents
CLINC	18,000	2,250	150
Banking	9,016	3,080	77
Transport	-	1,257	42
StackOverflow	18,000	1,000	20

Table 2: Dataset statistics.

4.2 Baselines

On Banking, StackOverflow, and our Transport dataset, we compare IDAS against the state-of-the-art in unsupervised intent discovery, i.e., the MTP-CLNN model (Zhang et al., 2022) that outperforms prior unsupervised methods, such as DEC (Xie et al., 2016b), DCN (Yang et al., 2017b), and DeepCluster (Caron et al., 2018b). As the MTP-CLNN model is pre-trained on the annotated training data of CLINC, directly comparing against it would be unfair. Instead, we compare our approach on CLINC with two state-of-the-art *semi-supervised* intent discovery methods, DAC (Zhang et al., 2021c) and SCL+PLT (Shen et al., 2021). Compared to the semi-supervised setting, the unsupervised setting without annotations is thus more challenging. We report results of DAC and SCL+PLT with an increasing "Known Class Ratio" (KCR) of 25%, 50%, and 75%, using the annotated data for the known intents of Shen et al. (2021).

4.3 Evaluation

Following Zhang et al. (2021c); Shen et al. (2021); Zhang et al. (2022), we assess cluster performance by comparing the predicted clusters to the ground truth intents using the (i) Adjusted Rand Index (ARI) (Steinley, 2004), (ii) Normalized Mutual Information (NMI), and (iii) Cluster Accuracy (ACC) based on the Hungarian algorithm (Kuhn, 1955). Since IDAS's label generation process may depend on the order in which utterances occur, we perform Steps 1–2 leading to utterance labels 5 times, shuffling the utterance order. We further conduct the final clustering Step 4 with 10 different seeds for each of those 5 label generation runs, to account for variation incurred by K-means. For each dataset, we then average the results in terms of means and standard variations across each of these 5 sets.

4.4 Implementation

Encoder: We use the same pre-trained encoder E in all steps of our approach, i.e., to (i) retrieve prototypes (§3.1), (ii) mine the n demonstrations

$\mathcal{N}_n(x)$ for utterance x (§3.2), and (iii) encode utterances with their labels using Eqs. (1)–(2) (§3.3). To rule out performance differences stemming purely from the encoder, we employ the same pre-trained encoder as the baseline we compare with: we use the MTP encoder for Banking, StackOverflow, and Transport, where we compare to MTP-CLNN (Zhang et al., 2022), and the SBERT encoder `paraphrase-mpnet-base2` (i.e., SMPNET) (Reimers and Gurevych, 2019) for CLINC, where we compare to DAC (Zhang et al., 2021c) and SCL+PLT (Shen et al., 2021).

Language models and prompts: `IDAS` uses the `text-davinci-003` GPT-3 model (Ouyang et al., 2022) as its LLM for label generation. We adopt the OpenAI playground default values, except for the temperature, which we set to 0 to minimize variation among generated labels of utterances with the same latent intent. To generate prototypical labels (§3.2), we use the instruction "`Describe the domain question in a maximum of 5 words`", where the domain is *banking*, *chatbot*, or *transport* for the corresponding dataset. Since StackOverflow is a topic rather than an intent classification dataset, we adopt a slightly different prototypical prompt. To generate labels for non-prototypical utterances with ICL (§3.2), we use "`Classify the domain question into one of the provided labels`" for all 4 datasets. See Appendix A.2 for full prompts and examples.

Nearest neighbor retrieval: The function s is implemented with cosine similarity. We use $n = 8$ demonstrations $\mathcal{N}_n(x)$ to generate label ℓ for utterance x (§3.2), based on Min et al. (2022c) and Lyu et al. (2022), who report that further increasing n does not improve ICL's performance. The number of smoothing samples n' is determined by running the final K-means (§3.4) multiple times with n' ranging from 5 to 45 and selecting the value that maximizes the average silhouette score.

5 Results and Discussion

5.1 Main Results

In *unsupervised* clustering, no labels are available and thus there is only a test set, used to evaluate the model's induced clusters against gold standard labels (Xie et al., 2016a; Yang et al., 2017a; Hadifar et al., 2019; Zhang et al., 2021a). In the *semi-supervised* intent detection setting, intent labels are available for a subset of intents: there is an additional labeled training set — which can be exploited, e.g., for (pre-)training a sentence encoder.

Zhang et al. (2022) evaluated their MTP and MTP-CLNN models by (pre-)training the encoder based on an unlabeled training set different from the test set where (new) intent clusters are induced, i.e., they evaluate on a held-out test set unseen during any (pre-)training phase. Since in our `IDAS`, no encoder is trained, we perform Steps 1–4 on the (unlabeled) test set following (Xie et al., 2016a; Yang et al., 2017a; Hadifar et al., 2019; Zhang et al., 2021a). To ensure a fair comparison we also consider an MTP-CLNN that uses that same test set in (pre-)training its encoder (i.e., for the $\mathcal{D}^{\text{unlabeled}}$ as defined in Zhang et al. (2022); results marked by ♠ in Table 3). Note that the test sets for a particular dataset are identical across all reported results.

First, we compare `IDAS` against the state-of-the-art in the *unsupervised* setting, i.e., MTP-CLNN, with results reported in Table 3. Both in the original settings of Zhang et al. (2022) (keeping the test data unseen during training, ♢) as well as when using the unlabeled test data in training MTP(-CLNN) (♠), our `IDAS` significantly surpasses it, with gains averaged over three datasets of +3.19–3.94%, +1.79–2.86% and +1.96–3.34% in respectively ARI, NMI and ACC. We further find that `IDAS` consistently outperforms MTP-CLNN on all metrics and datasets, except for Banking, where `IDAS` and MTP-CLNN perform similarly (when comparing them in similar settings, i.e., both using unlabeled test data in training phase). Note that both `IDAS` and MTP-CLNN perform worse on StackOverflow and Banking in our settings (♠) compared to the original results of Zhang et al. (2022) (♢), likely because in case of ♠, the MPT(-CLNN) encoder(s) were trained on a substantially lower number of samples, i.e., only 5.5% for StackOverflow (1,000 for ♠ vs. 18,000 for ♢) and 34% for Banking (3,080 for ♠ vs. 9,016 for ♢).

Second, we assess our `IDAS`'s performance in the *semi-supervised* task setting, where a subset of intents has labeled data. Note however that our `IDAS` does not use the labels for those utterances in any way. The results for CLINC presented in Table 4 show that `IDAS` outperforms both semi-supervised SCL+PLT and DAC methods for KCR's of 25% and 50%. Notably, `IDAS` surpasses SCL+PLT and DAC for KCR of 50%, with improvements in the range of 5.77–6.76%, 1.61–2.32%, and 4.78–4.89% in ARI, NMI, and ACC, respectively. Even for

	Banking			StackOverflow			Transport			Average		
Model	ARI	NMI	ACC	ARI	NMI	ACC	ARI	NMI	ACC	ARI	NMI	ACC
MTP$^\diamondsuit$	47.33	77.32	57.99	48.71	63.85	66.18	-	-	-	48.02	70.59	62.09
MTP-CLNN$^\diamondsuit$	55.75	81.80	65.90	67.63	78.71	81.43	-	-	-	61.69	80.26	73.67
IDAS	**57.56**	**82.84**	**67.43**	**72.20**	**81.26**	**83.82**	-	-	-	**64.88**$_{\pm 1.07}$	**82.05**$_{\pm 0.68}$	**75.63**$_{\pm 0.82}$
MTP$^\spadesuit$	39.52	72.03	51.66	29.66	47.46	48.97	44.51	74.71	57.51	37.90$_{\pm 0.48}$	64.73$_{\pm 0.31}$	52.69$_{\pm 0.60}$
MTP-CLNN$^\spadesuit$	52.47	79.46	**64.06**	62.53	73.52	78.82	50.33	77.77	61.60	55.11$_{\pm 1.32}$	76.92$_{\pm 0.74}$	68.16$_{\pm 1.02}$
IDAS	**53.31**	**80.43**	63.77	**66.08**	**77.25**	**82.11**	**57.75**	**81.66**	**68.51**	**59.05**$_{\pm 1.92}$	**79.78**$_{\pm 0.91}$	**71.46**$_{\pm 1.57}$
ΔMTP-CLNN$^\diamondsuit$	+1.81	+1.04	+1.53	+4.57	+2.55	+2.39	-	-	-	+3.19	+1.79	+1.96
ΔMTP-CLNN$^\spadesuit$	+0.84	+0.97	−0.29	+3.55	+3.73	+3.39	+7.42	+3.89	+6.91	+3.94	+2.86	+3.34

Table 3: Comparison against *unsupervised* state-of-the-art. $\diamondsuit$: results from Zhang et al. (2022). $\spadesuit$: results from (pre-)training MTP(-CLNN) on the test set (rather than a distinct unlabeled training set). The **best** model is typeset in bold and the runner-up is underlined. ΔMTP-CLNN values are the absolute gains of our IDAS.

		CLINC		
KCR	Model	ARI	NMI	ACC
0%	SMPNET	63.82	89.01	71.30
	IDAS	79.02$_{\pm 1.14}$	93.82$_{\pm 0.38}$	85.48$_{\pm 0.84}$
25%	DAC$^\heartsuit$	65.36	89.12	75.20
	SCL+PLT$^\heartsuit$	64.78	89.31	73.77
50%	DAC$^\heartsuit$	72.26	91.50	80.70
	SCL+PLT$^\heartsuit$	73.25	92.21	80.59
75%	DAC$^\heartsuit$	79.56	93.92	86.40
	SCL+PLT$^\heartsuit$	**83.44**	**95.25**	**88.68**

Table 4: Comparison against *semi-supervised methods* DAC and SCL+PLT. $\heartsuit$: results from Shen et al. (2021). Bold indicates **best** model. KCR: known class ratio.

KCR = 75%, it performs just slightly worse than DAC, further confirming IDAS's effectiveness.

5.2 Ablations

Below, we investigate the impact of (i) the encoding strategies from §3.3, and (ii) ICL from §3.2 on IDAS's performance. The results for each ablation are averaged over 5 runs with the utterances' order corresponding to those used for presenting the main results, i.e., with IDAS's default parameters values. Due to computation budget constraints, we only provide ablations on StackOverflow for (ii), since it requires GPT-3. For (i), we report results for Banking, StackOverflow, Transport, and CLINC.

Effect of the encoding strategies: Table 5 compares the cluster performance of these four encoding strategies: (1) $E(x)$ encodes only utterances; (2) $E(\ell)$ encodes only generated labels; (3) $\phi_{\text{AVG}}(x, \ell)$ (Eq. (1)) averages utterance and label encodings into a single vector representation; (4) $\phi_{\text{SMOOTH}}(x, \ell)$ (Eq. (2)) smooths the averaged vector representations. All encoding methods leveraging the generated labels ℓ outperform the baseline $E(x)$ using only the utterance, leading to ARI, NMI, and ACC gains between 5.12–19.23%, 3.82–16.75%, and 4.32–13.87%, respectively. This confirms our main hypothesis that abstractly summarizing utterances improves intent discovery. Moreover, combining utterance and label encodings ($\phi_{\text{AVG}}(x, \ell)$) further improves upon using the label alone (performing on par only for CLINC). Adding smoothing ($\phi_{\text{SMOOTH}}(x, \ell)$) boosts performance even more.

Inferring the number of smoothing neighbors: Smoothing requires selecting the number of neighbors n'. Our proposed IDAS selects the value of $n' \in \{5, \ldots, 45\}$ that yields the highest silhouette score. To assess the effect of that chosen n' value, we plot the ARI, NMI, and ACC scores for varying n' in Fig. 2. We observe that the ARI, AMI, and ACC scores obtained with the automatically inferred n' are nearly identical to the best achievable performance, demonstrating that the silhouette score is an effective heuristic for selecting a suitable number of smoothing neighbors.

Random vs. nearest neighbor demonstrations: IDAS employs KATE (Liu et al., 2022) to select the n ICL demonstrations most similar to x, i.e., $\mathcal{N}_n(x)$, for generating x's label (§3.2). To evaluate KATE's effectiveness for intent discovery, we present results for IDAS where n (= 8) demonstrations are instead selected randomly. Table 6 shows a substantial improvement of KATE over the random selection method, where the latter only marginally outperforms IDAS *without* any demon-

Encoding	Banking			StackOverflow			Transport			CLINC		
	ARI	NMI	ACC	ARI	NMI	ACC	ARI	NMI	ACC	ARI	NMI	ACC
$E(x)$	47.33	77.32	57.99	48.71	63.85	66.18	44.51	74.71	57.51	63.82	89.01	71.30
$E(\ell)$	52.45	81.14	62.31	67.94	80.60	80.05	54.37	80.68	64.66	75.01	93.04	81.27
$\phi_{\text{AVG}}(x,\ell)$	54.47	82.35	63.25	69.20	80.76	81.29	55.91	81.11	65.94	75.65	93.33	81.04
$\phi_{\text{SMOOTH}}(x,\ell)$	**57.56**	**82.84**	**67.43**	**72.20**	**81.26**	**83.82**	**57.75**	**81.66**	**68.51**	**79.02**	**93.82**	**85.48**

Table 5: *Effect of the encoding strategies.*

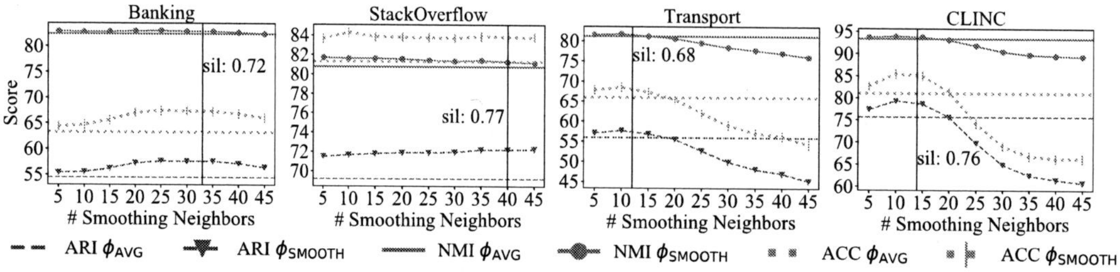

Fig. 2: *Inferring the number of smoothing neighbors n'.* The vertical lines represent the automatically determined number of smoothing neighbors corresponding to the highest silhouette score (sil).

strations (No ICL, $n = 0$). This follows the intuition that the LLM can pick a label from one of the n-NN instances, which likely shares an intent with the utterance to be labeled, thus effectively limiting label variation and improving clustering performance.

Varying the number of ICL demonstrations: We generate labels (1) *without* ICL, adopting the static prompt for generating the prototypical labels, without any demonstrations, and (2) *with* ICL for varying numbers of demonstrations $n \in \{1, 2, \ldots, 16\}$. Table 6 shows that (i) using any number of demonstrations leads to superior performance compared to using no demonstrations (No ICL); (ii) by varying small amounts of demonstrations ($n = 1$, 2, or 4) no significant differences are found; (iii) the best performance is achieved by using more demonstrations, i.e., 8 or 16. Consistent with the results of Min et al. (2022c); Lyu et al. (2022), increasing n from 8 to 16 does not result in further improvements, thus confirming that $n = 8$ demonstrations is a good default value.

Method	StackOverflow ARI	StackOverflow NMI	StackOverflow ACC
No ICL ($n = 0$)	$66.21_{\pm 0.13}$	$77.27_{\pm 0.04}$	$80.42_{\pm 0.13}$
KATE, $n = 1$	$68.91_{\pm 1.25}$	$79.11_{\pm 0.53}$	$83.09_{\pm 0.86}$
KATE, $n = 2$	$68.88_{\pm 1.40}$	$79.06_{\pm 0.86}$	$82.67_{\pm 0.98}$
KATE, $n = 4$	$69.97_{\pm 1.32}$	$79.76_{\pm 0.79}$	$82.94_{\pm 0.97}$
KATE, $n = 8$	$\underline{72.20}_{\pm 1.53}$	$\underline{81.26}_{\pm 0.93}$	$\underline{83.82}_{\pm 0.91}$
KATE, $n = 16$	$72.49_{\pm 1.75}$	$82.07_{\pm 1.18}$	$83.50_{\pm 0.88}$
random, $n = 8$	$66.80_{\pm 0.90}$	$78.72_{\pm 0.85}$	$81.37_{\pm 0.93}$
$K{\times}2$ ($n = 8$)	$71.43_{\pm 0.66}$	$80.76_{\pm 0.28}$	$83.51_{\pm 0.56}$

Table 6: ICL ablations. IDAS default settings are $n = 8$. The $K \times 2$ result uses twice the number of gold standard intents for the initial (Step 1, §3.1) clustering (i.e., 40 instead of 20 for StackOverflow).

Overestimating the number of prototypes: Following Hadifar et al. (2019); Zhang et al. (2021a,c, 2022), IDAS assumes a known number K of intents, both for the initial clustering (Step 1, retrieving prototypes, §3.1) and for the final clustering (Step 4, recovering latent intents, §3.4). While K can be *estimated* from a subset of utterances, determining it exactly is difficult. Unlike MTP-CLNN (Zhang et al., 2022), IDAS does not assume that the number of *samples* of each latent intent is known. To probe the robustness of IDAS's label generation to an incorrect number of prototypes, we conduct the initial K-means clustering with twice the gold number of intents. The $K \times 2$ row in Table 6 shows that this results in only a minor performance drop, indicating that IDAS's label generation process is sufficiently robust to such overestimation. In fact, we hypothesize that having multiple prototypes representing the same intent is less harmful than an insufficient number or incorrectly selected prototypes that do not accurately represent each intent.

6 Conclusions

Unlike existing methods that *train* unsupervised sentence encoders, our IDAS approach employs a *frozen* pre-trained encoder since it increases the (dis)similarity of (un)related utterances in the textual space by abstractly summarizing utterances into "labels". Our experiments demonstrate that IDAS substantially outperforms the current state-of-the-art in unsupervised intent discovery across multiple datasets (i.e., Banking, StackOverflow, and our private Transport), and surpasses two recent semi-supervised methods on CLINC, despite not using any labeled intents at all. Our findings suggest that our alternative strategy of abstractly summarizing utterances (using a general purpose LLM) is more effective than the dominant paradigm of training unsupervised encoders (specifically on dialogue data), and thus may open up new perspectives for novel intent discovery methods. Since our generated labels provide a better measure of intent-relatedness, we hypothesize that they could also enhance the performance of existing methods that train unsupervised encoders, e.g., by (i) reducing the number of false positive contrastive pairs for MTP-CLNN (Zhang et al., 2022), or (ii) improving the purity of clusters induced by methods that iteratively cluster utterances and update the encoder with (self-)supervision from cluster assignments (Xie et al., 2016a; Caron et al., 2018b; Hadifar et al., 2019). To facilitate such follow-up work, we release our generated labels for the Banking, StackOverflow, and CLINC datasets.[2]

Limitations

Our work is limited in the following senses. First, all presented results relied on the ground truth number of intents to initialize the number of clusters for conducting K-means to retrieve prototypes (§3.1) and infer latent intents (§3.4). In practice, however, the ground truth number of intents is unknown and needs to be estimated by examining a subset of utterances. However, our ablations in §5.2 investigated the impact of overestimating the number of ground truth intents by a factor of two, and found that IDAS's performance did not degrade much. While we did not explore this for the final K-means to infer latent intents, future work could investigate cluster algorithms that do not require the number of dialogue states as input, e.g., DBSCAN (Ester et al., 1996), Mean shift (Comaniciu and Meer, 2002), or Affinity propagation (Frey and Dueck, 2007).

Second, we generated labels with the GPT-3 (175B) `text-davinci-003` model, which may be prohibitively expensive and slow to run for very large corpora. In our initial experiments, we tried using smaller-sized models such as `text-curie-001`, `text-babbage-001`, and `text-ada-001`, as well as `Flan-T5-XL` (Chung et al., 2022), but found that the generated labels were of lower quality compared to those of `text-davinci-003`. In future work, it would thus be interesting to further explore how to more effectively exploit such smaller-sized and/or open-source language models.

Ethics Statement

Since IDAS automatically recovers intents from utterances, e.g., those exchanged between users and support agents, any prejudices that may be present in these utterances may become apparent or even amplified in intents inferred by our model, since clearly IDAS does not eliminate such prejudices. Hence, when designing conversational systems based on such inferred intents, extra care should be taken to prevent them from carrying over to conversational systems deployed in the wild.

Moreover, since IDAS's label generation process relies on LLMs, biases that exist in the data used to train these LLMs may be reinforced, leading to generated labels that may discriminate against or be harmful to certain demographics.

Acknowledgements

This work was funded in part by Flanders Innovation & Enterpreneurship (VLAIO), through Baekeland project-HBC.2019.2221 in collaboration with Sinch Chatlayer; and in part by the Flemish government under the "Onderzoeksprogramma Artificiële Intelligentie (AI) Vlaanderen" program.

[2]https://github.com/maarten-deraedt/IDAS-intent-discovery-with-abstract-summarization.

References

Somnath Banerjee, Krishnan Ramanathan, and Ajay Gupta. 2007. Clustering short texts using wikipedia. In *Proceedings of the 30th annual international ACM SIGIR conference on Research and development in information retrieval*, pages 787–788.

Tom Brown, Benjamin Mann, Nick Ryder, Melanie Subbiah, Jared D Kaplan, Prafulla Dhariwal, Arvind Neelakantan, Pranav Shyam, Girish Sastry, Amanda Askell, et al. 2020. Language models are few-shot learners. *Advances in neural information processing systems*, 33:1877–1901.

Mathilde Caron, Piotr Bojanowski, Armand Joulin, and Matthijs Douze. 2018a. Deep clustering for unsupervised learning of visual features. In *Proceedings of the European conference on computer vision (ECCV)*, pages 132–149.

Mathilde Caron, Piotr Bojanowski, Armand Joulin, and Matthijs Douze. 2018b. Deep clustering for unsupervised learning of visual features. In *Computer Vision – ECCV 2018*, pages 139–156, Cham. Springer International Publishing.

Iñigo Casanueva, Tadas Temčinas, Daniela Gerz, Matthew Henderson, and Ivan Vulić. 2020. Efficient intent detection with dual sentence encoders. In *Proceedings of the 2nd Workshop on Natural Language Processing for Conversational AI*, pages 38–45, Online. Association for Computational Linguistics.

Yanda Chen, Ruiqi Zhong, Sheng Zha, George Karypis, and He He. 2022. Meta-learning via language model in-context tuning. In *Proceedings of the 60th Annual Meeting of the Association for Computational Linguistics (Volume 1: Long Papers)*, pages 719–730, Dublin, Ireland. Association for Computational Linguistics.

Hyung Won Chung, Le Hou, Shayne Longpre, Barret Zoph, Yi Tay, William Fedus, Eric Li, Xuezhi Wang, Mostafa Dehghani, Siddhartha Brahma, Albert Webson, Shixiang Shane Gu, Zhuyun Dai, Mirac Suzgun, Xinyun Chen, Aakanksha Chowdhery, Sharan Narang, Gaurav Mishra, Adams Yu, Vincent Zhao, Yanping Huang, Andrew Dai, Hongkun Yu, Slav Petrov, Ed H. Chi, Jeff Dean, Jacob Devlin, Adam Roberts, Denny Zhou, Quoc V. Le, and Jason Wei. 2022. Scaling instruction-finetuned language models.

Dorin Comaniciu and Peter Meer. 2002. Mean shift: A robust approach toward feature space analysis. *IEEE Transactions on pattern analysis and machine intelligence*, 24(5):603–619.

Alexis Conneau, Douwe Kiela, Holger Schwenk, Loïc Barrault, and Antoine Bordes. 2017. Supervised learning of universal sentence representations from natural language inference data. In *Proceedings of the 2017 Conference on Empirical Methods in Natural Language Processing*, pages 670–680, Copenhagen, Denmark. Association for Computational Linguistics.

Martin Ester, Hans-Peter Kriegel, Jörg Sander, and Xiaowei Xu. 1996. A density-based algorithm for discovering clusters in large spatial databases with noise. In *Proceedings of the Second International Conference on Knowledge Discovery and Data Mining*, pages 226–231.

Brendan J Frey and Delbert Dueck. 2007. Clustering by passing messages between data points. *science*, 315(5814):972–976.

Tianyu Gao, Xingcheng Yao, and Danqi Chen. 2021. SimCSE: Simple contrastive learning of sentence embeddings. In *Proceedings of the 2021 Conference on Empirical Methods in Natural Language Processing*, pages 6894–6910, Online and Punta Cana, Dominican Republic. Association for Computational Linguistics.

Amir Hadifar, Lucas Sterckx, Thomas Demeester, and Chris Develder. 2019. A self-training approach for short text clustering. In *Proceedings of the 4th Workshop on Representation Learning for NLP (RepL4NLP-2019)*, pages 194–199, Florence, Italy. Association for Computational Linguistics.

Andreas Hotho, Steffen Staab, and Gerd Stumme. 2003. Ontologies improve text document clustering. In *Third IEEE international conference on data mining*, pages 541–544. IEEE.

Xiaohua Hu, Xiaodan Zhang, Caimei Lu, Eun K Park, and Xiaohua Zhou. 2009. Exploiting wikipedia as external knowledge for document clustering. In *Proceedings of the 15th ACM SIGKDD international conference on Knowledge discovery and data mining*, pages 389–396.

Ryan Kiros, Yukun Zhu, Russ R Salakhutdinov, Richard Zemel, Raquel Urtasun, Antonio Torralba, and Sanja Fidler. 2015. Skip-thought vectors. *Advances in neural information processing systems*, 28.

Harold W Kuhn. 1955. The hungarian method for the assignment problem. *Naval research logistics quarterly*, 2(1-2):83–97.

Stefan Larson, Anish Mahendran, Joseph J. Peper, Christopher Clarke, Andrew Lee, Parker Hill, Jonathan K. Kummerfeld, Kevin Leach, Michael A. Laurenzano, Lingjia Tang, and Jason Mars. 2019. An evaluation dataset for intent classification and out-of-scope prediction. In *Proceedings of the 2019 Conference on Empirical Methods in Natural Language Processing and the 9th International Joint Conference on Natural Language Processing (EMNLP-IJCNLP)*, pages 1311–1316, Hong Kong, China. Association for Computational Linguistics.

Ting-En Lin, Hua Xu, and Hanlei Zhang. 2020. Discovering new intents via constrained deep adaptive clustering with cluster refinement. In *Proceedings of the AAAI Conference on Artificial Intelligence*, volume 34, pages 8360–8367.

Jiachang Liu, Dinghan Shen, Yizhe Zhang, Bill Dolan, Lawrence Carin, and Weizhu Chen. 2022. What makes good in-context examples for GPT-3? In *Proceedings of Deep Learning Inside Out (DeeLIO 2022): The 3rd Workshop on Knowledge Extraction and Integration for Deep Learning Architectures*, pages 100–114, Dublin, Ireland and Online. Association for Computational Linguistics.

Stuart Lloyd. 1982. Least squares quantization in pcm. *IEEE transactions on information theory*, 28(2):129–137.

Xinxi Lyu, Sewon Min, Iz Beltagy, Luke Zettlemoyer, and Hannaneh Hajishirzi. 2022. Z-icl: Zero-shot in-context learning with pseudo-demonstrations. *arXiv preprint arXiv:2212.09865*.

George A Miller. 1995. Wordnet: a lexical database for english. *Communications of the ACM*, 38(11):39–41.

Sewon Min, Mike Lewis, Hannaneh Hajishirzi, and Luke Zettlemoyer. 2022a. Noisy channel language model prompting for few-shot text classification. In *Proceedings of the 60th Annual Meeting of the Association for Computational Linguistics (Volume 1: Long Papers)*, pages 5316–5330, Dublin, Ireland. Association for Computational Linguistics.

Sewon Min, Mike Lewis, Luke Zettlemoyer, and Hannaneh Hajishirzi. 2022b. MetaICL: Learning to learn in context. In *Proceedings of the 2022 Conference of the North American Chapter of the Association for Computational Linguistics: Human Language Technologies*, pages 2791–2809, Seattle, United States. Association for Computational Linguistics.

Sewon Min, Xinxi Lyu, Ari Holtzman, Mikel Artetxe, Mike Lewis, Hannaneh Hajishirzi, and Luke Zettlemoyer. 2022c. Rethinking the role of demonstrations: What makes in-context learning work? In *Proceedings of the 2022 Conference on Empirical Methods in Natural Language Processing*, pages 11048–11064, Abu Dhabi, United Arab Emirates. Association for Computational Linguistics.

Long Ouyang, Jeffrey Wu, Xu Jiang, Diogo Almeida, Carroll Wainwright, Pamela Mishkin, Chong Zhang, Sandhini Agarwal, Katarina Slama, Alex Gray, et al. 2022. Training language models to follow instructions with human feedback. In *Advances in Neural Information Processing Systems*.

Fabian Pedregosa, Gaël Varoquaux, Alexandre Gramfort, Vincent Michel, Bertrand Thirion, Olivier Grisel, Mathieu Blondel, Peter Prettenhofer, Ron Weiss, Vincent Dubourg, et al. 2011. Scikit-learn: Machine learning in python. *the Journal of machine Learning research*, 12:2825–2830.

Nils Reimers and Iryna Gurevych. 2019. Sentence-BERT: Sentence embeddings using Siamese BERT-networks. In *Proceedings of the 2019 Conference on Empirical Methods in Natural Language Processing and the 9th International Joint Conference on Natural Language Processing (EMNLP-IJCNLP)*, pages 3982–3992, Hong Kong, China. Association for Computational Linguistics.

Peter J Rousseeuw. 1987. Silhouettes: a graphical aid to the interpretation and validation of cluster analysis. *Journal of computational and applied mathematics*, 20:53–65.

Ohad Rubin, Jonathan Herzig, and Jonathan Berant. 2022. Learning to retrieve prompts for in-context learning. In *Proceedings of the 2022 Conference of the North American Chapter of the Association for Computational Linguistics: Human Language Technologies*, pages 2655–2671, Seattle, United States. Association for Computational Linguistics.

Xiang Shen, Yinge Sun, Yao Zhang, and Mani Najmabadi. 2021. Semi-supervised intent discovery with contrastive learning. In *Proceedings of the 3rd Workshop on Natural Language Processing for Conversational AI*, pages 120–129, Online. Association for Computational Linguistics.

Taylor Sorensen, Joshua Robinson, Christopher Rytting, Alexander Shaw, Kyle Rogers, Alexia Delorey, Mahmoud Khalil, Nancy Fulda, and David Wingate. 2022. An information-theoretic approach to prompt engineering without ground truth labels. In *Proceedings of the 60th Annual Meeting of the Association for Computational Linguistics (Volume 1: Long Papers)*, pages 819–862, Dublin, Ireland. Association for Computational Linguistics.

Karen Sparck Jones. 1972. A statistical interpretation of term specificity and its application in retrieval. *Journal of documentation*, 28(1):11–21.

Douglas Steinley. 2004. Properties of the hubert-arable adjusted rand index. *Psychological methods*, 9(3):386.

Tingting Wei, Yonghe Lu, Huiyou Chang, Qiang Zhou, and Xianyu Bao. 2015. A semantic approach for text clustering using wordnet and lexical chains. *Expert Systems with Applications*, 42(4):2264–2275.

Junyuan Xie, Ross Girshick, and Ali Farhadi. 2016a. Unsupervised deep embedding for clustering analysis. In *International conference on machine learning*, pages 478–487. PMLR.

Junyuan Xie, Ross Girshick, and Ali Farhadi. 2016b. Unsupervised deep embedding for clustering analysis. In *Proceedings of The 33rd International Conference on Machine Learning*, volume 48 of *Proceedings of Machine Learning Research*, pages 478–487, New York, New York, USA. PMLR.

Jiaming Xu, Peng Wang, Guanhua Tian, Bo Xu, Jun Zhao, Fangyuan Wang, and Hongwei Hao. 2015. Short text clustering via convolutional neural networks. In *Proceedings of the 1st Workshop on Vector Space Modeling for Natural Language Processing*, pages 62–69, Denver, Colorado. Association for Computational Linguistics.

Bo Yang, Xiao Fu, Nicholas D Sidiropoulos, and Mingyi Hong. 2017a. Towards k-means-friendly spaces: Simultaneous deep learning and clustering. In *international conference on machine learning*, pages 3861–3870. PMLR.

Bo Yang, Xiao Fu, Nicholas D. Sidiropoulos, and Mingyi Hong. 2017b. Towards k-means-friendly spaces: Simultaneous deep learning and clustering. In *Proceedings of the 34th International Conference on Machine Learning*, volume 70 of *Proceedings of Machine Learning Research*, pages 3861–3870. PMLR.

Dejiao Zhang, Feng Nan, Xiaokai Wei, Shang-Wen Li, Henghui Zhu, Kathleen McKeown, Ramesh Nallapati, Andrew O. Arnold, and Bing Xiang. 2021a. Supporting clustering with contrastive learning. In *Proceedings of the 2021 Conference of the North American Chapter of the Association for Computational Linguistics: Human Language Technologies*, pages 5419–5430, Online. Association for Computational Linguistics.

Hanlei Zhang, Xiaoteng Li, Hua Xu, Panpan Zhang, Kang Zhao, and Kai Gao. 2021b. TEXTOIR: An integrated and visualized platform for text open intent recognition. In *Proceedings of the 59th Annual Meeting of the Association for Computational Linguistics and the 11th International Joint Conference on Natural Language Processing: System Demonstrations*, pages 167–174, Online. Association for Computational Linguistics.

Hanlei Zhang, Hua Xu, Ting-En Lin, and Rui Lyu. 2021c. Discovering new intents with deep aligned clustering. *Proceedings of the AAAI Conference on Artificial Intelligence*, 35(16):14365–14373.

Haode Zhang, Yuwei Zhang, Li-Ming Zhan, Jiaxin Chen, Guangyuan Shi, Xiao-Ming Wu, and Albert Y.S. Lam. 2021d. Effectiveness of pre-training for few-shot intent classification. In *Findings of the Association for Computational Linguistics: EMNLP 2021*, pages 1114–1120, Punta Cana, Dominican Republic. Association for Computational Linguistics.

Yuwei Zhang, Haode Zhang, Li-Ming Zhan, Xiao-Ming Wu, and Albert Lam. 2022. New intent discovery with pre-training and contrastive learning. In *Proceedings of the 60th Annual Meeting of the Association for Computational Linguistics (Volume 1: Long Papers)*, pages 256–269, Dublin, Ireland. Association for Computational Linguistics.

Encoding	Banking			StackOverflow			CLINC			Average		
	ARI	NMI	ACC	ARI	NMI	ACC	ARI	NMI	ACC	ARI	NMI	ACC
MTP or `paraphrase-mpnet-base-v2`												
- $E(x)$	47.33	77.32	57.99	48.71	63.85	66.18	63.82	89.01	71.30	53.29	76.73	65.16
- $E(\ell)$	52.45	81.14	62.31	67.94	80.60	80.05	75.01	93.04	81.27	65.13	84.93	74.54
- $\phi_{\text{AVG}}(x, \ell)$	54.47	82.35	63.25	69.20	80.76	81.29	75.65	93.33	81.04	66.44	85.48	75.19
- $\phi_{\text{SMOOTH}}(x, \ell)$	57.56	82.84	67.43	72.20	81.26	83.82	79.02	93.82	85.48	69.59	85.97	78.91
`all-mpnet-base-v2`												
- $E(x)$	54.09	81.29	64.27	57.69	72.40	71.72	69.24	91.05	76.04	60.34	81.58	70.68
- $E(\ell)$	52.33	81.51	63.29	66.96	82.37	81.13	77.48	93.91	83.08	65.59	85.93	75.83
- $\phi_{\text{AVG}}(x, \ell)$	57.90	83.87	67.55	70.92	83.81	82.56	78.86	94.40	83.58	69.23	87.36	77.90
- $\phi_{\text{SMOOTH}}(x, \ell)$	**59.88**	**84.13**	**70.07**	**78.27**	**85.09**	**87.02**	**82.26**	**94.93**	**87.80**	**73.47**	**88.05**	**81.84**

Table 7: *Effect of using a more powerful sentence encoder.* The first four rows show the main results presented in §5.1, i.e., with the MTP encoder for Banking and StackOverflow, and with `paraphrase-mpnet-base-v2` for CLINC. The last four rows show the results of performing the final clustering (Step 4) with encoder `all-mpnet-base-v2`.

A Appendix

In §A.1, we analyze how using a more powerful pre-trained sentence encoder affects the cluster performance of `IDAS`. Additionally, we present and discuss the prompts in §A.2, and conduct a qualitative analysis of the generated labels produced by our `IDAS` approach in §A.3. Finally, in §A.4, we provide a brief overview of the implementation details of our experiments.

A.1 Effect of using a more powerful encoder

Here, we assess the impact of using a more powerful frozen pre-trained encoder on the clustering performance of `IDAS`. Specifically, we provide results of the four encoding strategies using the SBERT encoder `all-mpnet-base-v2` (Reimers and Gurevych, 2019) in Table 7. The overall results, presented in the three rightmost columns as the average of the scores across the three datasets, show that each encoding strategy for `all-mpnet-base-v2` (bottom half of the table) consistently improves upon the corresponding results for the encoder used in our previous main results (as repeated here in the top rows). However, the label-only encoding strategy ($E(\ell)$) achieves similar results for different encoders, likely because the labels already are a short disambiguated version of their associated utterances. Conversely, the other three strategies that exploit the original utterances x deliver substantially better results for `all-mpnet-base-v2`, as the advanced encoder can more effectively disambiguate utterances based on their latent intents, thus improving cluster performance. Notably, using `all-mpnet-base-v2` for the smoothing strategy ($\phi_{\text{SMOOTH}}(x, \ell)$) compared to using MTP (Banking, Stackoverflow) or `paraphrase-mpnet-base-v2` (CLINC), results in gains of +3.88%, +2.08%, and +2.93% in ARI, NMI, and ACC, respectively.

These results validate that employing more powerful pre-trained sentence encoders can further improve cluster performance out-of-the-box. It should be noted that, due to limitations in computation budget, we only replaced the encoder for Step 4 to induce intent clusters. However, we anticipate that using `all-mpnet-base-v2` also for Steps 1–2 could result in additional improvements.

A.2 Prompts

Figures 3–4 present the static prompts used to generate prototypical labels in Step 2.1 (§3.2) without demonstrations, as well as the ICL prompts for generating labels of non-prototypical utterances in Step 2.2 (§3.2). One advantage of instructing LLMs is the ability to specify additional information in the prompts. When clustering topic datasets, there typically is a general understanding of the broad topic according to which utterances should be partitioned, and this topic can be specified in the prompts used to instruct LLMs. Since StackOverflow pertains to topics rather than intents, we adopted a more specific prototypical label generation prompt to instruct the LLMs to directly summarize the utterances based on the "technology" they refer to. While this approach may not be effective for intent discovery (i.e., a single conversational dataset can contain intents from multiple topics as well as non-topic intents), we speculate that it could be applied to other topic classification datasets, e.g., News or Biomedical, where a prototypical prompt could instruct the LLM to identify the "news category" or "medical drug", "disease", etc. We defer exploring IDAS for topic clustering beyond StackOverflow to future work.

A.3 Qualitative Analysis

We conduct a qualitative analysis of IDAS's generated labels. Tables 8–10 show the generated labels for a subset of clusters induced in Step 4 for the corresponding StackOverflow, Banking, and CLINC datasets. For each presented cluster, we report (i) the generated labels with their associated counts in that cluster, and (ii) the majority gold intent, i.e., the most prevalent gold intent among utterances in that cluster, and the number of utterances within that cluster belonging to the majority gold intent.

Main findings: Overall, Tables 8–10 reveal that there is little variation among generated labels within a specific cluster. Specifically, for the majority of clusters, the most frequently occurring generated label has a notably higher count than the other generated labels, e.g., the first row in Table 8 shows that the label "*Magento*" is generated for 47 out of 49 utterances in that cluster. These findings further support our main hypothesis that abstract summarization increases the similarity in the input space of utterances with the same latent intent. Given the low variation across generated labels within clusters, we hypothesize that our generated labels could also make clusters more easy to interpret compared to utterance-only clustering, thereby potentially reducing the time required for manually inspecting clusters in real-world settings.

Slightly specific labels: While most clusters clearly contain a single label that appears much more frequently than other labels, there are some clusters, e.g., `pto_request`, `plug_type`, `reminder_update`, and `calories` for CLINC (Table 10), where this is not the case. However, a closer examination of these clusters reveals that the labels still exhibit low variation since they share the same syntactic and lexical structure. For instance, the `plug_type` cluster's generated labels mostly follow the "Plug Converter ⟨noun adjunct⟩" pattern, with only the noun adjunct being specific to the utterance from which the label is generated. Note that for our intent discovery purpose, these slightly more specific labels do not negatively impact cluster performance, as long as there is a high overlap in syntactical and lexical structure among generated labels.

Overly general labels: Although some utterances are summarized into slightly more specific labels, others may be summarized into overly general labels. For instance, in the banking cluster `exchange_via_app` (Table 9) the label "*Foreign currency exchange*" appears 25 times. However, 6 of those 25 utterances do not have `exchange_via_app` as their gold intent, despite having obtained the same generated label as those other 19 utterances that do. This is due to the fact that generated labels corresponding to more high-level intents may be assigned to utterances that belong to different intents but share that common more high-level intent. For instance, the utterances "*Can this app help me exchange currencies?*" and "*I want to make a currency exchange to EU*" have respective gold intents `exchange_via_app` and `fiat_currency_support`, yet both are summarized into a more high-level "*Foreign currency exchange*" label. In contrast to generated labels that are slightly too specific, overly general labels can adversely affect cluster performance, as they may incorrectly group together utterances that belong to different intents despite sharing a common high-level intent.

A.4 Implementation Details

For all presented experiments, the utterances are encoded (Steps 1, 3–4) on a 2.6 GHz 6-Core Intel Core i7 CPU, using a frozen pre-trained sentence encoder. Similarly, both the initial and final K-means clustering to respectively retrieve prototypes (Step 1) and infer latent intents (Step 4), are conducted on CPU. We adopt the K-means implementation of `scikit-learn` (Pedregosa et al., 2011), with default parameter values, i.e., using the algorithm of Lloyd (1982) and `n_init` = 10.

Banking

Describe the banking question in a maximum of 5 words.
question: {prototype} **label:**

Transport

Describe the transport question in a maximum of 5 words.
question: {prototype} **label:**

CLINC

Describe the chatbot question in a maximum of 5 words.
question: {prototype} **label:**

StackOverflow

Identify the technology in question.
question: {prototype} **technology:**

Fig. 3: *Static prototypical label generation prompts.* Note that since StackOverflow is a topic rather than an intent classification dataset, we adopt a slightly different prompt.

Transport

Classify the transport question into one of the provided labels.
(1) question: {demonstration 1}
(1) label: {label 1}
(2) question: {demonstration 2}
(2) label: {label 2}
...
(8) question: {demonstration 8}
(8) label: {label 8}

question: {input question}
label:

Banking

Classify the banking question into one of the provided labels.
(1) question: My card is about to expire. How do I get a new one?
(1) label: Get new card expiring
(2) question: Can I get a spare card for someone else to use?
(2) label: Additional card
...
(8) question: What do I do when my card is about to expire?
(8) label: Get new card expiring

question: Since my card is about to expire, I need a new one.
label:

CLINC

Classify the chatbot question into one of the provided labels.
(1) question: Please tell me what kind of gas this car needs
(1) label: Car gas type query
(2) question: Is there a type of gas i need to use for this car
(2) label: Car gas type query
...
(8) question: how many miles per gallon do i get
(8) label: Car gas mileage

question: What kind of gas will i need to put in this car
label:

StackOverflow

Classify the question into one of the provided technologies.
(1) question: When doing a tortoise svn merge, it includes a bunch of directories ...
(1) technology: Subversion (SVN)
(2) question: SVN how to resolve new tree conflicts when file is added on two branches
(2) technology: Subversion (SVN)
...
(8) question: how to put linq to sql in a separate project?
(8) technology: LINQ to SQL

question: Using svn for general purpose backup.
technology:

Fig. 4: *Prompts for non-prototypical label generation with ICL.*

Majority gold topic (# $y_{\text{GOLD}}/\lvert\mathcal{C}\rvert$)	**Generated labels** (# ℓ)		
`topic_20` (49/49)	Magento (47)	Magento CodeIgniter (1)	Shipping Method (1)
`topic_17` (44/45)	Drupal (35) Drupal and Ruby on Rails (1) Drupal and Microsoft SQL Server and Microsoft IIS 7 (1)	Drupal 6 (5) Drupal Ubercart (1)	Drupal 5 (1) Web View (1)
`topic_10` (43/49)	BASH scripting (30) BASH scripting (2) Shell scripting (1) Scriptaculous (1) SSH scripting (1)	Shell Scripting (5) Scripting (1) Pipe-separated files (1) Shell Scripting (1)	Bash (Unix Shell) (2) Scripting (1) Readline (1) Bash scripting (1)
`topic_6` (46/46)	Matlab (35) MATLAB (1) Matlab and C# (1) Ezplot (Matlab plotting tool) (1)	Matlab Octave (3) MatLab Mathematica (1) N/A (1)	Matrix (1) MatLab (1) Image Processing (1)
`topic_19` (45/46)	Haskell (40) Haskell HDBC (1) GHCi (Glasgow Haskell Compiler Interactive) (1)	Haskell Cabal (1) General Programming (1) GHCI (Glasgow Haskell Compiler Interactive) (1)	General Programming (1)
`topic_16` (42/45)	Qt (32) Qt4 (1) Qt (C++) (1) Real Time Video Capture (1)	Qt C++ (2) QT (1) QuickTime (1) QT (1)	Qt (C++ library) (2) QtScript (1) IP Camera (1) Quicksilver (1)
`topic_1` (45/48)	WordPress (38) Open Atrium (1) HTTP POST (1) WordPress, RESTful, SOAP, InterWoven TeamSite (1)	jQuery and cycle (1) Disqus (1) Blogging (1) Commenting (1)	Drupal and WordPress (1) WordPress, PHP (1) WordPress and Django (1)
`topic_5` (45/45)	Microsoft Excel (40) Microsoft Excel, Internet Information Services (IIS) (1)	Excel VBA (1) Microsoft Excel, Visual Basic (1)	Perl (1) Google Earth (1)
`topic_3` (47/53)	Subversion (SVN) (42) Apache web server and Subversion (SVN) (1) Subversion (SVN) and WebDAV (1) Subversion (SVN) and Apache web server (1)	File System (3) Subversion (SVN) and SharpSvn (1) Subversion (SVN) and Windows (1) Concurrent Versions System (CVS) (1)	Subversion (SVN) (1) Version Control (1)

Table 8: Generated labels that occur in selected `IDAS` clusters for StackOverflow, as well as the number of times # ℓ each label ℓ occurs in corresponding cluster $\mathcal{C}$. The majority gold topic y_{GOLD} of cluster $\mathcal{C}$ is the most prevalent gold topic among all utterances in y_{GOLD}, and # y_{GOLD} denotes the number of utterances in $\mathcal{C}$ with $y = y_{\text{GOLD}}$. Generated labels of utterances that have gold intents different than y_{GOLD} are highlighted in red. Since no descriptive topic names are provided for StackOverflow, we refer to them simply as numbered topics (`topic_x`)

Majority gold intent (# $y_{\text{GOLD}}/|\mathcal{C}|$)	**Generated labels** (# ℓ)	
lost_or_stolen_phone (38/38)	Lost phone banking app (37)	Switching phones banking app (1)
atm_support (35/35)	ATM card acceptance (25)	Find nearest ATM (10)
card_acceptance (24/27)	Card usage limits (24)	Card usage (3)
virtual_card_not_working (31/33)	Virtual card not working (31)	Virtual card not received (2)
contactless_not_working (37/39)	Contactless banking issue (37)	Banking login issues (2)
compromised_card (24/42)	Unauthorized card usage (24)	Unauthorized card usage (18)
age_limit (39/39)	Age requirement for banking (30)	Opening an account for family members (9)
terminate_account (40/41)	Close bank account (39) Change bank name (1)	Account closure advice (1)
card_about_to_expire (17/20)	Get new card expiring (17) Renew card banking (1)	Get new card swallowed (3)
card_delivery_estimate (13/13)	Delivery time in US (9) Delivery date selection (2)	Delivery time request (2)
country_support (17/17)	Banking countries operated in (14) Supported countries (1)	Banking locations (2)
automatic_topic (27/27)	Automated top-up option (14) Low balance top-up feature (5)	Auto top-up location query (7) Auto top-up activation issue (1)
receiving_money (14/18)	Banking - Salary Deposit (14) Banking - Types of Deposits (1)	Banking, Payment, Check (2) Banking, Deposit, Cheque (1)
receiving_money (10/19)	Configure salary in GBP (8) Convert currency to GBP (1) Convert currency to AUD (6)	Convert currency to GBP (2) Deposit Money in GBP (1) Convert currency to AUD GBP (1)
apple_pay_or_google_pay (40/40)	Top up with Google Pay (10) Apple Pay issue (10) Cost of Apple Pay (1)	Top up with Apple Pay (10) Top up with Apple Watch (8) Set up Apple Pay (1)
getting_spare_card (22/25)	Get second card banking (11) Link existing bank card (4) Get spare card banking (1)	Add card for family member (6) Link card to website (2) Choose bank card (1)
visa_or_mastercard (36/40)	Credit card offerings (19) Credit card application process (4) Credit card acceptance (1)	Credit card decision making (12) Card payment acceptance (3) Credit card eligibility (1)
balance_not_updated_after_cheque_or_cash_deposit (36/38)	Cash deposit not posted (25) Cheque deposit processing time (1) Cash deposit flagged (1) Direct Deposit not posted (1)	Cash deposit pending query (6) Cash deposit not accepted (1) Cash deposit to account (1)
exchange_via_app (27/51)	Foreign currency exchange (19) Currency conversion (1) Foreign currency exchange (6) Receive payment in foreign currency (5)	Currency exchange process (7) Cryptocurrency exchange (7) Cross-border payments (1) Discounts for frequent currency exchange (5)

Table 9: Generated labels that occur in selected IDAS clusters for Banking, as well as the number of times # ℓ each label ℓ occurs in corresponding cluster $\mathcal{C}$. The majority gold intent y_{GOLD} of cluster $\mathcal{C}$ is the most prevalent gold intent among all utterances in y_{GOLD}, and # y_{GOLD} denotes the number of utterances in $\mathcal{C}$ with $y = y_{\text{GOLD}}$. Generated labels of utterances that have gold intents different than y_{GOLD} are highlighted in red.

Majority gold intent (# $y_{\text{GOLD}}/|C|$)	**Generated labels** (# ℓ)	
`find_phone` (15/15)	Locate Phone Request (15)	
`vaccines` (15/15)	Travel Vaccination Needed (15)	
`exchange_rate` (15/15)	Currency Exchange Rate (15)	
`share_location` (15/15)	Share Location Request (15)	
`international_fees` (15/15)	International Transaction Fees (15)	
`report_fraud` (13/13)	Fraudulent Transaction Inquiry (11)	Report Fraudulent Activity (2)
`change_speed` (15/15)	Speak slower please (8)	Speak faster please (7)
`tire_pressure` (15/15)	Tire Air Pressure Query (14)	Tire air pressure query (1)
`international_visa` (15/16)	Need International Visa (15)	Intercontinental Meaning (1)
`pto_request_status` (13/17)	Vacation Request Status (12) Vacation Request Process (3)	Vacation request status (1) Vacation Request (1)
`weather` (15/17)	Weather forecast query (14) AC Temperature Query (1)	Meteorological Data for Tallahassee (1) Set AC Temperature (1)
`balance` (14/15)	Bank Account Balance (11) bank account balance (1)	Check Account Balance (2) Bank Account Balance (1)
`cancel_reservation` (15/16)	Cancel restaurant reservation (8) Cancel Reservations (1) Cancel reservation for Network (1)	Cancel dinner reservation (4) Call restaurant to cancel reservation (1) Cancel Appointment (1)
`pto_request` (11/11)	PTO request for March (3) PTO request for June (2) PTO request for First to Ninth (1) PTO request for July (1)	PTO request for May (2) PTO request for January (1) PTO request for January to February (1)
`plug_type` (15/15)	Plug Type Query (3) Plug Converter El Salvador (1) Plug Converter Mexico (2) Plug Converter Denmark (1) Plug Converter Z (1) Plug Converter Guam (1)	Plug Converter Barcelona (2) Plug in electronics? (1) Plug Converter Thailand (1) Plug Converter Israel (1) Plug Converter Cairo (1)
`reminder_update` (14/28)	Ask Reminder List (9) Set Reminder (3) Confirm Reminder Laundry (1) Set Reminder Trash Out (1) Set Reminder Movie (1) Set Reminder Bring Jacket (1) Set Reminder Conference (1) Set Reminder Booking (1)	Remind of Forgotten Task (3) Set Reminder Later (2) Set Reminder Later (1) Set Reminder Dog Medicine (1) Set Reminder Pick Up Stan (1) Set Reminder Take Out Oven (1) Set Reminder Pay Bills (1)
`calories` (15/21)	Calorie content of apple (2) Calorie content of peanut butter (1) Calorie content of Coke (1) Calorie content of bacon (1) Calorie content of KitKat (1) Calorie content of Cheetos (1) Nutrition Info for Brownies (1) Health benefits of avocados (1) Health benefits of chocolate (1) Calorie content of Peanut Butter and Jelly Sandwich (1)	Caloric value of cookie (1) Calorie content of fries (1) Calorie content of whole cashews (1) Calorie content of cookie (1) Calorie content of bagels (1) Calorie content of chocolate ice cream (2) Nutrition Facts for Cheerios (1) Health benefits of apples (1) Nutrition Info for Lay's Potato Chips (1)

Table 10: Generated labels that occur in selected IDAS clusters for CLINC, as well as the number of times # ℓ each label ℓ occurs in corresponding cluster C. The majority gold intent y_{GOLD} of cluster C is the most prevalent gold intent among all utterances in y_{GOLD}, and # y_{GOLD} denotes the number of utterances in C with y=y_{GOLD}. Generated labels of utterances that have gold intents different than y_{GOLD} are highlighted in red.

User Simulator Assisted Open-ended Conversational Recommendation System

Qiusi Zhan[1], Xiaojie Guo[2], Heng Ji[1], Lingfei Wu[3]
[1]University of Illinois Urbana-Champaign
[2]IBM Thomas J. Watson Research Center, [3]Pinterest
{qiusiz2, hengji}@illinois.edu
xguo7@gmu.edu, teddy.lfwu@gmail.com

Abstract

Conversational recommendation systems (CRS) have gained popularity in e-commerce as they can recommend items during user interactions. However, current open-ended CRS have limited recommendation performance due to their short-sighted training process, which only predicts one utterance at a time without considering its future impact. To address this, we propose a User Simulator (US) that communicates with the CRS using natural language based on given user preferences, enabling long-term reinforcement learning. We also introduce a framework that uses reinforcement learning (RL) with two novel rewards, i.e., recommendation and conversation rewards, to train the CRS. This approach considers the long-term goals and improves both the conversation and recommendation performance of the CRS. Our experiments show that our proposed framework improves the recall of recommendations by almost 100%. Moreover, human evaluation demonstrates the superiority of our framework in enhancing the informativeness of generated utterances. [1]

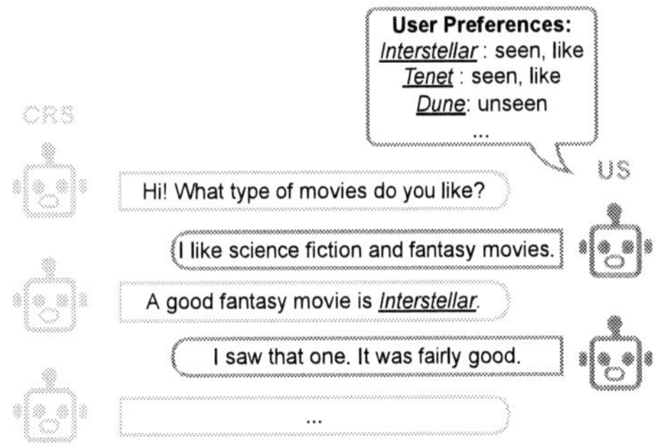

Figure 1: Overview of our proposed framework. The User Simulator (US) can interact with the Conversational Recommendation System (CRS) based on certain user preferences.

1 Introduction

Conversational Recommendation Systems (CRS) (Li et al., 2018; Chen et al., 2019; Zhou et al., 2020; Liang et al., 2021; Lei et al., 2020b; Deng et al., 2021; Yang et al., 2022) are of growing interest. Unlike traditional recommendation systems, CRS extract user preferences directly and recommend items during their interaction with users. Traditional CRS (Deng et al., 2021; Lei et al., 2020b,a) recommend an item or ask about the user preference of a specific attribute at a turn and use predefined question templates with item/attribute slots in practical applications, which are denoted as attribute-centric CRS. In addition, they often use reinforcement learning to learn a policy of recommending items and asking about attributes. Although such attribute-centric CRS are popular in industry due to its easy implementation, the user experience is unsatisfactory due to its lack of flexibility and interactivity. In addition, limited user information is collected by the CRS due to the constrained interaction format. To this end, open-ended CRS(Li et al., 2018; Chen et al., 2019; Zhou et al., 2020; Liang et al., 2021; Yang et al., 2022) are proposed to provide more flexible interactions with users. Such CRS can interact with the user like a real human-being, which focus on understanding user preferences according to their utterances and generating fluent responses to recommend items.

Although open-ended CRS can engage in natural and fluent conversations with users, their recommendation quality are often suboptimal. This is partly because these systems are typically trained using maximum likelihood estimation (MLE) to predict one utterance at a time, which hinders their ability to learn a long-term recommendation policy (Li et al., 2016b). Moreover, such MLE training fails to directly address the primary goal of CRS, which is to gradually explore user preferences and provide accurate, informative recommendations.

[1]Our code is released at https://github.com/ZQS1943/CRS_US.

Proceedings of the 5th Workshop on NLP for Conversational AI (NLP4ConvAI 2023), pages 89–101
July 14, 2023 ©2023 Association for Computational Linguistics

For instance, systems trained with MLE may generate generic and unhelpful responses, such as "*You're welcome. Bye.*"

Traditional attribute-centric CRS can learn effective recommendation policies by using reinforcement learning to enable a global view of the conversation. However, adapting this strategy to open-ended CRS is challenging due to the lack of a suitable User Simulator (US) for them. Developing a US for open-ended CRS is much harder than for attribute-centric CRS because it needs to generate natural-sounding utterances that are consistent with specific user preferences, rather than simply providing signal-level feedback as in the US for attribute-centric CRS. The US can serve not only as an environment for reinforcement learning but also provide more diverse and realistic human-like conversation scenarios and patterns than fixed training datasets. A suitable US for open-ended CRS would be a significant step toward improving their recommendation quality and making them more effective in real-world applications.

This paper proposes a framework that includes a CRS and a US to facilitate RL of the CRS. Specifically, we first develop a US for open-ended CRS, comprising three preference-aware modules that generate user utterances based on any given user preferences. Building on recent work in applying RL for dialogue generation (Tseng et al., 2021; Papangelis et al., 2019; Das et al., 2017; Li et al., 2016b), we propose optimizing the long-term performance of pre-trained CRS using RL during interaction with the US. We also introduce two rewards: the recommendation reward and the conversation reward, to better reflect the true objective of CRS. To the best of our knowledge, this is the first framework for training open-ended CRS in reinforcement learning strategies.

The contributions of this work are summarized as follows:

- We present the first US that can interact with the CRS using natural language based on specific user preferences. With three preference-aware modules, the proposed US not only gives the correct feedback to the CRS recommended items, but also expresses its preference actively to let the CRS know more about the user in a short dialog.

- We present the first framework for fine-tuning a pre-trained open-ended CRS with RL and introduce two rewards to improve both conversation and recommendation performance.

- Comprehensive experiments are conducted, which demonstrate that the proposed framework is powerful in improving both the accuracy of the recommendation and the informativeness of the generated utterances.

2 Methods

2.1 Overall Architecture

Formally, in the CRS scenario, we use u to denote a user from the user set $\mathcal{U}$ and i to denote an item from the item set $\mathcal{I}$. A dialog context can be denoted as a sequence of alternating utterances between the CRS and the user: $\{x_1^{crs}, x_1^{us}, x_2^{crs}, x_2^{us}, \cdots, x_t^{crs}, x_t^{us}\}$. In the t-th turn, the CRS generates an utterance x_t^{crs} that recommends the item $i_t \in \mathcal{I}$. Note that i_t can be None if x_t^{crs} is a chit-chat response or is a query to clarify the user preference and does not need to recommend. The user then provides a response x_t^{us}.

Our goal is to train the CRS with reinforcement learning to improve its long-term performance. Since online human interactive learning costs too much effort in training, a US is utilized to assist the RL process of the CRS, by simulating natural and personalized dialogue contexts. To train the overall framework, we first train a US that can simulate user utterances based on specific user preferences in each dialog, using supervised learning. We then fine-tune a pre-trained CRS by encouraging two novel rewards during the interaction with the US through reinforcement learning.

2.2 User Simulator

In this section, we present our US, which aims to interact with CRS using natural language based on any given user preferences. However, developing such a US comes with two main challenges: (1) the US must be able to express its preferences both actively and passively. It should provide accurate feedback on recommended items and actively express its preferences to quickly provide the CRS with more information in a short dialogue. (2) preserving the long-term preferences of the user creates a large search space for item selection, which can burden the US. Additionally, users are only interested in a small set of items in each dialogue, requiring the US to model dynamic user preferences

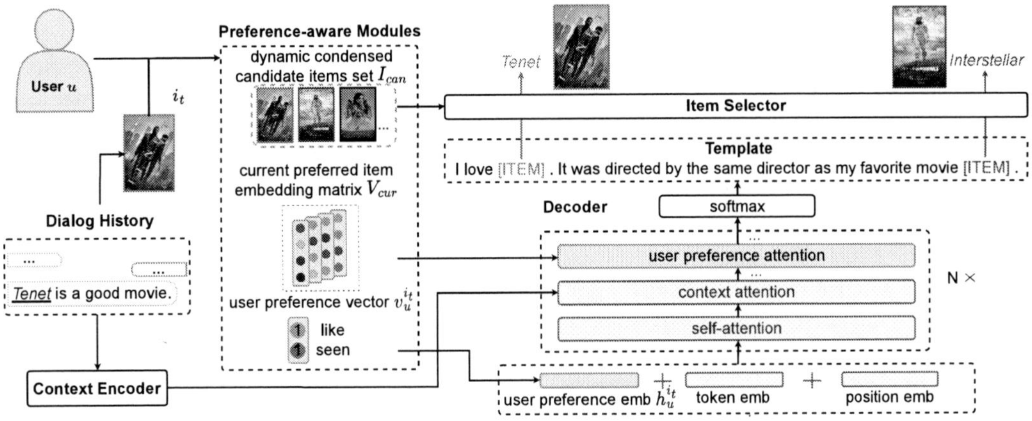

Figure 2: Our proposed User Simulator. Given the dialog history, a transformer-based Encoder-Decoder module enhanced with *user preference embedding* and *user preference attention* is used to generate a personalized response template with item slots. An Item Selector is used to select the appropriate items from the *dynamic condensed candidate items set* I_{can} based on the context and the user preference.

in the current dialogue. To address the first challenge, we propose two components: *User Preference Embedding* to capture the user's personalized characteristics for a recommended item, enabling the US to generate appropriate feedback, and *User Preference Attention* to prompt the US to express its preferred items. To tackle the second challenge, we employ the use of *Dynamic Condensed Candidate Item Set*, which captures the user's short-term preferences, thereby reducing the search space for item selection.

Figure 2 shows an overview of our proposed US, which is based on a dialog generation model NRTD (Liang et al., 2021). Given the dialogue context, we first utilize a knowledge-enhanced encoder-decoder-based template generator, depicted as the "context encoder" and "decoder" in Figure 2, to generate an utterance template with item slots. In the decoder module of the template generator, we incorporate *user preference embedding* to enhance token embedding with information about the last recommended item and add a *user preference attention* layer to incorporate user preferred items into the generated templates. Next, we use a template-aware item selector to select the appropriate items from a preference-based *dynamic condensed candidate items set*. We introduce these three preference-aware modules (*User Preference Embedding*, *User Preference Attention*, and *Dynamic Condensed Candidate Items Set*) in the following sections. We refer the reader to (Zhou et al., 2020) and (Liang et al., 2021) for more details of the whole model.

User Preference Embedding

When the CRS recommends an item, US is expected to provide the correct feedback for it. To achieve this, for each user u, we represent their *user preference vector* for item i as $v_u^i \in \mathbb{R}^{n_f}$, where n_f is the number of features to consider, such as a score indicating the user's liking for the item or a binary value indicating whether the user has purchased the item or not. We then map v_u^i to a continuous space using the following equation:

$$h_u^i = Wv_u^i \tag{1}$$

where $h_u^i \in \mathbb{R}^d$ represents the *user preference embedding*, and $W \in \mathbb{R}^{d \times n_f}$ is a learnable matrix.

When generating user utterances, we incorporate the user u's preference embedding of the last recommended item i_t, *i.e.*,$h_u^{i_t}$, into each word embedding to assist the US in generating accurate feedback for the recommended item i_t.

User Preference Attention

In addition to providing accurate feedback for recommended items, a good US should also actively express its preferences to provide the CRS with more information about the user. A user may have a large set of preferred items in the long-term, but in a short-term, during a current dialogue, they may be looking for specific types of items such as comedies, scary movies, etc. To this end, we define the user's *current preferred item set* $\mathcal{I}_{cur}$ as the set of user's short-term preferred items mentioned in a single dialogue in the dataset. We then use $V_{cur} \in \mathbb{R}^{d \times |\mathcal{I}_{cur}|}$ to denote *current preferred item embedding matrix*, where each column is a learnable representation of a preferred item enhanced by an external knowledge graph.

Then we add a multi-head attention layer, *i.e.*, $\mathrm{MHA}(Q, K, V)$, to each layer of the decoder to incorporate this user preference information:

$$R' = \mathrm{MHA}(R, V_{cur}, V_{cur}) \tag{2}$$

where $R \in \mathbb{R}^{d \times l}$ and $R' \in \mathbb{R}^{d \times l}$ are the embedding matrix before and after user preference attention in each layer of the decoder.

Dynamic Condensed Candidate Items Set

Searching through a large space of candidate items can impose a significant burden on the US in generating accurate and controllable utterances, especially when dealing with a large number of candidate items as seen in real-world scenarios. Furthermore, users' short-term preferences can change dynamically throughout a dialogue, which can affect the distribution of preferred items in the search space. To address this, we propose the use of a *dynamic condensed candidate item set* $\mathcal{I}_{can}$ which limits the number and quality of items, and the item selector can only select items from $\mathcal{I}_{can}$ for recommendation.

There are two key considerations in constructing the dynamic condensed candidate item set. First, as previously discussed, the US is expected to provide accurate feedback on the last recommended item i_t, therefore the last recommended item must be included in the set. Second, to accommodate the dynamic short-term preference of the users, the current preferred item set is also included, as $\mathcal{I}_{can} = \mathcal{I}_{cur} \cup \{i_t\}$.

Optimization of US

The entire User Simulator (US) is trained end-to-end, using human-written dialogues as supervision. For template generation, we use a standard cross-entropy loss L_{gen}. For item selection, we calculate the loss as the negative log-likelihood of the ground-truth item for an item slot, denoted as L_{sle}. We then combine the two losses with a weighting hyperparameter as follows:

$$L = \lambda L_{gen} + L_{sle} \tag{3}$$

We refer the reader to (Liang et al., 2021) for more details.

2.3 Reinforcement Learning of CRS

With the proposed US, we can fine-tune any pre-trained CRS using RL, based on its interactions with the US. Our US is able to create diverse training scenarios for the CRS by altering user preferences, which it uses as a basis for generating user utterances. In each dialog session, the CRS is fine-tuned based on a fixed user's *current preferred item set* $\mathcal{I}_{cur}$ from a dialog in the training set, with the aim of recommending items in $\mathcal{I}_{cur}$. This approach enables the CRS to model the long-term effects of a generated utterance and more closely imitate the true goal of a CRS, which is to recommend items that users will like, by utilizing designed rewards (Li et al., 2016b).

RL Components

An **action** a refers to a dialogue utterance generated by the CRS; the **state** is represented by the previous dialogue history c; the **policy** of the CRS model is represented by $p(a|c)$, defined by its parameters; r represents the **reward** obtained for each action.

Reward Design

Compared to RL in the task-oriented dialog (Tseng et al., 2021; Papangelis et al., 2019), the main challenge of RL in CRS is that there are no predefined dialog acts to use, and the model must take into account both the recommendation and the conversation performance, rather than simply selecting the best dialog act. To address this, we design two novel rewards for reinforcement learning in CRS training.

For the *recommendation reward*, inspired by the studies of attribute-centric CRS (Lei et al., 2020a,b; Deng et al., 2021), which use RL to enhance the efficiency of recommendations, our environment contains two types of rewards: (1) r_{rec_suc}, a positive reward when the user likes the recommended item, *i.e.*, the recommended item is in the user's *current preferred item set* I_{cur}, and (2) r_{rec_fail}, a negative reward when the user dislikes the recommended item.

For the *conversation reward*, we first provide a slightly positive reward r_{con_rec} when the generated utterance recommends an item, to encourage the CRS to make recommendations. Additionally, when recommending an item, the CRS should also explain why it chose the item, making it more persuasive. For instance, in the movie domain, the CRS may recommend a movie that shares the same actor as the user's favorite movie mentioned earlier. To encourage this, we construct a list of non-informative words, based on word frequency, excluding informative words about attributes of movies, such as movie genres and actor names. If the generated utterance contains a word that is not on this list of non-informative words, we consider it to be an informative utterance and provide a positive reward r_{con_info}. During our experiments, we also found that the CRS tends to use repeated templates to recommend different items in a single dialogue, which can make the conversation monotonous. To address this, we give slightly negative rewards r_{con_rep} to repeated templates.

Finally, the total reward is calculated as follows:

$$\begin{aligned} r =& \alpha(r_{rec\_suc} + r_{rec\_fail}) + \\ & \beta(r_{con\_rec} + r_{con\_info} + r_{con\_rep}) \end{aligned} \tag{4}$$

where α, β are weight hyperparameters.

Optimization of CRS

The model parameters are initialized using the pre-trained CRS model. We then use *Policy Gradient Theorem* (Sutton et al., 1999) to find parameters that maximize the expected reward, which can be written as

$$J(\theta) = \mathbb{E}[\sum_{i=1}^{T} R(a_i, c_i)] \tag{5}$$

where $R(a_i, c_i)$ denotes the reward resulting from action a_i given context c_i. We use the likelihood ratio trick (Williams, 1992; Li et al., 2016b) for gradient updates:

$$\nabla J(\theta) \approx \sum_{i} \nabla \log p(a_i|c_i) \sum_{i=1}^{i=T} R(a_i, c_i) \tag{6}$$

.

3 Experimental

3.1 Dataset

We conduct all the experiments on the *REcommendations through DIALog* (REDIAL) dataset(Li et al., 2018). It is collected on Amazon Mechanical Turk (AMT) platform where paired workers, recommender and seeker, make conversations about movie seeking and recommendation. It consists of 10006 dialogues with an average of 18.2 turns. 738 workers play the seeker roles at least in one dialog. There are 51699 movie mentions, of which 16278 are mentioned by the seeker and 35421 are recommended by the recommender. After the two workers complete the conversation, the system would ask the seeker to complete a table about whether he/she likes each mentioned movie or not and has seen it or not, which are the two features we use to model the user preferences. The seekers like most movies with more than 95% of all movie mentions are liked by the seekers. We first use the dialogues in the dataset to train the US in a supervision style. For the reinforcement learning of the CRS, at each round, we start the conversation based on the above-mentioned dataset, and continue the training of CRS during its interaction with the US, which is based on the user preference from the training data.

3.2 Evaluation Metrics

Following the previous open-ended work, we evaluate the CRS in terms of recommendation and conversation performance. However, existing works only evaluate the conversation quality locally, namely, one-round conversation, and the input dialogue history of the CRS is always the human-written utterances without any self-generated context. Thus, to evaluate the CRS in terms of its global performance in one dialog, we propose two novel global metrics in addition to the local evaluation. The details of the local metrics and the global metrics are provided as follows.

Local Metrics For recommendation evaluation, previous work often use *recall in response* (ReR), which shows whether the ground-truth item suggested by human is included in the final generated response. However, this deviates from the true goal of the CRS, which is to recommend user-liked items. Thus, we suggest expending the target item set to the user *current preferred item set* $\mathcal{I}_{cur}$, and using *recall of preferred items* (ReP) to measure whether the recommended item is included in $\mathcal{I}_{cur}$. For the evaluation of conversation, following previous work, we use *perplexity* (PPL) and *distinct n-gram* (Dist-n) (Li et al., 2016a) to measure the fluency and distinctiveness of generated utterances. We also use human evaluation to measure fluency and information quality.

Global Evaluation We propose two global metrics to evaluate the recommendation performance of the CRS during its interaction with the US. *Global recall* (GlobalRe) is calculated as the percentage of items recommended in the entire dialog that are in the user *current preferred item set* $\mathcal{I}_{cur}$. We also use *success rate* (Succ) where success means that the CRS has recommended at least one item that is in $\mathcal{I}_{cur}$ within a certain number of maximum turns. During the evaluation, the US employs user preferences, i.e., the *current preferred item set* $\mathcal{I}cur$ from the test set. This means that each user in a dialogue is treated as a distinct entity, and their $Icur$ represents the set of items mentioned in the dialogue that are liked by that particular user.

3.3 Implementation Details

Our framework can theoretically be paired with any CRS models.[2] In this experiment, we implement our model based on the CRS model NTRD (Liang et al., 2021), which consists of a recommendation component and a conversation component. We freeze the parameters of one component and train another one at a time using the corresponding reward to make the training process more stable. Both components are optimized with Adam optimizer with a batch size of 16. The maximum number of turns is set to 5. We train the recommendation component with a learning rate of 1e-4 for 20 epochs and the conversation component with a learning rate of 1e-7 for 40 epochs. On average, it takes approximately one hour to train an epoch with a Tesla P100GPU with 16GB of DRAM. For more implementation details, including the training of the US and the exact number of each reward, please refer to the Appendix.

3.4 Baselines

- **REDIAL** (Li et al., 2018): original model proposed with the dataset.
- **KBRD** (Chen et al., 2019): based on transformer, utilizing an external knowledge graph to enhance the item representations.
- **KGSF** (Zhou et al., 2020): utilized two external knowledge graphs to further enhance the user preference modelling.
- **NTRD** (Liang et al., 2021): proposes the two-step framework with a template generator and an item selector to better incorporate the recommended items into the generated responses.
- **RID** (Wang et al., 2021): utilizes the pre-trained language model to improve the CRS.
- **MESE** (Yang et al., 2022): also utilizes the pre-trained language model but use items meta information instead of the KG as the external knowledge.

3.5 Experimental Results

Machine-based Evaluation Table 1 shows the machine-based evaluation results of the models. Compared to the NTRD base model, our framework consistently improves the performance of the model in all metrics. In particular, our framework improves all recommendation metrics by almost 100%. This indicates that the CRS learns a good policy of recommending through the interaction with the US with the designed rewards. Note that after fine-tuning with our framework, the NTRD even outperforms the RID, which leverages a pre-trained language model (PLM) in terms of the recommendation.

The ablation study shows that both the recommendation reward and the conversation reward contribute to the final results. The conversation reward also improves the recommendation performance, which may be because a more informative response helps the model choose the correct items. The conversation reward improves the distinctiveness of generated utterances, since it encourages the model to generate more informative utterances.

Human-based Evaluation We asked three workers to read 100 randomly selected contexts and the generated response of each model and to give a score between 0 and 2 to evaluate both the fluency and the informativeness of the responses. Table 2 shows the average score of the human evaluation results. The intraclass correlation coefficient(ICC) between workers is 0.49 for fluency scores and 0.71 for informativeness scores. Our framework improves the performance of the base model NTRD, especially in terms of informativeness, which shows the effectiveness of the proposed design of the conversation reward.

Case Study of the US

In this section, we present an example to demonstrate the quality of our proposed US. Please refer to the Appendix for more cases. In Table 3, we compare the output of our proposed US with the

[2]We do not incorporate the proposed framework into CRSs (Yang et al., 2022; Wang et al., 2021) with pre-trained language models since it costs too much memory to perform reinforcement learning.

Model	Recommendation metrics				Conversation metrics			
	Local metrics		Global metrics					
	ReR ↑	ReP ↑	GlobalRe ↑	Succ ↑	PPL ↓	Dist2 ↑	Dist3 ↑	Dist4 ↑
ReDial	0.7	-	-	-	28.1	0.225	0.236	0.228
KBRD	0.8	-	-	-	17.9	0.263	0.368	0.423
KGSF	1.1	-	-	-	8.3	0.302	0.431	0.508
NTRD	1.7	11.7	5.7	26.7	6.41	0.569	0.804	0.940
Ours (NTRD)	**3.2**	**22.3**	**12.2**	**50.5**	**6.23**	0.528	0.807	1.010
- w/o con-R	2.8	18.3	11.5	49.8	6.41	0.449	0.670	0.807
- w/o rec-R	1.9	14.2	6.7	29.9	**6.23**	**0.671**	**0.965**	**1.169**
RID*	3.1	-	-	-	54.1	0.518	0.624	0.598
MESE*	6.4	-	-	-	12.9	0.822	1.152	1.313

Table 1: **Machine-based Evaluation.** * indicates leveraging of pre-trained transformer-based models. We **bold** the best result on the same base model NTRD; underline the best result on all models.

Model	Fluency	Informativeness
NTRD	1.44	0.46
Ours (NTRD)	**1.65**	**0.79**

Table 2: **Human-based Evaluation.**

Case Study of the User Simulator	
User Preferences	*Iron Man 2*: seen, liked *The Avengers*: seen, liked *It*: unseen, liked *Ant Man*: seen, liked
Human:	I would like to watch any movie. Tell me any movie Like *Ant Man*.
CRS:	Have you seen *The Avengers*?
US:	I have seen that one. I also liked *Iron Man 2*.
- w/o PAM:	I haven't see that one. Is it good?
Human:	I really enjoyed that one. Yes and I liked it. Which another one would you recommend me?
CRS:	Do you like scary movies? Have you seen *It*?
US:	I have not seen that one. I will check it out.
- w/o PAM:	I have not seen that one.
Human:	I watched *Iron Man 2* and I liked it.
	...

Table 3: A case study comparing the user utterances generated by our model, the baseline, and the ground truth. We mark the item mentions in blue color.

baseline which has no preference-aware modules (PAM) and with the human written response. The US without PAM generates utterances simply with higher probability; that is, the user has not seen the movie recommended by the CRS. This may be contradictory to user preferences: When the CRS recommends the movie *The Avengers*, the baseline says that it has not seen the movie, which is not true, since the user has seen and liked it. Instead, our US with preference-aware modules provides the correct feedback for two recommendations, *The Avengers* and *It*. Furthermore, our US can actively express its preference to help the CRS know more about it: it actively says that it likes the movie *Iron Man 2*.

Case Study of the CRS Table 4 shows some examples of the responses generated by NTRD and our model given the same context. In the first case, the NTRD generates a general response that is not fluent with the context, while our model, which is the RL fine-tuned NTRD, recommends a movie with a description of the movie. In the second case, our model recommends the movie *It* which is a scary movie consistent with the user's short-term preference. These indicate that our framework can improve the informativeness of the responses by providing more details of the recommended movie. In the third case, our model recommends a movie and introduces its actress. However, the actress does not play any role in the movie, which shows the limitation of current CRSs, that is, it cannot guarantee the correctness of the generated information in a fine-grained way.

Remaining Challenges

Though effective, improvements in the CRS are highly dependent on the good quality of the US. Currently, we only use reinforcement learning to optimize the CRS. However, previous work (Tseng et al., 2021) shows that joint-learning of the dialog system and the US can further enhance the performance of the dialog system. We leave the joint learning of the CRS and the US for future work.

Case Study of the Conversational Recommendation System			
Context		CRS responses	
...		NTRD:	I think you will like it.
CRS:	If you like action movies that are also sci-fi, there's *Star Wars*.	Ours:	*Jumanji* is a good action packed comedy.
User:	Yes, I did like all of the *Star Wars* movies. I also like *Paycheck*.		
...		NTRD:	I like *Freddy vs. Jason*.
CRS:	I think *Scream* was a fail as far as being scary, but it was a good movie overall.	Ours:	*It* is a good one if you like scary movie.
User:	I have seen all of the *Halloween* and *Jason X*.		
CRS:	Hello. How is your night going?	NTRD:	*Fargo* is a good one.
User:	Hi. I'm looking for a movie. One that is funny but not too stupid.	Ours:	*The Naked Gun* is a funny movie with Jennifer Lawrence.

Table 4: Case studies comparing the CRS responses generated by the original NTRD and our improved model given the same contexts. We only give the last turn of the dialog history to save space here. We mark the item mentions in blue color, and the user preferences in red color.

4 Related Work

Conversational Recommendation System Current CRS studies can be roughly categorized into two directions (Liang et al., 2021): (1)Attribute-centric CRS (Deng et al., 2021; Lei et al., 2020b,a; Zhang et al., 2022). These systems ask questions about the user preferences of certain attributes or make recommendations at each turn and gradually narrow down the hypothesis space of items to make optimal recommendations. These studies focus on the recommendation part and use question/answer templates with attribute or item slots. They often use reinforcement learning to achieve better recommending and asking policies. (2)Open-ended CRS (Li et al., 2018; Chen et al., 2019; Zhou et al., 2020; Liang et al., 2021; Yang et al., 2022). These studies focus on understanding user preferences according to user utterances and generating fluent responses to recommend items. Compared to attribute-centric CRSs, open-ended CRSs have more free-style recommendations and more flexible interactions, which provides a better user experience. In this paper, we focus on open-ended CRSs and borrow the idea of improving the recommendation by reinforcement learning from the studies of attribute-centric CRSs.

User Simulator Traditional USs are rule-based such as the agenda-based user simulator (ABUS) (Schatzmann and Young, 2009; Li et al., 2016c). For different tasks, ABUS needs to design different hand-crafted structures, which poses challenges in scenario shifting. Data-driven US(Asri et al., 2016; Gur et al., 2018) is another line of work. A seq2seq model is used to generate semantic-level dialog acts (Asri et al., 2016; Gur et al., 2018; Tseng et al., 2021) or natural languages (Kreyssig et al., 2018). However, most of the USs are designed for task-oriented dialog systems and cannot be directly used for CRS. To the best of our knowledge, our work is the first to explore US for open-ended CRS that can generate consistent responses based on certain user preferences.

5 Conclusion

In this paper, we propose a framework to be packed with any CRS to improve its recommendation accuracy and language informativeness. We first build a User Simulator for open-ended CRS with three preference-aware modules to give the appropriate feedback to the CRS based on certain user preferences. We then fine-tune a pre-trained CRS with reinforcement learning based on its interaction with the US with two types of designed rewards. Experiments demonstrate that our framework can significantly improve the recall of the recommendation, and human evaluation shows that the generated language is more informative with more descriptions of the recommended items. For future work, the first is to use joint optimization of CRS and US to further improve the interactive qualities, and the second is to explore the generalizability of the framework to other domains of recommendation.

6 Limitations

The proposed framework has a limitation in terms of the large GPU resources required, as it necessitates double the memory compared to training a CRS alone. Due to this limitation, we have to forego the use of pre-trained language models such as BERT, which could have been beneficial in enhancing language quality, but their extreme memory requirements make it infeasible.

References

Layla El Asri, Jing He, and Kaheer Suleman. 2016. A sequence-to-sequence model for user simulation in spoken dialogue systems. In *Interspeech 2016, 17th Annual Conference of the International Speech Communication Association, San Francisco, CA, USA, September 8-12, 2016*, pages 1151–1155. ISCA.

Qibin Chen, Junyang Lin, Yichang Zhang, Ming Ding, Yukuo Cen, Hongxia Yang, and Jie Tang. 2019. Towards knowledge-based recommender dialog system. In *Proceedings of the 2019 Conference on Empirical Methods in Natural Language Processing and the 9th International Joint Conference on Natural Language Processing, EMNLP-IJCNLP 2019, Hong Kong, China, November 3-7, 2019*, pages 1803–1813. Association for Computational Linguistics.

Abhishek Das, Satwik Kottur, José M. F. Moura, Stefan Lee, and Dhruv Batra. 2017. Learning cooperative visual dialog agents with deep reinforcement learning. In *IEEE International Conference on Computer Vision, ICCV 2017, Venice, Italy, October 22-29, 2017*, pages 2970–2979. IEEE Computer Society.

Yang Deng, Yaliang Li, Fei Sun, Bolin Ding, and Wai Lam. 2021. Unified conversational recommendation policy learning via graph-based reinforcement learning. In *SIGIR '21: The 44th International ACM SIGIR Conference on Research and Development in Information Retrieval, Virtual Event, Canada, July 11-15, 2021*, pages 1431–1441. ACM.

Izzeddin Gur, Dilek Hakkani-Tür, Gökhan Tür, and Pararth Shah. 2018. User modeling for task oriented dialogues. In *2018 IEEE Spoken Language Technology Workshop, SLT 2018, Athens, Greece, December 18-21, 2018*, pages 900–906. IEEE.

Florian Kreyssig, Iñigo Casanueva, Pawel Budzianowski, and Milica Gasic. 2018. Neural user simulation for corpus-based policy optimisation of spoken dialogue systems. In *Proceedings of the 19th Annual SIGdial Meeting on Discourse and Dialogue, Melbourne, Australia, July 12-14, 2018*, pages 60–69. Association for Computational Linguistics.

Wenqiang Lei, Xiangnan He, Yisong Miao, Qingyun Wu, Richang Hong, Min-Yen Kan, and Tat-Seng Chua. 2020a. Estimation-action-reflection: Towards deep interaction between conversational and recommender systems. In *WSDM '20: The Thirteenth ACM International Conference on Web Search and Data Mining, Houston, TX, USA, February 3-7, 2020*, pages 304–312. ACM.

Wenqiang Lei, Gangyi Zhang, Xiangnan He, Yisong Miao, Xiang Wang, Liang Chen, and Tat-Seng Chua. 2020b. Interactive path reasoning on graph for conversational recommendation. In *KDD '20: The 26th ACM SIGKDD Conference on Knowledge Discovery and Data Mining, Virtual Event, CA, USA, August 23-27, 2020*, pages 2073–2083. ACM.

Jiwei Li, Michel Galley, Chris Brockett, Jianfeng Gao, and Bill Dolan. 2016a. A diversity-promoting objective function for neural conversation models. In *NAACL HLT 2016, The 2016 Conference of the North American Chapter of the Association for Computational Linguistics: Human Language Technologies, San Diego California, USA, June 12-17, 2016*, pages 110–119. The Association for Computational Linguistics.

Jiwei Li, Will Monroe, Alan Ritter, Dan Jurafsky, Michel Galley, and Jianfeng Gao. 2016b. Deep reinforcement learning for dialogue generation. In *Proceedings of the 2016 Conference on Empirical Methods in Natural Language Processing, EMNLP 2016, Austin, Texas, USA, November 1-4, 2016*, pages 1192–1202. The Association for Computational Linguistics.

Raymond Li, Samira Ebrahimi Kahou, Hannes Schulz, Vincent Michalski, Laurent Charlin, and Chris Pal. 2018. Towards deep conversational recommendations. In *Advances in Neural Information Processing Systems 31: Annual Conference on Neural Information Processing Systems 2018, NeurIPS 2018, December 3-8, 2018, Montréal, Canada*, pages 9748–9758.

Xiujun Li, Zachary C. Lipton, Bhuwan Dhingra, Lihong Li, Jianfeng Gao, and Yun-Nung Chen. 2016c. A user simulator for task-completion dialogues. *CoRR*, abs/1612.05688.

Zujie Liang, Huang Hu, Can Xu, Jian Miao, Yingying He, Yining Chen, Xiubo Geng, Fan Liang, and Daxin Jiang. 2021. Learning neural templates for recommender dialogue system. In *Proceedings of the 2021 Conference on Empirical Methods in Natural Language Processing, EMNLP 2021, Virtual Event / Punta Cana, Dominican Republic, 7-11 November, 2021*, pages 7821–7833. Association for Computational Linguistics.

Alexandros Papangelis, Yi-Chia Wang, Piero Molino, and Gökhan Tür. 2019. Collaborative multi-agent dialogue model training via reinforcement learning. In *Proceedings of the 20th Annual SIGdial Meeting on Discourse and Dialogue, SIGdial 2019, Stockholm, Sweden, September 11-13, 2019*, pages 92–102. Association for Computational Linguistics.

Jost Schatzmann and Steve J. Young. 2009. The hidden agenda user simulation model. *IEEE Trans. Speech Audio Process.*, 17(4):733–747.

Richard S. Sutton, David A. McAllester, Satinder Singh, and Yishay Mansour. 1999. Policy gradient methods for reinforcement learning with function approximation. In *Advances in Neural Information Processing Systems 12, [NIPS Conference, Denver, Colorado, USA, November 29 - December 4, 1999]*, pages 1057–1063. The MIT Press.

Bo-Hsiang Tseng, Yinpei Dai, Florian Kreyssig, and Bill Byrne. 2021. Transferable dialogue systems and user simulators. In *Proceedings of the 59th Annual*

Meeting of the Association for Computational Linguistics and the 11th International Joint Conference on Natural Language Processing, ACL/IJCNLP 2021, (Volume 1: Long Papers), Virtual Event, August 1-6, 2021, pages 152–166. Association for Computational Linguistics.

Lingzhi Wang, Huang Hu, Lei Sha, Can Xu, Kam-Fai Wong, and Daxin Jiang. 2021. Finetuning large-scale pre-trained language models for conversational recommendation with knowledge graph. *CoRR*, abs/2110.07477.

Ronald J. Williams. 1992. Simple statistical gradient-following algorithms for connectionist reinforcement learning. *Mach. Learn.*, 8:229–256.

Bowen Yang, Cong Han, Yu Li, Lei Zuo, and Zhou Yu. 2022. Improving conversational recommendation systems' quality with context-aware item meta-information. In *Findings of the Association for Computational Linguistics: NAACL 2022, Seattle, WA, United States, July 10-15, 2022*, pages 38–48. Association for Computational Linguistics.

Yiming Zhang, Lingfei Wu, Qi Shen, Yitong Pang, Zhihua Wei, Fangli Xu, Bo Long, and Jian Pei. 2022. Multiple choice questions based multi-interest policy learning for conversational recommendation. In *WWW '22: The ACM Web Conference 2022, Virtual Event, Lyon, France, April 25 - 29, 2022*, pages 2153–2162. ACM.

Kun Zhou, Wayne Xin Zhao, Shuqing Bian, Yuanhang Zhou, Ji-Rong Wen, and Jingsong Yu. 2020. Improving conversational recommender systems via knowledge graph based semantic fusion. In *KDD '20: The 26th ACM SIGKDD Conference on Knowledge Discovery and Data Mining, Virtual Event, CA, USA, August 23-27, 2020*, pages 1006–1014. ACM.

A Appendix

A.1 User Preferences Extension

For each user u, we know its preference vectors of a constrained set of movies $\mathcal{I}^u_{known}$ from the dataset. We need to extend the user preference to each movie $i \in \mathcal{I}$, since during the interaction between the US and the CRS, the CRS may recommend a movie that is not in $\mathcal{I}^u_{known}$. Therefore, for each movie i_{unk} that is not in $\mathcal{I}^u_{known}$, we consider that the user u has not seen it. We then calculate the cosine similarities between i_{unk} and each movie in $\mathcal{I}^u_{known}$ and set the like/dislike label of i_{unk} the same as the closest movie to it, *i.e.*,

$$i^* =_{i \in \mathcal{I}_{known}} \cos\left((i), (i_{unk})\right) \tag{7}$$

, where (i) returns the embedding of the movie i, and the user u has the same like/dislike label to i_{unk} and i^*.

A.2 Hyper-parameters for Reproducing

The Hyper-parameters of RL

In this section, we introduce the detailed setting of reinforcement learning of the Conversational Recommendation System (CRS). To train the recommendation component, we only use recommendation rewards *i.e.*, $\alpha = 1, \beta = 0$, and for the conversation component, we only use conversation rewards *i.e.*, $\alpha = 0, \beta = 1$. Detailed reward values are listed in Table 5.

Reward Type	Value
r_{rec_suc}	5
r_{rec_fial}	0
r_{con_rec}	1
r_{con_info}	5
r_{con_rep}	-5

Table 5: The reward values of the RL of CRS.

The Hyper-parameters of the User Simulator

In this section, we introduce the hyper-parameters of the architecture of the User Simulator (US). The US consists of a template generator and an item selector, where the backbone of each component is a transformer with multi-head attentions. We use $\lambda = 5$ as the weight for generation loss L_{gen} and item selection loss L_{sle}. We train the US using Adam optimizer with a learning rate of 1e-3 and a batch size of 32 for 90 epochs. Detailed hyper-parameters for architecture are listed in Table 6.

Hyper-parameters	Value
num_attention_heads	2
num_hidden_layers	2
embedding_size	300
hidden_size	128
intermediate_size	300
gradient_clipping	0.1
dropout_prob	0.1
attention_dropout_prob	0
hidden_act	"relu"
relu_dropout_prob	0.1
max_context_length	256
max_response_length	30
vocab_size	17641

Table 6: The detailed hyper-parameters of the US.

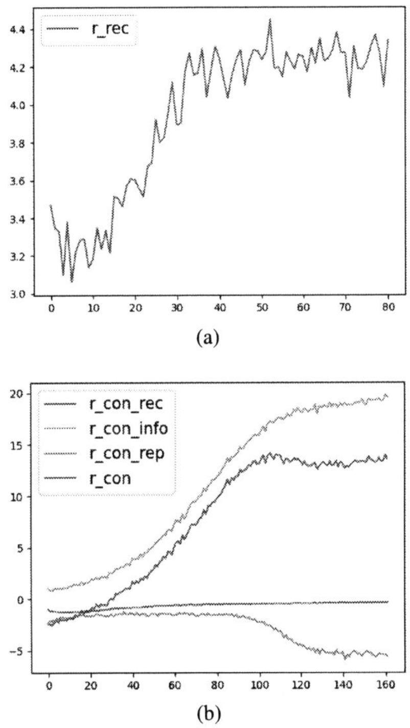

Figure 3: Averaged recommendation rewards (a) and conversation rewards (b) curve of the policies.

A.3 Reward Curves of RL

Figure 3 shows the average reward the policies receive at each 2000 steps during the training process. For the recommendation component, the rewards quickly converge, as the action space is limited by the number of the entire set of items $\mathcal{I}$. However, the reinforcement learning of the conversation component is much more unstable, since it needs to generate fluent utterances, and the action space

	NTRD with the US	Ours (NTRD) with the US
User Preferences:	*Taken*: unseen, like *Avengers: Infinity War (2018)*: seen, like *Die Hard*: unseen, like *Spider-Man*: seen, like	*Black Panther*: seen, like *The Sixth Battalion*: unseen, like *Thor: Ragnarok*: unseen, like *The Avengers*: unseen, like
(given) CRS:	What kind of movies do you like? Have you seen *Avengers: Infinity War*? or *Spider-Man*?	
(given) US:	Yes and i liked them. Those are awesome. I like that kind of movies.	
CRS:	*Thor: Ragnarok* is a good one.	*Black Panther* is a great comedy movie.
US:	I haven't seen that one yet.	Yes, I have seen that one. I liked it.
CRS:	*The Avengers* is a good one.	*The Avengers* is a great movie!
US:	I haven't seen that one yet.	I have not seen that one yet.
CRS:	I haven't seen that one. I'll check it out.	*Spider-Man* is a great movie.
US:	I will have to check it out.	Yes, I have seen that one. It was great.
CRS:	I hope you enjoy them!	*Die Hard* is a great movie.
US:	I will have to check it out.	I have not seen that one yet.
CRS:	I hope you enjoy them!	*Taken* is a classic.
US:	Thank you for your help.	I have not seen that one yet.
User Preferences:	*Porky's*: unseen, like *The Avengers*: unseen, like *Fist Fight*: unseen, like *Homecoming*: seen, like *Taken*: unseen, like	*Pineapple Express*: seen, like *The Hangover*: unseen, like *Animal House*: unseen, like *House*: seen, like
(given) CRS:	Hi there. Do you like movies?	
(given) US:	Hi. I like fun movies. I like *Homecoming*.	
CRS:	I have not seen that one. Is it a good one.	Have you seen *Porky's*?
US:	I have not seen that one.	I haven't seen either of those.
CRS:	*Pineapple Express* is a good one.	*Animal House* is a great comedy with Kevin Hart.
US:	I have not seen that one.	I haven't seen that one yet.
CRS:	*The Avengers* is a good one.	*Fist Fight* is a good comedy also.
US:	I have not seen that one.	I 'm not sure if I have seen that one.
CRS:	I have not seen that one. Is it a good one.	*The Hangover* is a good comedy with Bradley Cooper.
US:	I have not seen that one.	I haven't seen that one either.
CRS:	I have not seen that one. Is it a good one.	*Taken* is a classic.
US:	I have not seen that one.	I have not seen that one yet.

Table 7: Interactive Cases. Comparison of CRSs before (NTRD) and after (Ours) fine-tuning with reinforcement learning.

is infinite. Thus, we use a small learning rate and more steps to train the component. During training, the total reward (red curve) increases and converges. However, the convergence status consists of a high informative reward and a low repetition reward, which is caused by the model keeping generate simple but informative utterances like "xxx is a good comedy". This shows a limitation of our design of informative rewards: Though simple and effective, it is only a binary reward with informative or noninformative, which lacks the ability to judge the level informativeness. Therefore, the utterance "xxx is a good sci-fi" and "xxx is a sci-fi about a human trying to find another habitable planet." would get the same informative score, but obviously the latter one contains more information about the movie and deserves a higher score. In future work, we will design a better informative reward to encourage the model to generate more informative utterances and make the recommendations more persuasive.

A.4 Interactive Cases

Table 7 shows two cases of interactive conversations between the US and CRSs before and after fine-tuning with reinforcement learning. Given the first turn of the conversation, the US and CRS continue to interact for 5 turns. In each dialog, the US is based on different user preferences. Generally speaking, our CRS has a more fluent conversation with the US. The NTRD tends to generate generic utterances, and the conversation becomes stuck in an infinite loop of repetitive responses. Another improvement of our CRS is that it generates more informative utterances when recommending items, which are highlighted with red. However, as we discussed in the paper, there may be some mistakes when talking about actors / actresses: while Bradley Cooper plays an important role in *The Hangover*, Kevin Hart does not play any role in *Animal House*.

Evaluating Inter-Bilingual Semantic Parsing for Indian Languages

Divyanshu Aggarwal[1*], **Vivek Gupta**[2*], **Anoop Kunchukuttan**[3,4]
[1]American Express, AI Labs; [2]University of Utah; [3]Microsoft; [4]AI4Bharat
divyanshu.aggarwal1@aexp.com; vgupta@cs.utah.edu ; ankunchu@microsoft.com

Abstract

Despite significant progress in Natural Language Generation for Indian languages (IndicNLP), there is a lack of datasets around complex structured tasks such as semantic parsing. One reason for this imminent gap is the complexity of the logical form, which makes English to multilingual translation difficult. The process involves alignment of logical forms, intents and slots with translated unstructured utterance. To address this, we propose an Inter-bilingual Seq2seq Semantic parsing dataset IE-SEMPARSE for 11 distinct Indian languages. We highlight the proposed task's practicality, and evaluate existing multilingual seq2seq models across several train-test strategies. Our experiment reveals a high correlation across performance of original multilingual semantic parsing datasets (such as mTOP, multilingual TOP and multiATIS++) and our proposed IE-SEMPARSE suite.

1 Introduction

Task-Oriented Parsing (TOP) is a Sequence to Sequence (seq2seq) Natural Language Understanding (NLU) task in which the input utterance is parsed into its logical sequential form. Refer to Figure 1 where logical form can be represented in form of a tree with intent and slots as the leaf nodes (Gupta et al., 2018; Pasupat et al., 2019). With the development of seq2seq models with self-attention (Vaswani et al., 2017), there has been an upsurge in research towards developing *generation* models for complex TOP tasks. Such models explore numerous training and testing strategies to further enhance performance (Sherborne and Lapata, 2022; Gupta et al., 2022). Most of the prior work focus on the English TOP settings.

However, the world is largely multilingual, hence new conversational AI systems are also expected to cater to the non-English speakers. In that regard works such as mTOP (Li et al.,

[*]Equal Contribution

Figure 1: TOP vs Bilingual TOP.

2021), multilingual-TOP (Xia and Monti, 2021), multi-ATIS++ (Xu et al., 2020; Schuster et al., 2019), MASSIVE dataset (FitzGerald et al., 2022) have attempted to extend the semantic parsing datasets to other multilingual languages. However, the construction of such datasets is considerably harder since mere translation does not provide high-quality datasets. The logical forms must be aligned with the syntax and the way sentences are expressed in different languages, which is an intricate process.

Three possible scenarios for parsing multilingual utterances exists, as described in Figure 1. For English monolingual TOP, we parse the English utterance to it's English logical form, where the slot values are in the English language. Seq2Seq models (Raffel et al., 2019; Lewis et al., 2020) tuned on English TOP could be utilized for English specific semantic parsing. Whereas, for multi lingual setting, a *Indic* multilingual TOP (e.g. Hindi Multilingual TOP in Figure 1) is used to parse Indic utterance to it's respective Indic logical form. Here, the slot values are also Indic (c.f. Figure 1).[1]

The English-only models, with their limited input vocabulary, produce erroneous translations as it requires utterance translation. The multilingual models on the other side require larger multilingual vocabulary dictionaries (Liang et al., 2023; Wang et al., 2019). Although models with large vocabulary sizes can be effective, they may not perform equally well in parsing all languages, resulting in

[1] In both English and Indic Multilingual TOP, the utterance and it's corresponding logic form are in same language, English or Indic respectively.

Proceedings of the 5th Workshop on NLP for Conversational AI (NLP4ConvAI 2023), pages 102–122
July 14, 2023 ©2023 Association for Computational Linguistics

overall low-quality output. Moreover, managing multilingual inputs can be challenging and often requires multiple dialogue managers, further adding complexity. Hence, we asked ourselves: *"Can we combine the strengths of both approaches?"*

Therefore, we explore a third distinct setting: Inter-bilingual TOP. This setting involves parsing Indic utterances and generating corresponding logical forms with English slot values (in comparison, multilingual top has non-english multilingual slot values). For a model to excel at this task, it must accurately parse and translate simultaneously. The aim of inter-bilingual semantic parsing is to anticipate the translation of non-translated logical forms into translated expressions, which presents a challenging reasoning objective. Moreover, many scenarios, such as e-commerce searches, music recommendations, and finance apps, require the use of English parsing due to the availability of search vocabulary such as product names, song titles, bond names, and company names, which are predominantly available in English. Additionally, APIs for tasks like alarm or reminder setting often require specific information in English for further processing. Therefore, it is essential to explore inter-bilingual task-oriented parsing with English slot values.

In this spirit, we establish a novel task of Inter-Bilingual task-Oriented Parsing (Bi-lingual TOP) and develop a semantic parsing dataset suite a.k.a IE-SEMPARSE for Indic languages. The utterances are translated into eleven Indic languages while maintaining the logical structures of their English counterparts.[2] We created inter-bilingual semantic parsing dataset IE-SEMPARSE Suite (IE represents Indic to English). IE-SEMPARSE suite consists of three Interbilingual semantic datasets namely IE-mTOP, IE-multilingualTOP, IE-multiATIS++ by machine translating English utterances of mTOP, multilingualTOP and multiATIS++ (Li et al., 2021; Xia and Monti, 2021; Xu et al., 2020) to eleven Indian languages described in §3. In addition, §3 includes the meticulously chosen automatic and human evaluation metrics to validate the quality of the machine-translated dataset.

We conduct a comprehensive analysis of the performance of numerous multilingual seq2seq models on the proposed task in §4 with various input combinations and data enhancements. In our experiments, we demonstrate that interbilingual parsing is more complex than English and multilingual parsing, however, modern transformer models with translation fine-tuning are capable of achieving results comparable to the former two. We also show that these results are consistent with those obtained from semantic parsing datasets containing slot values in the same languages as the utterance. Our contributions to this work are the following:

1. We proposed a novel task of Inter-Bilingual TOP with multilingual utterance (input) and English logical form (output). We introduced IE-SEMPARSE, an Inter-Bilingual TOP dataset for 11 Indo-Dravidian languages representing about 22% of speakers of the world population.
2. We explore various seq2seq models with several train-test strategies for this task. We discuss the implications of an end-to-end model compared to translation followed by parsing. We also compare how pertaining, prefinetuning and structure of a logical form affect the model performance.

The IE-SEMPARSE suite along with the scripts will be available at `https://iesemparse.github.io/`.

2 Why Inter Bilingual Parsing?

In this section, we delve deeper into the advantages of our inter-bilingual parsing approach and how it affects the dialogue management and response generation. We will address the question: *"Why preserve English slot values in the logical form?"*.

Limited Decoder Vocabulary: Using only English logical forms simplifies the seq2seq model decoder by reducing its vocabulary to a smaller set. This will make the training process more stable and reduce the chances of hallucination which often occurs in decoders while decoding long sequences with larger vocabulary size (Raunak et al., 2021).

Multi-lingual Models Evaluation: In this work, we explore the unique task of translating and parsing spoken utterances into logical forms. We gain valuable insights into the strengths and weaknesses of current multilingual models on this task. Specifically, we investigate how multilingual models compare to monolingual ones, how translation finetuning affects performance, and how the performance of Indic-specific and general multilingual models

[2] Like previous scenarios, the slot tags and intent operators such as METHOD_TIMER and CREATE_TIMER are respectively preserved in the corresponding English languages.

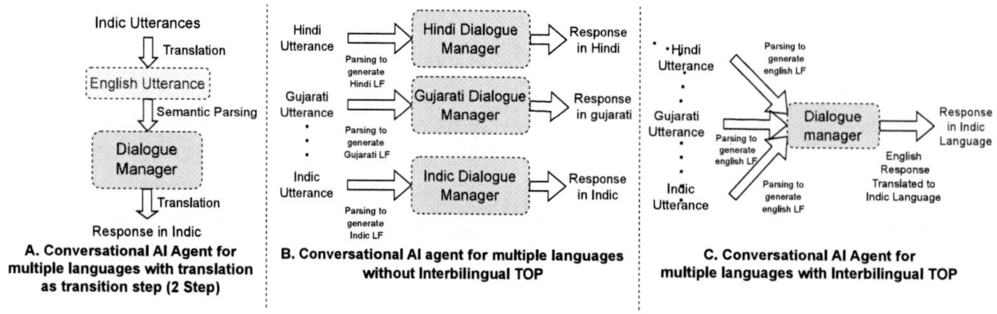

Figure 2: Conversational AI Agents comparisons with (w/o) inter-bilingual parsing. LF refers to logical form.

differ. We also analyze the predictions of the two best models across languages in §4.2, which is a novel aspect of our task. These insights enhance our understanding of existing multilingual models on IE-SEMPARSE.

Improved Parsing Latency: In figure 2, we illustrate three multilingual semantic parsing scenarios:

1. In **scenario A**, the Indic utterance is translated to English, parsed by an NLU module, and then a dialogue manager delivers an English response, which is translated back to Indic language.
2. In **scenario B**, language-specific conversational agents generate a logical form with Indic slot values, which is passed to a language-specific dialogue manager that delivers an Indic response.
3. In **scenario C**, a multilingual conversation agent generates a logical form with English slot values, which is passed to an English Dialogue Manager that delivers an English response, which is translated back into Indic language.

We observe that our approach scenario C is 2x faster than A. We further discuss the latency gains and the performances differences in appendix §A. Scenario B, on the other hand, has a significant developmental overhead owing to multilingual language, as detailed below.

Handling System Redundancy: We argue that IE-SEMPARSE is a useful dataset for developing dialogue managers that can handle multiple languages without redundancy. Unlike existing datasets such as mTOP (Li et al., 2021), multilingual-TOP (Schuster et al., 2019), and multi-ATIS++ (Xu et al., 2020), which generate logical forms with English intent functions and slot tags but multilingual slot values, our dataset generates logical forms with English slot values as well. This avoids the need to translate the slot values or to create separate dialogue managers for each language, which would introduce inefficiencies and complexities in the system design. Therefore, our approach offers a practical trade-off between optimizing the development process and minimizing the inference latency for multilingual conversational AI agents. Finally, the utilization of a multilingual dialogue manager fails to adequately adhere to the intricate cultural nuances present in various languages (Jonson, 2002).

3 IE-SEMPARSE Creation and Validation

In this section, we describe the IE-SEMPARSE creation and validation process in details.

IE-SEMPARSE Description: We create three inter-bilingual TOP datasets for eleven major *Indic* languages that include Assamese ('as'), Gujarat ('gu'), Kannada ('kn'), Malayalam ('ml'), Marathi ('mr'), Odia ('or'), Punjabi ('pa'), Tamil ('ta'), Telugu ('te'), Hindi ('hi'), and Bengali ('bn'). Refer to the appendix §A, for additional information regarding the selection of languages, language coverage of models, and the selection of translation model. The three datasets mentioned are described below:

1. **IE-mTOP:** This dataset is a translated version of the multi-domain TOP-v2 dataset. English utterances were translated to Indic languages using IndicTrans (Ramesh et al., 2021), while preserving the logical forms.
2. **IE-multilingualTOP**: This dataset is from the multilingual TOP dataset, where utterances were translated and logical forms were decoupled using the pytext library.[3]
3. **IE-multiATIS++**: This dataset comes from the multi-ATIS++, where utterances were translated and the logical forms were generated from labelled dictionaries and decoupled, as described in appendix §3.

[3] https://github.com/facebookresearch/pytext

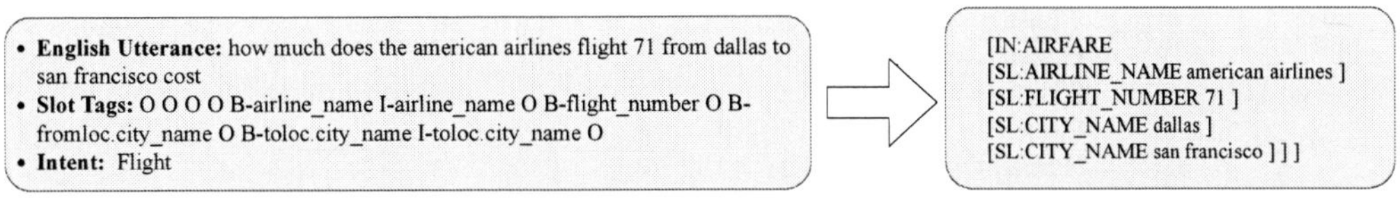

Figure 3: IE-multiATIS++ Logical Form Generation

Score	Dataset	as	bn	gu	hi	kn	ml	mr	or	pa	ta	te
BertScore	**Samanantar**	0.83	0.83	0.85	0.87	0.86	0.85	0.85	0.84	0.87	0.87	0.87
	IE-mTOP	0.83	0.85	0.85	0.87	0.86	0.85	0.86	0.85	0.87	0.87	0.87
	IE-multilingualTOP	0.98	0.98	0.98	0.96	0.98	0.98	0.99	0.98	0.97	0.98	0.98
	IE-multiATIS++	0.83	0.85	0.86	0.87	0.86	0.85	0.85	0.85	0.86	0.87	0.87
CometScore	**Samanantar**	0.12	0.12	0.11	0.12	0.12	0.12	0.13	0.13	0.12	0.12	0.12
	IE-mTOP	0.12	0.13	0.12	0.12	0.12	0.13	0.13	0.13	0.14	0.12	0.12
	IE-multilingualTOP	0.13	0.14	0.14	0.13	0.14	0.14	0.14	0.14	0.14	0.14	0.14
	IE-multiATIS++	0.13	0.13	0.13	0.13	0.13	0.13	0.13	0.13	0.13	0.13	0.13
BT_BertScore	**Samanantar**	0.95	0.96	0.96	0.97	0.96	0.96	0.96	0.96	0.97	0.96	0.96
	IE-mTOP	0.92	0.94	0.93	0.94	0.94	0.93	0.94	0.93	0.93	0.93	0.93
	IE-multilingualTOP	0.93	0.93	0.89	0.93	0.92	0.96	0.93	0.9	0.92	0.91	0.91
	IE-multiATIS++	0.91	0.92	0.92	0.93	0.93	0.92	0.92	0.91	0.92	0.92	0.92

Table 1: Automatic scores on IE-SEMPARSE and Benchmark Dataset Samanantar.

IE-multiATIS++ Logical Form Creation The logical forms are generated from the label dictionaries, where the Intent was labeled with 'IN:' tag and Slots were labelled with 'SL:' Tags and decoupled like IE-multilingualTOP dataset. The process of generating logical forms out of intent and slot tags from the ATIS dataset is illustrated in figure 3.

IE-SEMPARSE **Processing:** To construct IE-SEMPARSE we perform extensive pre and post processing, as described below:

Pre-processing We extensively preprocess IE-SEMPARSE. We use Spacy NER Tagger[4] to tag date-time and transform them into their corresponding lexical form. E.g. tag date time *"7:30 pm on 14/2/2023."* is transformed to *"seven thirty pm on fourteen february of 2023."*

Post-processing For many languages some words are commonly spoken and frequently. Therefore, we replace frequently spoken words in IE-SEMPARSE with their transliterated form, which often sounds more fluent, authentic, and informal than their translated counterparts.

To accomplish this, we replace commonly spoken words with their transliterated form to improve understanding. We created corpus-based transliteration token dictionaries by comparing Hindi mTOP, translated mTOP, and transliterated mTOP datasets. We utilize the human-translated Hindi set of mTOP dataset to filter frequently transliterated phrases and repurpose the same Hindi dictionary to post-process the text for all other Indic languages.

[4] https://spacy.io/api/entityrecognizer

3.1 IE-SEMPARSE Validation

As observed in past literature, machine translation can be an effective method to generate high quality datasets (K et al., 2021; Aggarwal et al., 2022; Agarwal et al., 2022b). However, due to inherent fallibility of the machine translation system, translations may produce incorrect utterance instances for the specified logical form. Consequently, making the task more complicated and generalizing the model more complex. Thus, it is crucial to examine the evaluation dataset quality and alleviate severe limitations accurately. Early works, including Bapna et al. (2022); Huang (1990); Moon et al. (2020a,b), has established that quality estimation is an efficacious method for assessing machine translation systems in the absence of reference data a.k.a the low-resource settings.

Using Quality Estimation: In our context, where there is a dearth of reference data for the IE-SEMPARSE translated language, we also determined the translation quality of IE-SEMPARSE using a (semi) automatic quality estimation technique. Most of recent works on quality estimation compare the results with some reference data and then prove the correlation between reference scores and referenceless quality estimation scores (Fomicheva et al., 2020; Yuan and Sharoff, 2020; Cuong and Xu, 2018). Justifying and interpreting quality estimation metrics, however, remains a stiff challenge for real-world referenceless settings.

IE-SEMPARSE **Automatic Benchmarking:** When a parallel corpus in both languages is

Dataset	Statistics	as	bn	gu	hi	kn	ml	mr	or	pa	ta	te
IE-multiATIS++	**Human Eval**	3.15	3.07	3.65	4.1	3.7	4.12	4	4.4	4.45	4.03	3.83
	Pearson	0.66	0.85	0.69	0.61	0.76	0.62	0.56	0.72	0.61	0.71	0.68
	Spearman	0.71	0.86	0.42	0.57	0.49	0.51	0.59	0.59	0.59	0.65	0.6
IE-multilingualTOP	**Human Eval**	3.06	3.21	3.92	4.46	4.33	4.13	4.24	4.74	4.47	4.22	3.84
	Pearson	0.55	0.79	0.56	0.53	0.45	0.5	0.65	0.42	0.67	0.58	0.59
	Spearman	0.57	0.74	0.54	0.53	0.45	0.46	0.62	0.63	0.51	0.5	0.49
IE-mTOP	**Human Eval**	3.1	3.39	4	4.42	4.28	3.99	4	4.61	4.42	4.16	4.13
	Pearson	0.66	0.74	0.64	0.55	0.61	0.63	0.73	0.45	0.51	0.5	0.62
	Spearman	0.67	0.7	0.6	0.45	0.4	0.64	0.67	0.41	0.5	0.45	0.5

Table 2: Human Evaluation Results: **Human Eval** represents the average score of 3 annotators for each language for each dataset. **Pearson** is the average pearson correlation of 1st and 2nd, 1st and 3rd and 2nd and 3rd annotators and similarly for **Spearman** which is spearman correlation.

not available, it is still beneficial to benchmark the data and translation model. In our context, we conducted an evaluation of the Samanantar corpus, which stands as the most comprehensive publicly accessible parallel corpus for Indic languages (Ramesh et al., 2021). The purpose of this assessment was to emulate a scenario wherein the Samanantar corpus serves as the benchmark reference parallel dataset, allowing us to provide a rough estimate of the scores produced by quality estimation models when evaluated in a referenceless setting on a gold standard parallel translation corpus.

We use two approaches to compare English and translated text directly. For direct quality estimation of English sentences and translated sentences in a reference-less setting, we utilize Comet Score (Rei et al., 2020) and BertScore (Zhang* et al., 2020) with XLM-RoBERTa-Large (Conneau et al., 2020) backbone for direct comparison of translated and english utterances. We also calculate BT BertScore (Agrawal et al., 2022; Moon et al., 2020a; Huang, 1990), which has shown to improve high correlation with human judgement (Agrawal et al., 2022) for our three datasets and Samanantar for reference. In this case, we translate the Indic sentence back to English and compare it with the original English sentence using BertScore (Zhang* et al., 2020). The scores for the Samanantar subset on a random subset of filtered 100k phrases and our datasets IE-SEMPARSE are provided in the table 1.

Original vs Machine Translated Hindi: As the human (translated) reference was available in mTOP and multi-ATIS for Hindi language, we leveraged that data to calculate Bert and Comet score to evaluate the translation quality of our machine translation model. We notice a high correlation between both datasets' referenceless and reference scores. Thus suggesting good translation quality for Hindi and other languages.

Dataset	Referenceless Score	Score
IE-mTOP	**Comet Score**	0.83
	Bert Score	0.96
	BT Bert Score	0.88
IE-multiATIS++	**Comet Score**	0.81
	Bert Score	0.85
	BT Bert Score	0.87

Table 3: Comet Score, BertScore and BT BertScore of Hindi dataset and translated Hindi dataset for IE-mTOP and IE-multiATIS++

In table 3 comet scores and Bert scores are scores keeping original English sentence as source, original Hindi sentence as reference and translated Hindi sentence as hypothesis. For the BT BertScore, the translated Hindi sentence and the original (human-translated) Hindi sentence are back-translated (BT) back onto English and their correlation is assessed using the Bert Score.

IE-SEMPARSE **Human Evaluation:** In our human evaluation procedure, we employ three annotators for each language [5]. We used determinantal point processes[6] (Kulesza, 2012) to select a highly diversified subset of English sentences from the test set of each dataset. We select 20 sentences from IE-multiATIS++, 120 from IE-multilingualTOP and 60 from IE-mTOP. For each dataset, this amounts to more than 1% of the total test population. We then got them scored between 1-5 from 3 fluent speakers of each Indic English and Indic language by providing them with a sheet with parallel data of English sentences and subsequent translation.

Analysis. We notice that the scores vary with resource variability where languages like "as" and "kn" have the lowest scores. However, most scores are within the range of 3.5-5 suggesting the high quality of translation for our dataset. Detailed scores are reported in Appendix §B table 7.

[5] every annotator was paid 5 INR for each sentence annotation each [6] `https://github.com/guilgautier/DPPy`

4 Experimental Evaluation

For our experiments, we investigated into the following five train-test strategies: **1. Indic Train:** Models are both finetuned and evaluated on Indic Language. **2. English+Indic Train:** Models are finetuned on English language and then Indic Language and evaluated on Indic language data. **3. Translate Test:** Models are finetuned on English data and evaluated on back-translated English data. **4. Train All:** Models are finetuned on the compound dataset of English + all other 11 Indic languages and evaluated on Indic test dataset. **5. Unified Finetuning:** IndicBART-M2O and mBART-large-50-M2O models are finetuned on all three datasets for all eleven languages creating unified multi-genre (multi-domain) semantic parsing models for all 3 datasets for all languages. This can be considered as data-unified extension of 4th Setting.

Models: The models utilized can be categorized into four categories as follows: (a.) MULTILINGUAL such as **mBART-large-50**, **mT5-base** such as (b.) INDIC SPECIFIC such as **IndicBART** (c.) TRANSLATION PREFINETUNED such as **IndicBART-M2O**, **mBART-large-50-M2O**, which are pre finetuned on XX-EN translation task (d.) MONOLINGUAL (ENGLISH) such as **T5-base**, **T5-large**, **BART-large**, **BART-base** used only in **Translate Test** Setting. The models are specified in the table's §8 *"Hyper Parameter"* column, with details in the appendix §C. Details of the fine-tuning process with hyperparameters details and the model's vocabulary augmentation are discussed in the appendix §D and §E respectively.

Evaluation Metric: For Evaluation, we use tree labelled F1-Score for assessing the performance of our models from the original TOP paper (Gupta et al., 2018). This is preferred over an exact match because the latter can penalize the model's performance when the slot positions are out of order. This is a common issue we observe in our outputs, given that the logical form and utterance are not in the same language. However, exact match scores are also discussed in appendix §F.5.

4.1 Analysis across Languages, Models and Datasets

We report the results of **Train All** and **Unified Finetuning** settings for all datasets in table 4 and 5 in the main paper as these were the best technique out of all. The scores for other train-test strategies such as translate test, Indic Train, English+Indic Train for all 3 datasets are reported in appendix §F.1 table 9, 10 and 11 respectively. However, we have discussed the comparison between train-test settings in the subsequent paragraphs.

Across Languages: Models perform better on high-resource than medium and low-resourced languages for **Train All** setting. This shows that the proposed inter-bilingual seq2seq task is challenging. In addition to linguistic similarities, the model performance also relies on factors like grammar and morphology (Pires et al., 2019). For other settings such as **Translate Test**, **Indic Train**, and **English+Indic**, similar observations were observed.

Across Train-Test Strategies: Translate Test method works well, however end-to-end English+Indic and Train All models perform best; due to the data augmentation setting, which increases the training size.[7] However, the benefits of train data enrichment are much greater in **Train All** scenario because of the larger volume and increased linguistic variation of the training dataset. We also discuss the comparisons in inference latency for a 2-step vs end-to-end model in §2.

Across Datasets: We observe that IE-multilingualTOP is the simplest dataset for models, followed by IE-mTOP and IE-multiATIS++. This may be because of the training dataset size, since IE-multilingualTOP is the largest of the three, followed by IE-mTOP and IE-multiATIS++. In addition, IE-multilingualTOP is derived from TOP(v1) dataset which have utterances with more simpler logical form structure (tree depth=1). IE-mTOP, on the other hand, is based on mTOP, which is a translation of TOP(v2), with more complex logical form having (tree depth>=2). We discuss the performance of models across logical form complexity in §4.2. For **Unified Finetuning** we observe an average performance gain of 0.2 in the tree labelled F1 score for all languages for all datasets as reported in table 5 in appendix.

Across Models: We analyse the performance across various models based on three criteria, language coverage, model size and translation finetuning, as discussed in detail below:

(a.) ***Language Coverage:*** Due to its larger size, mBART-large-50-M2O performs exceptionally well on high-resource languages, whereas IndicBART-M2O performs uniformly across all the languages due to its indic specificity. In addition, translation-optimized models perform better than

[7] By 2x (English + Indic) and 12x (1 English + 11 Indic).

Dataset	Model	Train All													ModAvg
		as	bn	gu	hi	kn	ml	mr	or	pa	ta	te	hi_{IE}	hi_O	
IE-mTOP	**IndicBART**	50	56	49	56	45	54	**67**	44	56	56	58	52	60	50
	mBART-large-50	51	53	51	**62**	51	55	51	32	53	48	52	58	66	51
	mT5-base	46	53	56	58	53	55	50	45	53	**58**	**58**	54	62	53
	IndicBART-M2O	54	57	57	**61**	59	58	58	57	59	57	**61**	59	63	58
	mBART-large-50-M2O	56	59	61	65	60	63	59	59	59	64	**65**	63	67	**61**
	Language Average	51	56	55	**60**	54	57	57	47	56	57	59	57	64	55
IE-multilingualTOP	**IndicBART**	44	50	57	**80**	43	42	50	37	67	70	77	–	–	56
	mBART-large-50	44	57	66	**77**	29	28	46	17	47	48	48	–	–	46
	mT5-base	49	54	57	60	56	55	52	50	53	53	**58**	–	–	54
	IndicBART-M2O	74	75	**79**	78	70	70	75	75	75	76	77	–	–	**75**
	mBART-large-50-M2O	54	57	60	**63**	58	58	53	56	57	57	61	–	–	58
	Language Average	51	56	55	**60**	54	57	57	47	56	57	59	–	–	55
IE-multiATIS++	**IndicBART**	51	58	52	**70**	50	41	63	25	50	39	56	66	76	54
	mBART-large-50	54	**86**	54	58	54	53	53	45	57	51	55	54	63	57
	mT5-base	67	**87**	73	73	72	78	64	59	70	68	74	70	77	72
	IndicBART-M2O	70	**90**	80	80	79	79	73	69	78	73	82	78	82	**78**
	mBART-large-50-M2O	73	**91**	83	81	77	79	75	65	78	73	79	79	83	**78**
	Language Average	63	82	68	72	66	66	66	53	67	61	69	69	76	68

Table 4: $Tree\_Labelled\_F1 * 100$ scores for the **Train All** setting. The bold numbers in the table indicate the row-wise maximum, i.e. the model's best language performance in the given context. The numbers in bold in the **ModAvg** (Model Average) column indicate the model with the best performance for the train-test strategy specified in the table's heading. Similarly, the numbers in bold in the **Language Average** row indicate the language with the best performance. Subsequently, hi_O refers to the original Hindi dataset from the dataset and hi_{IE} refers to the inter-bilingual dataset constructed by picking Hindi utterances and English logical form and joining them.

Dataset	Model	Unified Finetuning													ModAvg
		as	bn	gu	hi	kn	ml	mr	or	pa	ta	te	hi_{IE}	hi_O	
IE-mTOP	**IndicBART-M2O**	74	77	77	**81**	79	78	78	77	79	77	81	79	83	78
	mBART-large-50-M2O	76	79	81	**85**	80	83	79	79	79	84	85	83	87	**82**
	Language Average	75	78	79	**83**	80	81	79	78	79	81	83	81	85	80
IE-multilingualTOP	**IndicBART-M2O**	75	76	80	**79**	71	71	76	76	76	77	78	–	–	**76**
	mBART-large-50-M2O	55	58	61	**64**	59	59	54	57	58	58	62	–	–	59
	Language Average	65	67	71	**72**	65	65	65	67	67	68	70	–	–	67
IE-multiATIS++	**IndicBART-M2O**	80	80	90	**90**	89	89	83	79	88	83	92	88	92	**84**
	mBART-large-50-M2O	83	82	93	**91**	87	89	85	75	88	83	89	89	93	**84**
	Language Average	82	82	92	**91**	88	89	84	77	88	83	**91**	89	93	**84**

Table 5: $Tree\_Labelled\_F1 * 100$ scores of **IndicBART-M2O** and **mBART-large-50** model trained on all languages and all datasets. Other notations similar to that of Table 4.

those that are not. mBART-large-50 outperforms mT5-base despite its higher language coverage, while mBART-large-50's superior performance can be ascribed to its denoising pre-training objective, which enhances the model's ability to generalize for the *"intent"* and *"slot"* detection task. In section §4.2 we discuss more about the complexity of the logical forms.

(b.) ***Model Size:*** While model size has a significant impact on the Translate Test setting for monolingual models, we find that pre-training language coverage and Translation fine-tuning are still the most critical factors. For example, despite being a smaller model, IndicBART outperforms mT5-base on average for similar reasons. Another reason for better performance for IndicBART and mBART-large-50 denoising based seq2seq pre-training vs multilingual multitask objective of mT5-base.

(c.) ***Translation Finetuning:*** The proposed task is a mixture of semantic parsing and translation. We also observe this empirically, when models finetuned for translation tasks perform better. This result can be attributed to fact that machine translation is the most effective strategy for aligning phrase embeddings by multilingual seq2seq models (Voita et al., 2019), as emphasized by Li et al. (2021). In addition, we observe that the models perform best in the **Train All** setting, indicating that data augmentation followed by fine-tuning enhances performance throughout all languages on translation fine-tuned models.

Original vs Translated Hindi: We also evaluated the performance of Hindi language models on original datasets (hi_O) and (hi_{IE}) which combine Hindi utterances with logical forms of English of mTOP and multi-ATIS++ datasets, as shown in table 4. Inter-bilingual tasks pose a challenge and result in lower performance, but translation-finetuned models significantly reduce this gap. Model performance is similar for both ‘hi’ and ‘hi_{IE} ’, indicating the quality of translations. Additional details can be refered in Appendix §G.

Domain Wise Comparison: IE-mTOP dataset contains domain classes derived from mTOP. We compare the average F1 scores for different domains in IE-mTOP dataset for IndicBART-M2O and mBART-large-50-M2O in the **Train All** setting, as shown in Figure 4. We observe that mBART-large-50-M2O outperforms IndicBART-M2O for most domains except for people and recipes, where both perform similarly well due to cultural variations in utterances.

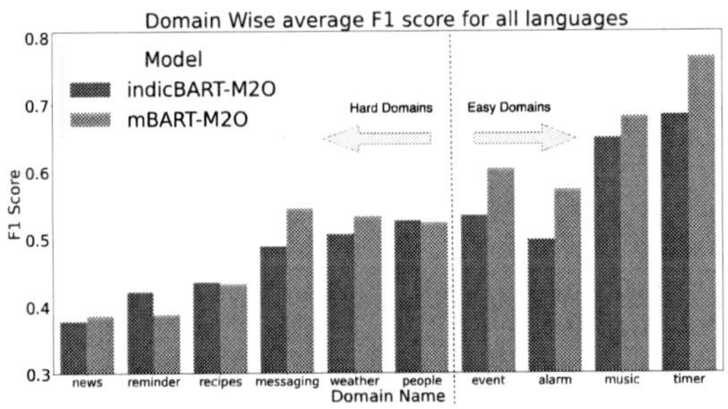

Figure 4: Domain Wise all language average F1 score in IE-mTOP dataset for IndicBART-M2O and mBART-large-50-M2O.

4.2 Analysis on Logical Forms

In this paper, we maintain the slot values in the English language and ensure consistency in the logical form across languages for each example in every dataset. This can be useful in assessing the model performance across language and datasets on the basis of logical form structure which we have analysed in this section. Previous works have shown a correlation between model performance and logical form structures (Gupta et al., 2022).

Logical Form Complexity: We evaluate the performance of the mBART-large-50-M2O model on utterances with simple and complex logical form structures in the Train All setting for IE-mTOP and IE-multilingualTOP datasets. Simple utterances have a flat representation with a single intent, while complex utterances have multiple levels [8] of branching in the parse tree with more than one intent. In IE-multiATIS++, instances are only attributed to simple utterances since they have a single unique intent. Figure 5 shows, that mBART-large-50-M2O performs better for complex utterances in IE-mTOP, while there is better performance for simple utterances in IE-multilingualTOP due to its larger training data size and a higher proportion of simple logical forms in training data.

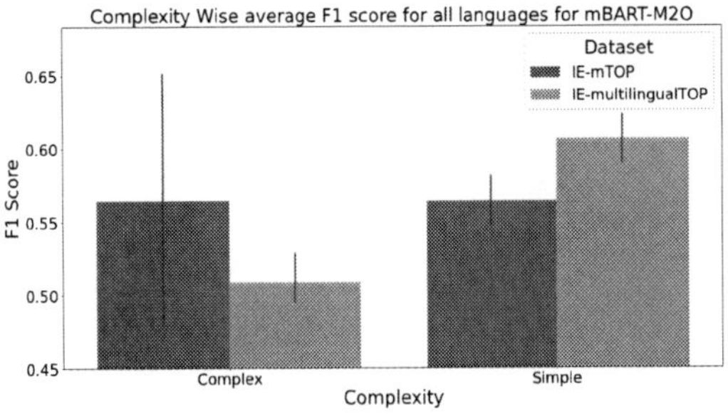

Figure 5: Complexity Wise all language average F1 score in IE-mTOP dataset for IE-mTOP and IE-multilingualTOP for mBART-large-50-M2O.

Effect of Frame Rareness: We compared mBART-large-50-M2O and IE-multilingualTOP on the Train All setting by removing slot values from logical forms and dividing frames into five frequency buckets[9]. A shown in figure 6, F1 scores increase with frame frequency, and IE-mTOP performs better for smaller frequencies while IE-multilingualTOP performs better for very large frequencies. This suggests that IE-mTOP has more complex utterances, aiding model learning with limited data, while IE-multilingualTOP’s larger training size leads to better performance in very high frequency buckets.

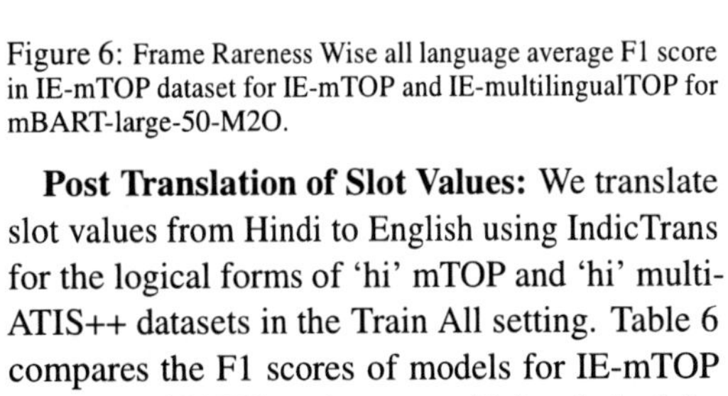

Figure 6: Frame Rareness Wise all language average F1 score in IE-mTOP dataset for IE-mTOP and IE-multilingualTOP for mBART-large-50-M2O.

Post Translation of Slot Values: We translate slot values from Hindi to English using IndicTrans for the logical forms of ‘hi’ mTOP and ‘hi’ multi-ATIS++ datasets in the Train All setting. Table 6 compares the F1 scores of models for IE-mTOP and IE-multiATIS++ datasets, which only had the original Hindi dataset available. Despite minor decreases in scores and visible translation errors, our

[8] depth >= 2

[9] namely very high, high, medium, low and very low.

approach yields accurate translations due to the short length of slot values and the high-resource nature of Hindi. However, we argue that our proposed task or multilingual TOP task is superior in terms of latency and performance, as discussed in §2 and §4.1.

Dataset	Model	F1
IE-mTOP	IndicBART	49
	mBART-large-50	55
	mT5-base	50
	IndicBART-M2O	56
	mBART-large-50-M2O	58
IE-multiATIS++	IndicBART	55
	mBART-large-50	67
	mT5-base	41
	IndicBART-M2O	68
	mBART-large-50-M2O	70

Table 6: Tree Labelled F1 scores of hindi dataset with post translation of slot values to english for IE-mTOP and IE-multiATIS++

Language Wise Correlation: We compared the logical form results of each language by calculating the average tree labelled F1 score between the datasets of one language to the other. We then plotted correlation matrices[10] and analysed performance on all datasets using IndicBART-M2O and mBART-large-50-M2O in **Train All** setting, as described in Figure 7, 8, and 9 in Appendix §F.4.

Our analysis shows that IndicBART-M2O has more consistent predictions than mBART-large-50-M2O. We also observed that models perform most consistently for the IE-multiATIS++ dataset. Additionally, related languages, such as 'bn' and 'as', 'mr' and 'hi', and 'kn' and 'te', have high correlation due to script similarity.

5 Related Work

Multi-Lingual Semantic Parsing: Recently, TOP has attracted a lot of attention due to the development of state-of-the-art seq2seq models such as BART (Lewis et al., 2020) and T5 (Raffel et al., 2019). Moreover, several works have extended TOP to the multilingual setting, such as mTOP, multilingual-TOP, and multi-ATIS++. The recent MASSIVE dataset (FitzGerald et al., 2022) covers six Indic languages vs eleven in our work, and only contains a flat hierarchical structure of semantic parse. Furthermore, the logical form annotations in MASSIVE are not of a similar format to those in the standard TOP dataset.

IndicNLP: Some works have experimented with code-mixed Hindi-English utterances for semantic parsing tasks, such as CST5 (Agarwal et al., 2022a). In addition to these advances, there have been significant contributions to the development of indic-specific resources for natural language generation and understanding, such as IndicNLG Suite Kumar et al. (2022), IndicBART Dabre et al. (2022), and IndicGLUE Kakwani et al. (2020). Also, some studies have investigated the intra-bilingual setting for multilingual NLP tasks, such as IndicXNLI (Aggarwal et al., 2022) and EI-InfoTabs (Agarwal et al., 2022b). In contrast to prior works, we focus on the complex structured semantic parsing task.

LLMs and Zero Shot: Our work is also related to zero-shot cross-lingual (Sherborne and Lapata, 2022) and cross-domain (Liu et al., 2021) semantic parsing, which aims to parse utterances in unseen languages or domains. Moreover, recent methods use scalable techniques such as automatic translation and filling (Nicosia et al., 2021) and bootstrapping with LLMs (Awasthi et al., 2023; Rosenbaum et al., 2022; Scao, 2022) to create semantic parsing datasets without human annotation. Unlike previous methods such as Translate-Align-Project (TAP) (Brown et al., 1993) and Translate and Fill (TAF) (Nicosia et al., 2021), which generate semantic parses of translated sentences, they propose a novel approach that leverages LLMs to generate semantic parses of multilingual utterances.

6 Conclusion and Future Work

We present a unique inter-bilingual semantic parsing task, and publish the IE-SEMPARSE suite, which consists of 3 inter-bilingual semantic parsing datasets for 11 Indic languages. Additionally, we discuss the advantages of our proposed approach to semantic parsing over prior methods. We also analyze the impact of various models and train-test procedures on IE-SEMPARSE performance. Lastly, we examine the effects of variation in logical forms and languages on model performance and the correlation between languages.

For future work, we plan to release a SOTA model, explore zero-shot parsing (Sherborne and Lapata, 2022), enhance IE-SEMPARSE with human translation (NLLB Team et al., 2022), explore zero-shot dataset generation (Nicosia et al., 2021), leverage LLM for scalable and diverse dataset generation(Rosenbaum et al., 2022; Awasthi et al., 2023), and evaluate instruction fine-tuning models.

[10] for 11 x 11 pairs

7 Limitations

One of the main limitations of our approach is the use of machine translation to create the IE-SEMPARSE suite. However, we showed that the overall quality of our dataset is comparable to Samanantar, a human-verified translation dataset. Furthermore, previous studies Bapna et al. (2022); Huang (1990); Moon et al. (2020a,b) have shown the effectiveness of quality estimation in reference-less settings. Lastly, we have also extensively evaluated our dataset with the help of 3 human evaluators for each language as described in §3. We can further take help of GPT4 in future to evaluate the translations in a scaled manner (Gilardi et al., 2023).

The second point of discussion focuses on the motivation for preserving logical form slot values in English. We explore the use cases where querying data in English is crucial, and how this approach can enhance models by reducing latency, limiting vocabulary size, and handling system redundancy. While open-source tools currently cannot achieve this, it would be valuable to evaluate the effectiveness of this task by comparing it with the other two discussed approaches. To accomplish this, we suggest using a dialogue manager and scoring the performance of its responses on the three TOP approaches outlined in the paper.

Another potential limitation of our dataset is that it may contain biases and flaws inherited from the original TOP datasets. However, we contend that spoken utterances are generally simpler and more universal than written ones, which mitigates the risk of cultural mismatches in IE-SEMPARSE dataset. Furthermore, our work is confined only to the Indo-Dravidian Language family of Indic languages due to our familiarity with them and the availability of high-quality resources from previous research. Nonetheless, our approach is easily extendable to other languages with effective translation models, enabling broader applications in various languages worldwide. In the future, we plan to improve our datasets by publicly releasing them through initiatives like NLLB or IndicTransV2, and by collaborating with larger organizations to have the test sets human-translated.

8 Acknowledgements

We express our gratitude to Nitish Gupta from Google Research India for his invaluable and insightful suggestions aimed at enhancing the quality of our paper. Additionally, we extend our appreciation to the diligent human evaluators who diligently assessed our dataset. Divyanshu Aggarwal acknowledges all the support from Amex, AI Labs. We also thank members of the Utah NLP group for their valuable insights and suggestions at various stages of the project; and reviewers their helpful comments. Vivek Gupta acknowledges support from Bloomberg's Data Science Ph.D. Fellowship.

References

Anmol Agarwal, Jigar Gupta, Rahul Goel, Shyam Upadhyay, Pankaj Joshi, and Rengarajan Aravamudhan. 2022a. Cst5: Data augmentation for code-switched semantic parsing.

Chaitanya Agarwal, Vivek Gupta, Anoop Kunchukuttan, and Manish Shrivastava. 2022b. Bilingual tabular inference: A case study on indic languages. In *Proceedings of the 2022 Conference of the North American Chapter of the Association for Computational Linguistics: Human Language Technologies*, pages 4018–4037, Seattle, United States. Association for Computational Linguistics.

Divyanshu Aggarwal, Vivek Gupta, and Anoop Kunchukuttan. 2022. IndicXNLI: Evaluating multilingual inference for Indian languages. In *Proceedings of the 2022 Conference on Empirical Methods in Natural Language Processing*, pages 10994–11006, Abu Dhabi, United Arab Emirates. Association for Computational Linguistics.

Sweta Agrawal, Nikita Mehandru, Niloufar Salehi, and Marine Carpuat. 2022. Quality estimation via backtranslation at the wmt 2022 quality estimation task. In *Proceedings of the Seventh Conference on Machine Translation*, pages 593–596, Abu Dhabi. Association for Computational Linguistics.

Abhijeet Awasthi, Nitish Gupta, Bidisha Samanta, Shachi Dave, Sunita Sarawagi, and Partha Talukdar. 2023. Bootstrapping multilingual semantic parsers using large language models.

Ankur Bapna, Isaac Caswell, Julia Kreutzer, Orhan Firat, Daan van Esch, Aditya Siddhant, Mengmeng Niu, Pallavi Baljekar, Xavier Garcia, Wolfgang Macherey, Theresa Breiner, Vera Axelrod, Jason Riesa, Yuan Cao, Mia Xu Chen, Klaus Macherey, Maxim Krikun, Pidong Wang, Alexander Gutkin, Apurva Shah, Yanping Huang, Zhifeng Chen, Yonghui Wu, and Macduff Hughes. 2022. Building machine translation systems for the next thousand languages.

Loïc Barrault, Ondřej Bojar, Fethi Bougares, Rajen Chatterjee, Marta R. Costa-jussà, Christian Federmann, Mark Fishel, Alexander Fraser, Yvette Graham, Paco Guzman, Barry Haddow, Matthias Huck, Antonio Jimeno Yepes, Philipp Koehn, André Martins, Makoto Morishita, Christof Monz, Masaaki Nagata, Toshiaki Nakazawa, and Matteo Negri, editors.

2020. *Proceedings of the Fifth Conference on Machine Translation*. Association for Computational Linguistics, Online.

Peter F. Brown, Stephen A. Della Pietra, Vincent J. Della Pietra, and Robert L. Mercer. 1993. The mathematics of statistical machine translation: Parameter estimation. *Computational Linguistics*, 19(2):263–311.

Alexis Conneau, Kartikay Khandelwal, Naman Goyal, Vishrav Chaudhary, Guillaume Wenzek, Francisco Guzmán, Edouard Grave, Myle Ott, Luke Zettlemoyer, and Veselin Stoyanov. 2020. Unsupervised cross-lingual representation learning at scale.

Hoang Cuong and Jia Xu. 2018. Assessing quality estimation models for sentence-level prediction. In *Proceedings of the 27th International Conference on Computational Linguistics*, pages 1521–1533, Santa Fe, New Mexico, USA. Association for Computational Linguistics.

Raj Dabre, Himani Shrotriya, Anoop Kunchukuttan, Ratish Puduppully, Mitesh Khapra, and Pratyush Kumar. 2022. IndicBART: A pre-trained model for indic natural language generation. In *Findings of the Association for Computational Linguistics: ACL 2022*, pages 1849–1863, Dublin, Ireland. Association for Computational Linguistics.

Jack FitzGerald, Christopher Hench, Charith Peris, Scott Mackie, Kay Rottmann, Ana Sanchez, Aaron Nash, Liam Urbach, Vishesh Kakarala, Richa Singh, Swetha Ranganath, Laurie Crist, Misha Britan, Wouter Leeuwis, Gokhan Tur, and Prem Natarajan. 2022. Massive: A 1m-example multilingual natural language understanding dataset with 51 typologically-diverse languages.

Marina Fomicheva, Shuo Sun, Lisa Yankovskaya, Frédéric Blain, Francisco Guzmán, Mark Fishel, Nikolaos Aletras, Vishrav Chaudhary, and Lucia Specia. 2020. Unsupervised Quality Estimation for Neural Machine Translation. *Transactions of the Association for Computational Linguistics*, 8:539–555.

Fabrizio Gilardi, Meysam Alizadeh, and Maël Kubli. 2023. Chatgpt outperforms crowd-workers for text-annotation tasks.

Sonal Gupta, Rushin Shah, Mrinal Mohit, Anuj Kumar, and Mike Lewis. 2018. Semantic parsing for task oriented dialog using hierarchical representations. In *Proceedings of the 2018 Conference on Empirical Methods in Natural Language Processing*, pages 2787–2792, Brussels, Belgium. Association for Computational Linguistics.

Vivek Gupta, Akshat Shrivastava, Adithya Sagar, Armen Aghajanyan, and Denis Savenkov. 2022. RetroNLU: Retrieval augmented task-oriented semantic parsing. In *Proceedings of the 4th Workshop on NLP for Conversational AI*, pages 184–196, Dublin, Ireland. Association for Computational Linguistics.

Barry Haddow and Faheem Kirefu. 2020. Pmindia – a collection of parallel corpora of languages of india.

Xiuming Huang. 1990. A machine translation system for the target language inexpert. In *COLING 1990 Volume 3: Papers presented to the 13th International Conference on Computational Linguistics*.

Rebecca Jonson. 2002. Multilingual nlp methods for multilingual dialogue systems.

Karthikeyan K, Aalok Sathe, Somak Aditya, and Monojit Choudhury. 2021. Analyzing the effects of reasoning types on cross-lingual transfer performance. In *Proceedings of the 1st Workshop on Multilingual Representation Learning*, pages 86–95, Punta Cana, Dominican Republic. Association for Computational Linguistics.

Divyanshu Kakwani, Anoop Kunchukuttan, Satish Golla, Gokul N.C., Avik Bhattacharyya, Mitesh M. Khapra, and Pratyush Kumar. 2020. IndicNLPSuite: Monolingual corpora, evaluation benchmarks and pre-trained multilingual language models for Indian languages. In *Findings of the Association for Computational Linguistics: EMNLP 2020*, pages 4948–4961, Online. Association for Computational Linguistics.

Alex Kulesza. 2012. Determinantal point processes for machine learning. *Foundations and Trends® in Machine Learning*, 5(2-3):123–286.

Aman Kumar, Himani Shrotriya, Prachi Sahu, Raj Dabre, Ratish Puduppully, Anoop Kunchukuttan, Amogh Mishra, Mitesh M. Khapra, and Pratyush Kumar. 2022. Indicnlg suite: Multilingual datasets for diverse nlg tasks in indic languages.

Mike Lewis, Yinhan Liu, Naman Goyal, Marjan Ghazvininejad, Abdelrahman Mohamed, Omer Levy, Veselin Stoyanov, and Luke Zettlemoyer. 2020. BART: Denoising sequence-to-sequence pre-training for natural language generation, translation, and comprehension. In *Proceedings of the 58th Annual Meeting of the Association for Computational Linguistics*, pages 7871–7880, Online. Association for Computational Linguistics.

Haoran Li, Abhinav Arora, Shuohui Chen, Anchit Gupta, Sonal Gupta, and Yashar Mehdad. 2021. MTOP: A comprehensive multilingual task-oriented semantic parsing benchmark. In *Proceedings of the 16th Conference of the European Chapter of the Association for Computational Linguistics: Main Volume*, pages 2950–2962, Online. Association for Computational Linguistics.

Davis Liang, Hila Gonen, Yuning Mao, Rui Hou, Naman Goyal, Marjan Ghazvininejad, Luke Zettlemoyer, and Madian Khabsa. 2023. Xlm-v: Overcoming the vocabulary bottleneck in multilingual masked language models.

Yinhan Liu, Jiatao Gu, Naman Goyal, Xian Li, Sergey Edunov, Marjan Ghazvininejad, Mike Lewis, and Luke Zettlemoyer. 2020. Multilingual denoising pre-training for neural machine translation. *Transactions of the Association for Computational Linguistics*, 8:726–742.

Zihan Liu, Genta Indra Winata, Peng Xu, and Pascale Fung. 2021. X2Parser: Cross-lingual and cross-domain framework for task-oriented compositional semantic parsing. In *Proceedings of the 6th Workshop on Representation Learning for NLP (RepL4NLP-2021)*, pages 112–127, Online. Association for Computational Linguistics.

Jihyung Moon, Hyunchang Cho, and Eunjeong L. Park. 2020a. Revisiting round-trip translation for quality estimation. In *Proceedings of the 22nd Annual Conference of the European Association for Machine Translation*, pages 91–104, Lisboa, Portugal. European Association for Machine Translation.

Jihyung Moon, Hyunchang Cho, and Eunjeong L. Park. 2020b. Revisiting round-trip translation for quality estimation. In *Proceedings of the 22nd Annual Conference of the European Association for Machine Translation*, pages 91–104, Lisboa, Portugal. European Association for Machine Translation.

Massimo Nicosia, Zhongdi Qu, and Yasemin Altun. 2021. Translate & Fill: Improving zero-shot multilingual semantic parsing with synthetic data. In *Findings of the Association for Computational Linguistics: EMNLP 2021*, pages 3272–3284, Punta Cana, Dominican Republic. Association for Computational Linguistics.

NLLB Team, Marta R. Costa-jussà, James Cross, Onur Çelebi, Maha Elbayad, Kenneth Heafield, Kevin Heffernan, Elahe Kalbassi, Janice Lam, Daniel Licht, Jean Maillard, Anna Sun, Skyler Wang, Guillaume Wenzek, Al Youngblood, Bapi Akula, Loic Barrault, Gabriel Mejia Gonzalez, Prangthip Hansanti, John Hoffman, Semarley Jarrett, Kaushik Ram Sadagopan, Dirk Rowe, Shannon Spruit, Chau Tran, Pierre Andrews, Necip Fazil Ayan, Shruti Bhosale, Sergey Edunov, Angela Fan, Cynthia Gao, Vedanuj Goswami, Francisco Guzmán, Philipp Koehn, Alexandre Mourachko, Christophe Ropers, Safiyyah Saleem, Holger Schwenk, and Jeff Wang. 2022. No language left behind: Scaling human-centered machine translation.

Panupong Pasupat, Sonal Gupta, Karishma Mandyam, Rushin Shah, Mike Lewis, and Luke Zettlemoyer. 2019. Span-based hierarchical semantic parsing for task-oriented dialog. In *Proceedings of the 2019 Conference on Empirical Methods in Natural Language Processing and the 9th International Joint Conference on Natural Language Processing (EMNLP-IJCNLP)*, pages 1520–1526, Hong Kong, China. Association for Computational Linguistics.

Telmo Pires, Eva Schlinger, and Dan Garrette. 2019. How multilingual is multilingual BERT? In *Proceedings of the 57th Annual Meeting of the Association for Computational Linguistics*, pages 4996–5001, Florence, Italy. Association for Computational Linguistics.

Colin Raffel, Noam Shazeer, Adam Roberts, Katherine Lee, Sharan Narang, Michael Matena, Yanqi Zhou, Wei Li, and Peter J. Liu. 2019. Exploring the limits of transfer learning with a unified text-to-text transformer.

Gowtham Ramesh, Sumanth Doddapaneni, Aravinth Bheemaraj, Mayank Jobanputra, Raghavan AK, Ajitesh Sharma, Sujit Sahoo, Harshita Diddee, Mahalakshmi J, Divyanshu Kakwani, Navneet Kumar, Aswin Pradeep, Kumar Deepak, Vivek Raghavan, Anoop Kunchukuttan, Pratyush Kumar, and Mitesh Shantadevi Khapra. 2021. Samanantar: The largest publicly available parallel corpora collection for 11 indic languages.

Vikas Raunak, Arul Menezes, and Marcin Junczys-Dowmunt. 2021. The curious case of hallucinations in neural machine translation. In *Proceedings of the 2021 Conference of the North American Chapter of the Association for Computational Linguistics: Human Language Technologies*, pages 1172–1183, Online. Association for Computational Linguistics.

Ricardo Rei, Craig Stewart, Ana C Farinha, and Alon Lavie. 2020. COMET: A neural framework for MT evaluation. In *Proceedings of the 2020 Conference on Empirical Methods in Natural Language Processing (EMNLP)*, pages 2685–2702, Online. Association for Computational Linguistics.

Andy Rosenbaum, Saleh Soltan, Wael Hamza, Yannick Versley, and Markus Boese. 2022. Linguist: Language model instruction tuning to generate annotated utterances for intent classification and slot tagging. In *COLING 2022*.

Teven Le Scao. 2022. Bloom: A 176b-parameter open-access multilingual language model. *ArXiv*, abs/2211.05100.

Sebastian Schuster, Sonal Gupta, Rushin Shah, and Mike Lewis. 2019. Cross-lingual transfer learning for multilingual task oriented dialog. In *Proceedings of the 2019 Conference of the North American Chapter of the Association for Computational Linguistics: Human Language Technologies, Volume 1 (Long and Short Papers)*, pages 3795–3805, Minneapolis, Minnesota. Association for Computational Linguistics.

Yongliang Shen, Kaitao Song, Xu Tan, Dongsheng Li, Weiming Lu, and Yueting Zhuang. 2023. Hugginggpt: Solving ai tasks with chatgpt and its friends in huggingface.

Tom Sherborne and Mirella Lapata. 2022. Zero-shot cross-lingual semantic parsing. In *Proceedings of the 60th Annual Meeting of the Association for Computational Linguistics (Volume 1: Long Papers)*, pages 4134–4153, Dublin, Ireland. Association for Computational Linguistics.

Yuqing Tang, Chau Tran, Xian Li, Peng-Jen Chen, Naman Goyal, Vishrav Chaudhary, Jiatao Gu, and Angela Fan. 2021. Multilingual translation from denoising pre-training. In *Findings of the Association for Computational Linguistics: ACL-IJCNLP 2021*, pages 3450–3466, Online. Association for Computational Linguistics.

Ashish Vaswani, Noam Shazeer, Niki Parmar, Jakob Uszkoreit, Llion Jones, Aidan N Gomez, Łukasz Kaiser, and Illia Polosukhin. 2017. Attention is all you need. In *Advances in neural information processing systems*, pages 5998–6008.

Elena Voita, Rico Sennrich, and Ivan Titov. 2019. The bottom-up evolution of representations in the transformer: A study with machine translation and language modeling objectives. In *Proceedings of the 2019 Conference on Empirical Methods in Natural Language Processing and the 9th International Joint Conference on Natural Language Processing (EMNLP-IJCNLP)*, pages 4396–4406, Hong Kong, China. Association for Computational Linguistics.

Elena Voita, Rico Sennrich, and Ivan Titov. 2021. Analyzing the source and target contributions to predictions in neural machine translation. In *Proceedings of the 59th Annual Meeting of the Association for Computational Linguistics and the 11th International Joint Conference on Natural Language Processing (Volume 1: Long Papers)*, pages 1126–1140, Online. Association for Computational Linguistics.

Hai Wang, Dian Yu, Kai Sun, Jianshu Chen, and Dong Yu. 2019. Improving pre-trained multilingual model with vocabulary expansion. In *Proceedings of the 23rd Conference on Computational Natural Language Learning (CoNLL)*, pages 316–327, Hong Kong, China. Association for Computational Linguistics.

Menglin Xia and Emilio Monti. 2021. Multilingual neural semantic parsing for low-resourced languages. In *Proceedings of *SEM 2021: The Tenth Joint Conference on Lexical and Computational Semantics*, pages 185–194, Online. Association for Computational Linguistics.

Weijia Xu, Batool Haider, and Saab Mansour. 2020. End-to-end slot alignment and recognition for cross-lingual NLU. In *Proceedings of the 2020 Conference on Empirical Methods in Natural Language Processing (EMNLP)*, pages 5052–5063, Online. Association for Computational Linguistics.

Linting Xue, Noah Constant, Adam Roberts, Mihir Kale, Rami Al-Rfou, Aditya Siddhant, Aditya Barua, and Colin Raffel. 2021. mT5: A massively multilingual pre-trained text-to-text transformer. In *Proceedings of the 2021 Conference of the North American Chapter of the Association for Computational Linguistics: Human Language Technologies*, pages 483–498, Online. Association for Computational Linguistics.

Yu Yuan and Serge Sharoff. 2020. Sentence level human translation quality estimation with attention-based neural networks. In *Proceedings of the 12th Language Resources and Evaluation Conference*, pages 1858–1865, Marseille, France. European Language Resources Association.

Tianyi Zhang*, Varsha Kishore*, Felix Wu*, Kilian Q. Weinberger, and Yoav Artzi. 2020. Bertscore: Evaluating text generation with bert. In *International Conference on Learning Representations*.

A Further Discussions

Why Indic Languages?: Indic languages are a set of Indo-Aryan languages spoken mainly in the Indian subcontinent. These languages combined are spoken by almost 22% of the total world population in monolingual, bilingual, or multilingual ways. these speakers also are the 2nd largest population of smartphone users, and almost everyone interacts with AI through chatbots. Hence it poses an excellent opportunity for NLP researchers to push state-of-the-art further for standard NLU tasks in these languages to benefit the digital business perspective and make technology more accessible to people through AI. However, most NLU benchmarks lack datasets in those languages despite some being high resource (such as 'hi,' 'bn,' and 'pa'). Moreover, with the introduction of various NLU models like IndicBERT (Kakwani et al., 2020), indicCorp, indicBART (Kumar et al., 2022), and state-of-the-art NMT module IndicTrans (Ramesh et al., 2021) that has opened new opportunities for researchers to innovate and contribute benchmark datasets which support building NLU models for Indic languages.

Lastly, discourse in languages other than English helps society understand more diverse perspectives and leads to a more inclusive society. As the world is mainly multilingual, various studies have proven that multilingual people can contribute more diverse societal perspectives through digital discourse.

Why IndicTrans translation? Furthermore we use IndicTrans because of the following three reasons, (a.) **Lightweight**: IndicTrans is an extremely lightweight yet state of the art machine translation model for Indic languages. (b.) **Indic Coverage**: IndicTrans covers the widest variety of Indic languages as compared to other models like mBART, mT5 and google translate and azure translate are not free for research. (c.) **Open Source:** IndicTrans is open source and free for research purposes, more on this is elaborated in Aggarwal et al. (2022).

Why Inter-Bilingual TOP task? Task-Oriented Parsing has seen significant advances in recent years with the rise of attention models in deep learning. There have been significant extensions of this dataset in the form of mTOP (Li et al., 2021) and multilingual-TOP (Xia and Monti, 2021). However, they remain limited in terms of language coverage, only covering a few major global languages and only Hindi in the Indic category.

These datasets are especially difficult to expand to other languages due to the fact that each language has a unique word order and the logical form of each sentence should be modified accordingly. They cannot be altered using a simple dictionary lookup or alignment technique to generate a high-quality dataset. In keeping with this, we propose an inter bilingual TOP task in which only input utterances are translated. As current computers continue to employ English to make decisions and interact with the outside world, modern dialogue managers can work with the logical forms of the English counterparts, construct a response, and translate it back to the input utterance's language.

This resolves the latency issue where the model must first convert the statement to English before parsing it with another seq2seq model. This was mentioned in section §4.1 which demonstrates that end to end models perform better than translate + parsing models in certain instances. Despite the difficulties of learning translation and parsing in a single set of hyper parameters, our research demonstrates that this is feasible with existing seq2seq models, especially models that have being pretrained with translation task.

Task Oriented Parsing in the era of ChatGPT: With the rising popularity of chatGPT [11] in open-domain conversational AI. It is still a challenge to actually use these large language models in a task-oriented manner. Moreover, these open domain models may not understand the intent of the user correctly or they may take incorrect actions provided a user utterance. These LLMs also have the risk of being biased and toxic. Recent works like HuggingGPT (Shen et al., 2023) have also shown that while these models may have outstanding language understanding capabilities, it is still better to use task specific models to execute tasks in a narrow scope.

[11] `https://openai.com/blog/chatgpt`

Model Coverages: Listed below is the language coverage for all employed multilingual models.

1. **mBART-large-50:** 'bn', 'gu', 'hi', 'ml', 'mr', 'ta', 'te'
2. **mT5-base:** 'bn', 'gu', 'hi', 'kn', 'ml', 'mr', 'pa', 'ta', 'te'
3. **IndicBART**: ''as', bn', 'gu', 'hi', 'kn', 'ml', 'mr', 'or', 'pa', 'ta', 'te'
4. **IndicBART-M2O**: ''as', bn', 'gu', 'hi', 'kn', 'ml', 'mr', 'or', 'pa', 'ta', 'te'
5. **mBART-large-50-M2O**: 'bn', 'gu', 'hi', 'ml', 'mr', 'ta', 'te'

Two-step vs End2End parsing: We measure the translation time of IndicTrans (Ramesh et al., 2021) on an NVIDIA T4 GPU and find that it takes 0.015 seconds on average to translate a single utterance from one language to another. In scenario A, this adds 0.03 seconds of latency per utterance, while our approach only adds 0.015 seconds ($\approx \frac{1}{2}$). In scenario B, where the logical form has slot values in Indic, there is no latency overhead for either approach, but there are significant development challenges due to multilingualism as discussed below.

B Details: Human Evaluation

In table 7 we show the detailed scores of human evaluation process discussed in the main paper §3.

C Details: Multilingual Models

1. **Generic Multilingual (Multilingual):** these models are generic Seq2Seq multilingual models, we used mBART-large-50, mT5-base (Liu et al., 2020; Xue et al., 2021) for experiments for this category.

2. **Indic Specific (Indic):** These seq2seq models are specifically pretrained on Indic data, we uexplore IndicBART for experiments (Dabre et al., 2022) in this category.

3. **Translation Finetuned (Translation):** These pretrained seq2seq models are finetuned on the translation task with a single target language i.e. English. The models we explored form this category areIndicBART-M2O and mBART-large-50-M2O (Dabre et al., 2022; Tang et al., 2021).

Dataset	Score	as	bn	gu	hi	kn	ml	mr	or	pa	ta	te
	Score_1	3.1	3	3.8	4.3	3.9	4.2	4.1	4.9	4.6	3.8	4.4
	Score_2	3	3	3.1	3.7	3.8	3.7	3.5	4	4.5	4.5	3.5
	Score_3	3.4	3.3	4.1	4.4	3.4	4.5	4.5	4.4	4.3	3.9	3.6
	$\text{Pearson}_{1,2}$	0.8	0.8	0.9	0.8	0.8	0.7	0.6	0.8	0.6	0.7	0.1
IE-multiATIS++	$\text{Pearson}_{1,3}$	0.6	0.9	0.2	0.5	0.8	0.7	0.4	0.6	0.7	0.7	0
	$\text{Pearson}_{2,3}$	0.6	0.8	0.1	0.5	0.6	0.5	0.6	0.7	0.6	0.8	0.7
	$\text{Spearman}_{1,2}$	0.8	0.8	0.8	0.7	0.4	0.5	0.6	0.6	0.3	0.7	0.1
	$\text{Spearman}_{1,3}$	0.7	0.9	0.2	0.5	0.8	0.8	0.5	0.6	0.5	0.7	0.1
	$\text{Spearman}_{2,3}$	0.6	0.9	0.2	0.6	0.3	0.3	0.7	0.6	0.1	0.6	0.7
	Score_1	2.9	3	4	4.6	4.4	4.4	4.3	4.9	4.7	4.1	4.4
	Score_2	3.1	3.2	3.7	4.2	4.3	4.2	4.2	4.7	4.5	4.1	3.6
	Score_3	3.2	3.5	4	4.6	4.3	3.8	4.3	4.7	4.3	4.5	3.5
	$\text{Pearson}_{1,2}$	0.7	0.8	0.5	0.7	0.5	0.7	0.6	0.6	0.7	0.6	0.4
IE-multilingualTOP	$\text{Pearson}_{1,3}$	0.6	0.7	0.4	0.5	0.3	0.4	0.7	0.4	0.7	0.4	0.5
	$\text{Pearson}_{2,3}$	0.4	0.8	0.7	0.4	0.6	0.4	0.6	0.2	0.6	0.8	0.9
	$\text{Spearman}_{1,2}$	0.7	0.8	0.4	0.5	0.4	0.5	0.6	0.5	0.5	0.6	0.4
	$\text{Spearman}_{1,3}$	0.6	0.7	0.4	0.3	0.3	0.4	0.7	0.3	0.5	0.3	0.4
	$\text{Spearman}_{2,3}$	0.4	0.8	0.8	0.3	0.6	0.4	0.6	0.1	0.5	0.6	0.7
	Score_1	2.9	3.2	4.2	4.3	4.5	4.3	4.1	4.8	4.7	4.2	4.5
	Score_2	2.8	3.5	3.8	4.2	4	3.9	3.9	4.4	4.2	4	4.3
	Score_3	3.2	3.6	4	4.7	4.3	3.8	4	4.6	4.4	4.3	3.6
	$\text{Pearson}_{1,2}$	0.8	0.7	0.6	0.7	0.5	0.6	0.8	0.4	0.4	0.4	0.3
IE-mTOP	$\text{Pearson}_{1,3}$	0.6	0.8	0.5	0.4	0.8	0.6	0.7	0.3	0.2	0.4	0.3
	$\text{Pearson}_{2,3}$	0.5	0.7	0.7	0.5	0.5	0.7	0.7	0.6	0.1	0.7	0.6
	$\text{Spearman}_{1,2}$	0.9	0.7	0.6	0.6	0.4	0.6	0.8	0.4	0.3	0.3	0.3
	$\text{Spearman}_{1,3}$	0.6	0.7	0.5	0.3	0.5	0.7	0.6	0.4	0.2	0.3	0.5
	$\text{Spearman}_{2,3}$	0.5	0.7	0.7	0.5	0.3	0.6	0.6	0.7	0.3	0.5	0.4

Table 7: Detailed Human Evaluation Scores. Score_x refers to the average score of the column language given by x annotator. $\text{Pearson}_{x,y}$ refers to the person correlation between the scores of annotators x and y for the column language and similarly for $\text{Spearman}_{x,y}$

4. **Monolingual (Monolingual):** These seq2seq models are pretrained on English data only. They were utilize only in the Translate Test setting. The models we explored form this category are T5-large, T5-base (Raffel et al., 2019) and BART-base, BART-large (Lewis et al., 2020).

D Hyperparameters Details

In Table 8 the hyperparamaters are abbreviated as mentioned below:

1. **PO:** Pre-training Objective.
2. **PD:** Pretraining Dataset,
3. **LR:** Learning Rate,
4. **BS:** Batch Size,
5. **NE:** Maximum Number of Epochs,
6. **WD:** Weight Decay,
7. **MSL:** Maximum Sequence Length,
8. **MS:** Model Size described as a number of parameters in millions,
9. **WS**: Warm-up Step.

All the experiments were run on RTX A5000 GPUs in Jarvis labs [12]. The code was written in PyTorch and Huggingface accelerate library [13]. We used early stopping callback in training process with patience of 2 epochs for each setting.

The Average runtime for each for T5-base, BART-base, IndicBART, IndicBART-M2O was 3 minutes for IE-mTOP, 1 minute for IE-multiATIS++ and 5 minutes for IE-multilingualTOP. The Average runtime for each for T5-large, BART-large, mT5-base,mBART-large-50, mBART-large-50-M2O was 5 minutes for IE-mTOP, 3 minute for IE-multiATIS++ and 10 minutes for IE-multilingualTOP.

E Vocabulary Augmentation

Unique Intents and slots from each dataset (IE-mTOP, IE-multilingualTOP, IE-multiATIS++) were extracted and added to the tokenizer and model vocabulary so that the models could predict them more accurately. In a typical slot and intent tagging task, these tags would have been treated as classes in the classification model. However, since our models are trained to not predict the entire word but only subwords (Raffel et al., 2019; Lewis et al., 2020) as usually done in modern self-attention architecture (Vaswani et al., 2017), we

[12] https://jarvislabs.ai/

[13] https://huggingface.co/docs/accelerate/index

Hyper Parameter	MS	LR	WD	MSL	BS	NE	PO	PD
BART-base	139	3.00e-3	0.001	64	128	50	Denoising Autoencoder	Wikepedia Data (Lewis et al., 2020)
BART-large	406	3.00e-5	0.001	64	16	50	Denoising Autoencoder	Wikepedia Data
T5-base	222	3.00e-3	0.001	64	256	50	Multi task Pretraining	C4 (Raffel et al., 2019)
T5-large	737	3.00e-5	0.001	64	16	50	Multi task Pretraining	C4
IndicBART	244	3.00e-3	0.001	64	128	50	Denoising Autoencoder	Indic Corp (Kakwani et al., 2020)
mBART-large-50	610	1.00e-4	0.001	64	16	50	Denoising Autoencoder	CC25(Liu et al., 2020)
mT5-base	582	3.00e-4	0.001	64	16	50	Multi task Pretraining	mC4 (Xue et al., 2021)
IndicBART-M2O	244	3.00e-3	0.001	64	128	50	Denoising Autoencoder	PM India (Haddow and Kirefu, 2020)
mBART-large-50-M2O	610	1.00e-4	0.001	64	16	50	Denoising Autoencoder	WMT16 (Barrault et al., 2020)

Table 8: Hyper Parameters and Pretraining Details

decided to include them in the vocabulary so that they can be generated easily during prediction runtime. This also contributed to the reduction of the maximum sequence length to 64 tokens, which improved generalisation as seq2seq models generalise better on shorter sequences (Voita et al., 2021). The Excel spreadsheet containing unique slots and intents will be made accessible alongside the code and supplemental materials.

F Additional Results

F.1 Other Train Test Settings

We include the results of all other settings except Train All (Already discussed in main paper) in table 9 till 15. We have discussed the comparisons of these settings in main paper §4.1.

F.2 Translate Test vs End2End models

While the performance of Monolingual models in the Translate Test setting is adequate, the performance of models in the end-to-end Train All setting outperform. Translation is prone to error, and the acquired logical form in English cannot be guaranteed to be precise. Moreover, a two-step approach to translation followed by parsing will incur greater execution time than a unified model.

F.3 Unified Models Results

In unified models, we observe a gain of atleast 0.15 in all languages for all datasets for both IndicBART-M2O and mBART-large-50-M2O.

F.4 Language verses Language

From figure 7, 8, 9 we observe that IndicBART-M2O is a more consistent than mBART-large-50-M2O.

F.5 Exact Match Results

We calculated modified exact match scores as inspired by Awasthi et al. (2023) which are agnostic of the positions of the slot tokens in the logical form. These scores are presented in tables 12, 13, 14, 15. We observed that exact match is a stricter metric as compared to tree labelled F1 (Gupta et al., 2018). We also observe that exact match scores are consistent with tree labelled F1 scores across languages, datasets and models.

G Original verses Interbilingual Hindi

As demonstrated by figure 1, we have data accessible in Hindi for all three settings. To produce Hindi bilingual TOP data, we utilize mTOP and multi-ATIS++ to internally combine Hindi and English data tables by unique id (uid). To construct our dataset, we filter the Hindi utterances column and the English logical form columns; we refer to these datasets as hi_{IE} in table 4. Furthermore, we conduct tests using original Hindi datasets (slot values in Hindi in logical form) and compare their performance to that of other languages. In the table 4, we refer to these datasets as hi_{O} for the mTOP dataset and multi-ATIS++ dataset both.

Analysis. We see a decline in F1 score for all models for hi_{IE} in both IE-mTOP and IE-multiATIS++. This might be due to data loss when hindi and english data are combined, as not all utterances of english data are included in both datasets. Furthermore, the hindi utterances in the original dataset may be more complex. The results for hi_{O} and hi_{O} enhances because the tokens were copied from the utterance and the model does not have to transform the tokens to English.

Dataset	Model	Translate Test											ModAvg
		as	bn	gu	hi	kn	ml	mr	or	pa	ta	te	
IE-mTOP	BART-base	28	37	35	**42**	35	38	39	35	36	41	33	36
	BART-large	30	41	38	44	38	41	41	39	38	**46**	36	39
	T5-base	31	44	41	**49**	41	43	43	41	42	47	41	42
	T5-large	29	43	39	**47**	39	42	42	40	40	44	38	40
	IndicBART	30	40	36	42	36	40	39	38	37	**42**	33	38
	mT5-base	34	43	40	48	40	43	43	38	40	**45**	38	41
	mBART-large-50	18	20	20	**23**	20	19	23	16	21	**23**	21	20
	IndicBART-M2O	35	44	43	51	44	46	44	41	42	**49**	41	44
	mBART-large-50-M2O	36	45	45	**50**	45	47	46	41	46	53	43	**45**
	Language Average	30	40	37	**44**	38	40	40	37	38	43	36	38
IE-multilingualTOP	BART-base	11	15	**16**	**16**	13	14	13	14	14	14	16	14
	BART-large	12	18	19	**20**	16	16	15	16	16	16	19	17
	T5-base	8	11	12	**13**	11	11	11	11	11	11	**13**	11
	T5-large	7	9	10	**11**	8	8	8	9	9	8	10	9
	IndicBART	20	29	31	**32**	27	29	25	26	27	25	31	27
	mT5-base	20	26	26	**28**	25	25	24	23	25	24	27	25
	mBART-large-50	26	34	35	**38**	34	35	33	30	34	32	36	33
	IndicBART-M2O	20	27	29	**30**	27	28	25	25	26	25	29	26
	mBART-large-50-M2O	30	42	45	**46**	41	44	41	38	41	39	45	**41**
	Language Average	17	23	25	26	22	23	22	21	23	22	25	23
IE-multiATIS++	BART-base	15	**20**	14	18	17	18	14	18	17	16	18	17
	BART-large	15	20	14	15	19	19	14	**21**	16	17	20	17
	T5-base	46	**70**	52	62	61	65	47	51	58	51	66	57
	T5-large	49	**74**	58	66	62	70	48	52	63	53	70	60
	IndicBART	44	**66**	46	56	54	63	47	46	58	49	63	54
	mT5-base	25	25	18	26	24	26	19	**27**	25	20	24	24
	mBART-large-50	55	70	58	70	66	**71**	60	56	68	59	68	64
	IndicBART-M2O	44	61	48	55	52	**68**	48	53	56	47	59	54
	mBART-large-50-M2O	53	70	68	**76**	67	73	63	62	69	56	71	**66**
	Language Average	38	**53**	42	49	47	**53**	40	43	48	41	51	46

Table 9: $Tree\_Labelled\_F1 * 100$ scores for the all the dataset for **Translate Test** settings. **ModAvg** is shorthand for Model Average. The bold numbers in the table indicate the row-wise maximum, i.e. the model's best language performance in the given context. The numbers in bold in the **ModAvg** column indicate the model with the best performance for the train-test strategy specified in the table's heading. Similarly, the numbers in bold in the **Language Average** row indicate the language with the best performance for that train-test strategy.

Dataset	Model	Indic Train											Model Average
		as	bn	gu	hi	kn	ml	mr	or	pa	ta	te	
IE-mTOP	IndicBART	19	**55**	35	53	33	30	50	15	31	45	44	37
	mBART-large-50	41	51	14	**60**	22	25	25	4	44	0	57	31
	mT5-base	30	22	28	52	50	**54**	36	8	36	53	15	35
	IndicBART-M2O	50	55	45	61	55	58	58	53	13	56	**59**	51
	mBART-large-50-M2O	55	59	61	**66**	56	63	57	52	53	59	63	**59**
	Language Average	39	48	37	**58**	43	46	45	26	35	43	48	43
IE-multilingualTOP	IndicBART	36	29	24	**65**	48	9	56	30	37	42	40	38
	mBART-large-50	51	55	35	55	55	54	54	50	34	55	**57**	50
	mT5-base	45	**56**	**56**	20	23	49	47	47	10	37	**56**	41
	IndicBART-M2O	50	56	60	**63**	60	20	55	15	57	57	62	50
	mBART-large-50-M2O	52	60	62	**65**	60	59	57	57	51	58	64	**59**
	Language Average	47	51	47	**54**	49	38	**54**	40	38	50	56	48
IE-multiATIS++	IndicBART	12	16	8	**25**	15	19	22	22	23	22	18	19
	mBART-large-50	16	18	10	30	10	10	18	13	**33**	20	15	18
	mT5-base	15	**39**	16	18	24	18	25	6	11	35	28	22
	IndicBART-M2O	34	**86**	63	68	73	74	57	63	64	63	71	68
	mBART-large-50-M2O	71	**92**	82	81	69	80	72	4	66	74	82	**70**
	Language Average	30	**50**	36	44	38	40	39	22	39	43	43	39

Table 10: $Tree\_Labelled\_F1 * 100$ scores for the all the dataset for **Indic Train** setting. The numbers in bold in the **Model Average** column indicate the model with the best performance for the train-test strategy specified in the table's heading. Similarly, the numbers in bold in the **Language Average** row indicate the language with the best performance for that train-test strategy.

Dataset	Model	English+Indic Train											Model Average
		as	bn	gu	hi	kn	ml	mr	or	pa	ta	te	
IE-mTOP	**IndicBART**	34	37	42	**58**	41	35	54	10	42	44	43	40
	mBART-large-50	50	52	58	56	54	51	55	0	42	**59**	57	49
	mT5-base	31	25	45	**60**	48	36	44	21	6	46	48	37
	IndicBART-M2O	51	54	57	60	57	58	54	57	57	55	**62**	57
	mBART-large-50-M2O	57	60	60	65	62	**66**	58	55	58	65	64	**61**
	Language Average	45	46	52	**60**	52	49	53	29	41	54	55	49
IE-multilingualTOP	**IndicBART**	43	45	52	53	47	40	**57**	30	47	38	49	46
	mBART-large-50	0	35	35	39	0	56	48	22	58	0	**60**	32
	mT5-base	14	53	**56**	50	53	50	50	48	52	51	**56**	48
	mBART-large-50-M2O	56	60	63	**66**	61	60	57	57	60	60	64	60
	IndicBART-M2O	54	56	60	**63**	60	58	54	57	24	57	**63**	**55**
	Language Average	33	50	53	**54**	44	53	53	43	48	41	58	48
IE-multiATIS++	**IndicBART**	34	12	12	**58**	25	21	65	12	30	16	37	29
	mBART-large-50	43	22	69	**78**	14	54	58	12	36	10	66	42
	mT5-base	25	36	28	38	33	**44**	23	23	35	30	35	32
	mBART-large-50-M2O	21	**86**	78	74	73	76	56	64	72	65	75	**67**
	IndicBART-M2O	71	**87**	77	77	71	82	74	54	45	71	82	72
	Language Average	39	49	53	**65**	43	55	55	33	44	38	59	48

Table 11: $Tree\_Labelled\_F1 * 100$ scores for the all the dataset for **English+Indic Train** setting. The numbers in bold in the **Model Average** column indicate the model with the best performance for the train-test strategy specified in the table's heading. Similarly, the numbers in bold in the **Language Average** row indicate the language with the best performance for that train-test strategy.

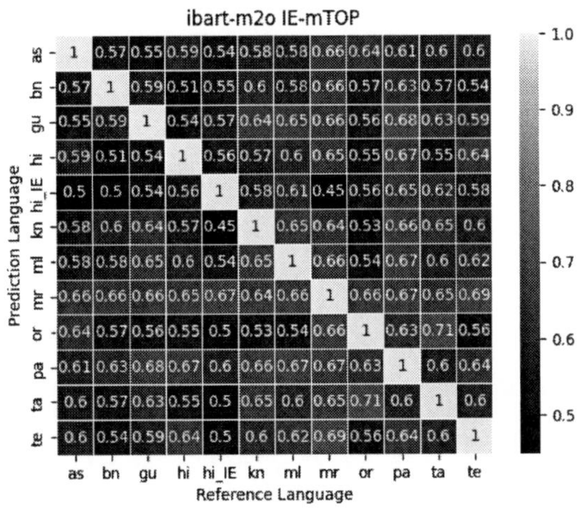

(a) IndicBART-M2O

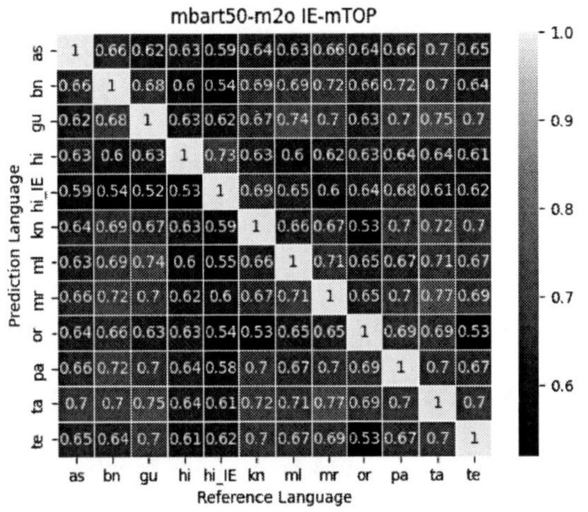

(b) mBART-large-50-M2O

Figure 7: Language wise f1 score of predictions of 2 languages for **IE-mTOP dataset** for **Train All** setting

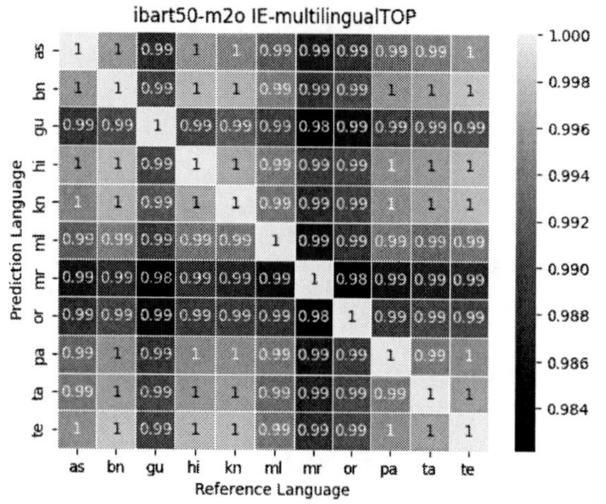

(a) IndicBART-M2O

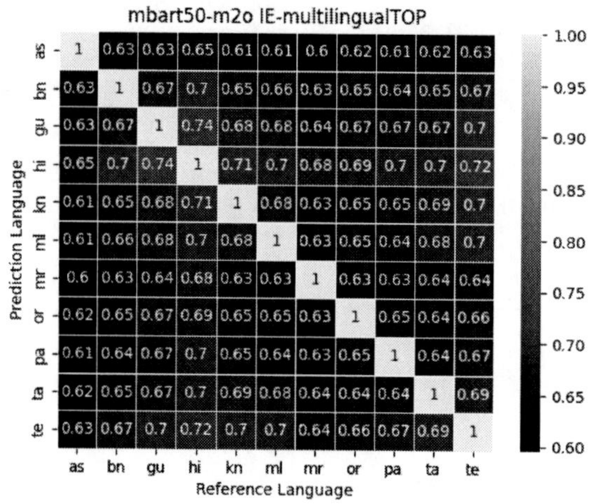

(b) mBART-large-50-M2O

Figure 8: Language wise f1 score of predictions of 2 languages for **IE-multilingualTOP Dataset** for **Train All** settings

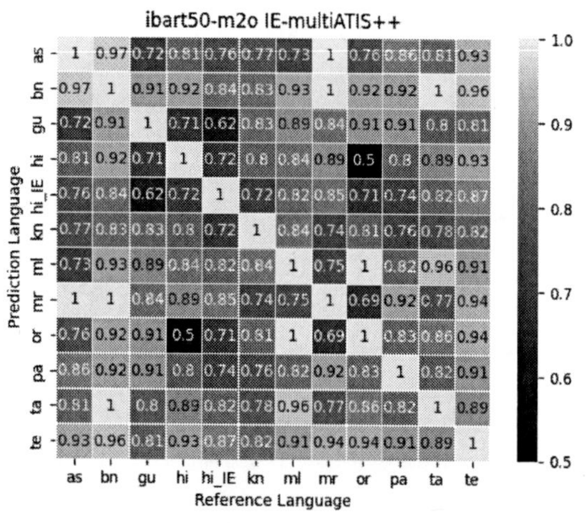

(a) IndicBART-M2O

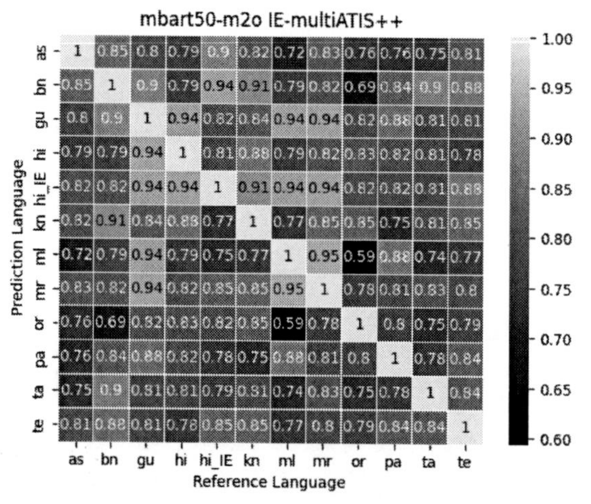

(b) mBART-large-50-M2O

Figure 9: Language wise f1 score of predictions of 2 languages for **IE-multiATIS++ Dataset** for **Train All** settings

Dataset	Model	Train All													ModAvg
		as	bn	gu	hi	kn	ml	mr	or	pa	ta	te	hi_O	hi_{IE}	
IE-mTOP	IndicBART	31	32	29	**42**	29	32	42	20	28	30	31	64	49	35
	IndicBART-M2O	42	40	46	48	46	52	47	47	48	48	**50**	68	53	49
	mBART-large-50	37	33	40	**48**	39	42	38	43	36	42	35	62	51	42
	mBART-large-50-M2O	48	45	50	50	50	53	49	50	47	**53**	51	67	54	**51**
	mT5-base	43	47	51	**52**	50	51	50	50	47	51	**52**	59	55	**51**
	Language Average	40	39	43	**46**	43	**46**	45	42	41	45	44	61	50	45
IE-multilingualTOP	IndicBART	35	38	42	**56**	39	37	47	22	38	36	43	-	-	39
	IndicBART-M2O	45	47	47	55	46	46	52	45	53	50	**57**	-	-	49
	mBART-large-50	37	41	43	**48**	41	41	36	40	40	41	47	-	-	41
	mBART-large-50-M2O	49	53	55	**60**	53	53	48	52	52	53	59	-	-	**53**
	mT5-base	43	49	52	**56**	52	50	47	45	49	48	54	-	-	50
	Language Average	28	31	33	**37**	32	31	31	27	30	30	34	-	-	31
IE-multiATIS++	IndicBART	37	20	23	**41**	32	23	37	13	39	38	19	34	16	29
	IndicBART-M2O	43	45	40	**59**	53	44	58	34	45	46	40	55	37	46
	mBART-large-50	60	85	73	**76**	75	76	60	59	67	66	72	36	18	63
	mBART-large-50-M2O	67	80	71	**73**	71	71	66	58	72	66	68	49	31	**65**
	mT5-base	45	70	58	**61**	60	**61**	45	44	52	51	57	34	16	50
	Language Average	50	60	53	**62**	58	55	53	42	55	53	51	42	24	51

Table 12: $Exact\_Match$*100 scores for the all the dataset for **Train All** settings. **ModAvg** is shorthand for Model Average. The bold numbers in the table indicate the row-wise maximum, i.e. the model's best language performance in the given context. The numbers in bold in the **ModAvg** column indicate the model with the best performance for the train-test strategy specified in the table's heading. Similarly, the numbers in bold in the **Language Average** row indicate the language with the best performance for that train-test strategy.

Dataset	Model	Translate Test											Model Average
		as	bn	gu	hi	kn	ml	mr	or	pa	ta	te	
IE-mTOP	IndicBART	29	40	38	**47**	38	40	41	39	37	43	34	**39**
	IndicBART-M2O	28	37	36	**46**	37	39	39	39	35	43	35	38
	BART-base	18	28	28	**35**	27	29	29	29	28	33	24	28
	BART-large	23	35	33	40	33	36	36	36	33	**41**	30	34
	mBART-large-50	13	14	15	**17**	15	13	18	15	16	16	14	15
	mBART-large-50-M2O	29	38	39	44	38	39	39	36	38	**46**	36	38
	mT5-base	26	36	33	**42**	33	36	36	33	32	38	31	34
	T5-base	21	33	31	**40**	30	31	33	35	31	37	32	32
	T5-large	20	33	29	**38**	29	31	32	35	30	35	29	31
	Language Average	23	33	31	**39**	31	33	34	33	31	37	29	32
IE-multilingualTOP	IndicBART	16	24	26	**28**	21	24	20	21	22	20	26	23
	IndicBART-M2O	13	20	23	**24**	20	21	18	19	19	19	22	20
	BART-base	12	13	13	**14**	11	12	11	11	12	11	13	12
	BART-large	10	15	16	**17**	13	14	12	14	13	14	16	14
	mBART-large-50	22	30	31	**35**	30	31	29	26	29	28	32	29
	mBART-large-50-M2O	26	38	40	**43**	36	38	36	33	35	34	40	**36**
	mT5-base	15	20	21	**23**	19	20	18	18	20	19	21	19
	T5-base	12	13	12	**15**	10	12	13	9	11	14	14	12
	T5-large	22	23	22	25	26	26	25	26	26	26	**27**	25
	Language Average	16	22	23	**25**	21	22	20	20	21	21	23	21
IE-multiATIS++	IndicBART	30	49	34	41	41	**51**	34	33	43	33	44	39
	IndicBART-M2O	32	51	39	44	40	**59**	37	42	43	35	46	43
	BART-base	31	**32**	**32**	30	31	30	30	30	30	30	30	31
	BART-large	31	**32**	**32**	30	31	30	30	30	31	31	31	31
	mBART-large-50	41	56	54	62	61	**66**	54	50	60	47	56	55
	mBART-large-50-M2O	40	60	66	**69**	62	66	57	58	60	47	59	**59**
	mT5-base	24	29	28	**35**	28	24	26	27	22	25	24	27
	T5-base	34	53	44	48	**55**	61	34	42	42	43	56	47
	T5-large	38	**60**	51	57	56	68	34	42	50	44	57	51
	Language Average	33	47	42	46	45	**51**	37	39	42	37	45	42

Table 13: $Exact\_Match$*100 scores for the all the dataset for **Translate Test** settings. The bold numbers in the table indicate the row-wise maximum, i.e. the model's best language performance in the given context. The numbers in bold in the **Model Average** column indicate the model with the best performance for the train-test strategy specified in the table's heading. Similarly, the numbers in bold in the **Language Average** row indicate the language with the best performance for that train-test strategy.

Dataset	Model	Indic Train											Model Average
		as	bn	gu	hi	kn	ml	mr	or	pa	ta	te	
IE-mTOP	IndicBART	24	26	29	33	28	24	**44**	12	25	23	23	26
	IndicBART-M2O	43	48	49	56	48	**53**	52	47	6	49	50	46
	mBART-large-50	34	44	43	**55**	40	44	45	27	36	0	50	38
	mBART-large-50-M2O	48	53	55	**62**	50	58	53	48	46	54	57	**53**
	mT5-base	22	29	21	**45**	42	46	29	24	28	25	24	30
	Language Average	34	40	39	**50**	42	45	45	32	28	30	41	39
IE-multilingualTOP	IndicBART	30	24	20	**61**	43	37	51	25	31	37	32	36
	IndicBART-M2O	45	54	56	**60**	56	15	51	20	54	53	59	48
	mBART-large-50	46	51	50	**57**	51	50	49	46	31	50	54	49
	mBART-large-50-M2O	49	56	59	**62**	56	55	53	53	46	54	60	**55**
	mT5-base	40	40	51	**61**	51	43	43	43	40	47	53	47
	Language Average	42	45	47	**60**	51	40	49	37	40	48	52	47
IE-multiATIS++	IndicBART	46	45	43	**54**	32	34	46	23	20	30	32	37
	IndicBART-M2O	56	56	54	**74**	44	55	68	47	40	50	52	54
	mBART-large-50	56	67	**76**	66	54	47	59	62	51	53	46	58
	mBART-large-50-M2O	66	**91**	81	81	60	65	72	78	69	65	60	**72**
	mT5-base	46	53	47	**56**	45	47	48	42	43	44	45	47
	Language Average	54	62	60	**66**	47	50	59	50	45	48	47	53

Table 14: $Exact\_Match{*}100$ scores for the all the dataset for **Indic Train** settings. The bold numbers in the table indicate the row-wise maximum, i.e. the model's best language performance in the given context. The numbers in bold in the **Model Average** column indicate the model with the best performance for the train-test strategy specified in the table's heading. Similarly, the numbers in bold in the **Language Average** row indicate the language with the best performance for that train-test strategy.

Dataset	Model	English+Indic Train											Model Average
		as	bn	gu	hi	kn	ml	mr	or	pa	ta	te	
IE-mTOP	IndicBART	27	29	36	**53**	34	28	49	17	34	37	36	35
	IndicBART-M2O	45	46	50	**54**	51	53	50	53	53	51	**54**	51
	mBART-large-50	43	46	50	50	47	45	50	0	37	**54**	50	43
	mBART-large-50-M2O	51	55	53	**61**	56	62	54	51	53	60	**61**	**56**
	mT5-base	23	30	37	**56**	41	27	38	16	27	38	39	34
	Langauge Average	38	41	45	**55**	46	43	48	27	41	48	48	44
IE-multilingualTOP	IndicBART	37	30	47	52	42	35	**53**	25	42	33	44	40
	IndicBART-M2O	48	52	56	59	56	54	50	53	16	53	**60**	51
	mBART-large-50	45	49	42	54	47	52	44	25	54	**56**	**56**	48
	mBART-large-50-M2O	51	56	**59**	63	57	56	53	53	56	57	61	**57**
	mT5-base	39	48	51	46	49	45	42	43	47	47	**52**	46
	Language Average	44	47	51	**55**	50	48	48	40	43	49	**55**	48
IE-multiATIS++	IndicBART	28	32	32	**63**	31	25	57	10	29	33	28	33
	IndicBART-M2O	74	**78**	76	**78**	72	80	40	54	64	53	68	**67**
	mBART-large-50	31	40	71	**83**	71	69	57	21	23	40	58	51
	mBART-large-50-M2O	64	84	73	78	70	**88**	71	46	66	70	76	71
	mT5-base	18	25	22	**35**	26	29	26	28	28	25	27	26
	Language Average	43	52	55	**67**	54	58	50	32	42	44	51	50

Table 15: $Exact\_Match{*}100$ scores for the all the dataset for **English+Indic Train** settings. The bold numbers in the table indicate the row-wise maximum, i.e. the model's best language performance in the given context. The numbers in bold in the **Model Average** column indicate the model with the best performance for the train-test strategy specified in the table's heading. Similarly, the numbers in bold in the **Language Average** row indicate the language with the best performance for that train-test strategy.

Zero-Shot Dialogue Relation Extraction by Relating Explainable Triggers and Relation Names

Ze-Song Xu Yun-Nung Chen
National Taiwan University, Taipei, Taiwan
r10922a07@csie.ntu.edu.tw y.v.chen@ieee.org

Abstract

Developing dialogue relation extraction (DRE) systems often requires a large amount of labeled data, which can be costly and time-consuming to annotate. In order to improve scalability and support diverse, unseen relation extraction, this paper proposes a method for leveraging the ability to capture triggers and relate them to previously unseen relation names. Specifically, we introduce a model that enables zero-shot dialogue relation extraction by utilizing trigger-capturing capabilities. Our experiments on a benchmark DialogRE dataset demonstrate that the proposed model achieves significant improvements for both seen and unseen relations. Notably, this is the first attempt at zero-shot dialogue relation extraction using trigger-capturing capabilities, and our results suggest that this approach is effective for inferring previously unseen relation types. Overall, our findings highlight the potential for this method to enhance the scalability and practicality of DRE systems.[1]

1 Introduction

Relation extraction (RE) is a key natural language processing (NLP) task that identifies the semantic relationships between arguments in various types of text data. It involves extracting relevant information and representing it in a structured form for downstream applications (Zhang et al., 2017; Cohen et al., 2020; Zhou and Chen, 2021; Huguet Cabot and Navigli, 2021). Dialogue relation extraction (DRE) is a specialized area of RE that focuses on identifying semantic relationships between arguments in conversations. Recent DRE research has used diverse methods to improve relation extraction performance, including constructing dialogue graphs (Lee and Choi, 2021), identifying explicit triggers (Albalak et al., 2022; Lin et al., 2022), and using prompt-based fine-tuning approaches (Son et al., 2022).

Supervised training for RE tasks can be time-consuming and expensive due to the requirement for a large amount of labeled data. Models trained on limited data can only predict the relations they have been trained on, making it challenging to identify similar but unseen relations. Hence, recent research has explored methods that require only a few labeled examples or no labeled examples at all, such as prompt-based fine-tuning (Schick and Schütze, 2020; Puri and Catanzaro, 2019). Additionally, Sainz et al. (2021) improved zero-shot performance by transforming the RE task into an entailment task. However, this approach has not yet been applied to DRE due to the challenge of converting long conversations into NLI format.

In this work, we observe that different relations may be dependent on each other, such as the *parent-child* relationship listed in Table 1. Prior work has treated all relations independently and modeled different labels in a multi-class scenario, making it impossible for models to handle unseen relations even if they are relevant to previously seen relations. Therefore, this paper focuses on enabling zero-shot relation prediction. Specifically, if we encounter an unseen relation during testing but have previously seen a similar relation, we can relate them through explicitly mentioned trigger words, such as per:children (seen relation) → "mom" (trigger) → per:parents (unseen relation).

To achieve this, we need to identify the key information of the relation as a tool for relation reasoning during inference. We adopt the approach proposed in Lin et al. (2022), which achieves remarkable results in DRE by capturing explainable keywords in a dialogue for guiding relation extraction. By leveraging such trigger-capturing capabilities, our proposed model can better deduce unseen relations from known relations and associated triggers. Therefore, the proposed DRE model is more practical, as it can generalize to unseen relations.

[1]Code: https://github.com/MiuLab/UnseenDRE.

Proceedings of the 5th Workshop on NLP for Conversational AI (NLP4ConvAI 2023), pages 123–128
July 14, 2023

DialogRE Relation	Similar DialogRE Relation
per:positive_impression	per:negative_impression
per:boss	per:subordinate
per:children	per:parents
gpe:residents_of_place	per:place_of_residence
per:place_of_birth	gpe:births_in_place
org:students	per:schools_attended
per:visited_place	gpe:visitors_of_place
per:employee_or_member_of	org:employees_or_members

Table 1: Similar relation examples in DialogRE.

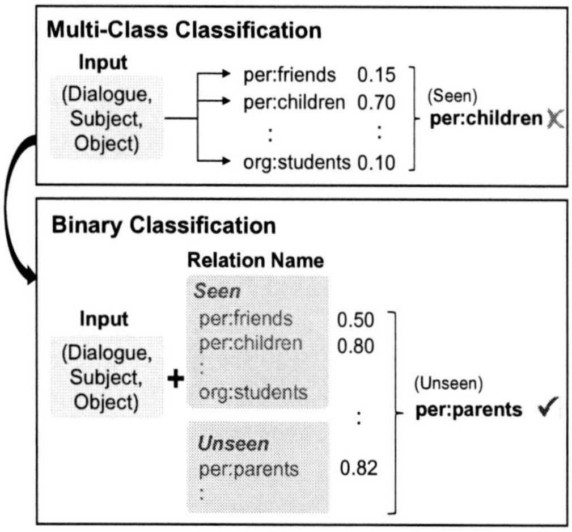

Figure 1: The illustration of our proposed zero-shot relation extraction model.

2 Proposed Approach

Prior work on classical DRE has treated it as a multi-class classification problem, which makes it challenging to scale to unseen relation scenarios. To enable a zero-shot setting, we reformulate the multi-class classification task into multiple binary classification tasks by adding each relation name as input, as illustrated in Figure 1. The binary classification task predicts whether the subject and object in the dialogue belong to the given relation. This approach is equivalent to predicting whether a set of subject-object relations is established, which can estimate any relations based only on their names (or natural language descriptions).

2.1 Model Architecture

Our model is illustrated in Figure 2, where there are three components in our architecture.

Trigger Prediction Inspired by Lin et al. (2022), we incorporate a trigger predictor into our model, allowing us to employ explicit cues for identifying subject-object relationships within a dialogue. Specifically, we adapt techniques from question-answering models to predict the start and end positions of the trigger span. By detecting these triggers, our model not only reasons the potential unseen relations but also enhances the interpretability of the task, making it more practical for real-world applications. To identify the keywords associated with `(Subject, Object, RelationType)` in a dialogue, we formulate the task as an extractive question-answering problem (Rajpurkar et al., 2016). In this setting, the dialogue can be viewed as a document, where the subject-object pair represents the question, and the answer corresponds to the span of keywords that explain the associated relation, i.e., the triggers.

Relation Name Injection In contrast to most prior work (Lee and Choi, 2021; Lin et al., 2022; Albalak et al., 2022), our input format includes the relation name after `[CLS]`, and we use the `[CLS]`-associated embeddings as relation name embeddings shown in Figure 2. By doing so, the model has access to *natural language descriptions* of the given relation, which facilitates more accurate capture of trigger words and further enables the zero-shot capability of the proposed model.

Binary Relation Prediction In our model, the relation predictor takes as input the learned relation name embedding and a predicted trigger span, as illustrated in the upper part of Figure 2. To establish the relationship between the relation name and its associated trigger words, we employ a general attention mechanism, where the relation name embedding serves as the query, while the trigger words are encoded by BERT and used as keys and values. The resulting features are then concatenated and fed through a fully connected layer, which generates the final prediction indicating whether the input subject and object have the given relation as

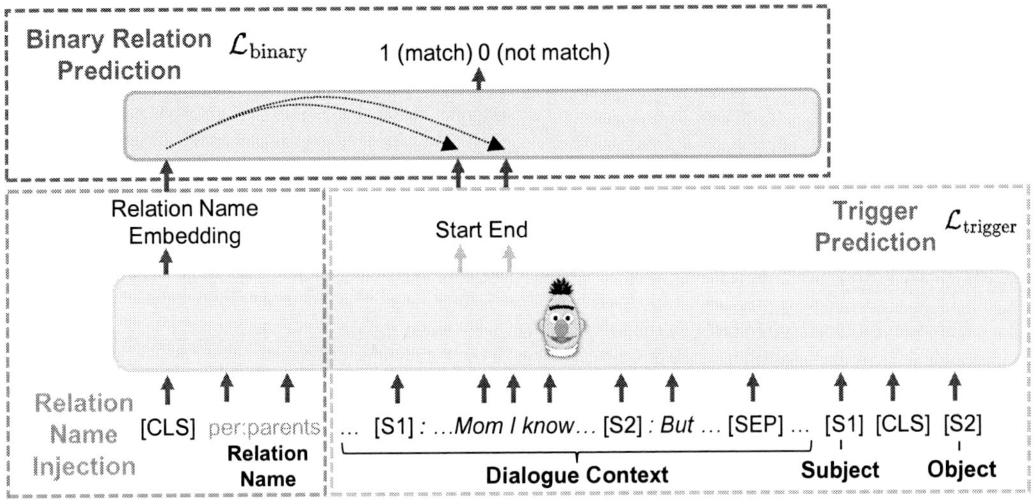

Figure 2: The illustration of our proposed model architecture.

expressed in the dialogue.

2.2 Training

As depicted in Figure 2, the input (`Dialogue, Subject, Oubject, RelationType`) will be initially expanded into a sequence resembling BERT's input format. The model is trained to perform two tasks. Firstly, it learns the ability to find the trigger span, and secondly, it learns to incorporate the triggers into the relation prediction.

Negative Sampling In accordance with Mikolov et al. (2013), we have adopted the negative sampling method in our training process. Specifically, we randomly select some relations from the set of previously observed relations that do not correspond to the given subject-object pair to create negative samples. Notably, the trigger spans of these negative samples remain unchanged.

Multi-Task Learning The trigger prediction task involves identifying the most likely trigger positions, and is treated as a single-label classification problem using cross-entropy loss $\mathcal{L}_{Trigger}$. On the other hand, the relation prediction task employs binary cross-entropy loss $\mathcal{L}_{Binary}$ to compute the prediction loss. To train the model simultaneously on both tasks, we employ multi-task learning. We use a linear combination of the two losses as the objective function. This enables us to train the entire model in an end-to-end fashion.

2.3 Inference

During inference, our model follows a similar setting to the one used during training. However, we have observed that the model tends to predict the seen relation when the captured trigger words are present in the training data. To prevent the model from overfitting to the seen relations, we replace the trigger span with a general embedding (the embedding of `[CLS]`), which is assumed to carry the information of the entire sentence. This embedding is used as the input for our relation prediction. By doing so, our model can better generalize to unseen scenarios and can avoid the tendency to predict the seen relation when capturing seen trigger words. This approach enhances the model's ability to handle diverse unseen relations during inference.

3 Experiments

We conducted experiments using the DialogRE dataset, which is widely used as a benchmark in the field. To assess our model's zero-shot capability, we divided the total of 36 relations into 20 seen and 16 unseen types detailed in the Appendix. We only train our model on data related to seen relation types. During training, we set the learning rate to 3e-5 and used a GeForce RTX 2080 Ti. The training process involves 10 epochs without early stopping[2], and the number of negative samples was 3. To ensure a fair comparison with prior work (Lin et al., 2022; Yu et al., 2020), we use the same testing set for evaluation.

3.1 Evaluation Metric

After performing multiple binary classification tasks, our model can rank the relation candidates

[2]The models with early stopping achieve similar performance.

Model	Unseen		Seen		Overall[2]	
	Top 1	Top 2	Top 1	Top 2	Top 1	Top 2
Multi-class BERT	0.0	0.0	60.6	-	48.5	-
TUCORE-GCN (Lee and Choi, 2021)	0.0	0.0	65.5[1]	-	48.4[1]	-
TREND (Lin et al., 2022)	0.0	0.0	**66.8**[1]	-	53.4[1]	-
Binary-Reformulated BERT	24.5	28.9	57.0	45.5	50.5	42.2
Proposed (with predicted triggers)	23.5	**34.8**	66.7	**51.5**	58.0	**48.2**
Proposed (with relation name embeddings)	**32.5**	**34.8**	65.6	51.0	**60.0**	47.8
Proposed with gold triggers	35.6	40.4	70.4	53.2	63.4	50.6

Table 2: The micro-F1 performance of DialogRE in terms of unseen, seen, and overall settings (%).

based on their predicted scores. Typically, the model outputs the relation with the highest score, as done in prior work, and micro-F score is calculated for evaluation. However, since our task is focused on zero-shot performance, we are also interested in whether our model can correctly rank the unseen relations, even if the top-ranked relation is incorrect. To better understand how our model estimates all relation candidates, we evaluate our model not only on the top-ranked relation but also on the top-2 ranked relations in our experiments. This allows us to gain insight into how well our model can rank the correct relations, even if they are not the top-ranked ones.

3.2 Model Setting

We perform different model settings on BERT-Base for fair comparison.

- **Multi-class BERT** is a baseline, where BERT-Base (Devlin et al., 2019) is adopted and treated DRE as multi-class classification.
- **TUCORE-GCN** construct a dialogue graph to utilize the graph strucutre for prediction (Lee and Choi, 2021).
- **TREND** proposed to capture explicit triggers for better performance (Lin et al., 2022).[3]
- **Binary-reformulated BERT** performs binary classification shown in Figure 1, which is a proper baseline for zero-shot settings.
- **Proposed** has three settings in binary relation prediction during inference: 1) based on predicted triggers, 2) based on relation name embddings, 3) based on gold triggers. The third is listed as an upper bound for reference.[4]

[3]The scores are reported from the prior work for reference, which cannot be directly compared with our scores.

[4]Overall performance is estimated based on data size.

3.3 Results

Table 2 presents our results. Prior work achieves micro-F scores above 60% for seen relations but cannot predict unseen relations (0%) due to their multi-class formulation. The reformulated BERT serves as the baseline for zero-shot settings, achieving 24.9% and 28.9% for top 1 and top 2 ranked relations, respectively.

Our proposed method of inputting predicted triggers for relation prediction did not rank correct unseen relations as top 1 (23.5% vs. 24.5%). However, the performance of top 2 ranked relations significantly improved (from 28.9% to 34.8%), suggesting that trigger prediction is indeed useful. The lower top 1 relations score can be attributed to similar triggers for relevant relations, which easily favor seen relations. An example of incorrect prediction is provided in Table 3.

Replacing predicted triggers with relation name embeddings, our proposed model achieves the best performance for unseen relations (32.5% for top 1 and 34.8% for top 2). This indicates that this setting avoids overfitting to seen relations and allows prediction to better generalize to unseen scenarios.

Moreover, feeding gold triggers into relation extraction during inference yields the best results, indicating the potential for improvement with the proposed trigger mechanism. In sum, the experiments demonstrate that our proposed model can connect trigger words with relation names and enables zero-shot relation extraction.

In terms of performance on seen data, our proposed models outperform the reformulated BERT baseline by a significant margin. Moreover, our models achieve comparable scores to previous work (66.7% vs. 66.8% in top 1 scores), even though we consider more candidates. These results further validate the effectiveness of our model and its superior generalization capability.

S1: What about Ben? We can't bring a baby to a hospital. S2: We'll watch him. S1: I don't think so. S3: What? I have seven Catholic sisters. I've taken care of hundreds of kids. Come on, we wanna do it, don't we? S2: I was looking forward to playing basketball, but I guess that's out the window. S1: Ok, well, if you do take him out for his walk, you might wanna bring his hat, and there's extra milk in the fridge, and there's extra diapers in the bag. S3: Hat, milk, got it. S1: ??? Thro up a thro thro–a thro thro! S3: Consider it done. S2: You understood that? S3: Yeah, my uncle Sal has a really big tongue. S2: Is he the one with the beautiful wife?
(Subject, Object) : (Sal, S3) Predicted trigger: uncle Gold trigger: uncle Predicted relation: per:children Gold relation: per:other_family

Table 3: An incorrectly-predicted example.

After comprehensive analysis, we found that our proposed method incorporating a general context embedding not only leverages the trigger capturing capability but also assists the DRE task indirectly, leading to the best overall performance among all proposed models. The ability to relate trigger keywords to relation names enables the model to generalize better to unseen relations and overcome the limitations of relying on specific trigger words. The results of our experiments demonstrate the effectiveness of our proposed method and its potential for real-world applications.

3.4 Qualitative Study

Table 3 showcases an example about the predicted triggers and relations for the DialogRE dataset. As an instance, Sal is the uncle of Speaker 3, so the relation between them should be "other_family". Although the trigger word mechanism accurately captures the crucial keyword "uncle", the model still outputs the "children" relation from the seen relation category rather than the "other_family" relation from the unseen relation category. This suggests that while capturing significant subject and object information through trigger words, the model tends to prioritize predicting relations from the seen relation category.

4 Conclusion

This paper introduces a novel approach for zero-shot dialogue relation extraction by relating explainable trigger words and relation names. Our proposed method effectively utilizes trigger-capturing capability and demonstrates a significant improvement in inferring unseen relations. The experimental results on benchmark data show that our approach achieves better generalization and practicality, making it a promising solution for real-world applications.

Acknowledgements

We thank the reviewers for their insightful comments. This work was financially supported by the Young Scholar Fellowship Program by the National Science and Technology Council (NSTC) in Taiwan, under Grants 111-2222-E-002-013-MY3 and 111-2628-E-002-016.

References

Alon Albalak, Varun Embar, Yi-Lin Tuan, Lise Getoor, and William Yang Wang. 2022. D-REX: Dialogue relation extraction with explanations. In *Proceedings of the 4th Workshop on NLP for Conversational AI*, pages 34–46.

Amir D. N. Cohen, Shachar Rosenman, and Yoav Goldberg. 2020. Relation extraction as two-way span-prediction. *CoRR*, abs/2010.04829.

Jacob Devlin, Ming-Wei Chang, Kenton Lee, and Kristina Toutanova. 2019. BERT: Pre-training of deep bidirectional transformers for language understanding. In *Proceedings of the 2019 Conference of the North American Chapter of the Association for Computational Linguistics: Human Language Technologies, Volume 1 (Long and Short Papers)*, pages 4171–4186, Minneapolis, Minnesota. Association for Computational Linguistics.

Pere-Lluís Huguet Cabot and Roberto Navigli. 2021. REBEL: Relation extraction by end-to-end language generation. In *Findings of the Association for Computational Linguistics: EMNLP 2021*, pages 2370–2381, Punta Cana, Dominican Republic. Association for Computational Linguistics.

Bongseok Lee and Yong Suk Choi. 2021. Graph based network with contextualized representations of turns in dialogue. In *EMNLP 2021-2021 Conference on Empirical Methods in Natural Language Processing, Proceedings*, pages 443–455. Association for Computational Linguistics (ACL).

Po-Wei Lin, Shang-Yu Su, and Yun-Nung Chen. 2022. TREND: Trigger-enhanced relation-extraction network for dialogues. In *Proceedings of the 23rd Annual Meeting of the Special Interest Group on Discourse and Dialogue*, pages 623–629, Edinburgh, UK. Association for Computational Linguistics.

Tomas Mikolov, Kai Chen, Greg Corrado, and Jeffrey Dean. 2013. Efficient estimation of word representations in vector space.

Raul Puri and Bryan Catanzaro. 2019. Zero-shot text classification with generative language models. *CoRR*, abs/1912.10165.

Pranav Rajpurkar, Jian Zhang, Konstantin Lopyrev, and Percy Liang. 2016. SQuAD: 100,000+ questions for machine comprehension of text. In *Proceedings of the 2016 Conference on Empirical Methods in Natural Language Processing*, pages 2383–2392, Austin, Texas. Association for Computational Linguistics.

Oscar Sainz, Oier Lopez de Lacalle, Gorka Labaka, Ander Barrena, and Eneko Agirre. 2021. Label verbalization and entailment for effective zero- and few-shot relation extraction. *CoRR*, abs/2109.03659.

Timo Schick and Hinrich Schütze. 2020. Exploiting cloze questions for few-shot text classification and natural language inference. *CoRR*, abs/2001.07676.

Junyoung Son, Jinsung Kim, Jungwoo Lim, and Heuiseok Lim. 2022. GRASP: Guiding model with RelAtional semantics using prompt for dialogue relation extraction. In *Proceedings of the 29th International Conference on Computational Linguistics*, pages 412–423, Gyeongju, Republic of Korea. International Committee on Computational Linguistics.

Dian Yu, Kai Sun, Claire Cardie, and Dong Yu. 2020. Dialogue-based relation extraction. In *Proceedings of the 58th Annual Meeting of the Association for Computational Linguistics*, pages 4927–4940, Online. Association for Computational Linguistics.

Yuhao Zhang, Victor Zhong, Danqi Chen, Gabor Angeli, and Christopher D. Manning. 2017. Position-aware attention and supervised data improve slot filling. In *Proceedings of the 2017 Conference on Empirical Methods in Natural Language Processing*, pages 35–45, Copenhagen, Denmark. Association for Computational Linguistics.

Wenxuan Zhou and Muhao Chen. 2021. An improved baseline for sentence-level relation extraction. *CoRR*, abs/2102.01373.

A Criteria for Relation Dividing

We categorized the relations into two sets, namely, seen and unseen, as presented in Table 4. Our categorization was based on the similarity of relations, where dependent ones are assigned to different categories. For those not related, we assigned them randomly to either category. This categorization aims to train the model on seen relations to enhance its ability to predict unseen relations during testing.

B Prediction Distribution Comparison

We analyze the distribution of correctly predicted top 1 unseen relations for two models, one with predicted triggers and the other with relation name embeddings, and present the results in Table 5. We observe that the two methods exhibit a similar pattern of correctly predicted relations, with a concentration on particular unseen relations such as siblings and spouses, among others. However, the proposed method with the relation name embeddings significantly outperforms the one with the predicted triggers method in this aspect.

Seen Relations	**Unseen Relations**
per:positive_impression	per:subordinate
per:client	gpe:visitors_of_place
per:origin	per:place_of_residence
per:works	per:schools_attended
per:place_of_work	per:parents
per:title	gpe:births_in_place
per:alternate_names	org:employees/members
per:acquaintance	per:dates
per:alumni	per:other_family
per:friends	per:siblings
per:girl/boyfriend	per:spouse
per:neighbor	per:negative_impression
per:roommate	per:age
per:boss	per:date_of_birth
per:children	per:major
gpe:residents_of_place	per:pet
per:place_of_birth	
per:visited_place	
per:employee/member_of	
org:students	

Table 4: Seen and unseen relations in our experiments.

Unseen Relation	**Unseen**	
	Predict	**CLS**
per:siblings	26	42
per:spouse	21	30
per:negative_impression	4	11
per:parents	5	9
per:dates	0	4
per:major	2	2
per:age	1	1
gpe:births_in_place	0	0
org:employees/members	0	0
per:other_family	0	0
per:date_of_birth	0	0
per:pet	0	0
per:subordinate	0	0
gpe:visitors_of_place	0	0
per:place_of_residence	0	0
per:schools_attended	0	0

Table 5: The distribution of correct predictions in the predict trigger method and cls trigger method.

Generating Video Game Scripts with Style

Gaetan Lopez Latouche* and **Laurence Marcotte*** and **Ben Swanson**
Ubisoft La Forge
{gaetan.lopez-latouche,ben.swanson2}@ubisoft.com
laurencemarcotte@hotmail.ca

Abstract

While modern language models can generate a scripted scene in the format of a play, movie, or video game cutscene the quality of machine generated text remains behind that of human authors. In this work, we focus on one aspect of this quality gap; generating text in the style of an arbitrary and unseen character. We propose the Style Adaptive Semiparametric Scriptwriter (SASS) which leverages an adaptive weighted style memory to generate dialog lines in accordance with a character's speaking patterns. Using the LIGHT dataset as well as a new corpus of scripts from twenty-three AAA video games, we show that SASS not only outperforms similar models but in some cases can also be used in conjunction with them to yield further improvement.

Figure 1: An illustration of our approach. SASS reuses words present in the character's previous conversations to generate character specific stylized responses.

1 Introduction

As the affordances of large language models (LLMs) continue to reveal themselves, this technology hints at the possibility of transformative changes to narrative media such as scriptwriting, songwriting and journalism. In this work, we focus on scriptwriting for AAA[1] video game dialog, a domain similar to the scripts used in movies, television and theater but with its own unique flavor that often features larger-than-life characters and action-packed dialogs.

Our particular goal is to advance the ability to incorporate a character style or voice in responses generated by LLMs. The importance of this aspect is motivated by the observation that in a AAA game a character's lines will often be written by several scriptwriters asynchronously, meaning that any assistance in maintaining a consistent style is a boon.

Central to the problem is the representation of a character's style, with recent work using attributes such as target styles (Zhou et al., 2018), character description (Rashkin et al., 2018), previous character utterances (Madotto et al., 2021; Han et al., 2022a) and conversation history (Boyd et al., 2020). The approaches presented can be partitioned into two categories; the first, which we call *explicit style*, consists of a short text sample that explicitly describes the character, their profession, age, interests, and other traits. The second, which we will call *implicit style*, uses a list of previously authored utterances from a character instead.

Considering the ultimate application of these techniques in AAA game development, we propose the use of implicit style provided at inference time as most suitable for several reasons. First, it can be too limiting to summarize the style of a character

*These authors contributed equally to this work.

[1]The term "AAA" refers to multi-million dollar budget productions often with hundreds of highly specialized contributors.

Proceedings of the 5th Workshop on NLP for Conversational AI (NLP4ConvAI 2023), pages 129–139
July 14, 2023

narrator: Marcus has hacked the final computer:
speakerA: Ladies. Gentlemen. Wrench. You are now talking to the DedSec master.
speakerB: Nice! So how did it end?
speakerA: Well... I signed up with the NSA in exchange for turning over personal data on every DedSec member.
speakerC: Marcus, I am going to hit you.
speakerA: It was a recruitment tool, like I thought. But I did a little extra and erased all traces I was ever there... along with the other two people who had filled the forms. Maybe when the NSA never calls them back, they'll turn to DedSec.
speakerC: Fingers crossed.

Table 1: Example Scene from an AAA game in the UBISCENES dataset.

with a few labels or utterances (Han et al., 2022a). Second, due to production constraints of the already complex narrative pipeline in the video game industry, models should be locked and not involve re-training if possible or else they risk becoming a pipeline blocker. Finally as the writing process naturally develops a character through the course of scriptwriting, using inference time implicit style allows the model to adapt as the character's lines manifest in other scenes of the game. It is worth noting that methods which employ small samples of implicit style (Han et al., 2022a; Suzgun et al., 2022; Reif et al., 2021; Boyd et al., 2020) achieve strong performance but do not fully leverage this continuous increase of character's lines.

To harness the signal of implicit style we build on the k-nearest neighbour language model (KNN-LM) (Khandelwal et al., 2019), adapting and improving it for the task of style-controlled generation. Our model, the Style Adaptive Semiparametric Scriptwriter (SASS), provides a drop-in replacement for a traditional language model architecture that scales well with the number of reference character lines supplied as implicit style, does not require added work from the script writers to keep up to date, and can be used orthogonally to other methods of style-controlled dialog generation. An illustration of our method is shown in Figure 1. Our automatic evaluations show that SASS generates responses that are more aligned with a target character style without sacrificing fluency when compared to both KNN-LM and a finetuned LLM baseline.

2 Related Work

We continue a long thread of study in style controlled dialog generation and the closely related topic of style transfer where the term style is heavily overloaded, often treating style as a categorical variable such as emotion, formality, or sentiment (Kong et al., 2021; Dathathri et al., 2019; Prabhumoye et al., 2018). We differentiate this notion of *ephemeral* style from the *character* style which is always present to some degree in a character's speech regardless of situation, of which the latter is our focus.

Recent research into methods incorporating explicit style has been fueled primarily by the PERSONA-CHAT (Zhang et al., 2018) and LIGHT datasets (Urbanek et al., 2019). Examples include Kim et al. (2022) which augments personas during inference and Madotto et al. (2021) which utilizes the persona in LLM prompting. Previous approaches to the use of implicit style vary from concatenation of the references to the conversation history (Boyd et al., 2020), to the construction of artificial prepended dialog (Han et al., 2022b), to approaches more similar to our own which seek to directly capture the frequent words used by a character as a proxy for their style (Fikri et al., 2021; Liu et al., 2020). Another approach to implicit style generation and transfer is learn a mapping to a vector style encoding (Li et al., 2020a; Riley et al., 2020a) which allows for inference time adaptation to arbitrary styles.

Our work also serves as a direct improvement to the k-nearest neighbour language model (Khandelwal et al., 2019) for which some previous attention has been paid to the intersection with style conditioning (Trotta et al., 2022).

3 Dataset

As no public dataset of video game dialog exists, we leverage our privileged access to the back catalog of all UBISOFT games to build one. From a pool of 23 games that are sufficiently narrative

	Train	*Valid*	*Test*
Games	16	3	4
Characters	3,514	477	291
Scenes	16,458	1,727	1,403
Utterances	107,222	14,058	12,170
Vocabulary Size	29,200	13,723	13,555
Utterance Length	15.82	15.11	16.20
Character/Scene	2.99	3.42	3.34
Utterance/Scene	6.51	8.14	8.67

Table 2: UBISCENES dataset statistics after filtering.

heavy, we collect 19,588 well filtered scenes featuring 4,282 characters and 133,450 lines of dialog, and refer to this dataset as UBISCENES. For filtering, we use a combination of thresholds on automatic metrics (the rate at which the same character speaks twice in a row as well as the entropy of the identity of the speaker across the scene) and game specific rules to accommodate the quirks of each production. Table 1 and Appendix A2 show examples of scenes that we collected. We split the dataset by game into training, validation, and test sets to avoid data leakage. Overall statistics of the collected dataset are given in table 2.

We also evaluate on the LIGHT dataset (Urbanek et al., 2019) which is, in our opinion, the most similar academic dataset to video game dialog despite its many differences. Specifically, we note the disparity in terms of writing quality between these two datasets: UBISCENES is composed of professionally authored text while LIGHT is created by crowdworkers. They also differ structurally as many dialogues in UBISCENES have a narrator involved which is not the case in LIGHT or other dialog datasets such as PERSONACHAT (Zhang et al., 2018), WIZ. OF WIKIPEDIA (Dinan et al., 2018), DAILY DIALOG (Li et al., 2017) or HLA-CHAT (Li et al., 2020b).

For both datasets, we replace all script cue names with an added special token *<speaker>* for a simple speaker or *<narrator>* for a narrator, although names are preserved in the dialog text. We evaluate only on dialogues where the target character has spoken strictly less than three times to avoid relying on the previous conversation history as a style indicator. 60% of the scenes are used to supply the indices of implicit style and we study the twenty characters with the highest number of lines in the remaining 40%.

4 Method

Our choice of model arises from our guiding hypothesis that a principal component of character style is simply their preferential choice of words that are either optional or semantically exchangeable with other words in context. SASS consists of two components:

- An autoregressive transformer (Vaswani et al., 2017) language model that encodes the dialog context.
- A non-parametric token retrieval module with access to each character's *style index*: a collection of all of their previously authored lines.

Both components provide a categorical distribution over the token vocabulary of the language model, and a *style adapter* combines these two components. Our model architecture draws on KNN-LM(Khandelwal et al., 2019) and Adaptive Semiparametric Language Models (Yogatama et al., 2021), improving on the gating mechanism of the latter to better choose when to leverage implicit style and when to rely on LLM generation.

4.1 Base Model

The transformer architecture (Vaswani et al., 2017) is our base model, using the GPT-J (Wang and Komatsuzaki, 2021) model from Huggingface Transformers (Wolf et al., 2019) as our initial pretrained language model. This model contains 6 billion parameters with a vocabulary size of 50,400 tokens.

This model is finetuned on the training split of our dataset and provides p_{LM}, the categorical language model probability of the next token of the dialog being generated. Note that at inference time the only representation of the character's style that is available to this model are the previous lines in the dialog.

4.2 Character Style Index

As in Trotta et al. (2022) each character has its own character style index with an average of 425 entries in the UBISCENES dataset and 1,404 in LIGHT. Given a character's implicit style as a list of strings $\mathcal{C}$, we formally define its style index $\mathcal{S}$ as the following set of key-value pairs:

$$\mathcal{S} = \bigcup_{s \in \mathcal{C}} \{(f(w_{i-}), w_i) \forall w_i \in s\}$$

where $f(w_{i-})$ is a vector encoding of the prefix of s at index i, but before the decision to produce w_i has been made.

Previous work has relied on the last layer hidden state of the LLM at index i as a definition of f (Khandelwal et al., 2019). Given the arbitrary relative scale and redundancy of the hidden state's parameters before its transformation into a predictive distribution over tokens, we propose the alternative use of the actual categorical probability distribution given by the language model at the i_{th} position to provide f. As the vocabulary size of GPT-J (Wang and Komatsuzaki, 2021) is high, we reduce the dimension of this probability distribution to a 768 long vector using PCA (Abdi and Williams, 2010).

At inference time we are given the input dialog context c and the style index of the currently speaking character, and we retrieve the k-nearest neighbors of $f(c)$ among the keys of S using L2 distance. Early qualitative analysis suggested that $k = 10$ gave reasonable results, and we leave the investigation of the impact of k on our method to future work.

As in the k-nearest neighbor language model (Khandelwal et al., 2019) we softmax a vector with a large negative number in all locations except for the retrieved tokens indices which are set to the negative L2 distance obtained during retrieval. This distribution over the LLM vocabulary is returned by the k-nearest neighbor component, which we will refer to as p_{kNN}.

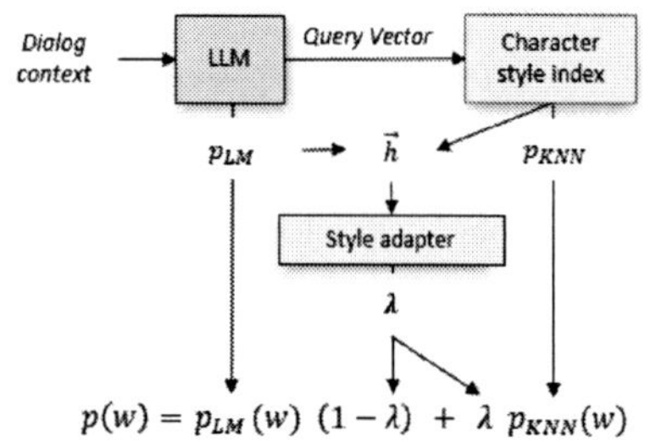

Figure 2: An illustration of SASS. Given a dialog context and a character style index, a query vector is constructed, a set of k nearest neighbors are retrieved and part of $\vec{h}$ is created. We extract from p_{LM} the probability of those k tokens and concatenate it to $\vec{h}$. $\vec{h}$ is then passed to a style adapter and returns the interpolation parameter λ.

4.3 Style Adapter

Once equipped with both p_{LM} and p_{kNN}, all that remains is to interpolate these distributions to predict the next token. We predict a linear interpolation parameter λ from the concatenation of the transformer's last hidden state, the raw distances (L2 distance between the query vector and the retrieval key) and the probability of the tokens retrieved under p_{LM} which we denote as $\vec{h_i}$ with dimension $d_{\vec{h_i}} = 2 * k + d_{embd}$ where d_{embd} is the dimension of the hidden states of the LLM. This gives the full token prediction probability distribution returned by SASS as

$$\begin{aligned} \lambda &= \sigma(\mathbf{W}\vec{h_i}) \\ p(w_{i+1}|w_{\leq i}) &= \lambda p_{\text{kNN}}(w_{i+1}|w_{\leq i}) \\ &\quad +(1-\lambda)p_{\text{LM}}(w_{i+1}|w_{\leq i}) \end{aligned}$$

where σ is the sigmoid function, and $\mathbf{W}$ is a parameter vector of size $d_{\vec{h_i}}$.

Intuitively, each component of $\vec{h_i}$ provides complementary information to the style adapter: the last hidden state gives a representation of the current dialog context, the raw distances show how confident the model is in the retrieved tokens, and the probability of the tokens retrieved under p_{LM} reveals the appropriateness of each retrieved token in the context. For nearest neighbor retrieval we use the FAISS library (Johnson et al., 2019) and use L2 as a distance metric as in Khandelwal et al. (2019). We train SASS with a learning rate of 2e-4 for the style adapter and 2e-5 for the LLM on the training set for one epoch. An illustration of SASS architecture is depicted in Figure 2.

5 Experiments

5.1 Evaluation

Following previous works on text style transfer (Li et al., 2018; Smith et al., 2020; Riley et al., 2020b) and style-controlled dialog agents (Han et al., 2022a), we train two multi-class classifiers on the utterances of the characters present in the test set (twenty characters per dataset) of UBISCENES and LIGHT(Urbanek et al., 2019) respectively. We denote $StyleAcc$ the classifier accuracy of predicting the target character, where a higher value indicates that generated text is more closely aligned to characters' styles.

To calculate $StyleAcc$ we use all dialog histories where the test characters have 0-2 previous lines. We also report $StyleAcc_0$ and $StyleAcc_1$,

Dataset	Context	5	10	25	50	100
UbiScenes	$knn_{p_{LM}}$	**44.03**	**48.98**	**54.79**	**58.95**	**62.61**
	knn^*	31.31	36.06	42.05	46.66	51.41
LIGHT	$knn_{p_{LM}}$	**38.85**	**45.63**	**53.60**	**59.33**	**64.52**
	knn^*	33.79	41.11	49.30	54.07	57.95

Table 3: Retrieval Recall for different k number of retrieved tokens. Using the language model probability p_{LM} improves recall for all k compared to the same method using the final hidden state state as a retrieval key (knn*).

the accuracy of the classifier when the character has exactly 0 or 1 previous lines in the dialogue history.

To measure how similar the vocabulary used in the generated responses is to its corresponding style index, we compute the n-gram overlap (where n=2) as done in (Han et al., 2022a) who define the n-gram overlap as the percent of n-grams in the generated line that appear anywhere in the style indices.

To check for a degenerate solution that represents style at the cost of fluency, we follow previous work on language models with external memory (Khandelwal et al., 2019; Trotta et al., 2022; Yogatama et al., 2021; Bhardwaj et al., 2022) and report perplexity. To validate the choice of our alternative encoding f of the retrieval key, we measure the quality of the retrieved tokens with recall over the retrieved tokens as in Bhardwaj et al. (2022).

5.2 Baseline Methods

Full-dataset Fine-tuning (SCRIPTWRITER): This straightforward baseline simply finetunes the vanilla GPT-J model on the training set, and is equivalent to fixing the style adapter's interpolation parameter λ to zero and ignoring p_{kNN}.

PDP Random Match: (PDP_r): PDP (Han et al., 2022a) constructs and prepends an artificial dialog before the input dialog context, effectively providing a Scriptwriter style model with a small selection of the style index. In their work, the authors use one of several pseudo-contexts, and present models that select the pseudo-context to be used based on the dialog history. We implement a variation of their Random Match method which selects the pseudo-context at random, with the difference that in our case we use a character's previous scenes directly. While this diverges from their exact approach, our goal of comparison in this case is not to show that one model is better than the other but instead to demonstrate that they can complement each other.

Adapted kNN-LM ($kNN\text{-}LM_r$): Our work is directly inspired by language models with external memory. Our approach is closely related to Khandelwal et al. (2019) with key modifications on the retrieval representation and the dynamic runtime calculation of the interpolation parameter. We use the SCRIPTWRITER as the base LLM required to compute the retrieval keys and tune lambda using the validation set. Comparing to this strong baseline allows us to determine if our style adapter has learned how to interpolate between the style of the character and the LLM more efficiently than using a constant interpolation term.

5.3 Additional Studies

In addition to the evaluation metrics presented above, we perform some extra experiments to validate our model. First, we shuffle the indices of each character to ensure that we observe a decrease in performance; if the model is simply leveraging game specific proper nouns as a proxy for character style then it would not be effected by using the wrong character index.

Second, we also perform data ablation on the size of the style indices to investigate at which point in the writing process our method can achieve improvements over simple finetuning.

6 Results & Discussion

Our results demonstrate that both our use of the PCA probability distribution as a retrieval key as well as a dynamic style adapter lead to improvements over the strong baseline of $kNN\text{-}LM_r$. We also show that SASS can be used in combination with other methods such as PDP (Han et al., 2022a) and explore the effects of size of the style index on performance.

Considering first the use of the PCA probability distribution as an alternative to the LLM hidden state used in k-nearest neighbor language models as a retrieval key, Table 3 demonstrates improved recall on both datasets.

	PPL	$StyleAcc$	$StyleAcc_0$	$StyleAcc_1$	$N-gram$
REAL	X	.6868	.701	.683	X
SCRIPTWRITER	35.873	.316	.232	.352	.186
$kNN\text{-}LM_r$	27.016	.409	.359	.427	.212
SASS	**23.055**	**.458**	**.413**	**.483**	**.233**
SASS SHUFFLED	38.700	.233	.160	.255	.177
PDP_r	32.786	.424	.364	.455	**.255**
$PDP_r + kNN\text{-}LM_r$	29.889	.473	.433	.493	.230
$PDP_r + SASS$	**27.394**	**.510**	**.467**	**.539**	.248

Table 4: Results for our automatic evaluation on UBISCENES. Best results are highlighted in bold for each metric. SASS generally outperforms its baseline method on all studied metrics.

UBISCENES: The results on our new dataset of AAA video game dialogs is shown in Table 4 and demonstrate that SASS outperforms all other baselines on all metrics except for N-Gram overlap where it is second best to PDP_r. Additionally, adding SASS or $kNN\text{-}LM_r$ to PDP_r(Han et al., 2022a) leads to better perplexity and generally superior style specific metrics compared to PDP_r alone.

The central result that deserves highlighting is that SASS outperforms the closely related $kNN\text{-}LM_r$ on all metrics, showing that our dynamic style adapter can effectively learn when to give importance to the style index of the character over the language model or vice versa. It is also worth noting the gap on the style metrics between all the models under experiment and the real scripts, hinting at the large amount of improvement still required to approach human authored quality. Example outputs of SASS can be found in Appendix A1.

LIGHT: Results for the LIGHT dataset are shown in Table 5. We first note that the performance of the classifier on the gold dialogs is considerably lower on this dataset compared to UBISCENES with an accuracy of 30.86% compared to 68.68%. We take this as evidence of our own qualitative assessment that characters in LIGHT do not have a strong style and as such it is difficult for the classifier to guess which utterance was written by whom. The smaller relative performance improvement of SASS and $kNN\text{-}LM_r$ over SCRIPTWRITER validate this hypothesis as does the fact that shuffling the character style index also has a low impact on style aware metrics. Overall, this demonstrates that LIGHT is not ideal for research in style based dialog and highlights the potential of professionally authored datasets such as UBISCENES.

6.1 Additional study results

Our data ablation study is especially important given our stated domain of AAA video game scriptwriting as our non-parametric design instantly integrates any lines spoken by a character as they are written, and data ablation viewed in reverse simulates this writing process. Figure 4 shows the results of this study. We also investigate the effect of randomly shuffling the characters' indices, expecting to see a drop in performance as long as our gains in style are not due to game level word frequencies like proper nouns but instead to actual character speaking patterns. Results of SASS SHUFFLED in table 4 reveals the outcome of this study.

Decreasing the number of entries in style index reduces performance, but, even at 10% of the original 60% of game data that was held out to create the style index SASS yields better perplexity and style specific scores compared to the SCRIPTWRITER baseline. This suggests that SASS has value even at the beginning of the writing process, which is perhaps when it can be most helpful to writers.

As hoped, replacing the character style index of our characters by the one of another character (SASS SHUFFLED) significantly decreases the performance in terms of both perplexity and style aware metrics. This demonstrates that not only do the characters in UBISCENES have their own style but also that SASS can leverage these styles effectively.

	PPL	$StyleAcc$	$StyleAcc_0$	$StyleAcc_1$	$N-gram$
REAL	X	.309	.330	.310	X
SCRIPTWRITER	29.567	.141	.113	.150	.370
$kNN\text{-}LM_r$	30.730	**.172**	**.150**	**.183**	.376
SASS	**26.759**	.157	.132	.166	**.390**
SASS SHUFFLED	27.474	.135	.105	.149	.379

Table 5: Results for our automatic evaluation on LIGHT. Best results are highlighted in bold for each metric. SASS and $kNN\text{-}LM_r$ generally outperforms the baseline method on style specific metrics.

6.2 Style adapter Analysis

We conduct some exploratory visualizations of the style adapter whose purpose is to adjust the importance of the non-parametric retrieved style at each generation step. Figure 3 shows histograms over the validation set of the distribution of values returned by our style adapter for λ when decoded with teacher forcing on the gold outputs.

We observe that in both LIGHT and UBISCENES lambda settles into a bimodal distribution with one peak near zero, which corresponds to ignoring the style index and relying on the language model instead. This Figure also reinforces the difference in performance gain of SASS on the two datasets; it is clear that with UBISCENES the values of λ are more varied which is evidence that the style adapter has found a signal with which to give a more nuanced prediction.

Finally we note that in both datasets λ is rarely much greater than .5, indicating that the style adapter is reluctant to fully disengage the language model. While this may indeed be optimal behavior, we suspect that this is a side effect of our architecture and potential avenue of improvement for this model class. To see the dilemma, consider that the gradient of lambda on a single prediction will only be positive if the gold token is actually retrieved regardless of the quality of the actual retrieved tokens which may be perfectly appropriate.

6.3 Discussion and Future Work

Our quantitative results demonstrate that SASS not only outperforms the strong baseline $kNN\text{-}LM_r$ but also can be used complementary to prompt editing based style control such as PDP_r. We performed qualitative pairwise comparison experiments with earlier versions of the model but did not achieve acceptable inter-annotator agreement. We attribute this to the subjectivity of choosing the better of two possible dialog lines once both lines are grammatically correct and coherent with the scene as are most outputs from all our models including the baseline. Furthermore, to provide raters with a rubric on which to base a choice of the more stylish output we must necessarily boil the character's style down into a short description or a few sample lines, which is a lossy and imprecise operation.

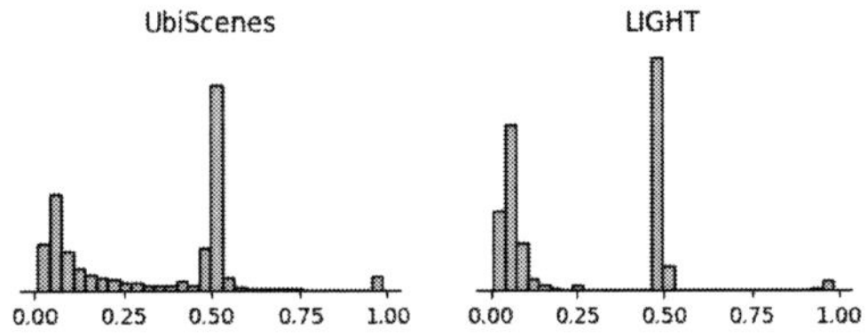

Figure 3: Distributions of values of λ on UBISCENES (left) and LIGHT (right) on the validation sets.

Our opinion is that the output of all of these models is "good enough" to be used as a writing aid, either to provide starter text for editing or simply to spur forward the creative process through inspiration. None of our models can be used as a substitute for actual professional scriptwriters, as is evidenced by the remaining gap in our automatic style metrics between SASS and the human authored lines. Nevertheless, we see clear qualitative evidence that SASS is making use of characters' speaking patterns without too much impact on fluency and coherence.

Our reliance on perplexity as a proxy for fluency is an area for improvement in our methodology, and there exist methods for formal quantization of coherence, topic and fluency in the literature (Aksitov et al., 2023). Although SASS leads to perplexity improvement, qualitative evaluations have shown that it could sometimes lead to a small decrease in fluency. We also note opportunities for further experimentation in the optimal choice of the number of retrieved neighbors k, as this could easily be

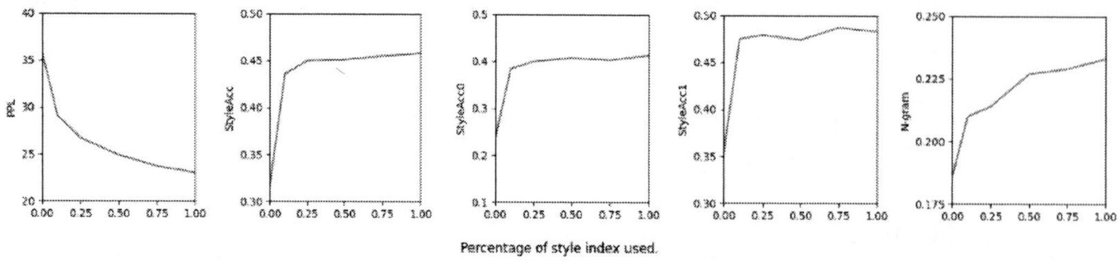

Figure 4: Effect of SASS character style index size on our studied metrics.

increased without sacrificing significant additional latency.

7 Conclusion

We present the Style Adaptive Semiparametric Scriptwriter (SASS), drawing inspiration from the closely related k nearest neighbor and adaptive semiparametric language models. In particular we propose new formulations of the encoder for retrieval as well as the determination of the style interpolation parameter and demonstrate that they lead to improved performance. Ablation studies reveal that the benefits of our approach manifest even with small amounts of reference style index material, and it is our intention to integrate this in our internal writing assistance tools in the near future.

We perform experiments on two datasets, the LIGHT dataset as well as a first of its kind dataset of video game script dialogs, UBISCENES, and demonstrate that the difference in style between professionally authored and crowdsourced text is a crucial consideration for style controlled generation research. We regret that we cannot release UBISCENES publicly due to concerns of its use in products that do not respect the intellectual property of their data sources. However, we are open to speak with academic collaborators that are interested in working with this data for targeted projects and invite them to reach out to the authors.

Limitations

The main limitation of our proposed method relies on the additional cost of retrieval. Even if the size of our character style indexes is small it still adds latency to our overall pipeline as retrieval must occur once per token. We expect that incorporating the recent work of He et al. (2021) on improving the efficiency of nearest neighbor language models should decrease this latency significantly.

As in most NLG work, another important limitation is in quality evaluation. We found qualitative evaluations to be too imprecise for appropriate inter-annotator agreement, and the quantitative evaluations that we present in this paper are all proxies that cannot be said to capture character style or fluency in full.

Another limitation of our work is the exclusion of models that are only accessible by calling or finetuning powerful external language model APIs due to the excessive monetary cost involved. It is almost certain that these larger models would outperform the 6B parameter model we use, and this may also change the relative performance of the techniques that we present. While we feel that this constraint is appropriate at this moment in history and that our position as major AAA developer gives us the authority to make such a claim, shifts in third party model availability and pricing could change the landscape.

Our work deals with data of a singular domain, video game scripts in English, but represents a wide variety of nationalities and ethnicities over the span of a large catalog of games.

References

Hervé Abdi and Lynne J Williams. 2010. Principal component analysis. *Wiley interdisciplinary reviews: computational statistics*, 2(4):433–459.

Renat Aksitov, Chung-Ching Chang, David Reitter, Siamak Shakeri, and Yunhsuan Sung. 2023. Characterizing attribution and fluency tradeoffs for retrieval-augmented large language models. *arXiv preprint arXiv:2302.05578*.

Rishabh Bhardwaj, George Polovets, and Monica Sunkara. 2022. Adaptation approaches for nearest neighbor language models. *arXiv preprint arXiv:2211.07828*.

Alex Boyd, Raul Puri, Mohammad Shoeybi, Mostofa Patwary, and Bryan Catanzaro. 2020. Large scale multi-actor generative dialog modeling. *arXiv preprint arXiv:2005.06114*.

Sumanth Dathathri, Andrea Madotto, Janice Lan, Jane Hung, Eric Frank, Piero Molino, Jason Yosinski, and Rosanne Liu. 2019. Plug and play language models: A simple approach to controlled text generation. *arXiv preprint arXiv:1912.02164*.

Emily Dinan, Stephen Roller, Kurt Shuster, Angela Fan, Michael Auli, and Jason Weston. 2018. Wizard of wikipedia: Knowledge-powered conversational agents. *arXiv preprint arXiv:1811.01241*.

Abdurrisyad Fikri, Hiroya Takamura, and Manabu Okumura. 2021. Stylistically user-specific response generation. *Journal of Natural Language Processing*, 28(4):1116–1140.

Seungju Han, Beomsu Kim, Jin Yong Yoo, Seokjun Seo, Sangbum Kim, Enkhbayar Erdenee, and Buru Chang. 2022a. Meet your favorite character: Open-domain chatbot mimicking fictional characters with only a few utterances. *arXiv preprint arXiv:2204.10825*.

Seungju Han, Beomsu Kim, Jin Yong Yoo, Seokjun Seo, Sangbum Kim, Enkhbayar Erdenee, and Buru Chang. 2022b. Meet your favorite character: Open-domain chatbot mimicking fictional characters with only a few utterances.

Junxian He, Graham Neubig, and Taylor Berg-Kirkpatrick. 2021. Efficient nearest neighbor language models. *arXiv preprint arXiv:2109.04212*.

Jeff Johnson, Matthijs Douze, and Hervé Jégou. 2019. Billion-scale similarity search with gpus. *IEEE Transactions on Big Data*, 7(3):535–547.

Urvashi Khandelwal, Omer Levy, Dan Jurafsky, Luke Zettlemoyer, and Mike Lewis. 2019. Generalization through memorization: Nearest neighbor language models. *arXiv preprint arXiv:1911.00172*.

Minju Kim, Beong-woo Kwak, Youngwook Kim, Hong-in Lee, Seung-won Hwang, and Jinyoung Yeo. 2022. Dual task framework for improving persona-grounded dialogue dataset. *CoRR*.

Xiangzhe Kong, Jialiang Huang, Ziquan Tung, Jian Guan, and Minlie Huang. 2021. Stylized story generation with style-guided planning. In *Findings of the Association for Computational Linguistics: ACL-IJCNLP 2021*, pages 2430–2436, Online. Association for Computational Linguistics.

Aaron W Li, Veronica Jiang, Steven Y Feng, Julia Sprague, Wei Zhou, and Jesse Hoey. 2020a. Aloha: Artificial learning of human attributes for dialogue agents. In *Proceedings of the AAAI Conference on Artificial Intelligence*, volume 34, pages 8155–8163.

Aaron W Li, Veronica Jiang, Steven Y Feng, Julia Sprague, Wei Zhou, and Jesse Hoey. 2020b. Aloha: Artificial learning of human attributes for dialogue agents. In *Proceedings of the AAAI Conference on Artificial Intelligence*, volume 34, pages 8155–8163.

Juncen Li, Robin Jia, He He, and Percy Liang. 2018. Delete, retrieve, generate: a simple approach to sentiment and style transfer. *arXiv preprint arXiv:1804.06437*.

Yanran Li, Hui Su, Xiaoyu Shen, Wenjie Li, Ziqiang Cao, and Shuzi Niu. 2017. Dailydialog: A manually labelled multi-turn dialogue dataset. *arXiv preprint arXiv:1710.03957*.

Siyi Liu, Ziang Leng, and Derry Wijaya. 2020. Learning to mirror speaking styles incrementally. *arXiv preprint arXiv:2003.04993*.

Andrea Madotto, Zhaojiang Lin, Genta Indra Winata, and Pascale Fung. 2021. Few-shot bot: Prompt-based learning for dialogue systems. *arXiv preprint arXiv:2110.08118*.

Shrimai Prabhumoye, Yulia Tsvetkov, Ruslan Salakhutdinov, and Alan W Black. 2018. Style transfer through back-translation. *arXiv preprint arXiv:1804.09000*.

Hannah Rashkin, Eric Michael Smith, Margaret Li, and Y-Lan Boureau. 2018. Towards empathetic open-domain conversation models: A new benchmark and dataset. *arXiv preprint arXiv:1811.00207*.

Emily Reif, Daphne Ippolito, Ann Yuan, Andy Coenen, Chris Callison-Burch, and Jason Wei. 2021. A recipe for arbitrary text style transfer with large language models. *arXiv preprint arXiv:2109.03910*.

Parker Riley, Noah Constant, Mandy Guo, Girish Kumar, David Uthus, and Zarana Parekh. 2020a. Textsettr: Few-shot text style extraction and tunable targeted restyling. *arXiv preprint arXiv:2010.03802*.

Parker Riley, Noah Constant, Mandy Guo, Girish Kumar, David Uthus, and Zarana Parekh. 2020b. Textsettr: Few-shot text style extraction and tunable targeted restyling. *arXiv preprint arXiv:2010.03802*.

Eric Michael Smith, Diana Gonzalez-Rico, Emily Dinan, and Y-Lan Boureau. 2020. Controlling style in generated dialogue. *arXiv preprint arXiv:2009.10855*.

Mirac Suzgun, Luke Melas-Kyriazi, and Dan Jurafsky. 2022. Prompt-and-rerank: A method for zero-shot and few-shot arbitrary textual style transfer with small language models. *arXiv preprint arXiv:2205.11503*.

Severino Trotta, Lucie Flek, and Charles Welch. 2022. Nearest neighbor language models for stylistic controllable generation. *arXiv preprint arXiv:2210.15762*.

Jack Urbanek, Angela Fan, Siddharth Karamcheti, Saachi Jain, Samuel Humeau, Emily Dinan, Tim Rocktäschel, Douwe Kiela, Arthur Szlam, and Jason Weston. 2019. Learning to speak and act in a fantasy text adventure game. *arXiv preprint arXiv:1903.03094*.

Ashish Vaswani, Noam Shazeer, Niki Parmar, Jakob Uszkoreit, Llion Jones, Aidan N Gomez, Łukasz Kaiser, and Illia Polosukhin. 2017. Attention is all you need. *Advances in neural information processing systems*, 30.

Ben Wang and Aran Komatsuzaki. 2021. Gpt-j-6b: A 6 billion parameter autoregressive language model.

Thomas Wolf, Lysandre Debut, Victor Sanh, Julien Chaumond, Clement Delangue, Anthony Moi, Pierric Cistac, Tim Rault, Rémi Louf, Morgan Funtowicz, et al. 2019. Huggingface's transformers: State-of-the-art natural language processing. *arXiv preprint arXiv:1910.03771*.

Dani Yogatama, Cyprien de Masson d'Autume, and Lingpeng Kong. 2021. Adaptive semiparametric language models. *Transactions of the Association for Computational Linguistics*, 9:362–373.

Saizheng Zhang, Emily Dinan, Jack Urbanek, Arthur Szlam, Douwe Kiela, and Jason Weston. 2018. Personalizing dialogue agents: I have a dog, do you have pets too? *arXiv preprint arXiv:1801.07243*.

Hao Zhou, Minlie Huang, Tianyang Zhang, Xiaoyan Zhu, and Bing Liu. 2018. Emotional chatting machine: Emotional conversation generation with internal and external memory. In *Proceedings of the AAAI Conference on Artificial Intelligence*, volume 32.

Appendix

Human Input: Join us, the show is about to start.
Eh character: Eh, it's a little soon for all that, we need to set up!
Huh character: I'm sorry I'm not in the mood to talk huh.
Speaker from an AAA game: Just don't get us killed, OK? This is not the place to play.
Speaker from an AAA game: Oh, thank God!
Narrator from an AAA game: Edward enters and walks in.
Narrator from an AAA game: ext. UNDERWORLD of THEATERS.

Table A1: Example outputs from SASS for different well known video game characters and two example characters (one usually starting its sentences by "Eh" and the other finishing with "huh").

narrator: This is the first line that plays during the dialog for big battles occurring at sea. It is followed by an accept/decline hub.
narrator: This greeting plays when Athens is on the offensive, and when the player is at a medium to high level in game.
speakerA: The mighty Eagle Bearer. Rumor has it you command one of the fiercest ships at sea. Maybe you'd be interested in making some drachmae off it?
speakerB: Depends how.
speakerA: Join Athens as we set sail to destroy the Spartan navy... that's all.

Table A2: Example Scene from an AAA game in the UBISCENES dataset.

A Survey of Challenges and Methods in the Computational Modeling of Multi-Party Dialog

Ananya Ganesh Martha Palmer Katharina Kann
University of Colorado Boulder
ananya.ganesh@colorado.edu

Abstract

Advances in conversational AI systems, powered in particular by large language models, have facilitated rapid progress in understanding and generating dialog. Typically, task-oriented or open-domain dialog systems have been designed to work with two-party dialog, i.e., the exchange of utterances between a single user and a dialog system. However, modern dialog systems may be deployed in scenarios such as classrooms or meetings where conversational analysis of multiple speakers is required. This survey will present research around computational modeling of "multi-party dialog", outlining differences from two-party dialog, challenges and issues in working with multi-party dialog, and methods for representing multi-party dialog. We also provide an overview of dialog datasets created for the study of multi-party dialog, as well as tasks that are of interest in this domain.

1 Introduction

Dialog systems are increasingly a part of our personal and professional lives, and have made their way into domains such as healthcare (Valizadeh and Parde, 2022), business (Sang and Bao, 2022), and education (Litman and Silliman, 2004). Predominantly, research on dialog systems investigates how to develop task-oriented or open-domain systems that individual users can interact with, to accomplish routine tasks or engage in chit-chat. Conversations in such settings tend to be two-party or *dyadic* conversations, that is, involve only two participants, the system and the user, who may typically alternate turns while speaking. However, for applications such as classroom tutoring assistants or meeting summarization, dialog systems need to be able to understand and participate in *multi-party* dialog – interactions between multiple humans.

However, multi-party dialog is structurally different from dyadic dialog, requiring systems to be designed with their characteristics in mind. For

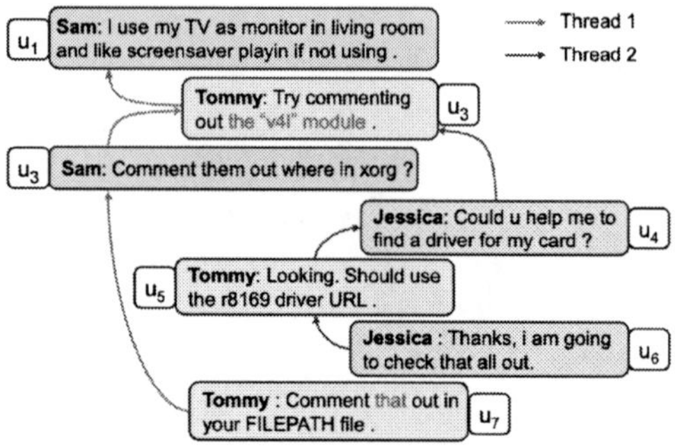

Figure 1: An example of a multi-party interaction, with speakers and threads marked. Figure from Shen et al. (2023)

instance, looking at the chat conversation in Figure 1, we see that the conversations are non-linear and interleaved, and utterances can be implicitly addressed to a specific participant(s). Conversational analysis of this interaction would require understanding each sub-dialog, and require resolving the speaker and addressees of each utterance. Responses by the dialog agent would also require determining which participant the response should be directed to. If multiple dialog agents are present, response management also requires determining which agent takes the turn. For the purposes of this study, we only consider scenarios with multiple human participants, and one dialog agent.

In this paper, we survey research that investigates the computational modeling of multi-party dialog [1]. We first introduce the characteristics of multi-party dialog based on early work in conversational analysis, focusing on ways in which they differ from two-party dialog. Based on these differences, we outline some of the challenges that face systems operating in this setting, and their solutions that have been investigated by the field. In Section 5, we present a comprehensive overview

[1]Unless stated otherwise, the systems and datasets we describe are focused on English dialog.

Proceedings of the 5th Workshop on NLP for Conversational AI (NLP4ConvAI 2023), pages 140–154

of representation learning methods for multi-party dialog, focusing on the merits of modeling information flow through graph structures, and discuss deep learning methods for obtaining and encoding these structures. Finally, we conclude with a discussion of opportunities for future work in multi-party dialog modeling.

2 Characteristics of Multi-Party Dialog

Participant Roles: The defining characteristic of multi-party dialog is the presence of multiple participants or interlocutors in a conversation. While in a two-party interaction, one participant takes on the role of the speaker in a turn and the other participant takes on the role of listener or "addressee", an utterance in a multi-party conversation not only has multiple candidate addressees, but could also be directed at multiple listeners at the same time. Traum (2004) further defines participant roles based on their degree of participation at various stages in the conversation: in-context listeners have heard all the previous utterances and may interpret the current utterance differently from a listener with no prior context; active participants are engaged in the conversation and play the roles of speakers and addressees, whereas overhearers may receive utterances but do not participate in the conversation.

Initiative and turn-taking: Traum (2004) observe that while many two-party dialog systems are mixed-initiative or user-initiative driven, multi-party dialog tends to be asymmetric in displaying initiative, with some participants dominating. Multi-party dialog may also include simultaneous conversations about multiple distinct topics (Elsner and Charniak, 2008). Aoki et al. (2006) analyze spontaneous social conversations in small groups, focusing on the nature of turn-taking in simultaneous conversations. Of particular interest are *conversational floors* (Sacks et al., 1974), which are structures that can be composed of one turn at a time such as in a therapy session, or can contain multiple alternating turns – for example, when a speaker has the floor and another speaker takes a turn to ask a question, but does not take the floor (Edelsky, 1981). They find that multi-party conversations tend to have multiple simultaneously active floors, with a single session (of up to an hour) having an average of 1.79 active floors, and a maximum of 4 active floors. They further find that floors are dynamic, particularly when the participants are young (ages 14-24) – in sessions with youth there are upto 70 distinct floors over the course of the conversation, each lasting about 44 seconds.

Dialog structure: Research has also studied how structures such as dialog acts or discourse relations can shed light on the nature of multi-party dialog. Ishizaki and Kato (1998) examine how dialog act structures differ between two-party and multi-party dialog (specifically, three-party dialog in their study). They first find that dialog act sequences most frequently involve only two speakers, particularly in sequences of length three to five. Looking at distances between utterances and their antecedents, Ginzburg and Fernández (2005) find that long range dependencies are more prevalent in multi-party dialog than in two-party dialog. Discourse relations prevalent in multi-party dialog also tend to be distinctive: Volha et al. (2011) find `feedback elicitation` to be more prevalent than in two-party dialog, whereas Asher et al. (2016) find that the most frequent relations are question-answer pairs or follow-up questions.

3 Challenges and Sub-Tasks

The unique characteristics of multi-party dialog imply the existence of challenges that cannot be handled by traditional two-party dialog systems. These challenges are occasionally treated as part of the larger system design (Ouchi and Tsuboi, 2016), but for the most part have been isolated as separate sub-tasks. We list a few major problems, and discuss solutions proposed in the literature.

3.1 Speaker and addressee recognition

In multi-party dialog, particularly in spoken or transcribed dialog, determining the speaker of the *current* utterance is a non-trivial task (Traum, 2004). *Closed-set* speaker identification is formulated as a classification task, where given an utterance, the goal is to determine the speaker from a list of known participants (Reynolds and Rose, 1995). Early work on text-independent speaker recognition makes use of acoustic features extracted from speech (Brunelli and Falavigna, 1995; Campbell et al., 2006) for classification, as well as multimodal signals such as gestures (Bohus and Horvitz, 2010b) or the movement of lips in videos (Haider and Al Moubayed, 2012). Utterance-aware (Gu et al., 2022b) or text-dependent speaker identification uses the content of the utterance, typically from transcribed text, in order to determine the speaker. Work along these lines include Ma et al.

(2017), who classify speakers based on utterances from multiple transcripts and find success using a convolutional neural network, Meng et al. (2018) who use a hierarchical RNN (Serban et al., 2016) to encode content as well as temporal information indicated by speaker order.

Addressee identification is an important sub-task in which work follows two directions: 1) identifying the participant at whom each utterance is directed enables the construction of a graphical structure to represent information flow and 2) selecting the addressee to whom a response generated by a dialog agent should be addressed. For 1), Traum (2004) propose an algorithm looking at "vocative expressions" in the utterance, as well as speakers and content of current and previous utterances. Other features investigated for this task include gaze and acoustic features (Jovanovic et al., 2006; Jovanovic and op den Akker, 2004), and dialog acts (Gupta et al., 2007; Galley et al., 2004).

For 2), Ouchi and Tsuboi (2016) propose the task of *addressee and response selection*, where given a context of utterances with their speakers, the system predicts an addressee and a response. They propose two modeling frameworks, which both learn a vector representation for each participant (or agent), which is then encoded with the utterance context using an RNN: the *static* setting uses a fixed agent vector computed based on the speaking order of all agents, while the *dynamic* model updates the agent vector corresponding to the speaker of the current utterance at each timestep during training. However, since this doesn't capture the interaction between different agents, Zhang et al. (2018) propose an improvement that updates the embeddings of all active participants at each timestep. Wang et al. (2020) integrate addressee identification into a multi-task learning model that also performs topic prediction and response selection.

3.2 Turn taking

Turn-taking in natural conversations refers to the process by which humans coordinate participation, through verbal as well as non-verbal cues (Traum, 2004; Bohus and Horvitz, 2010b). Dialog systems, even in a two-party setting, need to perform turn management to identify when they can speak. Computational modeling of turn-taking in dialog is therefore a task that has received much attention (Hawes et al., 2009; Raux and Eskenazi, 2009; Bohus and Horvitz, 2010a; de Bayser et al., 2019). Bohus and Horvitz (2010a) define four kinds of "floor management" actions – *Hold, Release, Take* and *Null* to describe how turns move from one participant to another, and use heuristics based on response intervals to design a turn management system that chooses the appropriate action (Bohus and Horvitz, 2010b). Raux and Eskenazi (2009) use a similar formulation, and present a finite state machine that is optimized to minimize gaps and overlaps in a conversation.

Turn-taking is also modeled in some work as the task of predicting the next speaker, given a context consisting of speakers and utterances from previous turns. Hawes et al. (2009) treat this as a sequence labeling problem, and propose a second-order CRF in combination with features such as discourse markers (Marcu, 1997) and pronoun references. In more recent work, Skantze (2017) use lexical and acoustic features with an LSTM model; de Bayser et al. (2019) comparatively investigate SVM, CNN and LSTM models, achieving best results with the CNN models; Ishii et al. (2016) additionally use multi-modal features such as gaze to predict the next speaker as well as the time at which the next utterance will be made.

3.3 Conversation disentanglement

The presence of multiple simultaneous conversation floors (Section 2) results in distinct threads of conversation being entangled in a single session of multi-party dialogue. To enable understanding and responding to such conversations, the task of "conversation disentanglement" is important, which creates separate threads that are each about a specific topic. Elsner and Charniak (2008) introduce a corpus for this problem based on Internet Relay Chat (IRC) conversations, where annotations mark utterances that belong to the same conversational thread. They present a two-stage framework for disentanglement that first classifies pairs of utterances as to whether they are part of the same thread or not based on discourse and content features. Then, they perform correlation clustering to partition all utterances into clusters greedily. In follow-up work, Elsner and Charniak (2011) experiment with incorporating discourse coherence models (Lapata et al., 2005; Soricut and Marcu, 2006) for disentanglement, and find mixed results on the IRC corpus: models of local coherence help with assigning individual utterances into the right threads, but not in disentangling entire conversations.

The two-stage setup described here has been iteratively improved in future work, particularly by improving the classification component using deep learning models. Mehri and Carenini (2017) make use of discourse structure by annotating reply-to relations, and include two additional RNN-based classifiers to the Elsner and Charniak (2008) model, one for classifying pair-wise reply relations, and one for determining if an utterance follows a context. Jiang et al. (2018) achieve improvements to the same-thread classifier using Siamese CNNs. Kummerfeld et al. (2019) increase the scale of the IRC corpus by 30 times, creating a new benchmark for conversation disentanglement, and additionally propose an ensemble feedforward model that outperforms previous models. In contrast, more recent works investigate end-to-end models for this task, such as Liu et al. (2020) who develop a transition-based model that keeps track of states in discovered threads while assigning incoming utterances to existing or new threads in an online fashion. Liu et al. (2021) perform disentanglement on an unlabeled corpus by first creating pseudo data for the pairwise classifiers.

Time	User	Utterance
[12:21]	dell	well, can I move the drives?
[12:21]	cucho	dell: ah not like that
[12:21]	RC	dell: you can't move the drives
[12:21]	RC	dell: definitely not
[12:21]	dell	ok
[12:21]	dell	lol
[12:21]	RC	this is the problem with RAID:)
[12:21]	dell	RC haha yeah
[12:22]	dell	cucho, I guess I could just get an enclosure and copy via USB...
[12:22]	cucho	dell: i would advise you to get the disk

Sender	Recipient	Utterance
dell		well, can I move the drives?
cucho	dell	ah not like that
dell	cucho	I guess I could just get an enclosure and copy via USB
cucho	dell	i would advise you to get the disk
dell		well, can I move the drives?
RC	dell	you can't move the drives. definitely not. this is the problem with RAID :)
dell	RC	haha yeah

Figure 2: An interaction from Lowe et al. (2015), heuristically disentangled and tagged with addressees.

4 Datasets

Corpora for studying multi-party conversations span a variety of modalities – spoken (Renals et al., 2007), written (Lowe et al., 2015), or accompanied by video (Poria et al., 2019); they also span multiple genres, including chat forums for software discussions, movies and TV dialog, formal discourse in meetings and interviews, and informal discourse during gameplay. In this survey, we do not focus on comprehensively describing all available datasets, but provide an overview of three datasets which serve as benchmarks for modeling multi-party dialog, and have been extensively used in the models described below. For a detailed survey of datasets specifically, we refer the reader to Mahajan and Shaikh (2021).

Ubuntu IRC Corpora Internet Relay Chat (IRC), a text-based chat interface, contains channels for discussion about specialized topics. Typically, discussions consist of users posting questions, and other users replying with solutions, and all messages (or utterances), contain the identity of the sender (speaker). Corpora built from this interface have been used for the tasks of conversation disentanglement, speaker and addressee recognition, and response generation. Elsner and Charniak (2008) were the first to use conversations from the `##LINUX` channel, which they manually annotate for threads, for the task of disentanglement. This yields 80 conversations, with a total of about 1500 utterances. Uthus and Aha (2013) scrape six years of chats from the `##ubuntu` channel (which contains messages in English), as well as seven non-English channels including the languages Chinese, Russian, Spanish, Portuguese, Italian, Polish and Swedish. This corpus contains over 26 million messages, but without any annotations. Lowe et al. (2015) present the Ubuntu Dialog corpus, which contains 1 million English conversations totalling 7 million utterances. Each utterance contains speaker ID, and they also heuristically extract addressee IDs and disentangle conversations, as shown in Figure 2. Kummerfeld et al. (2019) present the largest manually annotated corpus from this domain, for the task of conversation disentanglement, with 70k utterances. Finally, Li et al. (2020) introduce the Molweni challenge corpus by annotating the Ubuntu corpus with reading comprehension style questions and answers, resulting in 33k question-answer pairs.

Meeting Corpora The AMI project (Kraaij et al., 2005; Renals et al., 2007) provides a corpus for multimodal conversational analysis of formal discourse – specifically, in multi-party meetings. The AMI corpus consists of 100 hours (175 sessions) of scenario-oriented meetings between four participants, where video and audio are recorded, along with artifacts such as digital pen movements and whiteboard content. They providing access to videos, manually transcribed speech, abstractive and extractive summaries of the conversations, and annotations for dialog acts, topic segments, gaze and positional information, and gestures. Other corpora under the umbrella of the AMI project includes the ICSI corpus (Janin et al., 2003), which contains 72 hours of naturally-occuring meetings (not elicited by a scenario).

MELD Corpus Another multi-modal multi-party dataset that is widely used in the models below is the MELD corpus (Poria et al., 2019), designed for emotion recognition from conversations. It consists of 1433 conversations from the TV show Friends, providing access to video, audio, and transcripts. They include annotations at the utterance level indicating one out of seven emotions (such as anger, surprise, etc.) expressed by the utterance.

5 Representation Learning for MPD

In this section, we will describe how machine learning models represent and encode multi-party dialog in order to leverage its inherent structural properties for tasks such as response generation. Early work such as Lowe et al. (2015) represent the entire conversational context sequentially, where all prior utterances to the current one that fall in a window are concatenated. Improvements such as Zhou et al. (2016) model relationships between the current utterance and the context through a hierarchical RNN. However, given that multi-party dialog can have multiple addressees, multiple replies, as well as simultaneous conversations, such sequential structures cannot represent all relationships between utterances in the dialog.

As a solution, recent successful models experiment with graph structures to represent the flow of information in multi-party dialog. Typically, this approach treats the utterances as nodes, and the relations between them (such as *reply-to*) as edges. The graphs thus obtained are encoded through a suitable neural network architecture (Kipf and Welling, 2017; Schlichtkrull et al., 2018), and the resulting embeddings are used for the downstream task, in combination with decoders or classification layers. Below, we look at specific sub-components and strategies for this workflow.

5.1 Dialog structure induction

Corpora such as the Ubuntu Dialog Corpus (Lowe et al., 2015), which serve as benchmarks for modeling multi-party dialog, contain explicit annotations for speakers and addressees. When annotations for dialog structure such as addressee information are not available, dialog structure needs to be learned from the conversation without explicit supervision, so that it can be used to perform downstream tasks While unsupervised methods for structure induction on task-oriented dialog have received some attention (Shi et al., 2019; Sun et al., 2021a; Xu et al., 2021), comparatively less work exists for multi-party dialog, the most prominent being Qiu et al. (2020), who propose a model to induce structure on both two-party and multi-party dialog. They propose a model for response generation, which consists of a Variational Recurrent Neural Network (VRNN) (Chung et al., 2015) into which *structured attention* layers are integrated, such that the latent state of the VRNN captures the underlying dialog structure. The model first encodes sentences with an LSTM, then the VRNN encodes a dialog history into a latent state, which is then decoded to produce a response. While training, they maximize the conditional likelihood of a response given the history, while also learning a latent dependency tree – here, nodes represents the utterances, and directed edges exist between nodes when one utterance is the parent of another. Evaluating on the Ubuntu Chat Corpus (Uthus and Aha, 2013), they find that the VRNN model performs comparably to a graph-based model that makes use of explicit speaker/addressee annotations (Hu et al., 2019). On comparing the learned utterance dependency tree with gold annotations for speaker and addressee relations, they find that the model achieves an accuracy of 68.5% in identifying the parents of each utterance.

5.2 Graph-based representations

Unlike Qiu et al. (2020), the predominant line of research on modeling multi-party dialog makes use of annotated speaker/addressee information in order to obtain the graph structures. Hu et al. (2019) propose a model for response generation that they call *Graph Structured Networks* (GSN), which was to our knowledge the first to successfully apply graphs to multi-party dialog. Similar to the framework discussed above, they formulate their graph as an utterance dependency graph, assuming access to annotated speaker/addressee information within the conversational data. The GSN consists of a word-level encoder to represent utterances, an utterance-level graph structured encoder to represent information flow, and a decoder to generate responses. Embeddings for an utterance are obtained from the graph using forward and backward information flow, and the speaker information. In experiments on the Ubuntu Dialog Corpus (Lowe et al., 2015), they find that their proposed model achieves a significant improvement over baselines that are based on sequential or hierarchical utterance encodings (Serban et al., 2016). They further find, through ablations, that the inclusion of speaker information flow is crucial to model performance.

For two-party and task-oriented dialog, Graph Convolutional Networks (Kipf and Welling, 2017; Schlichtkrull et al., 2018) have been successfully used for representing structure (Banerjee and Khapra, 2019), and have consequently been explored for multi-party dialog as well. Ghosal et al. (2019) propose a model called DialogueGCN for the task of emotion recognition from conversations, which is an utterance-level classification task. They represent each utterance as a node in the graph, and construct edges to represent the context – all utterances within a window prior and after the current utterance are marked. They also assign relational edges, to capture temporal dependency as well as speaker dependency between pairs of utterances. The graph is then encoded through Relational Graph Convolutional Networks (Schlichtkrull et al., 2018), which provides a representation for each node that aggregates information from its context nodes. The proposed model outperforms multiple strong baselines when evaluating on MELD (Poria et al., 2019), including DialogRNNs (Majumder et al., 2019). A similar framework is proposed by Ju et al. (2022), who include *personas* corresponding to each speaker in the vertex set, for the task of generating personalized responses. Edges are then constructed between personas and their corresponding utterances, as well as between consecutive utterances, before encoding through a GCN. As a baseline, they adapt DialogueGCNs for response generation by adding a decoder, and show the superiority of their persona-aware model according to automated and human evaluation metrics.

Similar to Ju et al. (2022), the idea of including nodes that are not just utterances has been explored by other work, resulting in graphs that are *heterogenous*. Gu et al. (2022a) propose *HeterMPC*, a graph-based model for response generation in multi-party dialog. Their graph treats utterances as well as participants as nodes, drawing edges between nodes to indicate six types of relations: *reply, reply-to, speak, spoken-by, address, addressed-by*. Utterance nodes are represented by embeddings from BERT, whereas interlocutors are represented by a speaker embedding initialized based on their position in the conversation. When updating the representations for nodes, they compute heterogeneous attention weights over source and target, conditioned on the edge type. Their proposed model outperforms GSNs with automated and human evaluations. Further, their ablations indicate the importance of interlocutor nodes as well as edge relations. Sang and Bao (2022) also make use of heterogeneous graphs that contain participant and utterance nodes, towards the task of financial risk prediction upon earnings call conferences. The edges in their graph connect speakers to their utterances, and the resulting graph is encoded with a Graph Attention Network (Veličković et al., 2018). From the graph encoder's output, they aggregate speaker embeddings separately from utterance embeddings using two separate contextual attention layers, which then represent the whole conversation, which is then classified for stock volatility. Lee and Choi (2021) include four types of nodes in their graph: dialog (utterance), turn, subject, and object; edges relate turns nodes to their respective utterances, connect utterances by the same speaker, and connect turns to arguments that are mentioned. They also encode their graph with a GCN, and evaluate on the tasks of relation extraction in dialogues, as well as emotion recognition. Liang et al. (2021) take heterogeneous graphs one step further with multimodal nodes – their nodes include utterances, facial expression features, emotion categories, and speakers, with seven kinds of edges capturing the relations between the different features. They encode this graph with a heterogeneous graph neural network (Zhang et al., 2019), and evaluate on the downstream task of response generation expressing a suitable emotion.

5.3 Utilizing discourse relations

Some research has investigated how the graph structures described above can include other task-specific or linguistic information, such as annotations for discourse.

Feng et al. (2021) present a dialog discourse aware graph-based model for the task of meeting summarization. Of interest are 16 discourse relations from Asher et al. (2016) including comment, QA, elaboration, etc. They obtain discourse relations from a dialog discourse parser (Shi and Huang, 2019), and transform it such that nodes are created for utterances as well as discourse relations, with directed edges marking the relations between utterances. They encode their graph with an R-GCN (Schlichtkrull et al., 2018). Experiments on the AMI and IMSI meeting corpora show improvements over sequential models (Serban et al., 2016). They find that performance is correlated with the quality of the discourse parser, as well as the number of discourse relations available. Discourse structures from an off-the-shelf parser are also used by Sun et al. (2021b) in their graph-based model for emotion recognition. Similar to Ghosal et al. (2019), they construct directed edges between utterance nodes, marking discourse relations in addition to speaker and temporal relations. The inclusion of discourse results in a significant improvement over DialogGCNs on the MELD corpus. Contemporaneously, Li et al. (2021) investigate discourse-aware graphs for machine reading comprehension on multi-party dialog as found in the Molweni challenge corpus (Li et al., 2020). They also model utterances as nodes, with dependencies as edges and discourse types denoted by edge relations, using DialogGCN for encoding. Additionally, an MRC module integrates a representation for the question, outputting an answer span.

5.4 Pretraining

Following the advancements in the representational capabilities of pretrained language models (Devlin et al., 2019; Radford and Narasimhan, 2018), models such as ToD-BERT (Wu et al., 2020) and DialoGPT (Zhang et al., 2020) have been developed with the goal of enhancing dialog representations in task-oriented or open-domain dialog. Pre-training has also been explored for multi-party dialog: Gu et al. (2021) propose MPC-BERT, in which they pretrain BERT on data from the Ubuntu Chat Corpus (Lowe et al., 2015), with five self-supervision tasks. These tasks are designed to model underlying interlocutor structure in multi-party dialog, as well as utterance semantics. Tasks for the first category include 1) *reply-to utterance recognition*, which involves predicting the preceding utterance that an utterance is replying to; 2) *identical speaker searching*, or identifying utterances that share a speaker; 3) *pointer-consistency distinction*, which involves maintaining a similar representation for pairs of utterances between the same speaker–addressee pair in order to model interlocutors. Tasks for the second category include 1) *masked shared utterance restoration*, where utterances that receive multiple replies are masked and reconstructed during training 2) *shared node detection*, where sub-threads of the same parent utterance are required to be correctly identified. The pretrained model thus obtained can be finetuned for downstream tasks – the authors finetune and evaluate on the tasks of addressee recognition, speaker identification, and response selection, outperforming previous methods significantly. Notably, all of the finetuning tasks are from the same domain (Ubuntu IRC) as the pre-training data, although the authors declare that they only use the train split for pre-training.

Other work that focuses on pre-training for multi-party conversation understanding includes Zhong et al. (2022), who focus on learning long-range dependencies across dialog, in order to solve problems like summarization and question answering. In contrast to MPC-BERT, and similar to BART (Lewis et al., 2019), their self-supervision objective involves denoising dialog based on windows – given a long dialog, they sample random windows to which noise is added, which is later reconstructed. The added noise takes the form of masking speaker identities, utterances, merging turns and shuffling utterances within a turn. With this objective, they train a Transformer-based model called UniLM (Dong et al., 2019) on the Movie Subtitles corpus (Lison and Tiedemann, 2016) and MediaSum interview corpus (Zhu et al., 2021). Finetuning on the tasks of summarization, dialog segmentation and question answering, they show improvements across automated and human evaluations. Wang et al. (2020) pretrain a BERT model on the task of topic prediction – determining if two utterances are about the same topic, in addition to masked language modeling. Their encoder, called TopicBERT, is then finetuned in a multi-task learning setup, on the tasks of response selection, topic prediction, and topic disentanglement.

6 Tasks of Interest

Response generation and selection: As seen above, a large body of work exists on response generation (Qiu et al., 2020; Hu et al., 2019; Gu et al., 2022a), given a multi-party dialog as context. To generate responses at the right time and towards the right speaker, this can be combined with the tasks of speaker prediction (Yang et al., 2019) and addressee selection (Liu et al., 2019). The generated responses are typically evaluated with a combination of automated metrics such as BLEU (Papineni et al., 2002) and METEOR (Banerjee and Lavie, 2005) given a reference from the conversation. Human evaluations, such as in Liu et al. (2019); Gu et al. (2022a); Ju et al. (2022) assess whether responses are fluent, consistent with the context, informative, and coherent. The task of response selection, formulated as *retrieving* the most appropriate next utterance from a set of candidates, is also of interest (Ouchi and Tsuboi, 2016; Zhang et al., 2018; Wang et al., 2020; Gu et al., 2021). Response selection is typically evaluated with classification-based metrics such as precision and recall, including $Recall_n@k$ to match n available candidates with top k retrieved candidates.

Modeling socio-cultural phenomena: Multi-party conversations are of interest from a computational social science perspective, to study interactional dynamics between participants. This includes determining when decision-making occurs (Frampton et al., 2009; Bui et al., 2009), analyzing bargaining and negotiation strategies (Petukhova et al., 2016; Joshi et al., 2021; Asher et al., 2016), and analyzing collaborative behavior such as entrainment (Litman et al., 2016; Rahimi et al., 2017), cohesion (Bangalore Kantharaju et al., 2020) and agreement (Hillard et al., 2003; Strzalkowski et al., 2010; Rosenthal and McKeown, 2015). Work on recognizing emotions from utterances, typically with multi-modal information, is also loosely related to this direction (Ghosal et al., 2019; Poria et al., 2019).

Other NLP tasks: Datasets and models have been developed for the task of summarization of multi-party conversations (Renals et al., 2007; Purver et al., 2007; Chen and Metze, 2012; Zhu et al., 2021). While Zhu et al. (2021) provide a dataset that disentangles the primary topic from secondary topics before summarization, an under-explored issue is performing summarization jointly with disentanglement so that multiple summaries are produced for the multiple sub-threads in the conversation. Other high-level NLP tasks that have been explored include answering reading comprehension questions over multi-party dialog (Li et al., 2020, 2021), and relation extraction (Albalak et al., 2022; Yu et al., 2020).

7 Discussion

One of the salient findings from our survey is that most recent work on multi-party dialog modeling, particularly using the graph-based methods, are centered around corpora from a limited set of domains; in fact, almost all of the models in Section 5 are evaluated on the Ubuntu chat corpus or on TV show transcript corpora. A possible reason for this is the availability of annotated structure in these datasets, including speaker and addressee information, as well as threads. However, we argue that the time is ripe for researchers to investigate how to extend modeling innovations to other available corpora and domains.

This is an important next step for two reasons, namely *real-world applicability*, and *robustness*. Natural dialog, such as spontaneous interactions between humans, is typically not well-represented in datasets such as typed chat, or scripted TV dialog. With the growing influence of dialog systems in daily lives, if our goal is to build better technology for the real world, like classrooms or businesses, we need to demonstrate that these state-of-the-art models perform equally well on probable, real-world conversations. Moreover, as seen in Mahajan and Shaikh (2021), numerous datasets satisfying these properties are actually available, although they do not necessarily contain explicit annotations for structure. However, as this survey shows, we have a large body of work that tells us how to go from natural conversations to more structured representations through tasks such as speaker and addressee recognition, turn prediction, and conversation disentanglement. Using these tasks as scaffolds for downstream tasks like response generation would enable us to leverage the expressivity of graph-based modeling on new and realistic domains.

In terms of other important next steps for this field of research, one interesting direction is exploring strategies for obtaining silver-standard graph structures through unsupervised methods – we so far only find one paper constructing a reply-to relation graph unsupervisedly. Additionally, to answer the robustness question, a systematic assessment of the advantages and shortcomings of graph-structured methods on rarer domains such as meetings (Petukhova et al., 2016) could be highly valuable, particularly for practitioners interested in studying the phenomena exhibited in such conversations. More broadly in this direction, given how the methods we have seen are predominantly focused on English multi-party dialog, the applicability of these methods to languages other than English (Liu et al., 2012), as well as conversations with code-switching (Hartmann et al., 2018), also needs to be evaluated. Finally, with the growing adoption and effectiveness of large language models (LLMs) in NLP research, a natural next question is to determine how these models can be used in understanding multi-party dialog, and what their limitations are. Current directions with promising results include using LLMs for conversation synthesis (Wei et al., 2023; Chen et al., 2023), where high-quality multi-party conversations are synthesized through prompting, and the conversations can be grounded in specific characters or personas. Such synthesized conversations may also help adapt methods for conversation analysis and response generation to rarer domains that may not be well-represented in natural corpora.

8 Conclusion

Our survey provides an overview of research in computationally modeling multi-party dialog. We identify major challenges based on differences from two-party dialog, and discuss how sub-tasks have been designed for solving them. We comprehensively describe recent advances in representation learning for multi-party dialog, focusing in particular on graph-based structures. Finally, we discuss some key directions that future work in this area can explore.

Acknowledgments

We thank the anonymous reviewers for their thoughtful feedback and suggestions. We also thank the members of the CU Boulder Computational Semantics group for their feedback on this survey. This research was supported by the NSF National AI Institute for Student-AI Teaming (iSAT) under grant DRL 2019805. The opinions expressed are those of the authors and do not represent views of the NSF.

References

Alon Albalak, Varun Embar, Yi-Lin Tuan, Lise Getoor, and William Yang Wang. 2022. D-REX: Dialogue relation extraction with explanations. In *Proceedings of the 4th Workshop on NLP for Conversational AI*, pages 34–46, Dublin, Ireland. Association for Computational Linguistics.

Paul M. Aoki, Margaret H. Szymanski, Luke Plurkowski, James D. Thornton, Allison Woodruff, and Weilie Yi. 2006. Where's the "party" in "multi-party"? analyzing the structure of small-group sociable talk. In *Proceedings of the 2006 20th Anniversary Conference on Computer Supported Cooperative Work*, CSCW '06, page 393–402, New York, NY, USA. Association for Computing Machinery.

Nicholas Asher, Julie Hunter, Mathieu Morey, Benamara Farah, and Stergos Afantenos. 2016. Discourse structure and dialogue acts in multiparty dialogue: the STAC corpus. In *Proceedings of the Tenth International Conference on Language Resources and Evaluation (LREC'16)*, pages 2721–2727, Portorož, Slovenia. European Language Resources Association (ELRA).

Satanjeev Banerjee and Alon Lavie. 2005. METEOR: An automatic metric for MT evaluation with improved correlation with human judgments. In *Proceedings of the ACL Workshop on Intrinsic and Extrinsic Evaluation Measures for Machine Translation and/or Summarization*, pages 65–72, Ann Arbor, Michigan. Association for Computational Linguistics.

Suman Banerjee and Mitesh M Khapra. 2019. Graph convolutional network with sequential attention for goal-oriented dialogue systems. *Transactions of the Association for Computational Linguistics*, 7:485–500.

Reshmashree Bangalore Kantharaju, Caroline Langlet, Mukesh Barange, Chloé Clavel, and Catherine Pelachaud. 2020. Multimodal analysis of cohesion in multi-party interactions. In *Proceedings of the Twelfth Language Resources and Evaluation Conference*, pages 498–507, Marseille, France. European Language Resources Association.

Dan Bohus and Eric Horvitz. 2010a. Computational models for multiparty turn taking. *Technical Report. Microsoft Research Technical Report MSR-TR 2010-115.*

Dan Bohus and Eric Horvitz. 2010b. Facilitating multiparty dialog with gaze, gesture, and speech. In *International Conference on Multimodal Interfaces and the Workshop on Machine Learning for Multimodal Interaction*, pages 1–8.

Roberto Brunelli and Daniele Falavigna. 1995. Person identification using multiple cues. *IEEE transactions on pattern analysis and machine intelligence*, 17(10):955–966.

Trung Bui, Matthew Frampton, John Dowding, and Stanley Peters. 2009. Extracting decisions from multi-party dialogue using directed graphical models and semantic similarity. In *Proceedings of the SIGDIAL 2009 Conference*, pages 235–243, London, UK. Association for Computational Linguistics.

William M Campbell, Joseph P Campbell, Douglas A Reynolds, Elliot Singer, and Pedro A Torres-Carrasquillo. 2006. Support vector machines for speaker and language recognition. *Computer Speech & Language*, 20(2-3):210–229.

Maximillian Chen, Alexandros Papangelis, Chenyang Tao, Seokhwan Kim, Andy Rosenbaum, Yang Liu, Zhou Yu, and Dilek Hakkani-Tur. 2023. PLACES: Prompting language models for social conversation synthesis. In *Findings of the Association for Computational Linguistics: EACL 2023*, pages 844–868, Dubrovnik, Croatia. Association for Computational Linguistics.

Yun-Nung Chen and Florian Metze. 2012. Intra-speaker topic modeling for improved multi-party meeting summarization with integrated random walk. In *Proceedings of the 2012 Conference of the North American Chapter of the Association for Computational Linguistics: Human Language Technologies*, pages 377–381, Montréal, Canada. Association for Computational Linguistics.

Junyoung Chung, Kyle Kastner, Laurent Dinh, Kratarth Goel, Aaron C Courville, and Yoshua Bengio. 2015. A recurrent latent variable model for sequential data. *Advances in neural information processing systems*, 28.

Maíra Gatti de Bayser, Paulo Rodrigo Cavalin, Claudio Santos Pinhanez, and Bianca Zadrozny. 2019. Learning multi-party turn-taking models from dialogue logs. *CoRR*, abs/1907.02090.

Jacob Devlin, Ming-Wei Chang, Kenton Lee, and Kristina Toutanova. 2019. BERT: Pre-training of deep bidirectional transformers for language understanding. In *Proceedings of the 2019 Conference of the North American Chapter of the Association for Computational Linguistics: Human Language Technologies, Volume 1 (Long and Short Papers)*, pages 4171–4186, Minneapolis, Minnesota. Association for Computational Linguistics.

Li Dong, Nan Yang, Wenhui Wang, Furu Wei, Xiaodong Liu, Yu Wang, Jianfeng Gao, Ming Zhou, and Hsiao-Wuen Hon. 2019. Unified language model pre-training for natural language understanding and generation. *Advances in neural information processing systems*, 32.

Carole Edelsky. 1981. Who's got the floor? *Language in Society*, 10(3):383–421.

Micha Elsner and Eugene Charniak. 2008. You talking to me? a corpus and algorithm for conversation disentanglement. In *Proceedings of ACL-08: HLT*, pages 834–842, Columbus, Ohio. Association for Computational Linguistics.

Micha Elsner and Eugene Charniak. 2011. Disentangling chat with local coherence models. In *Proceedings of the 49th Annual Meeting of the Association for Computational Linguistics: Human Language Technologies*, pages 1179–1189.

Xiachong Feng, Xiaocheng Feng, Bing Qin, and Xinwei Geng. 2021. Dialogue discourse-aware graph model and data augmentation for meeting summarization. In *Proceedings of the Thirtieth International Joint Conference on Artificial Intelligence, IJCAI-21*, pages 3808–3814. International Joint Conferences on Artificial Intelligence Organization. Main Track.

Matthew Frampton, Jia Huang, Trung Bui, and Stanley Peters. 2009. Real-time decision detection in multi-party dialogue. In *Proceedings of the 2009 Conference on Empirical Methods in Natural Language Processing*, pages 1133–1141, Singapore. Association for Computational Linguistics.

Michel Galley, Kathleen McKeown, Julia Hirschberg, and Elizabeth Shriberg. 2004. Identifying agreement and disagreement in conversational speech: Use of Bayesian networks to model pragmatic dependencies. In *Proceedings of the 42nd Annual Meeting of the Association for Computational Linguistics (ACL-04)*, pages 669–676, Barcelona, Spain.

Deepanway Ghosal, Navonil Majumder, Soujanya Poria, Niyati Chhaya, and Alexander Gelbukh. 2019. DialogueGCN: A graph convolutional neural network for emotion recognition in conversation. In *Proceedings of the 2019 Conference on Empirical Methods in Natural Language Processing and the 9th International Joint Conference on Natural Language Processing (EMNLP-IJCNLP)*, pages 154–164, Hong Kong, China. Association for Computational Linguistics.

Jonathan Ginzburg and Raquel Fernández. 2005. Scaling up from dialogue to multilogue: Some principles and benchmarks. In *Proceedings of the 43rd Annual Meeting of the Association for Computational Linguistics (ACL'05)*, pages 231–238, Ann Arbor, Michigan. Association for Computational Linguistics.

Jia-Chen Gu, Chao-Hong Tan, Chongyang Tao, Zhen-Hua Ling, Huang Hu, Xiubo Geng, and Daxin Jiang. 2022a. HeterMPC: A heterogeneous graph neural network for response generation in multi-party conversations. In *Proceedings of the 60th Annual Meeting of the Association for Computational Linguistics (Volume 1: Long Papers)*, pages 5086–5097, Dublin, Ireland. Association for Computational Linguistics.

Jia-Chen Gu, Chongyang Tao, and Zhen-Hua Ling. 2022b. Who says what to whom: A survey of multi-party conversations. In *Proceedings of the Thirty-First International Joint Conference on Artificial Intelligence, IJCAI*, pages 5486–5493.

Jia-Chen Gu, Chongyang Tao, Zhenhua Ling, Can Xu, Xiubo Geng, and Daxin Jiang. 2021. MPC-BERT: A pre-trained language model for multi-party conversation understanding. In *Proceedings of the 59th Annual Meeting of the Association for Computational Linguistics and the 11th International Joint Conference on Natural Language Processing (Volume 1: Long Papers)*, pages 3682–3692, Online. Association for Computational Linguistics.

Surabhi Gupta, John Niekrasz, Matthew Purver, and Dan Jurafsky. 2007. Resolving "you" in multi-party dialog. In *Proceedings of the 8th SIGdial Workshop on Discourse and Dialogue*, pages 227–230, Antwerp, Belgium. Association for Computational Linguistics.

Fasih Haider and Samer Al Moubayed. 2012. Towards speaker detection using lips movements for human-machine multiparty dialogue. In *The XXVth Swedish Phonetics Conference (FONETIK)*, pages 117–120. Citeseer.

Silvana Hartmann, Monojit Choudhury, and Kalika Bali. 2018. An integrated representation of linguistic and social functions of code-switching. In *Proceedings of the Eleventh International Conference on Language Resources and Evaluation (LREC 2018)*, Miyazaki, Japan. European Language Resources Association (ELRA).

Timothy Hawes, Jimmy Lin, and Philip Resnik. 2009. Elements of a computational model for multi-party discourse: The turn-taking behavior of supreme court justices. *Journal of the American Society for Information Science and Technology*, 60(8):1607–1615.

Dustin Hillard, Mari Ostendorf, and Elizabeth Shriberg. 2003. Detection of agreement vs. disagreement in meetings: Training with unlabeled data. In *Companion Volume of the Proceedings of HLT-NAACL 2003 - Short Papers*, pages 34–36.

Wenpeng Hu, Zhangming Chan, Bing Liu, Dongyan Zhao, Jinwen Ma, and Rui Yan. 2019. Gsn: A graph-structured network for multi-party dialogues. In *Proceedings of the Twenty-Eighth International Joint Conference on Artificial Intelligence, IJCAI-19*, pages 5010–5016. International Joint Conferences on Artificial Intelligence Organization.

Ryo Ishii, Kazuhiro Otsuka, Shiro Kumano, and Junji Yamato. 2016. Prediction of who will be the next speaker and when using gaze behavior in multiparty meetings. *ACM Trans. Interact. Intell. Syst.*, 6(1).

Masato Ishizaki and Tsuneaki Kato. 1998. Exploring the characteristics of multi-party dialogues. In *36th Annual Meeting of the Association for Computational Linguistics and 17th International Conference on Computational Linguistics, Volume 1*, pages 583–589, Montreal, Quebec, Canada. Association for Computational Linguistics.

Adam Janin, Don Baron, Jane Edwards, Dan Ellis, David Gelbart, Nelson Morgan, Barbara Peskin, Thilo Pfau, Elizabeth Shriberg, Andreas Stolcke, et al. 2003. The icsi meeting corpus. In *2003 IEEE International Conference on Acoustics, Speech, and Signal Processing, 2003. Proceedings.(ICASSP'03).*, volume 1, pages I–I. IEEE.

Jyun-Yu Jiang, Francine Chen, Yan-Ying Chen, and Wei Wang. 2018. Learning to disentangle interleaved conversational threads with a Siamese hierarchical network and similarity ranking. In *Proceedings of the 2018 Conference of the North American Chapter of the Association for Computational Linguistics: Human Language Technologies, Volume 1 (Long Papers)*, pages 1812–1822, New Orleans, Louisiana. Association for Computational Linguistics.

Rishabh Joshi, Vidhisha Balachandran, Shikhar Vashishth, Alan W. Black, and Yulia Tsvetkov. 2021. Dialograph: Incorporating interpretable strategy-graph networks into negotiation dialogues. *CoRR*, abs/2106.00920.

Natasa Jovanovic and Rieks op den Akker. 2004. Towards automatic addressee identification in multi-party dialogues. In *Proceedings of the 5th SIGdial Workshop on Discourse and Dialogue at HLT-NAACL 2004*, pages 89–92, Cambridge, Massachusetts, USA. Association for Computational Linguistics.

Natasa Jovanovic, Rieks op den Akker, and Anton Nijholt. 2006. Addressee identification in face-to-face meetings. In *11th Conference of the European Chapter of the Association for Computational Linguistics*, pages 169–176, Trento, Italy. Association for Computational Linguistics.

Dongshi Ju, Shi Feng, Pengcheng Lv, Daling Wang, and Yifei Zhang. 2022. Learning to improve persona consistency in multi-party dialogue generation via text knowledge enhancement. In *Proceedings of the 29th International Conference on Computational Linguistics*, pages 298–309, Gyeongju, Republic of Korea. International Committee on Computational Linguistics.

Thomas N. Kipf and Max Welling. 2017. Semi-supervised classification with graph convolutional networks. In *International Conference on Learning Representations*.

Wessel Kraaij, Thomas Hain, Mike Lincoln, and Wilfried Post. 2005. The ami meeting corpus.

Jonathan K. Kummerfeld, Sai R. Gouravajhala, Joseph J. Peper, Vignesh Athreya, Chulaka Gunasekara, Jatin Ganhotra, Siva Sankalp Patel, Lazaros C Polymenakos, and Walter Lasecki. 2019. A large-scale corpus for conversation disentanglement. In *Proceedings of the 57th Annual Meeting of the Association for*

Computational Linguistics, pages 3846–3856, Florence, Italy. Association for Computational Linguistics.

Mirella Lapata, Regina Barzilay, et al. 2005. Automatic evaluation of text coherence: Models and representations. In *Ijcai*, volume 5, pages 1085–1090.

Bongseok Lee and Yong Suk Choi. 2021. Graph based network with contextualized representations of turns in dialogue. In *Proceedings of the 2021 Conference on Empirical Methods in Natural Language Processing*, pages 443–455, Online and Punta Cana, Dominican Republic. Association for Computational Linguistics.

Mike Lewis, Yinhan Liu, Naman Goyal, Marjan Ghazvininejad, Abdelrahman Mohamed, Omer Levy, Veselin Stoyanov, and Luke Zettlemoyer. 2019. BART: denoising sequence-to-sequence pre-training for natural language generation, translation, and comprehension. *CoRR*, abs/1910.13461.

Jiaqi Li, Ming Liu, Min-Yen Kan, Zihao Zheng, Zekun Wang, Wenqiang Lei, Ting Liu, and Bing Qin. 2020. Molweni: A challenge multiparty dialogues-based machine reading comprehension dataset with discourse structure. In *Proceedings of the 28th International Conference on Computational Linguistics*, pages 2642–2652, Barcelona, Spain (Online). International Committee on Computational Linguistics.

Jiaqi Li, Ming Liu, Zihao Zheng, Heng Zhang, Bing Qin, Min-Yen Kan, and Ting Liu. 2021. Dadgraph: A discourse-aware dialogue graph neural network for multiparty dialogue machine reading comprehension. In *2021 International Joint Conference on Neural Networks (IJCNN)*, pages 1–8. IEEE.

Yunlong Liang, Fandong Meng, Ying Zhang, Yufeng Chen, Jinan Xu, and Jie Zhou. 2021. Infusing multi-source knowledge with heterogeneous graph neural network for emotional conversation generation. In *Proceedings of the AAAI Conference on Artificial Intelligence*, volume 35, pages 13343–13352.

Pierre Lison and Jörg Tiedemann. 2016. OpenSubtitles2016: Extracting large parallel corpora from movie and TV subtitles. In *Proceedings of the Tenth International Conference on Language Resources and Evaluation (LREC'16)*, pages 923–929, Portorož, Slovenia. European Language Resources Association (ELRA).

Diane Litman, Susannah Paletz, Zahra Rahimi, Stefani Allegretti, and Caitlin Rice. 2016. The teams corpus and entrainment in multi-party spoken dialogues. In *Proceedings of the 2016 Conference on Empirical Methods in Natural Language Processing*, pages 1421–1431, Austin, Texas. Association for Computational Linguistics.

Diane Litman and Scott Silliman. 2004. Itspoke: An intelligent tutoring spoken dialogue system. In *Demonstration papers at HLT-NAACL 2004*, pages 5–8.

Cao Liu, Kang Liu, Shizhu He, Zaiqing Nie, and Jun Zhao. 2019. Incorporating interlocutor-aware context into response generation on multi-party chatbots. In *Proceedings of the 23rd Conference on Computational Natural Language Learning (CoNLL)*, pages 718–727, Hong Kong, China. Association for Computational Linguistics.

Hui Liu, Zhan Shi, Jia-Chen Gu, Quan Liu, Si Wei, and Xiaodan Zhu. 2020. End-to-end transition-based online dialogue disentanglement. In *IJCAI*, volume 20, pages 3868–3874.

Hui Liu, Zhan Shi, and Xiaodan Zhu. 2021. Unsupervised conversation disentanglement through co-training. In *Proceedings of the 2021 Conference on Empirical Methods in Natural Language Processing*, pages 2345–2356, Online and Punta Cana, Dominican Republic. Association for Computational Linguistics.

Ting Liu, Samira Shaikh, Tomek Strzalkowski, George Aaron Broadwell, Jennifer Stromer-Galley, Sarah M Taylor, Umit Boz, Xiaoai Ren, and Jingsi Wu. 2012. Extending the mpc corpus to chinese and urdu-a multiparty multi-lingual chat corpus for modeling social phenomena in language. In *LREC*, pages 2868–2873.

Ryan Lowe, Nissan Pow, Iulian Serban, and Joelle Pineau. 2015. The Ubuntu dialogue corpus: A large dataset for research in unstructured multi-turn dialogue systems. In *Proceedings of the 16th Annual Meeting of the Special Interest Group on Discourse and Dialogue*, pages 285–294, Prague, Czech Republic. Association for Computational Linguistics.

Kaixin Ma, Catherine Xiao, and Jinho D. Choi. 2017. Text-based speaker identification on multiparty dialogues using multi-document convolutional neural networks. In *Proceedings of ACL 2017, Student Research Workshop*, pages 49–55, Vancouver, Canada. Association for Computational Linguistics.

Khyati Mahajan and Samira Shaikh. 2021. On the need for thoughtful data collection for multi-party dialogue: A survey of available corpora and collection methods. In *Proceedings of the 22nd Annual Meeting of the Special Interest Group on Discourse and Dialogue*, pages 338–352, Singapore and Online. Association for Computational Linguistics.

Navonil Majumder, Soujanya Poria, Devamanyu Hazarika, Rada Mihalcea, Alexander Gelbukh, and Erik Cambria. 2019. Dialoguernn: An attentive rnn for emotion detection in conversations. In *Proceedings of the AAAI conference on artificial intelligence*, volume 33, pages 6818–6825.

Daniel Marcu. 1997. From discourse structures to text summaries. In *Intelligent Scalable Text Summarization*.

Shikib Mehri and Giuseppe Carenini. 2017. Chat disentanglement: Identifying semantic reply relationships with random forests and recurrent neural networks. In *Proceedings of the Eighth International Joint Conference on Natural Language Processing (Volume 1: Long Papers)*, pages 615–623, Taipei, Taiwan. Asian Federation of Natural Language Processing.

Zhao Meng, Lili Mou, and Zhi Jin. 2018. Towards neural speaker modeling in multi-party conversation: The task, dataset, and models. In *Proceedings of the Eleventh International Conference on Language Resources and Evaluation (LREC 2018)*, Miyazaki, Japan. European Language Resources Association (ELRA).

Hiroki Ouchi and Yuta Tsuboi. 2016. Addressee and response selection for multi-party conversation. In *Proceedings of the 2016 Conference on Empirical Methods in Natural Language Processing*, pages 2133–2143, Austin, Texas. Association for Computational Linguistics.

Kishore Papineni, Salim Roukos, Todd Ward, and Wei-Jing Zhu. 2002. Bleu: a method for automatic evaluation of machine translation. In *Proceedings of the 40th Annual Meeting of the Association for Computational Linguistics*, pages 311–318, Philadelphia, Pennsylvania, USA. Association for Computational Linguistics.

Volha Petukhova, Christopher Stevens, Harmen de Weerd, Niels Taatgen, Fokie Cnossen, and Andrei Malchanau. 2016. Modelling multi-issue bargaining dialogues: Data collection, annotation design and corpus. In *Proceedings of the Tenth International Conference on Language Resources and Evaluation (LREC'16)*, pages 3133–3140, Portorož, Slovenia. European Language Resources Association (ELRA).

Soujanya Poria, Devamanyu Hazarika, Navonil Majumder, Gautam Naik, Erik Cambria, and Rada Mihalcea. 2019. MELD: A multimodal multi-party dataset for emotion recognition in conversations. In *Proceedings of the 57th Annual Meeting of the Association for Computational Linguistics*, pages 527–536, Florence, Italy. Association for Computational Linguistics.

Matthew Purver, John Dowding, John Niekrasz, Patrick Ehlen, Sharareh Noorbaloochi, and Stanley Peters. 2007. Detecting and summarizing action items in multi-party dialogue. In *Proceedings of the 8th SIGdial Workshop on Discourse and Dialogue*, pages 18–25, Antwerp, Belgium. Association for Computational Linguistics.

Liang Qiu, Yizhou Zhao, Weiyan Shi, Yuan Liang, Feng Shi, Tao Yuan, Zhou Yu, and Song-Chun Zhu. 2020. Structured attention for unsupervised dialogue structure induction. In *Proceedings of the 2020 Conference on Empirical Methods in Natural Language Processing (EMNLP)*, pages 1889–1899, Online. Association for Computational Linguistics.

Alec Radford and Karthik Narasimhan. 2018. Improving language understanding by generative pretraining.

Zahra Rahimi, Anish Kumar, Diane Litman, Susannah Paletz, and Mingzhi Yu. 2017. Entrainment in Multi-Party Spoken Dialogues at Multiple Linguistic Levels. In *Proc. Interspeech 2017*, pages 1696–1700.

Antoine Raux and Maxine Eskenazi. 2009. A finite-state turn-taking model for spoken dialog systems. In *Proceedings of human language technologies: The 2009 annual conference of the North American chapter of the association for computational linguistics*, pages 629–637.

Steve Renals, Thomas Hain, and Hervé Bourlard. 2007. Recognition and understanding of meetings the ami and amida projects. In *2007 IEEE Workshop on Automatic Speech Recognition & Understanding (ASRU)*, pages 238–247. IEEE.

Douglas A Reynolds and Richard C Rose. 1995. Robust text-independent speaker identification using gaussian mixture speaker models. *IEEE transactions on speech and audio processing*, 3(1):72–83.

Sara Rosenthal and Kathy McKeown. 2015. I couldn't agree more: The role of conversational structure in agreement and disagreement detection in online discussions. In *Proceedings of the 16th Annual Meeting of the Special Interest Group on Discourse and Dialogue*, pages 168–177, Prague, Czech Republic. Association for Computational Linguistics.

Harvey Sacks, Emanuel A. Schegloff, and Gail Jefferson. 1974. A simplest systematics for the organization of turn-taking for conversation. *Language*, 50(4):696–735.

Yunxin Sang and Yang Bao. 2022. DialogueGAT: A graph attention network for financial risk prediction by modeling the dialogues in earnings conference calls. In *Findings of the Association for Computational Linguistics: EMNLP 2022*, pages 1623–1633, Abu Dhabi, United Arab Emirates. Association for Computational Linguistics.

Michael Schlichtkrull, Thomas N Kipf, Peter Bloem, Rianne Van Den Berg, Ivan Titov, and Max Welling. 2018. Modeling relational data with graph convolutional networks. In *The Semantic Web: 15th International Conference, ESWC 2018, Heraklion, Crete, Greece, June 3–7, 2018, Proceedings 15*, pages 593–607. Springer.

Iulian Serban, Alessandro Sordoni, Yoshua Bengio, Aaron Courville, and Joelle Pineau. 2016. Building end-to-end dialogue systems using generative hierarchical neural network models. In *Proceedings of the AAAI conference on artificial intelligence*, volume 30.

Weizhou Shen, Xiaojun Quan, and Ke Yang. 2023. Generic dependency modeling for multi-party conversation. *ArXiv*, abs/2302.10680.

Weiyan Shi, Tiancheng Zhao, and Zhou Yu. 2019. Unsupervised dialog structure learning. In *Proceedings of the 2019 Conference of the North American Chapter of the Association for Computational Linguistics: Human Language Technologies, Volume 1 (Long and Short Papers)*, pages 1797–1807, Minneapolis, Minnesota. Association for Computational Linguistics.

Zhouxing Shi and Minlie Huang. 2019. A deep sequential model for discourse parsing on multi-party dialogues. In *Proceedings of the AAAI Conference on Artificial Intelligence*, volume 33, pages 7007–7014.

Gabriel Skantze. 2017. Towards a general, continuous model of turn-taking in spoken dialogue using LSTM recurrent neural networks. In *Proceedings of the 18th Annual SIGdial Meeting on Discourse and Dialogue*, pages 220–230, Saarbrücken, Germany. Association for Computational Linguistics.

Radu Soricut and Daniel Marcu. 2006. Discourse generation using utility-trained coherence models. In *Proceedings of the COLING/ACL 2006 Main Conference Poster Sessions*, pages 803–810.

Tomek Strzalkowski, George Aaron Broadwell, Jennifer Stromer-Galley, Samira Shaikh, Sarah Taylor, and Nick Webb. 2010. Modeling socio-cultural phenomena in discourse. In *Proceedings of the 23rd International Conference on Computational Linguistics (Coling 2010)*, pages 1038–1046, Beijing, China. Coling 2010 Organizing Committee.

Yajing Sun, Yong Shan, Chengguang Tang, Yue Hu, Yinpei Dai, Jing Yu, Jian Sun, Fei Huang, and Luo Si. 2021a. Unsupervised learning of deterministic dialogue structure with edge-enhanced graph autoencoder. In *Proceedings of the AAAI conference on artificial intelligence*, volume 35, pages 13869–13877.

Yang Sun, Nan Yu, and Guohong Fu. 2021b. A discourse-aware graph neural network for emotion recognition in multi-party conversation. In *Findings of the Association for Computational Linguistics: EMNLP 2021*, pages 2949–2958, Punta Cana, Dominican Republic. Association for Computational Linguistics.

David Traum. 2004. Issues in multiparty dialogues. In *Advances in Agent Communication: International Workshop on Agent Communication Languages, ACL 2003, Melbourne, Australia, July 14, 2003. Revised and Invited Papers*, pages 201–211. Springer.

David C Uthus and David W Aha. 2013. The ubuntu chat corpus for multiparticipant chat analysis. Technical report, NAVAL RESEARCH LAB WASHINGTON DC.

Mina Valizadeh and Natalie Parde. 2022. The AI doctor is in: A survey of task-oriented dialogue systems for healthcare applications. In *Proceedings of the 60th Annual Meeting of the Association for Computational Linguistics (Volume 1: Long Papers)*, pages 6638–6660, Dublin, Ireland. Association for Computational Linguistics.

Petar Veličković, Guillem Cucurull, Arantxa Casanova, Adriana Romero, Pietro Liò, and Yoshua Bengio. 2018. Graph attention networks. In *International Conference on Learning Representations*.

Petukhova Volha, Laurent Prevot, and Bunt Harry. 2011. Multi-level discourse relations between dialogue units. In *The Sixth Joint ISO-ACL SIGSEM Workshop on Interoperable Semantic Annotation*, pages 18–27.

Weishi Wang, Steven C.H. Hoi, and Shafiq Joty. 2020. Response selection for multi-party conversations with dynamic topic tracking. In *Proceedings of the 2020 Conference on Empirical Methods in Natural Language Processing (EMNLP)*, pages 6581–6591, Online. Association for Computational Linguistics.

Jimmy Wei, Kurt Shuster, Arthur Szlam, Jason Weston, Jack Urbanek, and Mojtaba Komeili. 2023. Multi-party chat: Conversational agents in group settings with humans and models.

Chien-Sheng Wu, Steven C.H. Hoi, Richard Socher, and Caiming Xiong. 2020. TOD-BERT: Pre-trained natural language understanding for task-oriented dialogue. In *Proceedings of the 2020 Conference on Empirical Methods in Natural Language Processing (EMNLP)*, pages 917–929, Online. Association for Computational Linguistics.

Jun Xu, Zeyang Lei, Haifeng Wang, Zheng-Yu Niu, Hua Wu, and Wanxiang Che. 2021. Discovering dialog structure graph for coherent dialog generation. In *Proceedings of the 59th Annual Meeting of the Association for Computational Linguistics and the 11th International Joint Conference on Natural Language Processing (Volume 1: Long Papers)*, pages 1726–1739.

Qichuan Yang, Zhiqiang He, Zhiqiang Zhan, Jianyu Zhao, Yang Zhang, and Changjian Hu. 2019. Mids: End-to-end personalized response generation in untrimmed multi-role dialogue. In *2019 International Joint Conference on Neural Networks (IJCNN)*, pages 1–8.

Dian Yu, Kai Sun, Claire Cardie, and Dong Yu. 2020. Dialogue-based relation extraction. In *Proceedings of the 58th Annual Meeting of the Association for Computational Linguistics*, pages 4927–4940, Online. Association for Computational Linguistics.

Chuxu Zhang, Dongjin Song, Chao Huang, Ananthram Swami, and Nitesh V Chawla. 2019. Heterogeneous graph neural network. In *Proceedings of the 25th ACM SIGKDD international conference on knowledge discovery & data mining*, pages 793–803.

Rui Zhang, Honglak Lee, Lazaros Polymenakos, and Dragomir Radev. 2018. Addressee and response selection in multi-party conversations with speaker interaction rnns. In *Proceedings of the AAAI conference on artificial intelligence*, volume 32.

Yizhe Zhang, Siqi Sun, Michel Galley, Yen-Chun Chen, Chris Brockett, Xiang Gao, Jianfeng Gao, Jingjing Liu, and Bill Dolan. 2020. DIALOGPT : Large-scale generative pre-training for conversational response generation. In *Proceedings of the 58th Annual Meeting of the Association for Computational Linguistics: System Demonstrations*, pages 270–278, Online. Association for Computational Linguistics.

Ming Zhong, Yang Liu, Yichong Xu, Chenguang Zhu, and Michael Zeng. 2022. Dialoglm: Pre-trained model for long dialogue understanding and summarization. In *Proceedings of the AAAI Conference on Artificial Intelligence*, volume 36, pages 11765–11773.

Xiangyang Zhou, Daxiang Dong, Hua Wu, Shiqi Zhao, Dianhai Yu, Hao Tian, Xuan Liu, and Rui Yan. 2016. Multi-view response selection for human-computer conversation. In *Proceedings of the 2016 Conference on Empirical Methods in Natural Language Processing*, pages 372–381, Austin, Texas. Association for Computational Linguistics.

Chenguang Zhu, Yang Liu, Jie Mei, and Michael Zeng. 2021. MediaSum: A large-scale media interview dataset for dialogue summarization. In *Proceedings of the 2021 Conference of the North American Chapter of the Association for Computational Linguistics: Human Language Technologies*, pages 5927–5934, Online. Association for Computational Linguistics.

Conversational Recommendation as Retrieval: A Simple, Strong Baseline

Raghav Gupta, Renat Aksitov, Samrat Phatale, Simral Chaudhary, Harrison Lee, Abhinav Rastogi
Google Research
{raghavgupta, raksitov, samratph, simral, harrisonlee, abhirast}@google.com

Abstract

Conversational recommendation systems (CRS) aim to recommend suitable items to users through natural language conversation. However, most CRS approaches do not effectively utilize the signal provided by these conversations. They rely heavily on explicit external knowledge e.g., knowledge graphs to augment the models' understanding of the items and attributes, which is quite hard to scale. To alleviate this, we propose an alternative information retrieval (IR)-styled approach to the CRS item recommendation task, where we represent conversations as queries and items as documents to be retrieved. We expand the document representation used for retrieval with conversations from the training set. With a simple BM25-based retriever, we show that our task formulation compares favorably with much more complex baselines using complex external knowledge on a popular CRS benchmark. We demonstrate further improvements using user-centric modeling and data augmentation to counter the cold start problem for CRSs.

1 Introduction

Recommendation systems have become ubiquitous in recent years given the explosion in massive item catalogues across applications. In general, a recommendation system learns user preference from historical user-item interactions, and then recommends items of user's preference. In contrast, CRSs directly extract user preferences from live dialog history to precisely address the users' needs. An example dialogue from the popular ReDial benchmark (Li et al., 2018) for CRSs is shown in Table 1: the CRS' task is to recommend items (in this case, movies) based on the user's indicated preference.

Generally, a CRS integrates two modules: a **dialogue module** which generates natural language responses to interact with users, and a **recommendation module** which recommends desirable items to users using the dialog context and external knowledge. We focus on the latter module in this work: we posit that once the correct item to recommend is identified, newer pretrained language models (PLMs) can easily generate fluent agent responses.

Role	Message
User	Hello! I am looking for some movies.
Agent	What kinds of movie do you like? I like animated movies such as Frozen (2013).
Rec. item	Frozen (2013)
User	I do not like animated films. I would love to see a movie like Pretty Woman (1990) starring Julia Roberts. Know any that are similar?
Agent	Pretty Woman (1990) was a good one. If you are in it for Julia Roberts you can try Runaway Bride (1999).
Rec. item	Runaway Bride (1999)

Table 1: An example dialogue from ReDial. The items to recommend are in blue, with their inferred attributes in red. The ground truth recommended items for agent utterances are also shown.

It is notable that the conversational context provides sufficient signal to make good recommendations (Yang et al., 2021). E.g., in Table 1, attributes about the items to recommend (e.g., genre and cast, in red) provide potentially sufficient information to the model to recommend relevant items.

Most approaches to CRS rely heavily on external knowledge sources, such as knowledge graphs (KGs) and reviews (Lu et al., 2021). Such approaches require specific sub-modules to encode information from these sources like graph neural networks (Kipf and Welling, 2016), which are hard to scale with catalog additions. Existing approaches require either re-training the entire system when the KG structure changes (Dettmers et al., 2018) or adding complex architectures on top to adapt (Wu et al., 2022). Newer approaches utilize PLMs (Radford et al.; Lewis et al., 2020), but they often encode item information in model parameters, making it hard to scale to new items without retraining.

Looking for a fast, more scalable approach, we re-formulate the item recommendation task for

Proceedings of the 5th Workshop on NLP for Conversational AI (NLP4ConvAI 2023), pages 155–160
July 14, 2023

CRSs as an information retrieval (IR) task, with recommendation-seeking conversations as queries and items to recommend as documents. The document content for retrieval is constructed using plain text metadata for the item paired with conversations where the said item is recommended, in order to enhance semantic overlap between the queries which are themselves conversations.

We apply a standard non-parametric retrieval baseline - BM25 - to this task and show that the resulting model is fast and extensible without requiring complex external knowledge or architectures, while presenting improvements over more complex item recommendation baselines. Our contributions are summarized as follows:

- We present an alternate formulation of the CRS recommendation task as a retrieval task.
- We apply BM25 to this task, resulting in a simple, strong model with little training time and reduced reliance on external knowledge.
- We further improve the model using user-centric modeling, show that the model is extensible to new items without retraining, and demonstrate a simple data augmentation method that alleviates the cold start problem for CRSs.

2 Related Work

Conversational recommendation systems constitute an emerging research area, helped by datasets like REDIAL (Li et al., 2018), TG-REDIAL (Zhou et al., 2020b), INSPIRED (Hayati et al., 2020), DuRecDial (Liu et al., 2020, 2021), and CPCD (Chaganty et al., 2023). We next describe the recommender module architectures of CRS baselines.

ReDial (Li et al., 2018) uses an autoencoder to generate recommendations. CRSs commonly use knowledge graphs (KGs) for better understanding of the item catalog: DBpedia (Auer et al., 2007) is a popular choice of KG. KBRD (Chen et al., 2019) uses item-oriented KGs, while KGSF (Zhou et al., 2020a) further incorporates a word-based KG (Speer et al., 2017). CR-Walker (Ma et al., 2021) performs tree-structured reasoning on the KG, CRFR (Zhou et al., 2021) does reinforcement learning and multi-hop reasoning on the KG. UniCRS (Wang et al., 2022) uses knowledge-added prompt tuning with and KG & a fixed PLM. Some methods also incorporate user information: COLA (Lin et al., 2022) uses collaborative filtering to build a user-item graph, and (Li et al., 2022) aims to find lookalike users for user-aware predictions.

Eschewing KGs, MESE (Yang et al., 2022) trains an item encoder to convert flat item metadata to embeddings then used by a PLM, and TSCR (Zou et al., 2022) trains a transformer with a Cloze task modified for recommendations. Most above approaches, however, either rely on complex models with KGs and/or need to be retrained for new items, which is very frequent in present-day item catalogs.

3 Model

We formally define the item recommendation task, followed by our retrieval framework, details of the BM25 retrieval model used, and finally our user-aware recommendation method on top of BM25.

3.1 Conversational Item Recommendation

A CRS allows the user to retrieve relevant items from an item catalog $V = \{v_1, v_2 \cdots v_N\}$ through dialog. In a conversation, let a be an agent response containing an item(s) from V recommended to the user. Let $d_t = \{u_1, u_2, \cdots u_t\}$ be the t turns of the conversation context preceding a, where each turn can be spoken by the user or the agent.

We model the recommendation task as masked item prediction, similar to Zou et al. (2022). For each agent response a where an item $v_i \in V$ is recommended, we mask the mention of v_i in a i.e. replace it with the special token `[REC]`, yielding the masked agent response a'. We now create training examples with input $q = d_t \oplus a'$ and ground truth v_i ($\oplus$ denotes string concatenation).

We define Q^{train} and Q^{test} as the set of all conversational contexts $q = d_t \oplus a'$ with an item to predict, from the training and test sets respectively. For each item v_i, we also define $\boldsymbol{Q_{v_i}^{train}} \subset Q^{train}$ as the set of all conversational contexts in Q^{train} where v_i is the ground truth item to recommend.

3.2 Item Recommendation as Retrieval

Information retrieval (IR) systems are aimed at recommending documents to users based on the relevance of the document's content to the user query. We reformulate masked item prediction as a retrieval task with Q^{train} or Q^{test} as the set of queries to calculate relevance to, and V as the set of items/documents to recommend from.

To match a query $q \in Q^{test}$ to a document/item $v_i \in V$, we define the document's content using two sources: **metadata** in plaintext about item v_i, and $\boldsymbol{Q_{v_i}^{train}}$ i.e. all conversational contexts from the training set where v_i is the recommended item, concatenated together, similar to document expansion (Nogueira et al., 2019). Our motivation for adding $Q_{v_i}^{train}$ to the document representation is that it is easier to match queries (which are conversations) to conversations instead of plain metadata since conversations can be sparse in meaningful keywords. For an item v_i we create a document as:

$$Doc(v_i) = Metadata(v_i) \oplus Q_{v_i} \quad (1)$$

For test set prediction, we can now apply retrieval to recommend the most relevant document $Doc(v_i), v_i \in V$, for each test set query $q \in Q^{test}$.

3.3 Retrieval Model: BM25

BM25 (Robertson et al., 2009) is a commonly used sparse, bag-of-words ranking function. It produces a similarity score for a given document, *doc* and a query, q, by matching keywords efficiently with an inverted index of the set of documents. Briefly, for each keyword in each document, we compute and store their term frequencies (TF) and inverse document frequencies (IDF) in an index. For an input query, we compute a match score for each query keyword with each document using a function of TF and IDF, and sum this score over all keywords in the query. This yields a similarity score for the query with each document, which is used to rank the documents for relevance to the query.

3.4 User Selection

Our IR formulation also gives us a simple way to incorporate user information for item recommendation. Let $U = \{u_1, u_2 \dots u_J\}$ be the set of all users in the dataset. Each conversation context in Q^{train} be associated with a user $u_j \in U$. We use a simple algorithm for user-aware recommendations:

- For each user $u \in U$, we obtain the set of items they like based on conversations in Q^{train}, and also construct a unique BM25 index for each user u_j using only conversations associated with u_j.
- For a test set query $q \in Q^{test}$, we identify movies liked by the seeker in the current q, and use it to find the M most similar users in the training set.
- We now compute and add up similarity scores for the query with all documents based on the per-user BM25 indices for these M selected users.
- Finally, we linearly combine these user-specific similarity scores per document with the similarity scores from the BM25 index in Section 3.3, and use these combined scores to rank all documents.

Model	R@1	R@10	R@50
ReDial (Li et al., 2018)	2.3	12.9	28.7
KBRD* (Chen et al., 2019)	3.0	16.4	33.8
KGSF* (Zhou et al., 2020a)	3.9	18.3	37.8
CR-Walker* (Ma et al., 2021)	4.0	18.7	37.6
CRFR* (Zhou et al., 2021)	4.0	20.2	39.9
COLA* (Lin et al., 2022)	4.8	22.1	42.6
UniCRS* (Wang et al., 2022)	5.1	22.4	42.8
MESE† (Yang et al., 2021)	5.6	25.6	45.5
TSCR* (Zou et al., 2022)	7.2	25.7	44.7
BM25 w/o Metadata	4.8	19.5	37.4
BM25†	5.2	20.5	38.5
BM25 + User Selection†	5.3	21.1	38.7

Table 2: Item recommendation results on the ReDial benchmark. Our BM25-based models outperform many baselines despite being much, lighter and not using complex KGs. * denotes models using DBPedia KG, † denotes models using plaintext IMDb metadata.

4 Experiments

4.1 Dataset and Evaluation

ReDial (Li et al., 2018) is a popular benchmark of annotated dialogues where a seeker requests movie suggestions from an agent. Figure 1 shows an example. It contains 956 users, 51,699 movie mentions, 10,006 dialogues, and 182,150 utterances.

For evaluation, we reuse Recall@k (or R@k) as our evaluation metric for ReDial from prior work. It evaluates whether the target human-recommended item appears in the top-k items produced by the recommendation system. We compare against baselines introduced in Section 2.

4.2 Training

For movie recommendations, we extract metadata from *IMDb.com* to populate $Metadata(v_i)$ for movies $v_i \in V$, which includes the movie's brief plot and names of the director and actors.

Parameters k_1 and b for BM25 are set to 1.6 and 0.7 respectively. For user selection, we select the $K = 5$ most similar users, and linearly combine the user-specific BM25 scores with the overall BM25 scores with a coefficient of 0.05 on the former. Constructing the BM25 index on the ReDial training set and inference on the test set took ~5 minutes on a CPU (+10 minutes for the user selection method). Alongside BM25 with and without user selection, we also experiment with a BM25 variant without metadata i.e. using only past conversation contexts as the document content for a movie/item.

5 Results

Table 2 shows $R@\{1, 10, 50\}$ on ReDial for the baselines and our models. Our BM25-based models perform strongly, outperforming many baselines which use complex KGs and/or complex model architectures e.g., tree-structured reasoning and reinforcement learning. Improvement is most visible on $R@1$ and less so on $R@50$. Our fairest comparison is with **MESE**, which uses the exact same data (text metadata + dialogues): our best model achieves 95% of its $R@1$ and 85% of its $R@50$ with a faster and simpler model. Note that all baselines except TSCR are jointly optimized for the item recommendation and response generation tasks, therefore their recommendation-only performance can potentially be better than reported.

A surprising result is **BM25 w/o Metadata** doing better than many baselines, without using any external knowledge whatsoever, in contrast to all other baselines except **ReDial**. This indicates that prior conversations indeed contain sufficient signal for good conversational item recommendation.

Our simple **user selection** raises recall by 1-3% across thresholds, with more potential gains from better user-centric modeling (Li et al., 2022).

6 Cold Start and Data Augmentation

Conversational recommenders often suffer from the **cold start problem**: it is difficult for a new item i.e. not seen during training, to be recommended, since not much is known about it beyond metadata.

Our model is not immune to this problem. The red lines in Figure 1 show $R@10$ values for the BM25 model for different sets of movies in ReDial based on how many times they are seen in the training set: the model never or rarely recommends movies with 10 or fewer occurrences in training.

To counteract this, we perform **data augmentation** using few-shot prompting (Liu et al., 2023). In particular, we randomly select 6 conversations from ReDial's training set, use them to prompt a PaLM 2-L model (Anil et al., 2023), and generate up to 20 dialogues per movie. We do this only for movies seen 10 or fewer times during training, since the model does the worst on these.

Figure 1's blue curve shows notably improved $R@10$ for the movies for which data was augmented, without hurting $R@10$ for more frequent movies. Overall $R@10$ also improves by ~8% using just ≤ 20 artificial dialogues per movie. Further combining augmentation with user selection lifts $\boldsymbol{R@1}$ to **5.9**, $\boldsymbol{R@10}$ to **22.3**, and $\boldsymbol{R@50}$ to **40.7**.

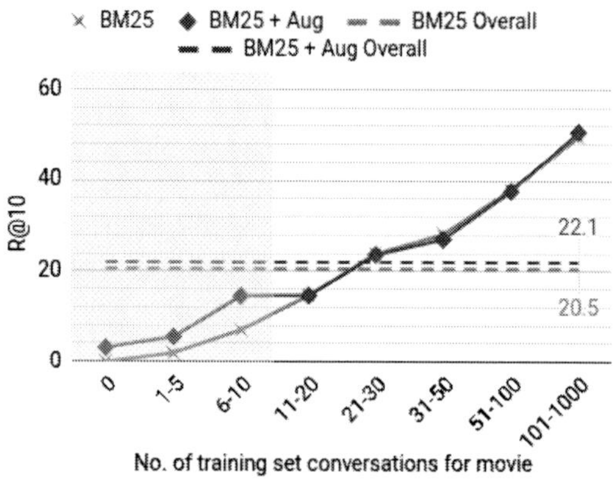

Figure 1: Impact of data augmentation on $R@10$. The shaded area represents the set of movies for which data augmentation was performed.

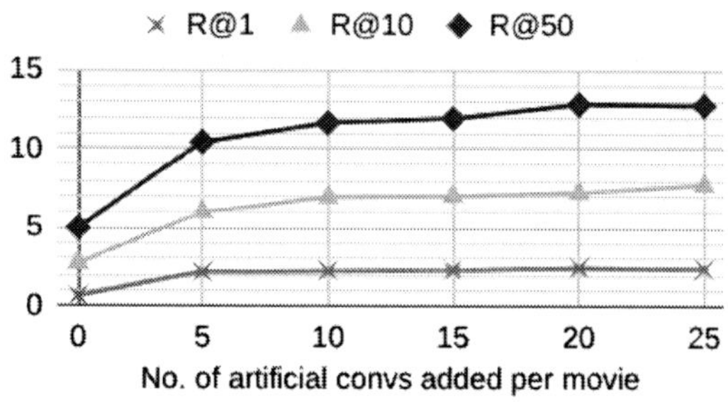

Figure 2: Recall for the BM25 model with varying amounts of augmented conversations.

Figure 2 plots recall for BM25 model with the number of artificial dialogues added for low-frequency movies. Based on this plot, we opted to generate at most 20 conversations per movie.

7 Conclusion

We present a retrieval-based formulation of the item recommendation task, used to build CRSs, by modeling conversations as queries and items as documents. We augment the item representation with conversations recommending that item; the retrieval task then reduces to matching conversations to conversations. Using BM25-based retrieval with this task results in a model that is very fast and inexpensive to train (~5 min on CPU) while being flexible to add-ons like user selection. We also show that new items can be easily added without retraining the model, and that simple data augmentation with as few as 20 conversations counters the cold start problem for new items: fewer than most neural network finetuning methods would need.

References

Rohan Anil, Andrew M Dai, Orhan Firat, Melvin Johnson, Dmitry Lepikhin, Alexandre Passos, Siamak Shakeri, Emanuel Taropa, Paige Bailey, Zhifeng Chen, et al. 2023. Palm 2 technical report. *arXiv preprint arXiv:2305.10403*.

Sören Auer, Christian Bizer, Georgi Kobilarov, Jens Lehmann, Richard Cyganiak, and Zachary Ives. 2007. Dbpedia: A nucleus for a web of open data. In *The Semantic Web: 6th International Semantic Web Conference, 2nd Asian Semantic Web Conference, ISWC 2007+ ASWC 2007, Busan, Korea, November 11-15, 2007. Proceedings*, pages 722–735. Springer.

Arun Tejasvi Chaganty, Megan Leszczynski, Shu Zhang, Ravi Ganti, Krisztian Balog, and Filip Radlinski. 2023. Beyond single items: Exploring user preferences in item sets with the conversational playlist curation dataset. *ArXiv*, abs/2303.06791.

Qibin Chen, Junyang Lin, Yichang Zhang, Ming Ding, Yukuo Cen, Hongxia Yang, and Jie Tang. 2019. Towards knowledge-based recommender dialog system. In *Proceedings of the 2019 Conference on Empirical Methods in Natural Language Processing and the 9th International Joint Conference on Natural Language Processing (EMNLP-IJCNLP)*, pages 1803–1813, Hong Kong, China. Association for Computational Linguistics.

Tim Dettmers, Pasquale Minervini, Pontus Stenetorp, and Sebastian Riedel. 2018. Convolutional 2d knowledge graph embeddings. In *Proceedings of the AAAI conference on artificial intelligence*, volume 32.

Shirley Anugrah Hayati, Dongyeop Kang, Qingxiaoyang Zhu, Weiyan Shi, and Zhou Yu. 2020. Inspired: Toward sociable recommendation dialog systems. In *Proceedings of the 2020 Conference on Empirical Methods in Natural Language Processing (EMNLP)*, pages 8142–8152.

Thomas N Kipf and Max Welling. 2016. Semi-supervised classification with graph convolutional networks. *arXiv preprint arXiv:1609.02907*.

Mike Lewis, Yinhan Liu, Naman Goyal, Marjan Ghazvininejad, Abdelrahman Mohamed, Omer Levy, Veselin Stoyanov, and Luke Zettlemoyer. 2020. Bart: Denoising sequence-to-sequence pre-training for natural language generation, translation, and comprehension. In *Proceedings of the 58th Annual Meeting of the Association for Computational Linguistics*, pages 7871–7880.

Raymond Li, Samira Ebrahimi Kahou, Hannes Schulz, Vincent Michalski, Laurent Charlin, and Chris Pal. 2018. Towards deep conversational recommendations. In *Advances in Neural Information Processing Systems 31 (NIPS 2018)*.

Shuokai Li, Ruobing Xie, Yongchun Zhu, Xiang Ao, Fuzhen Zhuang, and Qing He. 2022. User-centric conversational recommendation with multi-aspect user modeling. In *Proceedings of the 45th International ACM SIGIR Conference on Research and Development in Information Retrieval*, pages 223–233.

Dongding Lin, Jian Wang, and Wenjie Li. 2022. Cola: Improving conversational recommender systems by collaborative augmentation. *arXiv preprint arXiv:2212.07767*.

Pengfei Liu, Weizhe Yuan, Jinlan Fu, Zhengbao Jiang, Hiroaki Hayashi, and Graham Neubig. 2023. Pre-train, prompt, and predict: A systematic survey of prompting methods in natural language processing. *ACM Computing Surveys*, 55(9):1–35.

Zeming Liu, Haifeng Wang, Zheng-Yu Niu, Hua Wu, and Wanxiang Che. 2021. Durecdial 2.0: A bilingual parallel corpus for conversational recommendation. In *Proceedings of the 2021 Conference on Empirical Methods in Natural Language Processing*, pages 4335–4347.

Zeming Liu, Haifeng Wang, Zheng-Yu Niu, Hua Wu, Wanxiang Che, and Ting Liu. 2020. Towards conversational recommendation over multi-type dialogs. In *Proceedings of the 58th Annual Meeting of the Association for Computational Linguistics*, pages 1036–1049.

Yu Lu, Junwei Bao, Yan Song, Zichen Ma, Shuguang Cui, Youzheng Wu, and Xiaodong He. 2021. RevCore: Review-augmented conversational recommendation. In *Findings of the Association for Computational Linguistics: ACL-IJCNLP 2021*, pages 1161–1173, Online. Association for Computational Linguistics.

Wenchang Ma, Ryuichi Takanobu, and Minlie Huang. 2021. Cr-walker: Tree-structured graph reasoning and dialog acts for conversational recommendation. In *Proceedings of the 2021 Conference on Empirical Methods in Natural Language Processing*, pages 1839–1851.

Rodrigo Nogueira, Wei Yang, Jimmy Lin, and Kyunghyun Cho. 2019. Document expansion by query prediction. *arXiv preprint arXiv:1904.08375*.

Alec Radford, Karthik Narasimhan, Tim Salimans, Ilya Sutskever, et al. Improving language understanding by generative pre-training.

Stephen Robertson, Hugo Zaragoza, et al. 2009. The probabilistic relevance framework: Bm25 and beyond. *Foundations and Trends® in Information Retrieval*, 3(4):333–389.

Robyn Speer, Joshua Chin, and Catherine Havasi. 2017. Conceptnet 5.5: An open multilingual graph of general knowledge. In *Proceedings of the AAAI conference on artificial intelligence*, volume 31.

Xiaolei Wang, Kun Zhou, Ji-Rong Wen, and Wayne Xin Zhao. 2022. Towards unified conversational recommender systems via knowledge-enhanced prompt learning. In *Proceedings of the 28th ACM SIGKDD Conference on Knowledge Discovery and Data Mining*, pages 1929–1937.

Tianxing Wu, Arijit Khan, Melvin Yong, Guilin Qi, and Meng Wang. 2022. Efficiently embedding dynamic knowledge graphs. *Knowledge-Based Systems*, page 109124.

Bowen Yang, Cong Han, Yu Li, Lei Zuo, and Zhou Yu. 2021. Improving conversational recommendation systems' quality with context-aware item meta information. *arXiv preprint arXiv:2112.08140*.

Bowen Yang, Cong Han, Yu Li, Lei Zuo, and Zhou Yu. 2022. Improving conversational recommendation systems' quality with context-aware item meta-information. In *Findings of the Association for Computational Linguistics: NAACL 2022*, pages 38–48, Seattle, United States. Association for Computational Linguistics.

Jinfeng Zhou, Bo Wang, Ruifang He, and Yuexian Hou. 2021. Crfr: Improving conversational recommender systems via flexible fragments reasoning on knowledge graphs. In *Proceedings of the 2021 Conference on Empirical Methods in Natural Language Processing*, pages 4324–4334.

Kun Zhou, Wayne Xin Zhao, Shuqing Bian, Yuanhang Zhou, Ji-Rong Wen, and Jingsong Yu. 2020a. Improving conversational recommender systems via knowledge graph based semantic fusion. In *Proceedings of the 26th ACM SIGKDD International Conference on Knowledge Discovery & Data Mining*, pages 1006–1014.

Kun Zhou, Yuanhang Zhou, Wayne Xin Zhao, Xiaoke Wang, and Ji-Rong Wen. 2020b. Towards topic-guided conversational recommender system. In *Proceedings of the 28th International Conference on Computational Linguistics, COLING 2020, Barcelona, Spain, December 8-11, 2020*.

Jie Zou, Evangelos Kanoulas, Pengjie Ren, Zhaochun Ren, Aixin Sun, and Cheng Long. 2022. Improving conversational recommender systems via transformer-based sequential modelling. In *Proceedings of the 45th International ACM SIGIR Conference on Research and Development in Information Retrieval*, pages 2319–2324.

Author Index